The Later Mid

'This exceptionally wide-ranging, lucid and informative selection of texts pulls off a brilliant trick: it makes the strange places of the past accessible while revealing at the same time their fascinating variousness and complexity. It's not only a handbook for beginners but a treasure trove for those who already know their way around.' – **Felicity Riddy, formerly Professor of English and Related Literature and Deputy Vice-Chancellor, University of York, UK**

This substantial anthology of documents offers students of later medieval English literature, society and history a range of interdisciplinary perspectives through which to understand literary texts from the period 1350–1550. Informed by the latest scholarship and meticulous original research, it both includes classic texts and brings rare materials back into circulation. The documents illustrate and illuminate the languages of medieval England, its books and methods of manuscript production; as well as the diverse richness of the spirituality, chivalry and scientific knowledge that shaped the later medieval world.

Supported by a wide-range of pedagogically designed tools to help students find their way into the history, literature and culture of the period, *The Later Middle Ages: A Sourcebook* includes:

- an authoritative introduction outlining key historical events, social and political movements, and literary and cultural ideas of the time
- informative headnotes, footnotes and section introductions, supporting the material and providing insights into how individual documents aid the reading of major texts
- a timeline and a chronological list of the major literary events of the period
- a comprehensive guide to further reading and useful websites.

The Later Middle Ages: A Sourcebook makes available documents that are both important in their own right, and crucial for an understanding of the literary output of the period, challenging boundaries between text and context, literature and history. The rich source material and essential context that this book provides make it an invaluable resource for all students of Medieval Studies.

Carolyn P. Collette is Professor of English at Mount Holyoke College. Her recent books include *Species, Phantasms and Images: Vision and Medieval Psychology in the Canterbury Tales*, *Performing Polity: Women and Agency in the Anglo-French Tradition* and *The Legend of Good Women: Context and Reception.*

Harold Garrett-Goodyear is Professor of history at Mount Holyoke College.

Palgrave Sourcebooks

Series Editor: Steven Matthews

Published

Simon Bainbridge: **Romanticism**
Lena Cowen Orlin: **The Renaissance**
Steven Matthews: **Modernism**
Carolyn Collette and Harold Garrett-Goodyear: **The Later Middle Ages**

Forthcoming

John Plunkett, Ana Vadillo, Regenia Gagnier, Angelique Richardson, Rick Rylance and Paul Young: **Victorian Literature**
Nigel Wood: **The 'Long' Eighteenth Century**

Palgrave Soucebooks

Series Standing Order
ISBN 978–1–4039–4277–7 hardcover
ISBN 978–1–4039–4278–4 paperback
(outside North America only)

You can receive future titles in this series as they are published by placing a standing order. Please contact your bookseller or, in the case of difficulty, write to us at the address below with your name and address, the title of the series and the ISBN quoted above.

Customer Services Department, Macmillan Distribution Ltd
Houndmills, Basingstoke, Hampshire RG21 6XS, England

The Later Middle Ages

A Sourcebook

Carolyn P. Collette and Harold Garrett-Goodyear

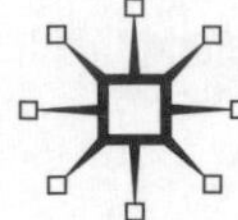

First published 2011 by
PALGRAVE MACMILLAN

Palgrave Macmillan in the UK is an imprint of Macmillan Publishers Limited, registered in England, company number 785998, of Houndmills, Basingstoke, Hampshire RG21 6XS.

Palgrave Macmillan in the US is a division of St Martin's Press LLC, 175 Fifth Avenue, New York, NY 10010.

Palgrave Macmillan is the global academic imprint of the above companies and has companies and representatives throughout the world.

Palgrave® and Macmillan® are registered trademarks in the United States, the United Kingdom, Europe and other countries

ISBN 978–0–230–55135–0 hardback
ISBN 978–0–230–55136–7 paperback

This book is printed on paper suitable for recycling and made from fully managed and sustained forest sources. Logging, pulping and manufacturing processes are expected to conform to the environmental regulations of the country of origin.

A catalogue record for this book is available from the British Library.

Library of Congress Cataloging-in-Publication Data

Collette, Carolyn P.
The later Middle Ages : a sourcebook / Carolyn Collette and Harold Garrett-Goodyear.
p. cm. — (Palgrave sourcebooks)
Summary: "More than a hundred primary documents offer students of later medieval English literature, society, and history intriguing original perspectives through which to understand the literary texts of the period 1350–1500 as well as the culture which created and received them. Complete with a substantial introduction, annotations and a timeline"— Provided by publisher.
ISBN 978-0-230-55136-7 (pbk.)
1. Great Britain—History—Medieval period, 1066–1485—Sources. 2. England—Civilization—1066–1485—Sources. 3. Middle Ages—Sources. I. Garrett-Goodyear, Harold. II. Title.
DA170.C65 2010
942.04—dc22 2010032622

10 9 8 7 6 5 4 3 2 1
20 19 18 17 16 15 14 13 12 11

Printed in China

Short Contents

Contents

Illustrations

Acknowledgments

It is a great pleasure to acknowledge and publicly thank the many people who helped with the production of this book. First of all we are grateful to Steven Matthews, editor of the Literary Contexts series at Palgrave for his critical insights and great good will in reading multiple drafts of this book. We would also like to thank Felicity Noble and Kate Haines of the editorial department at Palgrave for unfailingly timely and helpful advice, as well as encouragement.

At Mount Holyoke College a number of people helped us work through multiple problems of access and technology. Among the people at LITS we would particularly like to thank James Gehrt for his help exploring the frontiers of scanning aged and poorly-printed documents.

This book could not have been possible without the wonderful students we have taught together in interdisciplinary Medieval Studies courses over the years. In many ways this book is dedicated to our students, past and present, and to their sense of intellectual adventure and their unfailing engagement with medieval texts.

Finally, we owe a great debt to Cynthia Meehan, Senior Administrative Assistant to the Medieval Studies Program. Former student, colleague, friend, she is the still, calm center of our program, and of the work of assembling this book. We could not have done it without her.

The authors would also like to express their gratitude for the support of the Mount Holyoke College Faculty Grants Committee and the Benjamin Einhorn Fund.

The authors and publishers wish to thank the following for permission to reproduce copyright material:

Bodleian Library, University of Oxford, black and white reproduction of MS. Rawl, D. 939 section 3 recto (detail of couple embracing.), Figure 3.

Boydell Press, for pp. 120–3 from *The Armburgh Papers. The Brokholes INHERITANCE in Warwickshire, Hertfordshire and Essex c. 1417–c.1453*, edited by by Christine Carpenter (1998).

The British Library, for use of images reproduced from Additional MS 37049, f. 24v, Figure 1, and Arundel MS 83 II, f. 128v, Figure 2.

Cambridge University Press, for pp. 55–7 from *Johannes de Mirfeld of St Bartholomew's, Smithfield: His Life* (1936). Also, for pp. 51–3, 106–7, 118–22, 144–5, 201, and 205–7 from *The Plumpton Letters and Papers,* edited by Joan Kirby, Royal Historical Society Publications, Camden Fifth Series Vol. 8 (1996) © Royal Historical Society, published by the Cambridge University Press, and reproduced with permission. We also acknowledge with gratitude Joan Kirby's permission to use this material.

The Early English Text Society for permission to reprint ll. 3105–26, 5213–38, 5475–84, 5675–702, 6511–32, 7293–306, 8381–407, 10177–194, 10389–408 from *Sidrak and Bokkus: A Parallel Text Edition from Bodleian Library MS Laud Misc. 559 and British Library MS Lansdowne 793*, edited by T. L. Burton et al. (1998). The editors wish to thank the Society for enabling the use of many other medieval texts in this publication.

The Hakluyt Society for pp. 444–6 from *Mandeville's Travels*, edited by Malcolm Letts (1953).

Harvard University Press, for pp. 9, 11, and 13 reprinted by permission of the publisher from *Famous Women* by Giovanni Boccaccio, edited and translated by Virginia Brown, the I Tatti Renaissance Library, Cambridge Mass. Copyright © 2001 by the President and Fellows of Harvard College.

The History Press, for pp. 51–3 from Richard Kieckhefer, ed., *Forbidden Rites: A Necromancer's Manual of the Fifteenth Century* (1997).

Johns Hopkins University Press, for pp. 285–9 from *Handbook of Middle English*, edited by Fernand Mossé, trans. James A. Walker. © 1952 The Johns Hopkins University Press. Reprinted with permission of The Johns Hopkins University Press.

Lancashire and Cheshire Antiquarian Society, for pp. 42–52 from R. Sharpe France, "Two Custumals of the Manor of Cockerham, 1326 and 1483," in *Transactions of the Lancashire and Cheshire Antiquarian Society Publications*, Vol. 64 (1955).

Liverpool University Press for pp. 51–7 from *Nicole Oresme and the Astrologers*, edited by George William Coopland (1952).

Michigan State University Press, for pp. 293–7 from *A Zodiacal Lunary for Medical Professionals*, edited by Irma Tavitsainen (1994).

The National Archives, for generous approval for our use of crown copyright documents, identified throughout this present publication by the abbreviation "TNA," and in particular, to the Chancellor and Council of the Duchy of Lancaster for use of the Barnston manor court proceedings, TNA DL 30/58/721, published in *Select Cases in Manorial Courts. Property and Family Law. 1250–1500*, edited by L. R. Poos and Lloyd Bonfield, *Selden Society Publications*, 114 (1982), pp. 87–92.

Oxford University Press, for pp. 135–8 and 170 from *Life of the Black Prince by the Herald of Sir John Chandos*, edited and translated by Mildred K. Pope and Eleanor C. Lodge, Clarendon Press (1910); pp. 184–6 from *The Paston Letters. A Selection in Modern Spelling*, edited by Norman Davis (1963); pp. 224–7 from *A Book of London English 1384–1425*, edited by C. W. Chambers and Marjorie Daunt (1993); and pp. 185–9 from Nicholas Pronoy and John Taylor, *Parliamentary Texts of the Later Middle Ages* (1980); from *Romance of the Rose*, Guillaume de Lorris and Jean de Meun, translated with an introduction by Frances Horgan, ll. 8319–424, 16053–118 (1999); pp. 453–56 from the *Chaucer*

Tradition, Aage Brusendorff (1925); pp. 399–407 from *Walter of Henley and Other Treatises on Estate Management and Accounting*, edited by Dorothea Oschinsky (1971).

Palgrave Macmillan, for pp. xxviii–xxix from R. B. Dobson, ed., *The Peasants' Revolt of 1381*, 2nd ed. (1983). Reproduced with permission of Palgrave Macmillan.

Persea Books, for pp. 85–7, 168–70 from Christine de Pizan, *A Medieval Woman's Mirror of Honor: The Treasury of the City of Ladies*, translated by Charity Cannon Willard, translation copyright © 1989 by Persea Books, edited by Madeleine Pelner Cosman, Reprinted by permission of Persea Books, Inc., New York.

Richard III and Yorkist History Trust, for pp. 135–9 and 236–50 from *The Politics of Fifteenth-Century England. John Vale's Book*, by Margaret Lucille Kekewich, Colin Richmond, Anne F. Sutton, Livia Visser-Fuchs, and John L. Watts, Alan Sutton Publishing (1995).

Royal Historical Society, for pp. 196–200 and 202–6 from *Tracts of the Later Middle Ages*, edited by Jean-Philippe Genet, Royal Historical Society Publications, Camden Fourth Ser. Vol. 18 (1977). We also extend our thanks to Professor Genet, as well as The Master and Fellows of University College, Oxford, for use of these excerpts from "The III Considerations Right Necesserye to the Good Governance of a Prince," University College, Oxford. MS 85.

Selden Society, for pp. 143–5 from *Select Cases in the Court of King's Bench,:* Vol. 6: *Under Edward III*, edited by G. O. Sayles, Selden Society Vol. 82, 1965); pp. 83–5 and 192–4 from *Select Cases in the Court of King's Bench*, Vol. 7: *Richard II, Henry IV, and Henry V*, edited by G. O. Sayles, Selden Society Publications Vol. 88 (1971); pp. 1–6 and 130–7 from *Select Cases Before the King's Council in the Star Chamber 1477–1509*, edited by I. S. Leadam, Selden Society Publications Vol. 16 (1908); pp. 87–92 from *Select Cases in Manorial Courts. Property and Family Law. 1250–1500*, edited by L. R. Poos and Lloyd Bonfield, Selden Society Publications Vol. 114 (1982); pp. 42–6 from *Select Cases in the Court of Requests, 1497–1569*, edited by I. S. Leadam, Selden Society Publications Vol. 12 (1898).

Taylor & Francis Books (UK), for pp. 1094–5 from *English Historical Documents*, Vol. 4: *1327–1485*, edited by A. R. Myers, Eyre & Spottiswoode (© 1969), reissued by Routledge (©1996), reproduced by permission of Taylor & Francis Books UK.

Universitätsverlag Winter (Heidelberg) for pp. 78–9 from *The Middle English Translation of the Rosarium Theologie*, edited by Christina Von Nolcken (1979) © Universitätsverlag Winter; pp. 96–7 from *The Kalenre of the Newe Legende of England: from Pynson's printed edition, 1516*, edited by Manfred Gorlach (1994) © Universitätsverlag Winter.

University of California Press, for pp. 10–11, 57–8, 93–7, and 103–5 from *Philobiblon*, by Richard de Bury, edited by Archer Taylor. © 1948 by the Regents of the University of California; © renewed 1976 by Archer Taylor.

University of Pennsylvania Press, for pp. 87, 89, 91, and 95 from Richard W. Kaeuper and Elspeth Kennedy, ed. and trans., *The Book of Chivalry of Geoffroi de Charny* (1996), and for pp. 178–91 from Mary Frances Wack, *Lovesickness in the Middle Ages* (1990). Reprinted with permission of the University of Pennsylvania Press.

Every effort has been made to trace rights holders, but if any have been inadvertently overlooked the publishers would be pleased to make the necessary arrangements at the first opportunity.

Abbreviations

EETS	Early English Text Society.
	o.s. Original Series; e.s. Extra Series.
OED	*Oxford English Dictionary* available online.
Oxford DNB	Oxford *Dictionary of National Biography* available online.
RP	*Rotuli Parliamentorum et Petitiones in Parliamento* (1783), vols.
SR	Statues of the Realm (Record Commision, 1830–28), 12 vols.
TNA	The National Archives, Kew, London; formerly PRO, Public Record Office.

Series Editors' Preface

For at least twenty-five years, questions about the relation between literature and the historical period in which it was created have formed the central focus and methodology of critics. From the early 1980s, crucially, a range of literary scholars have sought to explore and define the parallels and differences between the representational language deployed in creative texts, and uses of similar rhetorical strategies in other contemporary cultural sources, such as journals, court documents, diaries and religious tracts. This kind of historicist reconsideration of literature has had far-reaching consequences in the academy and beyond, and the drive better to understand the dialogue established between texts and their originating period has brought new dynamism to ideas of context and contextualization.

The *Sourcebooks* series aims to provide a comprehensive and suggestive selection of original cultural sources for each of the major artistic moments from the medieval period onward. Edited by internationally renowned British and American experts in their chosen area, each volume presents within suitable subsections a panoply of materials relating to everything from historical background, to gender, philosophy, science and religion, which will be of use both to students and scholars seeking to contextualize creative work in any given period. It has been a particular ambition of the series to put back into circulation ephemeral original texts from magazines, newspapers, and even private sources, in order to offer a more representative sense of any one period's cultural debates and processes. Literature remains the primary focus of the volumes, but each contains documents relating to the broader artistic and cultural context which will be of interest and use to everyone working in the humanities area.

Each volume contains an informative general Introduction giving an overview of pertinent historical and cultural movements and pressures of its time. Each document is edited to a high scholarly standard through the use of headnotes and other supportive apparatus, in order to make the document accessible for further study. This apparatus is not prescriptive in determining the relation between any one literary text and these background resources, although each volume contains instances where documents directly alluded to by major writers are specifically excerpted. Generally, however, the series seeks to further historicist study and research by making available important or intriguing materials which might act to instigate further thought and reflection, so aiding to determine a more substantial picture of any literary work's moment of coming into being.

Steven Matthews

Timeline of Historical Events

1307–27	Reign of Edward II.
1309–77	"Babylonian Captivity" of the papacy: Pope Clement V established papal residence at Avignon.
1311	Pope Clement V ordered adoption of the Feast of Corpus Christi; it was introduced to England between 1320 and 1325; the earliest record of York's Corpus Christi Plays is 1376; by the fifteenth century, crafts in towns frequently were required to cooperate in its celebration.
1314–22	Baronial opposition to king's favorites, Gaveston, Edward and Hugh le Despenser, culminated in the revolt of Thomas of Lancaster.
1315–16	Great famine in England.
1327	Edward II deposed and murdered by Queen Isabella and Roger Mortimer.
1327–77	Reign of Edward III.
c.1325–1483	Stonor Family Letters. The handful of letters before 1400 are in French; thereafter, family members use English for correspondence.
1328	Edward III recognized Scottish independence in the Treaty of Edinburgh but supported Edward Balliol in opposition to David II between 1332 and 1341.
1339–1453	The Hundred Years' War, initiated by the confiscation of Aquitaine by Philip VI of France. Open hostilities between 1337 and 1360 included English victories in the naval action of Sluys (1340), the battle of Crecy (1347), and the capture of Calais (1347). Initial parliamentary unrest over costs of the war subsided after 1341, and Edward III's relations with parliament remained amicable until the mid-1370s.
1345–1500	Royal charters of incorporation were obtained by 42 towns during these years; even more significantly, between 1373, when Edward III granted Bristol incorporation and status as an

	autonomous county, and 1500, nine other towns were separated from their counties, to exercise autonomous jurisdiction within their boundaries: York, Newcastle, Norwich, Lincoln, Hull, Southampton, Nottingham, Coventry, and Canterbury.
1346	David II of Scotland captured at battle of Neville's Cross, halting a Scottish invasion.
1348	Order of the Garter established.
1348–50	Black Death ravaged Britain; population loss estimated at one-third to one-half.
*c.*1350	The first paper-mill in England.
1351	Statute of Labourers attempted to fix wages and prices following the Black Death; Statute of Provisors attempted to reduce foreign clergy in English benefices.
1356	Edward, the Black Prince, vanquished French army at the battle of Poitiers, capturing the King of France (Jean le Bon).
1357	Treaty of Berwick: ransom of David II.
1359–60	Edward III's last expedition in France; Treaty of Bretigny (1360), never implemented, marked a new direction in the war, as Edward III substituted autonomous authority over Gascony for his earlier claim to the French crown. The Black Prince, invested with the title "Prince of Aquitaine," alienated the support of French aristocracy in southern France.
1361	Return of the plague.
1362	Statute prescribing use of English for pleading and judgement in the courts.
1363	English used to explain the summoning of parliament.
1369	Renewed war between English and French. The Black Prince ordered the sack of Limoges in 1370, but the French were successful in reconquering lost territory between 1369 and 1375.
1371–8	John Wyclif (1330–84), associated with negotiations and policies of the Black Prince and John of Gaunt, preached on disendowment of the clergy in 1376, was condemned by Pope Gregory XI in 1377, and by the University of Oxford in 1381.
1376	The "Good Parliament," dissatisfied with the royal administration, impeached several royal advisors.
1377–99	Reign of Richard II, aged 10 when he inherited the crown.

1377	The "Bad Parliament" reversed reforms designed to rein in royal expenditures and voted the first general poll tax, taxing every married couple and single person regardless of wealth or income, exempting only beggars.
1378–1417	Great Schism of the papacy: rival popes in Rome and Avignon.
1381	The Peasants' Revolt, offering occasion for a strong display of courage and initiative by Richard, but leaving a deep anxiety at the prospect of similar resistance from peasants in the future.
1382	Richard II married Anne of Bohemia.
1385	Robert de Vere created Duke of Ireland. Richard II's Scottish expedition, which included the sack of Edinburgh, ended inconclusively.
1386	The "Wonderful Parliament" again attempted to impose oversight of the king's expenditures, warning Richard that kings who governed contrary to law and parliament could be deposed. John of Gaunt departed for Spain to pursue a tenuous claim to the crown of Spain.
1388	"Merciless Parliament" of Lords Appellant, led by Richard's uncle, Thomas duke of Gloucester, impeached and condemned five of Richard's advisors.
1388	Earl Douglas defeated English army at Battle of Otterburn ("Chevy Chase").
1394	Anne of Bohemia died.
1396	Richard married Isabelle, daughter of Charles VI of France, with a clause obliging the French to support him against his English enemies.
1397	Richard struck at the Lords Appellant, exiling, imprisoning or killing them, although the earl of Derby (Henry Bolingbroke, the future Henry IV) and the duke of Norfolk were not banished until 1398.
1398–9	Richard's second expedition to Ireland.
1399	Death of John of Gaunt. Deposition and murder of Richard II by Henry Bolingbroke.
1399–1413	Reign of Henry IV, whose ambiguous claim to the throne led to a concession that he would appoint his officials with the consent of parliament (subsequently revoked) and that money bills would ordinarily begin in the Commons, not the Lords.

1400–9	Welsh rising of Owain Glyndwr; parliaments at Machynlleth and Pennal, alliance with France (1404–6).
1401	Statute "On Burning Heretics" signaled vigorous suppression of Lollards, reformers associated with Wycliffe's views on the church. William Sawtry burned at Smithfield.
1402	Percies and northern barons halt Scottish invasion at Homildon Hill; Percy revolt quelled at the Battle of Shrewsbury (1403). Rebellion and execution of Richard Scrope, archbishop of York (1405).
1413–22	Reign of Henry V.
1413	Parliament recognized a new status, "gentleman," below the rank of esquire.
1414	Lollard revolt of Sir John Oldcastle (Lord Cobham); Oldcastle executed, 1417.
1414–18	Council of Constance, a gathering of churchmen intended to resolve the Schism and reform corrupt practices in the church; only the former was achieved. In 1415, the Council ordered the burning of Johan Hus for views similar to Wycliffe's.
1414–19	John Talbot, chief governor of Ireland, attempted to reverse demoralization and exodus of the Anglo-Irish colonial class.
1415	Henry V invaded France, capturing Harfleur and defeating the French army at Agincourt.
1415	Bridgettine order established in England at Syon Abbey.
1418–c.1509	Paston family correspondence.
1420	The Treaty of Troyes included recognition by Charles VI that Henry VI was the Duke of Normandy and heir to the crown of France.
1422–61	Reign of Henry VI.
1422	Humphrey, duke of Gloucester, uncle of the infant king, became regent in England, while another uncle, the duke of Bedford, managed English interests in France.
1430	Joan of Arc captured and delivered to the English; burned at Rouen, 1431.
1431	Henry VI crowned king of France in Paris.
1433–c.1550	Plumpton family correspondence.

1435	Treaty of Arras established peace between Philip of Burgundy and Charles VII of France, ending the Burgundian alliance with England.
1436	Henry VI assumed his regality, but Council remained in power; Charles VII re-entered Paris in the same year, signaling the decline in English power on the continent. By 1443, rivalry between supporters of Humphrey duke of Gloucester, and William de la Pole, duke of Suffolk, reduced the Council to impotence.
1445	Marriage of Henry VI to Margaret of Anjou, Charles VII's niece, but English failure to fulfil promise to withdraw from Maine led to renewed war in 1448, the loss of Normandy in 1450, Gascony in 1451, and Bordeaux in 1453; only Calais in what is now France remained in English hands, until 1558, and the "Hundred Years' War" effectively ended.
1447	Duke of Gloucester died under indictment for treason, initiated by duke of Suffolk; Suffolk, in 1450, forced to flee, was assassinated on his way to France.
1450	Henry VI carried debts several times the normal annual income of the crown; a squire, Jack Cade, led a rising that called for dismissal of unworthy advisors, the regency of the duke of York, and a return to rule of law, although he was killed before presentation of the petition. On the continent, Gutenberg printed Bible in Mainz.
1453	Henry VI, long known to be mentally handicapped, collapsed under pressure of military disasters abroad and politial confusion at home; increasingly, doubts voiced about legitimacy of Lancastrian claim to the throne. The fall of Constantinople to the Turks, and the end of the Roman Empire in the east, coincided with end of English pretensions to sovereignty in France.
1455	Rivalry among aristocrats over control of Henry VI and the monarchy broke into open conflict, subsequently known as Wars of the Roses, at the first battle of St Albans, where the duke of Somerset, representing interests of the Beaufort/Lancastrian faction, was killed, enabling Richard, duke of York, to become Protector of the Realm.
1460	Richard of York died in the battle of Wakefield, but his supporters, associated with white rose, won definitive victory at Towton the following year, at the Second Battle of St Albans.
1461–83	Reign of Edward IV.

1461	The son and heir of Richard of York, aged 19, acclaimed king as Edward IV, in debt to Neville family, and especially Richard Neville, earl of Warwick, for his victory, while Percy family threw support to the deposed Henry VI.
1464	Edward IV married Elizabeth Wydeville, precluding dynastic marriage diplomacy, and irritating Warwick, further alienated by Edward's decision to marry his sister to the duke of Burgundy, so abandoning Warwick's goal of improved relations with France.
1471	Warwick "the Kingmaker" briefly restored Henry VI, then died in Battle of Barnet. Henry VI was murdered in the Tower and Edward IV reassumed the throne. Lancastrian claims to throne subsequently represented by Henry Tudor, earl of Richmond, son of Edmund Tudor and Margaret Beaufort.
1475–83	Edward's war with France (funded by imposition of a "benevolence", 1474), concluded quickly; parliamentary reversals of grants made by Henry VI, careful management of the king's own estates, and avoidance of further military adventures enabled both Edward and his eventual successor Henry VII to escape major dependence on parliamentary taxation.
1476	William Caxton set up press in the Almonry, Westminster.
1483	Death of Edward IV in April, after a decade or so of relatively quiet relations between crown and nobility, was followed by accession of his son, Edward V, deposed in June and eliminated in murky circumstances by Edward IV's brother, Richard, duke of Gloucester, who would rule as Richard III.
1483–85	Reign of Richard III.
1485–1509	Reign of Henry VII, begun by the death of Richard III at Bosworth Field when Henry Tudor launched a military campaign from France.
1486	Henry Tudor, who asserted the weakest hereditary claim to the crown since William the Conqueror, married Elizabeth, daughter of Edward IV, symbolically linking the two roses, Lancastrian and Yorkist.
1487	Henry VII defeated Lambert Simnel, masquerading as a nephew of Edward IV. Star Chamber established.
1489	Yorkshire rising suppressed.
1491–9	Plot of Perkin Warbeck, Flemish pretender to the English crown.
1492	Voyage of Columbus; Henry VII invades France.

1495	Statute of Drogheda: Edward Poynings, Deputy in Ireland, subjects Irish legislature to the crown and parliament of England. Foundation of Aberdeen University.
1496	Treaty Magnus Intercursus ends dispute with Flanders. James IV invades Northumberland.
1497	Rising in Cornwall suppressed. Truce between England and Scotland. John Cabot's exploration of Newfoundland.
1499–1500	Desiderius Erasmus, at Oxford, met Thomas More.
1500	English conquest of Ireland.
1509–47	Reign of Henry VIII.
1514	James IV fell at the Battle of Flodden Field.
1517	Martin Luther posted 95 theses at Wittenberg; ban of the Edict of Worms, 1521.
1522	England at war with France and Scotland.
1528	England and France at war with Emperor Charles V. Wool staple moved from Antwerp to Calais. Rioting in Kent.
1529	Henry's proposed divorce from Katherine of Aragon submitted to universities for debate. Wolsey dismissed from his offices, succeeded by Thomas More.
1529–37	Reformation Parliament. Henry VIII proclaimed himself supreme head of the Church in England, 1531; submission of English clergy to the crown, 1532.

Timeline of Literary Events

1320s	Richard Rolle, hermit of Hampole (fl. c.1300–49), writing in Latin a series of mystical religious texts, including *Incendium Amoris*.
c.1330	Auchinleck Manuscript[1] created in London, containing mixture of religious texts and romances including *Beves, Degare, Floris and Blancheflur*.
1354	Henry of Lancaster, *Livre des Seynts Medecines* (in Anglo-French).
c.1360	*Pricke of Conscience.*
c.1360	*Speculum Christiani.*
1361–7	Jean Froissart writing in England in household of Queen Philippa in French.
c.1360s	Geoffrey Chaucer in household of Duke of Clarence, English translation of *Roman de la Rose.*
c.1362	William Langland, *Piers Plowman, A Text; B-Text* c.1377; *C-Text, c.* 1390.
c.1370	Chaucer, *Book of the Duchess.*
c.1373	Julian of Norwich (c.1342–1416?) "short version," *Book of Shewings* (*Revelations of Divine Love*); "long version," 1388.
c.1374	John Gower, *Cinkante Balades* in Anglo-French.
c.1374–9	John Gower, *Mirour de l'Omme* in Anglo-French.
1376	First reference to York Corpus Christi Play.
1376	John Barbour, *The Bruce.*
1380–2	Translation of Wycliffe Bible by Nicholas of Hereford and John Purvey.
c.1380	*The Cloud of Unknowing.*
c.1380	Geoffrey Chaucer, *House of Fame.*
c.1382	*Parliament of Fowls.*

1 For a detailed description of this important manuscript and for a list of its contents see The Auchinleck site online: http://www.nls.uk/auchinleck.

c.1381–5	*Troilus and Criseyde; Boece* (translation of Boethius' *Consolation of Philosophy).*
c.1385	*Legend of Good Women* ("F" Prologue).
c.1385	Chandos Herald, *Life of the Black Prince,* in Anglo-French.
c.1385	Thomas Usk, *Testament of Love.*
c.1385	John Gower, *Vox Clamantis* in Latin.
c.1386–90	*Confession Amantis,* revised 1393.
c.1385–7	John Trevisa, translation of Ranulf Higden's *Polychronicon.*
c.1390	Vernon Manuscript.[2]
1390s	*Pearl* Manuscript containing *Sir Gawain and the Green Knight, Patience,* and *Cleannesse.*
c.1387–1400	Geoffrey Chaucer, *The Canterbury Tales.*
c.1391	*Treatise on the Astrolabe.*
c.1392	Earliest mention of Coventry Corpus Christi play.
c.1395	*Pierce the Ploughman's Crede.*
c.1396	Walter Hilton, *Scale of Perfection.*
c.1398	John Trevisa, translation of *De Proprietatibus Rerum.*
c.1398	John Gower, *Traitié pour essampler les amantz marietz* in Anglo-French.
c.1400	*Cronica Tripartita.*
c.1399–1406	*Richard the Redeless* and *Mum and the Sothsegger.*
1402	Thomas Hoccleve, *Letter of Cupid,* translation of Christine de Pisan's *L'Epistre au Dieu d'Amours.*
c.1406	*La Male Regle.*
c.1408	John Lydgate, *Reason and Sensuality.*
c.1410	Edward, Duke of York, *The Master of Game.*
c.1410	*Dives and Pauper.*
c.1410	Nicholas Love, *Mirrour or the Blessed Lyf of Jesu Christ.*
c.1412	Thomas Hoccleve, *De Regimine Principum* (The Regiment of Princes).

2 For access to the editorial site for ths manuscript see: http://www.medievalenglish.bham.ac.uk/vernon/.

c.1412–20	John Lydgate, *Troy Book*, translated from Guido delle Colonne, *Historia Troiana*.
c.1416	*Life of Our Lady*.
c.1418–c.1509	Paston family correspondence.
c.1420	Margery Kempe, *The Book of Margery Kempe*.
1422	Earliest mention of Chester Corpus Christi play; c.1421–2.
	John Lydgate, *Siege of Thebes*.
c.1426–8	*Pilgrimage of the Life of Man*, translated from Guillaume de Deguileville, *Le Pelerinage de la Vie Humaine*.
c.1431–8	*Fall of Princes*, translated from Boccaccio, *De Casibus Virorum Illustrium*.
c.1436	*The Libell of English Policye*.
c.1440	Robert Thornton, *The Thornton Manuscript*.
c.1450–1500	The Townley play cycle (Wakefield Plays).
c.1450	*The Floure and the Leaf*.
c.1461–1500	*Croxton Play of the Sacrament*.
c.1470	Sir Thomas Malory, *Morte Darthur*.
c.1470	Morality plays *Wisdom* and *Mankind*.
c.1473	Sir John Fortescue, *On the Governance of England*.
1476	William Caxton sets up his press in Westminster Cathedral precinct. He prints:

1474	*The Dicts or Sayengis of the Philosophres*.
1478	*The Canterbury Tales*, *Parliament of Fowles*, *Boethius' Consolation of Philosophy*.
1479	*Book of Courtesy*.
1481	*Myrrour of the World*.
1482	*Troilus and Creseyde*, Trevisa's translation of Higden's *Polychronicon*.
1483	*The Golden Legend*.
1484	*Order of Chivalry*, *Book of the Knight of the Tower*.
1485	Malory's *Morte D'Arthur*.
c.1510	*Everyman*.

Introduction

Contextualizing late medieval English literature means reading it within an Anglo-European tradition of language and culture, as well as multiple insular traditions of custom, law and history. The canonical authors of the period of 1350 to 1530 – Geoffrey Chaucer, John Gower, the anonymous Gawain-poet, William Langland, Julian of Norwich, Margery Kempe, John Lydgate, Thomas Malory, the anonymous authors of the York and Chester Plays, of morality plays such as *Everyman* and *Wisdom*, and of romances – wrote for audiences who both shared a common general culture and also shared more narrow *sociolects*, that is the discourses, values and cultural memories of relatively defined groups within the larger society. The history of Middle English literature has been written largely in terms of binaries, of popular and courtly, of urban and rural, male and female without fully recognizing the multiple ways that individual members of the culture crossed multiple boundaries in their reading tastes. Citizens of London's urban culture are closely associated with the romances of the Auchinleck Manuscript; country gentry read Gower's works; there is increasing recognition that Langland's "country" poem, *Piers Plowman*, was popular in London circles; Caxton's Arthurian romances were intended for a mixed audience of gentle men and women.

Generic categories, too, break down under closer scrutiny. A religious lyric like William Herebert's praise of the Virgin contains a legal metaphor that suggests the author, a monk, lived and thought in multiple registers of expression and multiple fields of imagination – as Shakespeare did two centuries later. While we are used to thinking of later English literature as written by people who could be religious divines and passionate lovers, theatrical entrepreneurs and brilliant poets, we seem not to recognize such possibilities in medieval writers. Chaucer's life as a servant of the crown and member of parliament is almost invisible in the modern critical reception of his work.[1] One of the challenges of this volume is to try to recover some of the varied modes of thinking and registers of expression that English people used during the later Middle Ages.

The period addressed by this volume, the fourteenth to the early sixteenth centuries, is often referred to as a time of change; terms like "reformation" and "revolution" are employed to describe events, singly and cumulatively. Yet while it is a time when English culture was truly on the cusp of significant institutional and bureaucratic change, it was also – paradoxically and simultaneously – a

1 Carlson, David R., *Chaucer's Jobs* (New York: Palgrave Macmillan, 2004).

culture that insisted on the value of continuity and custom. Religion, social structure, production and polity are all in significant flux as earlier models devolve and evolve. The received narrative of this period focuses attention on several major events: the Hundred Years' War, a time of chronic conflict among and within English and French aristocracy; a virulent form of plague in the mid-fourteenth century that affected all aspects of social life throughout Europe; continuing political struggles that resulted in the deposition of Richard II in 1399; years of internecine Lancastrian and Yorkist contention for local advantage and access to the crown which finally culminated in the 1485 victory of Henry Tudor at the battle of Market Bosworth, and in the establishment of a Tudor dynasty to which credit is given for a Reformation of religion threatened, feared, and contained for nearly a hundred and fifty years from 1385 to 1534.

Such a narrative may exaggerate the disorder and turbulence of the period, direct too much attention to dynastic struggles and too little to the broader spectrum of communities that constitute culture. What is remarkable in this period is not so much evident change, but rather the surprising stability of the terms of political and religious debate and discourse and the conceptual paradigms within which debates and discourses are carried on. The fifteenth century may seem a period of confused polity and struggle, characterized by derivative literary expression because of our tendency to use binary paradigms of order and disorder or growth and decay. In this volume we are interested in the coexistence of disorder and continual adaptation as a productive synergy in the literary culture of this period. Fifteenth-century literature and culture form a continuum with past and future, a continuum in which authors revisit and reshape previous genres – witness, for instance, the abiding interest in foundation narratives like the *Brut* that combine history and romance. This literature flourishes in tandem with renewed attention to the virtue of *prudence* in household governance as well as statecraft; the classic definition of *prudence* as an ability to learn from the past in order to prepare for the future suggests the broad importance of the idea of the past of late medieval English culture.[2]

The major canonical writers of the period likewise evince a decided continuity of theme and concern; in many respects their literary efforts constitute a palimpsest, a continual re-writing of partially erased older works. The authority of previous writers defines the fields, but the urgency of emerging cultural concerns guarantees that older forms are renewed. In this respect Henryson's *Testament of Cresseid* is an instructive example, for Henryson works out of and against the influence of Chaucer's earlier depiction of Criseyde in *Troilus and Criseyde*. Chaucer is famously proclaimed as the father of English literature by his followers in the fifteenth century. His themes of love, romance, and history, his exemplary stories of religion and constancy, no less than his adept and

2 Ferster, Judith, *Fictions of Advice: the Literature and Politics of Counsel in Late Medieval England* (Philadelphia: University of Pennsylvania Press, 1996).

imaginative use of the English language, provide a steady influence on the literature of the period covered by this volume. Lydgate writes in admiration and emulation of Chaucer whose reputation is reinforced by Caxton's press and by later sixteenth-century admirers like Spenser whose archaisms provide an index to Chaucer's influence and to the fading accessibility of his language. Similarly, Gower's late-fourteenth-century works in English, Anglo-French and Latin, self-consciously announce both his project to instruct his readership and the moral and social value his works provide by drawing on classical stories. Their late-fourteenth-century contemporaries, Langland and the Gawain-poet, each in a very different way, write of concern with how individuals in society work singly or in groups to the best of their ability to fulfill their roles, often evoking a sense of a golden past as a standard for present and future. Late-fourteenth-century anxiety about chivalric values and their performance is echoed in Malory's Arthurian narratives where chivalric codes are tested in a variety of circumstance. Lydgate's *Troy book* and *Siege of Thebes* re-write the stories that form the back matter of so much of late-fourteenth-century literature, in works ranging from *Sir Gawain and the Green Knight* to the *Troilus*, the *Legend of Good Women* and the *Tales*.

English literature of this period is also characterized by self-conscious striving against measured standards of history and of contemporary Franco-Italian literary and courtly culture in which highly adapted versions of well-known tales shaped into exemplary stories figure prominently. This energetic selective adaptation has been interpreted as giving rise to irony or indeterminacy in such works at Gower's *Confessio* and Chaucer's *Legend of Good Women*, but it may more fruitfully be understood as part of a European literature of dynamic tension in which "morals" and messages are often apparently at odds with narrative flow, as in the narratives of Boccaccio's *Famous Women* and the lives of the pagan heroines Christine extols in the *City of Ladies*. Late medieval literature on both sides of the Channel is a literature capable of saying what it doesn't "mean" and meaning what it doesn't seem to say. This dynamic tension, often apparent in frequent instances of textual *mouvance*, arises from the fact that stories are versions of well-known narratives, selected and adapted for specific circumstances. Such adaptations inevitably recall "missing" details and themes, creating simultaneous literal and shadow texts, particularly in stories like those derived from the Classical narratives that are central to Lydgate's, Chaucer's and Gower's work.

Religious writers of the period, especially Julian of Norwich, whose polished prose style invites comparison to Chaucer's poetic achievement, write of faith in God's abiding love; yet their writing flowers in a time when the terms on which salvation can be achieved are hotly debated, and when such writing itself might be dangerous. The role of grace, of will, the nature of God's absolute power, the efficacy of the sacraments – all doctrinal topics "settled" earlier in the Middle Ages, are contested and re-examined in this period which culminates in the Reformation of religion in sixteenth-century England. The York Play, like other mystery play cycles at Chester and Wakefield, retells Biblical and commonly accepted apocryphal stories of Jesus' life and His Church through the imaginations of laypeople (priests were nominally forbidden to write the plays), interweaving doctrine and secular practice in ways that tell us a great deal about how polymorphous late medieval lay spirituality appropriated and adapted Christian tradition. In recent years abundant evidence of a rich spiritual literature written for and by women has reshaped the way we think about religious experience in late medieval England. The popularity of *prymers* – lay prayer books – from this period, and the role of monastic institutions in publishing and disseminating religious texts, as well as the continuing popularity of hagiographical literature throughout the period, all suggest a thriving religious culture, both secular and regular.

In its forms and messages, late medieval English literature constitutes a body of public performance focused on the self in relation to a variety of groups and institutions, religious, chivalric, political, economic. Individuals figure prominently in much of the literature of the time: single knights on chivalric quests like Gawain, or in search of more material rewards like Degrevant; Lydgate's Virgin Mary, Chaucer's ideal women – Custance, Dorigen, Griselda – often struggle in isolation, facing domestic, religious, or political challenges. Allegories like *Piers Plowman* transform concepts into tales of individuals striving, competing, and uniting. The civic drama translates biblical stories and doctrine into flesh and blood characters. Morality plays present concepts performing as if they were individual human beings. All these announce concern with the individual as part of multiple intersecting social communities and moral, ethical codes. In the importance of conduct literature in this period we read evidence of a continual re-examination of how individuals find their places in society, of how far and in what ways individual action can work for or against the common profit. As members of groups – families, households, guilds, orders of chivalry – individuals derive identity from corporate values even as they affirm and give substance to those values in the practices of their lives.

Late Medieval English Literature: Recent Critical Trends

The literature of late medieval England appears in a wide variety of genres, dialects, and formats. Until recently a canonical approach to the subject had narrowly defined those texts that could be termed literary. Supported by a master-narrative of the triumph of English at the end of the fourteenth century, the canon of late medieval English literature was a hierarchy of works in which the poetry and prose of Chaucer, Gower, Lydgate, Malory – all writers with significant ties to court and to courtly traditions – rested at the center. Attending this center were the works of the Gawain-poet, Langland's *Piers Plowman*, the religious texts of Julian of Norwich, Margery Kempe, and the mystical tradition of Richard Rolle. All of these authors composed texts that are fundamentally literary in the sense of the craft and artifice that underlay their verbal expression and figurative imaginations. The mystery plays were included as evidence of early interest in drama that would finally flourish in the works of the sixteenth-century London playwrights, above all Shakespeare. Much of late medieval English romance remained an unexplored domain in which critics were reluctant to quest, for fear of monstrous language and wandering plots. An implicit teleology linked Chaucer as the foundation and Shakespeare as the apex in this master narrative.

This neat paradigm was broken open in the last decades of the twentieth century by a series of critical movements which transformed how we read the original "canonical" authors, and the myriad of other authors who have been recognized now that the field is more broadly defined. In most cases these new approaches were adaptations of critical methods and principles first used to analyze more contemporary literature and culture. Feminist criticism, impelled by the basic desire to recover women's voices and deeds, asked questions first about women's presences and absences in texts; subsequent research asked where we heard women's voices, what women's reading habits were, how women were patrons as well as audience. This line of inquiry gave rise to scholarly attention to the household as a place where literacy, gender, and power intersected with religious and secular values. The numerous excellent books and essays on these subjects include Diane Watt's *Medieval Women's Writing: Works by and for Women in England, 1100–1500* (Cambridge, UK: Cambridge University Press, 2007), Jocelyn Wogan-Browne's *Medieval Women: Texts and Contexts in Late Medieval Britain: Essays for Felicity Riddy* (Turnhout: Brepols, 2000), and Carol Meale's *Women and Literature in Britain 1150–1500* (Cambridge, UK: Cambridge University Press, 1993).

Developments in conceptualizing women's place in literature and society led to new thinking about gender in relationship to community, faith, social and spiritual anxieties, creating a secondary literature that inquired into bonds that united individuals into communities, and into how individuals understood their relationships to one another. Richard Firth Green's *A Crisis of Truth: Literature and Law in Ricardian England* (Philadelphia: University of Pennsylvania Press, 1999) epitomizes the influence of anthropological paradigms on this line of analysis. Following a thorough discussion of the forms of legal institutions that underlay the importance of *truth* and truthful speech in Ricardian England, he concludes with an epilogue that considers law in the Nigerian novel and how that subject is connected to his medieval English subject. David Aers' work in the 1980s and 1990s engaged the subject of individual and community in several books which helped to shape the critical thought of the period, including *Community, Gender and Individual Identity: English Writing 1360–1430* (New York: Routledge, 1988) and *The Powers of the Holy: Religion, Politics and Gender in Late Medieval English Culture* (University Park, PA: Penn State Press, 1996), with Lynn Staley. Carolyn Dinshaw's writing, first in *Chaucer's Sexual Poetics* (Madison: University of Wisconsin Press, 1989), and subsequently in *Getting Medieval: Sexualities and Communities Pre- and Postmodern* (Durham, NC: Duke University

Press, 1999) encouraged readers to think about sexuality, gender, and difference in a literature never before read so broadly.

During the 1980s and 1990s, one element of the dominant paradigm of cultural studies, renewed attention to the reciprocal cultural dynamics that produce literature and influence culture, investigated the relationship among power, economics, and literary production. Eschewing ideas of authorial exceptionalism, New Historicist criticism sought always to locate authors within the terms of the culture that produced them. Strongly influenced by Foucault's answer to the question, "What is an author?," this way of thinking about authorship fit medieval textual production, often anonymous, often subject to scribal variation and reconstruction.

Critical studies opened ways to thinking about larger issues of literacy, audience, and writing, culminating in works like Steven Justice's *Writing and Rebellion: England in 1381* (Berkeley: University of California Press, 1994). It also opened the way to thinking about the play among literature, the self, and coercive power dynamics in works like David Wallace and Barbara Hanawalt's *Bodies and Disciplines: Intersections of Literature and History in Fifteenth Century England* (Minneapolis: University of Minnesota Press, 1996) and Wallace's later *Chaucerian Polity Absolutist Lineages and Associational Forms in England and Italy* (Stanford, CA: Stanford University Press, 1997). Joel Kaye, author of *Economy and Nature in the Fourteenth Century: Money, Market Exchange, and the Emergence of Scientific Thought* (Cambridge, UK: Cambridge University Press, 1998) has analyzed medieval economics, theories and assumptions about value and exchange, to offer new understanding of the role of the markets and money within the late medieval culture. Miri Rubin's study *Corpus Christi: The Eucharist in Late Medieval Culture* (Cambridge, UK: Cambridge University Press, 1991), is an early example of the insights that can be gained by asking what power dynamics underlie community ritual celebrations. Recently Sarah Stanbury's *The Visual Object of Desire in Late Medieval England* (Philadelphia: University of Pennsylvania Press, 2008), analyzes the power of images within a critical paradigm drawn from anthropology, focused on the value of the fetish.

Interest in vision and medieval psychology, medieval history and postcolonial theory, the relationship between art and literature in manuscript culture, has opened medieval studies to new ways of thinking and to ever increasing numbers of readers, both students and more casual inquirers. But a word of caution is always in order when discussing how well and to what extent contemporary theories reveal a hidden past. The dead are vulnerable. They speak, but only indirectly, because they speak only when invited to do so. Their words are selected and assembled by scholars in ways that create patterns of meaning that both do and do not reflect original circumstances or intention. The case of early Christine de Pizan scholarship is a case in point: in the early days of feminist criticism she was hailed as a proto-feminist, a medieval voice of feminist resistance. And, to be sure, she was resistant to misogyny in her own time, but she was also highly accepting of cultural codes and restrictions that limited women's speech, and action, as *Le livre des trois vertus* shows (see 7.11).

A degree of caution is necessary, too, in assuming that what we have access to from late medieval English culture represents the full spectrum of writing and thinking of that time. Paul Strohm has spoken of the "sponsored survivorship" of the manuscripts and texts we have today – they exist because successive generations thought they ought to be preserved, and so they were. What about the texts that were not so lucky? Many unknown texts, as well as copies of preserved texts, have undoubtedly disappeared over the centuries. Judging from the number of unique copies we have of what we regard as major medieval texts – *Sir Gawain and the Green Knight, The Book of Margery Kempe, and* the earlier *Beowulf/Judith* manuscript – we can rightly infer that these texts could not have all been singular exemplars, rather that they represent large classes of literature and literary production now lost to us through the accidents of time or the deliberate predation and destruction of monastic and spiritual texts during the extended period of the Protestant Reformation. Generalization is a luxury few medievalists can indulge.

Recovering Texts

One rule of thumb in assessing the popularity of a medieval text is the number of manuscript witnesses to that text. The greater the number, the greater the presumed popularity and dissemination of a text. Chaucer's *Canterbury Tales* exist in about 100 manuscripts, the *Pricke of Conscience* (see 2.8) exists in 117 manuscripts. We study the former, but very few know anything of the latter. Over the last quarter century the work of recovering medieval texts, a labor first undertaken a hundred and fifty years ago by a generation of Victorian scholars whose knowledge and dedication are still available to students in the publications of the Early English Text Society, has become the focus of much scholarly attention. A new period of manuscript study and editing has contributed immense knowledge as well as access. Derek Pearsall, in a series of studies and edited volumes over the last 25 years has disseminated a great deal of knowledge about manuscript culture and production.[3]

Similarly Martha Driver's work on early book production, particularly images, has helped draw attention to the conventions and assumptions of early printed illustrations (see *The Image in Print: Book Illustration in Late Medieval England and Its Sources* (London: the British Library, 2004). The scholarship concerning late medieval manuscript production has been immeasurably enriched by the research of Kathryn Kerby-Fulton, who has worked extensively on the production and circulation of Langland manuscripts in the British Isles, as well as on

3 See *Manuscripts and Readers in Fifteenth Century England: The Literary Implications of Manuscript Study* (Cambridge, UK: D. S. Brewer, 1983); *Book Production and Publishing in Britain 1375–1475*, ed. with Jeremy Griffiths (Cambridge, UK: Cambridge University Press, 1989); and *New Directions in Later Medieval Manuscript Studies* (Rochester, NY: York Medieval Press, 2000).

evidence of the interactivity between manuscript and reader most often recorded in marginal glosses (see, for example, *The Medieval Professional Reader at Work: Evidence from the Manuscripts of Chaucer, Langland, Kempe, and Gower*, ed. with Maidie Hilmo (Victoria, BC, Canada: University of Victoria, 2001). Kathleen L. Scott's two-volume *Later Gothic Manuscripts 1390–1490* (London: H. Miller, 1996) is the fruit of years of analysis and comparison that have enabled her to identify the hands of various scribes working in multiple manuscripts, and so to deduce new information about the organization and processes of late medieval manuscript production in London. Linne R. Mooney's exceptional patience, imagination, and hard work yielded not only the name, but also a good deal of information about the circumstances of the scribe whom Chaucer called *Adam Scriveyn* and who was closely associated with the production of early manuscripts of *The Canterbury Tales* (see, "Chaucer's Scribe," *Speculum* 81 [2006], pp. 97–138).[4]

Other lines of recovery, often supported by contemporary theory, include investigations into the relationship between the written word and its aural reception, as well as its oral performance. Joyce Coleman's *Public Reading and the Reading Public in Late Medieval England and France* (Cambridge, UK: Cambridge University Press, 1996) and William A. Quinn's *Chaucer's Rehersynges: the Perfomability of the Legend of Good Women* (Washington, DC: Catholic University of American Press, 1994) both emphasized the complex relationships among text, reading, literacy, and performance during the late medieval period. Similarly, scholars have begun to pay attention to the importance of regionalism and to medieval voices speaking of local exchanges and influences; Gail McMurray Gibson's *The Theater of Devotion: East Anglian Drama and Society in the Late Middle Ages* (Chicago: University of Chicago Press, 1989) is a salient example of explaining the value of recognizing the cultural importance of East Anglia's close contact with the spirituality of the Lowlands.

Looking back at the scholarship of late medieval English literature written in the last quarter century one sees emergent patterns of connections. Interest in household literature, the household as the site of reading, writing, and patronage meshes with important work in recovering not only spiritual texts, often written for women, but also romance literature. The essays in Nicola McDonald's *Pulp Fictions of Medieval England: Essays in Popular Romance* (Manchester: Manchester University Press/Palgrave, 2004) explore romance expressions of love and desire, as well as cannibalism and polity. Similarly, a nexus of interest in vision, visuality, memory, and psychology has produced a variety of books on medieval seeing, art, memory, and psychology by Michael Camille, Mary Caruthers, Carolyn Collette, and Susan Akbari.

4 Thirty years ago printed editions and facsimiles were the only source of access to manuscripts; today one can access manuscripts all over the world, sitting at a computer. For teaching purposes certain manuscripts are available for detailed and close study, so that reading a digital edition of the Hengwrt manuscript of the *Tales* alongside a standard print edition allows students to see editorial choices and manuscript variability immediately and clearly.

Arguably, one of the most significant and most recent changes in the field of late medieval English literature is recognition of the rich interplay of the languages of England addressed to a variety of audiences throughout the centuries from the Conquest to the end of the fifteenth century. Recognition of the abiding presence and utility of French as an English language, fostered by the work of Jocelyn Wogan-Browne and scholars like Tim Machan, David Trotter, and Serge Lusignan has re-written the history of vernacular writing in England. The years between the Conquest and the end of the fourteenth century, which for the last hundred years have seemed almost devoid of imaginative literature, are now known to have been full of creative writing, expressed not only in English but also in Anglo-Norman, a form of French which, along with Latin, was an English language. The late Ruth Dean's volume with Maureen Bolton, *Anglo-Norman Literature: A Guide to Texts and Manuscripts* (London: Anglo-Norman Text Society, 1999), catalogues hundreds of texts and thousands of manuscripts written either in the form of French recognized as Anglo-Norman, or in other French dialects employed by writers in England.

As a result, today we see late medieval English literature not so much as the sudden flowering of a newly vitalized English language, or as a sign of national self-definition in distinction from French culture; rather, given the rich history of twelfth and thirteenth-century literary production in England, later medieval literature appears as part of a continuing tradition of writing, a tradition of multilingualism evidenced by texts like *Ancrene Riwle* and *Brut* which appear in multiple languages over the course of time. Certainly the writing associated with the English court at the end of the fourteenth and throughout the fifteenth centuries is demonstrably influenced by French models. Indeed, look wherever one will, one sees abundant evidence of French lexical influence in virtually all late medieval texts, even in *Sir Gawain and the Green Knight*, a text produced in the Northwest Midlands, far from London court circles, and in Scots dialect as well.

Master Narratives

The history of later medieval England is full of widely accepted master narratives: the rise of English as a national tongue; the evolution of a strong central administration; the on-going struggle between royal interests and those of major nobles resolved by the iron determination of the Tudors; the triumph of proto-Protestant religious principles closely linked to literacy; the transformation of an agrarian landscape inhabited by tenant farmers to an agrarian landscape farmed for maximum utility and profit by major landholders. Each of these narratives is true, but none can stand by itself without extensive modification. The master narrative of the chronology of the period covered by this volume contains two extended and briefly overlapping periods of warfare and internecine dispute. The first, the Hundred Years' War, essentially began in the late thirteenth century when the French crown seized the territory of Gascony, subject of a long-simmering dispute over land in France claimed by the English nobility. The phrase "Hundred Years' War" refers to more than a hundred years of intermittent English raids on French territory, French and Scottish raids on English territory, and various victories and defeats, including the famous English victories at the battles of Crecy (1346) and Agincourt (1415). Between 1303 and 1451 periods of warfare were interrupted by extended periods of peace, especially during the reign of Richard II (1377–1399). Although the English succeeded in occupying much of central France during the early fifteenth century, ultimately they were repulsed by the French armies of Charles VII inspired by Joan of Arc.

In many ways the triumphs the English achieved proved to be pyrrhic: Henry V's victory at Agincourt led to his marriage with a royal French princess, Katherine (daughter of Charles VI), who brought a strain of madness into the Lancastrian bloodline that helped to create the instability of the English dynastic disputes known as the Wars of the Roses. Katherine and Henry V's son, Henry VI, proved to be a weak and ineffectual king; his cousin, Edward IV, successfully challenged him for the throne of England. Eventually, in 1485, at the battle of Market Bosworth, Henry Tudor made good his somewhat tenuous claim to the English throne by the right of conquest. Those English people who lived through these disruptions and conflicts were undoubtedly aware of the instability they created, but, as the documents in the chapters devoted to governance suggest, they experienced the effects of instability in local circumstances, through disputes between local magnates and their dependants.

The master narrative of this period also focuses on the fact that the bubonic plague struck Europe in 1348 in the first of what would be waves of pestilence occurring for nearly three hundred years. Europe had not experienced a major pandemic of the sort since the Justinian plagues of the sixth century. Europeans had little immunity to the disease, although some people did survive infection and illness. Moreover, because of a so-called mini ice age in the fourteenth century, the European population had been weakened by years of small or failed harvests. Records suggest that in densely populated communities, especially cities and monastic communities, mortality reached 30 to 40 percent. It is certainly true that the plague effectively reduced the working population of England, and that English people were aware of the change and anxious to minimize its effect on pre-plague exchange values and wages. The records of the later fourteenth century are full of references to disputes over the tenure of land, over wages, the right to work, and secondary effects of altered patterns of land usage, culminating in the incursion of sheep onto land formerly reserved for tillage.

Another element of the master narrative of the instability of the period focuses on strains within the Catholic Church, in respect to its leadership and its doctrines. The papal exile from Rome to Avignon (1309–77, when French popes led the Catholic Church), and the following Papal Schism when Italian pontiffs disputed the election of French popes and sought to move the seat of the Papacy back to Rome (1378–1417, resolved at the Council of Constance) coincided with a series of attempts at renewal in the Christian Church. Mysticism, with its focus on individual access to spiritual truth revealed privately, challenged Church doctrines that asserted the need for priestly intermediaries for salvation. The rise of Wycliffite thought with its suspicions of corrupt Church practices, its attack on the doctrines of transubstantiation, and its sponsorship of access to scripture in the vernacular, posed a challenge to the established Church. In their criticism of the ecclesiastical hierarchy and its de facto assault on secular power through a parallel legal system and a parallel ability to raise money from a subject population, Wycliffites became defenders of state against the Church, as we see in 2.22.

In addition to these familiar plot lines, accepted half-truths about the period are also fixed firmly in popular assumption. That the kings of England were exceedingly powerful is one; in fact the history of English kingship is one of negotiation and cooperation with both powerful nobles and the commons. At times this delicate system was so challenged it broke down, and the king was deposed, as happened to Edward II, to Richard II, and, to some extent, to Henry VI. Another popular myth is that medieval people were either nobles or peasants, and, if peasants, largely without power, doomed to work their land. The documents throughout this volume show a complex social hierarchy which seems to have fostered multiple routes of access to various courts and intermediaries, both official, as in the legal system, and unofficial, as in the system of patronage and affiliation which facilitated social advancement and change. Women are also thought to have been essentially powerless, when the fact is that although the learned clerical tradition worked very hard to create women as a separate, inferior class, their contributions to household and to production were highly necessary and therefore highly valued. Literacy is commonly thought to have been restricted to the gentry classes, but evidence shows the importance of literacy and numeracy for anyone who dealt in trade or, indeed, in farming.

Historical Contexts

One of the challenges of this project has been to contend with the assumptions of modern categories. England was a nation during the late medieval period, in the sense that medieval English used the term *nation*, that is in the sense of a people who lived in England and imagined themselves related and alike in fundamental ways. But England was not a nation state in the way we understand nation states today. It is true that the crown was able to collect taxes (if parliament was agreeable), administer justice (with increasing efficiency during this period), and wage war, defensive and offensive. But English people's lives were not necessarily nation-centered, or as centered in London and the royal court as much of our criticism suggests. England was a country of local and regional cultures. Multiplicity of languages, of literary forms and genres during this period is matched by multiple *sociolects*. People in the north were not quite the same as people in the south, as we see in 1.1.

Contextualizing the literature of such a dynamic culture is a daunting challenge. How does one select documents both broadly representative and comprehensible to the modern reader? Does one select sources for what seem today, from a modern perspective, to be the "major" trends of the period, important in hindsight, but not universally widespread in late medieval England – Lollardy, for instance? Or does one concentrate on more widespread doctrines and practices, like Marian devotion? The answer, of course, must be both, but the question requires continual attention. The authors of this volume have made several open as well as deliberate choices, realizing that transparency of purpose can alleviate, if not prevent, the inevitable displacements and appropriations that modern culture inflicts on the past. We have decided to try to contextualize literary works by representing a broad cross-section of intellectual, religious, and political practices. We believe the best context for the literature of the period is the broad context of the culture in which it is produced. Wherever possible, we have striven for documents that represent general praxis: what did late medieval men and women throughout the country of England actually do? What did they hear in churches, think about the created world, and about human sexuality? How did they create and settle disputes? Why does violence seem a hallmark of this age? What purposes did violence serve? These are some of the questions we asked, and to which this volume offers some preliminary answers. We offer the texts here as indications of lines of thinking and ways of organizing the world of late medieval culture. The documents that follow represent the world that produced them. But no set of documents, no matter how extensive, can fully define that world.

The choice of sources for this volume posed many challenges, but some of the challenges are a cause for gratitude: Medieval English people made and kept lots of records of their activities, their disputes and negotiations, their thoughts and their feelings, which made the selection difficult but also fun. Organizing them also proved challenging but engaging, given the many different dimensions of culture, society, and consciousness that any individual item might be used to illustrate, or at least partly explain. We do not claim the logic which governed our final decisions about the divisions into which we placed sources, or the order in which we arrange them, is required by the sources themselves; finally, our decisions stemmed from our common sense of what gave promise of being most useful for our readers. Our commitment in shaping this volume has been to contextualize late medieval English literature by trying to represent salient values, institutions, struggles, and aspirations of the people that produced and read it.

We begin with "The English Languages," to establish from the outset the fundamental, shaping importance of the multiplicity of languages English people in the late Middle Ages used to express their ideas, record their doings, and communicate with one another. In English law courts, a version of French remained the language for reporting about law cases in the early sixteenth century, and Latin remained universal for the official records of cases in common law courts; but in Chancery and prerogative courts, complaints and pleadings were ordinarily in English. Immediately following are two chapters designed to describe and illuminate two dominant cultural paradigms in late medieval England: Chapter 2, "Spiritual Affirmations, Aspirations and Anxieties," and Chapter 3, "Violence and the Work of Chivalry." In both chapters we focus on praxis, on what was done, and on instructions for how things ought to be done in these two crucial spheres of cultural performance. But neither chivalry nor Christianity had a monopoly on cultural authority, and we proceed from them to Chapter 4, "Scientia: Knowledge Practical, Theoretical and Historical," which undertakes a brief but, we hope, illuminating survey of what kinds of knowledge mattered to English people, as well as an indication of the immense value they placed on ancient literature and authority. And from a collection of sources intended to enable an understanding of what people regarded as important to know about themselves and the world they lived in, we move to fifteenth-century production and circulation of books which brought the worlds of knowledge and literature into the lives of increasing numbers of English people. Chapter 5, "Book Production: The World of Manuscripts, Patrons, and Readers," offers information on how books were created, requested, shared, sold, and valued as objects of cultural importance, and as objects which encoded dangers to the smooth functioning of society.

Full appreciation of what late medieval literature contained, of the culture it simultaneously reflected and transformed, requires attention to the work performed in the countryside and in towns and cities. Managing and controlling the work of peasants and rural laborers, of craftsmen and artisans, did not simply provide the framework for cultural production; so vigorously were the relations and terms of work and production contested, that it could be said to be itself the most important cultural product of the period. Chapter 6, "Producing and Exchanging: Work in Manors and Towns," is an attempt both to illuminate the lives of workers on whom the edifice of ideas and values ultimately depended, and to show the active contribution that these workers made to shaping late medieval cultural and social institutions. Indeed, they contributed also to shaping the political structures within which English people, of high and low status alike, negotiated terms for living together.

We end this collection with Chapter 7, sources about "Polity and Governance, Unity and Disunity." This final chapter is about royal government, and aristocratic participation in that government; about the troubled alliance between royal government and spiritual authorities; about how – whether the domain was that of the household or the kingdom – English people struggled to reconcile a deep commitment to harmony and unity with preservation of a hierarchy of status and class that bound together, but also pitted against each other, governors and governed.

How to Use This Book

The varied texts that constitute the chapters of this book share a focus on action, either proposed or recorded: they testify to a commitment to negotiation through verbal appeals, legal recourse, and political petition, all enlisted to serve a desire for *common profit* that grows out of harmonious unity and community within household, cities, estates, and the realm. While not all of these texts directly contextualize literary production of the period, all represent the imaginative paradigms in which late medieval English people conceived individuality, social relations, and political structures. They give us a sense of the fundamental beliefs and cultural structures that constitute the matrix in which literary expression is grounded. Our aim in this book has been to assemble an array of texts not easily accessible,[5] voices speaking of what may be unfamiliar and perhaps surprising values to modern readers.

Because we have drawn on such a wide variety of sources we have had to treat our sources in a variety of ways. Wherever it was feasible without too much inconvenience to a modern reader, we have kept the original Middle English language of our sources. While Middle English may at first seem quite different from modern English, it is not so different that it cannot be read. Vocabulary presents the first challenge, as medieval English people lived in a different culture and their language is full terms for the material and abstract constructs of their world. We have glossed all the Middle English extracts; if you find words that are not clear from context and are not glossed, both the *Oxford English Dictionary* and the *Middle English Dictionary* are available online.

Alphabet presents a second major challenge to modern readers of medieval texts. The alphabet medieval English people used was different from ours: they had a sign for "th" termed *thorn* and represented by the symbol þ, and a sign that represented both "y" and "gh," termed *yogh*, and represented by the symbol 3. We have modernized both of these to current spelling throughout the text. The Middle English alphabet did not distinguish between "i" and "y" in any regular way, so the two appear as vowels almost interchangeably throughout these texts. Similarly our modern distinction of "u" and "v" does not appear in these texts where either one is used for both modern sounds. Middle English texts, depending on date and dialect, used two sets of personal pronouns, one derived from the Norse, and used today, *they, their, them,* while Anglo-Saxon personal pronouns *he, hire, hem* also appeared throughout the medieval period. To prevent confusion about pronouns, which are often drawn from both Norse and Anglo-Saxon, one informal rule of thumb in reading these texts is to ask if a word beginning with an "h" would be more familiar if you imagined a "t" before

5 Because this book is primarily intended for undergraduates, we have not generally indicated the manuscripts from which the print editions of texts we cite are edited. In virtually every case an inquiring reader can discover the original manuscript(s) by consulting the print editions.

the "h." Finally, we have preserved early print punctuation that reflected manuscript practice in Caxton's prologues and epilogues.

We have footnoted the signal orthographical[6] features of different dialects. Medieval scribes wrote what they heard, and as sounds differed from region to region, so did the spelling of manuscripts, which can often retain traces of the dialect in which they were composed and traces of a scribe's own, different dialect. We have not engaged pronunciation at all, in part because it is dialect specific. What we can say, though, is if a passage is difficult, try sounding it out – your ear may recognize what your eye cannot. Middle English pronounced all the letters on a page, even "k" before "n" and all "-es" endings.[7] Most of all, we hope that you will feel free to make this book your own by skipping from text to text and subject to subject, following your interest and curiosity. As we have said before, medieval culture defies modern categories; it is hard to separate religion from politics, and politics from household. In reading in these texts we hope you will come to share our sense of the rich, surprising diversity of thought and culture they represent and to realize that the Middle Ages are even more fascinating in fact than they seem be in contemporary popular culture.

6 Orthography: spelling system

7 A simple and helpful guide to pronunciation of later Middle English appears in the introduction to the *Riverside Works of Geoffrey Chaucer*, widely available in academic and public libraries.

1
The English Languages

Introduction

The language and literature of later medieval England reflect the complicated cultural history of Britain,[1] a fertile island rich in natural resources. In the mid-twelfth century Geoffrey of Monmouth described Britain in this way at the beginning of his account of the various nations and tribes who had successively invaded, occupied, defended, and lost control of Britain:

> Britain, the best of islands, is situated in the Western Ocean, between France and Ireland. It stretches for eight hundred miles in length and for two hundred in breadth. It provides in unfailing plenty everything that is suited to the use of human beings. It abounds in every kind of mineral. It has broad fields and hillsides which are suitable for the most intensive farming and in which, because of the richness of the soil, all kinds of crops are grown in their seasons. It also has open woodlands which are filled with every kind of game. Through its forest glades stretch pasture-lands which provide the various feeding-stuffs needed by cattle, and there too grow flowers of every hue which offer their honey to the flitting bees. At the foot of its windswept mountains it has meadows green with grass, beauty-spots where clear springs flow into shining streams which ripple gently and murmur an assurance of deep sleep to those lying on their banks.[2]

Because of its fertility, and its proximity to Europe, Britain received waves of invaders, settlers, and raiders in the 1,300 years before the late Middle Ages. Geoffrey of Monmouth's narrative tells part of the story of how the Britons coped with the Romans, the Angles and the Saxons. Subsequent invasions by Vikings, Danes, and Normans ensured that the people of Britain would be a diverse, at times unsettled population, and that their language, like the land they inhabited, would be the product of a continual process of fertile renewal.

---

1 The island of Britain comprises the modern nations England, Scotland and Wales.

2 Geoffrey of Monmouth, *The History of the Kings of Britain*, trans. Lewis Thorpe (New York: Penguin Books, 1966), p. 53.

Historians of the English language have generally concentrated their narratives on three major elements of English: its roots in Germanic languages, the influence of Latin on its vocabulary, especially on the formation of an ecclesiastical discourse during the Anglo-Saxon period, and the influence of two forms of French.[3] The first was Anglo-Norman, the French spoken and written in England after the Norman Conquest of 1066 until the later thirteenth century. This form of French became the basis of the legal language of England termed "law French."[4] From the beginning of the fourteenth century through the period this book covers, a second wave of French influence, largely in the form of new and "re-borrowed" vocabulary, expanded the language's capacity for abstraction and its ability to express religious, theological, and political discourses in an English vernacular which rapidly Anglicized French borrowings. David Crystal estimates that in the last quarter of the fourteenth century 2,500 new French words, largely abstractions, entered English.[5] By the late fourteenth century, the English language demonstrated evidence of the history of Britain. English was structurally a Germanic language in respect to its core vocabulary and grammar: for instance, the verb *to be* in Middle English (ME) *been/beon* developed from Old English (OE) *beon*; *to see,* ME *seen/seon,* came from OE *seon*; the prepositions, *in, at, to, from* derived from OE as did common nouns like the words for *wife, brother, sister, father, home, land, water.* Allowing for dialectical differences in orthography,[6] all are essentially the same words in Old English, Middle English, and Modern English. Medieval English used the singular third person pronouns of OE, *he, she, hit,* but a set of Old Norse plurals, familiar to us today as the English *they, their, them,* largely supplanted OE plural pronouns, first in the Northern dialect, and by the end of the fifteenth century throughout England. Invasion and settlement patterns also influenced spelling, place names, and dialects. Suffixes such as *-by* and *-thorpe,* common in the North of England that was once part of the Danelaw,[7] indicated different communities of settlers and inscribed a history of invasion into the geography of the country.[8] The net result was that by the later fourteenth century English-speaking people in

3 See bibliography for references to some of the plethora of texts now available on the history of the English language.

4 For an informed early twentieth-century discussion about the persistence of French in the English until the seventeenth century and its evolution, see http://www. orbilat.com/Influences_of_Romance/English/RIFL-English-French-The_Anglo-French_Law_Language. html.

5 David Crystal, *The Stories of English* (New York: Overlook Press, 2004), p. 154.

6 Spelling.

7 A large area of Eastern England settled by Danish immigrants; by the middle of the ninth century, the Danelaw was recognized as a distinct cultural region of Britain.

8 The suffix *-by* in names like Whitby and Rugby occurs in areas occupied by the Danes; the suffix derives from a Danish word meaning "farm" or "town." The suffix *-thorp(e)* in place names like Althorp derives from a Scandinavian word for village.

Britain seem to have been self-consciously aware of the diverse forms their language took, aware that English sounded different and was written differently in various parts of the country.[9] Although there was no fixed orthography in English at this point, the written record preserves a number of texts that begin to identify Northern and Southern dialects as less or more "correct" and, by implication, to define the North as lacking against a Southern standard. This division of "North and South" would continue to dominate English political and social thought into the twentieth century. By the end of the fourteenth century writers in the south of England, especially those associated with the royal court at London, began self-consciously to shape English into a literary language. Their work, and the London dialect they used, became the foundation of a future national language, one distinct from Latin or romance languages, with its own style and a rich capacity for multiple registers of expression through which to present English people and their thoughts to one another and to the rest of the world.

In addition to reflecting persistent concern about the inconvenience of linguistic diversity in English, the documents in this chapter reflect some of the concern English writers felt about the capacity of their language to function as an adequate vehicle for translation and for elegant expression. A recurrent anxiety about the difference between English's imputed "rudeness" and the smooth eloquence of French appears in some of these documents. The documents that create apologies for translation demonstrate an awareness of the value of the vernacular, an implicit challenge to the hegemony of Latin and clerical culture. Such an emphasis on the need for translation and the utility of the vernacular was not unique to England. Earlier in the fourteenth century Dante made a plea for the utility and capacity of the vernacular in *De Vulgari Eloquentia, and* in the middle years of the century Nicole Oresme, one of Charles V's great court translators, argued passionately for the French vernacular as a language of literature and culture. Many of the documents in this section, particularly the ones written in London English, show that English was capable of creating a variety of registers of expression that produced lively and engaging writing. Finally, this section also contains documents that demonstrate how easily late medieval English people moved among Latin, French, and English; wills, civic records, and even love poetry demonstrate the multi-lingualism of this culture.

---

9 For a detailed presentation of Middle English dialect difference, see *A Linguistic Atlas of Late Medieval English*, Angus McIntosh, M. L. Samuels, Michael Benskin with the assistance of Margaret Laing and Keith Williamson (Aberdeen: Aberdeen University Press, 1986).

The English Vernacular: Voice(s) of the Mother Tongue

1.1 John Trevisa, "Concerning the Language of the Inhabitants of Britain," from a Translation of Higden's *Polychronicon*, based on Fernand Mossé, *A Handbook of Middle English*, James A. Walker, trans. (Baltimore: Johns Hopkins, 1966), pp. 286–9.

In the mid 1380s John Trevisa[10] *translated Higden's* Polychronicon, *an immensely popular mid-fourteenth-century "universal" history which survives in more than a hundred manuscripts, from Latin into English. The passage below, an excerpt from that translation, documents the linguistic diversity of late medieval England, its bi-lingualism, as well as its several dialects linked to geography and economics. An investigation of its lexicon will show that Trevisa relies on both Germanic and Romance (French) vocabulary in translating the Latin text. Perhaps the most significant element of this famous passage is Higden's recognition of the evolving status of French and of English in the years before and after the Black Death. Reference to the grammar innovations of John Cornwall have been linked to a John Cornwall who taught Latin grammar in Oxford in the middle years of the fourteenth century. Baugh and Cable note, "his name appears in the accounts of Merton in 1347, as does that of Pencrich a few years later." The innovation was probably due to a scarcity of competent teachers. At any rate, after 1349 English began to be used in the schools and by 1385 the practice had become general.*[11]

De incolarum linguis (Concerning the language of the Inhabitants)[12]

As hyt ys yknowe how meny maner people buth[13] in this ylond, ther buth also of so meny people longages and tonges; notheles Walschmen and Scottes, that buth not ymelled[14] with other nacions, holdeth wel ny here

10 John Trevisa (c. 1342–1402) was educated at Oxford, spending approximately eighteen years at Queen's College, during which time he translated the *Polychronicon*, from 1384–87 (David C. Fowler, *John Trevisa*, English Writers of the Middle Ages Series [Brookfield, VT: Ashgate, 1993], p. 14). While in the service of Thomas, Lord Berkeley, whom he served as "priest and bedesman" (Fowler, 23), he translated two other major Latin works in addition to the *Polychronicon*: Bartholomaeus Anglicus' *On the Properties of Things*, and Aegidius Romanus' *De Regimine Principum* during the period 1394–98.

11 Albert C. Baugh and Thomas Cable, *A History of the English Language*, 4th ed. (Englewood Cliffs, NJ: Prentice Hall, 1993), p. 147.

12 The orthography of this document reflects Trevisa's southwestern dialect (he was born in Cornwall); it uses "u" where modern English uses "i" or "e"; at other times, as in "Bote," "o" is used where modern orthography uses "u" or "a"; past participles are denoted by the prefix "y" as in the first line "yknowe."

13 Are.

14 Mixed together.

furste[15] longage and speche, bote yef[16] Scottes, that were som tyme confederat and wonede[17] with the Pictes, drawe somwhat after here speche. Bote[18] the Flemmynges[19], that woneth[20] in the west syde of Wales, habbeth[21] yleft here strange speche and speketh Saxonlych[22] ynow.[23] Also Englischmen, thogh hy[24] hadde fram the bygynnyng thre maner speche, Southeron, Northeron, and Myddel speche in the myddel of the lond, as hy come of thre maner people of Germania; notheles, by commyxstion and mellyng, furst with Danes and afterward with Normans, in menye[25] the contray longage ys apeyred,[26] and som vseth strange wlaffyng, chyteryng, harryng, and garryng, grisbittyng.[27] This apeyryng of the burth tonge ys bycause of twey[28] thinges. On ys for[29] chyldern[30] in scole, agenes[31] the vsage and manere of al other nacions, buth compelled for to leue here[32] oune longage, and for to construe here lessons and here thinges a Freynsch, and habbeth suththe[33] the Normans come furst into Engelond. Also, gentilmen children buth ytaught for to speke Freynsch fram tyme that a[34] buth yrokked in here cradel, and conneth[35] speke and playe with a child hys brouch[36]; and oplondysch[37] men wol lykne hamsylf[38] to gentil men, and fondeth[39] with gret bysynes for to speke Freynsch, for to be more ytold[40] of.

15 First.
16 "Except that."
17 Dwelled.
18 But.
19 Henry II favored the immigration of Flemings who settled in the area Trevisa describes as the "west syde" of Wales, i.e. Pembrokeshire.
20 Dwell.
21 Have.
22 In the manner of Saxons.
23 Although this spelling usually designates a form of the modern word "enough," here it seems to be an unusual variant spelling of "now" (see OED).
24 Though they.
25 Many.
26 Impaired, i.e. deteriorated; it was thought that such mixture as is described injures language.
27 This string of words is intended to be onomatopeic; it translates as stammering, chattering, snaffling, grating and grinding of teeth.
28 Two.
29 Because.
30 Children.
31 Against, in distinction to.
32 Their.
33 Since.
34 They; here and below "a" functions as a third person plural pronoun.
35 Know.
36 A child's plaything.
37 Rustic, rural, unsophisticated.
38 Liken themselves.
39 Attempt, try.
40 To be held in high esteem.

Thys manere was moche y-vsed tofore the furste moreyn,[41] and ys seth[42] the somdel ychaunged.[43] For Iohan Cornwal, a mayster of gramere, chayngede the lore in gramerscole and construccion[44] of Freynsch into Englysch; and Richard Pencrych lurnede that manere techyng of hym, and other men of Pencrych, so that now, the yer of oure Lord a thousond thre hondred foure score and fyue, of the secunde kyng Richard after the conquest nyne, in al the gramerscoles of Engelond childern leueth[45] Frensch, and construeth and lurneth an Englysch, and habbeth therby avauntage in on syde, and desavauntage yn another; here avauntage ys that a lurneth here gramer yn lasse tyme than childern wer ywoned[46] to do; disavauntage ys that now childern of gramerscole conneth no more Frensch than can hire lift heele,[47] and that ys harm for ham and a scholle passe the se and trauayle in strange londes,[48] and in meny caas also. Also gentil men habbeth now moche yleft for to teche here childern Frensch. Hyt semeth a gret wondur how Englysch, that ys the burth-tonge of Englyschmen, and here oune longage and tonge, ys so dyuers[49] of soun[50] in this ylond; and the longage of Normandy ys comlyng[51] of another lond, and hath on maner soun among al men that speketh hyt aryght in Engelond.[52] Notheles ther ys as meny dyuers maner Frensch yn the rem[53] of Fraunce as ys dyuers manere Englysch in the rem of Engelond.

* * *

Al the longage of the Northhumbres, and specialych at York, ys so scharp, slyttyng, and frotyng, and unschape,[54] that we Southeron men may that longage unnethe undurstonde.[55] Y[56] trowe[57] that that ys bycause that a buth nygh[58] to strange men and aliens, that speketh strangelych, and also bycause

41 Death, plague; or sickness of animals; here the plague of 1348–9.
42 Since.
43 Somewhat changed.
44 Translation, interpretation.
45 Leave.
46 Used to.
47 Left heel.
48 And that is harmful for them if they should travel across the sea and work in strange lands.
49 Diverse.
50 Sound.
51 A stranger, come from another land.
52 French, having come from abroad, is a more unified and less diverse language – it has "on maner soun," one kind of sound.
53 Realm.
54 Piercing, grinding, and unformed.
55 Scarcely understand.
56 I.
57 Believe.
58 That they are close to.

that the kynges of Engelond woneth[59] alwey fer fram that contray: For a buth more yturnd[60] to the south contray; and yef a goth[61] to the north contray, a goth with gret help and strengthe. The cause why a buth more in the south contray than in the north may be betre cornlond, more people, more noble cytés, and more profytable hauenes.[62]

1.2 John Trevisa, *Dialogue between a Lord and a Clerk* (c. *1387*), from J. A. Burrow and Thorlac Turville-Petre, *A Book of Middle English*, 3rd ed. (Oxford: Blackwell, 2005), pp. 237–42.

At the beginning of his translation of Higden, Trevisa created a "dialogue" between a Lord and a Clerk, a form of exposition common in Latin scholastic writing. In a politic reversal of role, the Lord instructs the Clerk by arguing for the utility and importance of knowledge to be gained by translating from Latin into the English vernacular. Translation from Latin and French sources constituted a major source of English literature for the hundred years between Chaucer and Caxton. Chaucer, Gower, Hoccleve, Lydgate, Malory all "Englished" works from other European vernaculars or Latin. Chaucer refers continually to his work as a translator, especially in the retraction at the end of The Canterbury Tales, *and in the prologue to* The Legend of Good Women.

Trevisa's argument is but one of many made particularly during the last two decades of the fourteenth century, linking "the mother tongue" and access to valuable knowledge. His concern is not so much access to what we would term literature, but to the learning and knowledge of past times and other cultures.

And so Ranulph monk of Chester[63] wrot yn Latyn hys bookes of cronykes[64] that discreveth[65] the world aboute yn lengthe and yn brede,[66] and maketh mencyon and muynde[67] of doyngs and of dedes, of mervayls[68] and of wondres, and rekneth the yeres to hys laste dayes fram the vurste[69] makyng of hevene and of erthe.[70] And so tharynne ys noble and gret informacion and lore to hem that can tharynne rede and understonde. Tharvore ich wolde

59 Dwell; are used to be, inhabit.
60 They are more turned to, i.e. oriented to.
61 If they go to the north country, they go.
62 Havens; properties.
63 Ranulph Higden, who was from Chester.
64 Chronicles.
65 Describe.
66 Breadth.
67 Makes mention and brings to mind.
68 Marvels.
69 First.
70 Reckons the years to his last days from the first making of heaven and earth; that is, he wrote a chronicle of the history of the world.

have[71] theus[72] bokes of cronyks translated out of Latyn ynto Englysch, for the mo[73] men scholde hem[74] understonde and have thereof konnyng,[75] informacion and lore."

[In his arguments against the Clerk's position, the Lord defends translation as an historical phenomenon and essential aspect of translatio studii *– the inexorable and appropriate transmission of learning from generation to generation and from nation to nation. In late medieval Italy, France, and England authors were keenly desirous of claiming the mantle of the classical tradition.]*

Dominus[76]*:* Hyt is wonder that thou makest so feble argementys and hast ygo[77] so long to scole. Aristoteles bokes and othere bokes also of logyk and of philosofy were translated out of Gru[78] into Latyn. Also, atte prayng[79] of Kyng Charles [Charles the Bold], John Scot[80] translatede Seint Denys hys bokes out of Gru ynto Latyn. Also holy wryt was translated out of Hebrew ynto Gru and out of Gru into Latyn, and thanne out of Latyn ynto Frensch.[81] Thanne what hath Englysch trespased[82] that hyt myght noght be translated into Englysch? Also Kyng Alvred, that foundede the unyversité of Oxenford,[83] translatede the beste lawes into Englysch tonge and a gret del[84] of the Sauter[85] out of Latyn into Englysch, and made Wyrefryth byschop of Wyrcetre,[86] translate Seint Gregore hys bokes Dialoges out of Latyn ynto Saxon.[87] Also Cedmon of Whyteby was inspired of the Holy Gost and made wonder poesyes[88] an Englysch nygh of al[89] the storyes of holy wryt. Also the holy man Beda[90]

71 I would have.
72 These (theus is a SW dialect form).
73 More.
74 Them.
75 Cunning, knowledge.
76 The lord.
77 Gone.
78 Greek.
79 Request.
80 John Scotus Erigena, c. 810–c. 877, translated works by Dionysius the Areopagite from Greek into Latin.
81 French vernacular translation of the Bible dates from the thirteenth century, nearly a hundred years before the English translation.
82 How has English failed, or done wrong.
83 King Alfred (c. 849–99) was mistakenly thought to have founded Oxford.
84 Deal.
85 Psalter, book of Psalms.
86 Werforth, Bishop of Worcester; Trevisa's parish of Berkeley was in the Worcester diocese.
87 Four Books on the lives and miracles of the Saints in Italy, and on the immortality of the soul.
88 Poems; Caedmon's hymn is an example of spiritual inspiration resulting in religious poetry composed by a simple farm laborer.
89 In English nearly all of.
90 Bede c. 673–735, historian and author of *The English Church and People*.

translatede Seint John hys gospel out of Latyn ynto Englysche. Also thou wost where the Apocalips ys ywryte in the walles and roof of a chapel bothe in Latyn and yn Freynsch.[91] Also the gospel and prophecy and the ryght fey[92] of holy churche mot be taught and ypreched to Englyschmen that conneth no Latyn. Thanne the gospel and prophecy and the ryght fey of holy cherche mot be told ham an Englysch, and that ys noght ydo bote by Englysch translacion.[93] Vor[94] such Englysch prechyng ys verrey[95] Englysch translacion, and such Englysch prechyng ys good and neodful; thanne Englysch translacion is good and neodfol.

[*By the time the debate concludes, Clericus submits to Dominus' arguments, and articulates a credal statement of the central elements of Christian doctrine in which writing becomes a metaphor for salvation. At the day of judgement:*]

Thanne al men that buth ywryte yn the bok of lyf schal wende with hym [Christ] ynto the blysse of hevene, and be there in body and in soul, and se and knowe hys godhede and manhede in joye without eny ende. *Explicit Dialogus.*

1.3 From the Prologue to *The Holy Bible . . . from the Latin Vulgate by John Wycliffe and His Followers (c. 1384–95)*, ed. Josiah Forshall and Sir Frederic Madden, 2 vols (Oxford: 1850), p. 59.

The excerpt below, from the Prologue to the Wycliffe translation of the Bible into English, repeats some of the arguments that appear in Trevisa's exchange above. It uses them to support widely held convictions about the appropriate, indeed necessary, translation of the Bible, knowledge of which was increasingly deemed essential to salvation by English people critical of the corrupt state of the Catholic Church throughout the later medieval period. The excerpt below focuses not so much on the importance of access to Holy Scripture as a matter of salvation, as on the importance of access to scripture in the vernacular, one's own birth tongue. It is an early assault on clerical privilege and the Roman Church's hegemony in the matter of salvation.

The Prologue to the "Wycliffe Bible" introduces the first translation of the Old and New Testaments into the English vernacular after the Norman Conquest. The

91 Burrow and Thorlac-Petre note that, "Passages from an Anglo-Norman translation of the Book of Revelation are still to be seen inscribed on the roof beams in the morning room, formerly the chapel, of Berkeley Castle" (p. 241).

92 Faith.

93 Told to them in English, and that cannot be done except by English translation.

94 For.

95 Truly.

translators recognize the exceptional nature of their undertaking, and, in the passage below, reflect on the dangers of misunderstanding leading to mistranslation. The arguments in the Prologue to the Wycliffe Bible echo similar arguments made at almost the same time in France in the translation projects authorized by Charles V. Nicole Oresme argued in the prologues to his translations of Aristotle's Politics *and* Ethics *commissioned by Charles (1370s), that French people ought to have access to the learning of the past in their own tongue, just as the ancient Romans (termed Latyns in the Bible passage below) had access to ancient wisdom in their own vernacular, or mother tongue. Both English and French translators recognized the inherent difficulties of any translation project, realizing the need for neologisms to expand their lexicon. The passage below reflects the influence of Latin terms conveyed through French into English.*

> Yit[96] worldli clerkis axen gretli what spiryt makith idiotis hardi to translate now the bible into English, sithen the foure greete doctouris dursten neuere do this?[97] This replicacioun[98] is so lewid,[99] that it nedith[100] noon answer, no but stillnesse, eithir curteys scorn;[101] for these greete doctouris weren noon English men, neither thei weren conuersaunt among English men, neithir in caas thei kouden the langage of English,[102] but thei ceessiden neuere til thei hadden holi writ in here modir tunge, of here owne puple. For Jerom, that was a Latyn man of birthe, translatide the bible, bothe out of Ebru[103] and out of Greek, into Latyn, and expounide ful myche therto;[104] and Austyn, and manie mo Latyns[105] expouniden the bible, for manie partis, in Latyn, to Latyn men, among whiche thei dwelliden, and Latyn was a comoun langage to here[106] puple aboute Rome, and biyondis, and on this half, as Englishe is comoun langage to oure puple, and yit this day the comoun puple in Italie spekith Latyn corrupt, as trewe men seyn, that han ben in Italie; and the noumbre of translatouris out of Greek into Latyn passith mannis knowing, as Austyn witnessith in the ij. book of Cristene Teching, and seith thus, "the translatouris out of Ebru into Greek moun be noumbrid,[107] but Latyn translatouris,

96 Yet.
97 Yet worldly clerks often ask what spirit makes the unlearned [layperson] now bold to translate the Bible into English, considering that the four great doctors [of the Church] never dared to do this.
98 Rejoinder.
99 Ignorant.
100 Needs.
101 But silence or polite scorn.
102 Nor could they know the English language.
103 Hebrew.
104 Explained, explicated it extensively as well.
105 Romans; users of Latin.
106 Their.
107 Might be counted.

either thei that translatiden into Latyn, moun not be noumbrid in ony manere." For in the firste tymes of feith,[108] ech[109] man, as a Greek book came to him, and he semyde to him silf to haue sum kunnyng[110] of Greek and of Latyn, was hardi to translate;[111] and this thing helpide more than lettide[112] vndurstonding, if rederis ben not necligent, forwhi the biholding of manie bokis hath shewid ofte, eithir declarid, summe derkere sentencis.[113] This seith Austyn there. Therfore Grosted seith, that it was Goddis wille, that diuerse men translatiden, and that diuerse translacions be in the chirche, for where oon seide derkli,[114] oon either mo seiden openli. Lord God! sithen at the bigynnyng of feith so manie men translatiden into Latyn, and to greet profyt of Latyn men, lat oo symple[115] creature of God translate into English, for profyt of English men; for if worldli clerkis loken wel here croniclis[116] and bokis, thei shulden fynde, that Bede[117] translatide the bible, and expounide myche in Saxon, that was English, either[118] comoun langage of this lond, in his tyme; and not oneli Bede, but also king Alured,[119] that foundide Oxenford, translatide in hise laste daies the bigynning of the Sauter[120] into Saxon, and wolde more, if he hadde lyued lengere. Also Frenshe men, Beemers,[121] and Britons han the bible, and othere bokis of deuocioun and of exposicioun, translatid in here modir langage ; whi shulden[122] not English men haue the same in here modir langage, I can not wite,[123] no but for falsnesse and necgligence of clerkis, either for oure puple is not worthi to haue so greet grace and gifte of God, in peyne of here olde synnes.[124] God for his merci amende these euele causis, and make oure puple to haue, and kunne, aud kepe truli holi writ, to lijf and deth![125] But in translating of wordis

108 Faith.
109 Each.
110 And if it seemed to him that he had some knowledge.
111 Bold to translate.
112 Hindered.
113 If readers are not negligent, because the reading of many books has often shown or made clear some obscure [dark] meanings.
114 Grosseteste; was obscure.
115 One simple.
116 Read their chronicles carefully.
117 Bede, monk of Jarrow, author of *The English Church and People,* d. 735.
118 Or.
119 King Alfred.
120 Translated in his later life the beginning of the Psalter.
121 An uncertain term thought to refer to Bohemians and/or residents of the low countries.
122 Should.
123 Know.
124 I do not understand, except for the falseness and negligence of clerks, or because our people is not worthy to have so great a grace and gift from God, because of their ancient sins.
125 Know and keep truly holy writ, in life and death.

equiuok,[126] that is, that hath manie significacions vndur oo lettre,[127] mai lightli be pereil,[128] for Austyn seith in the ij. book of Cristene Teching, that if equiuok wordis be not translatid into the sense, either vndur-stonding, of the autour, it is errour. . . .

1.4 "A shorte epiloge excusatorie of the translatours rudnesse," from Osbern Bokenham, *Mappula Angliae*, ed. Carl Horstmann, *Englische Studien, 10* (1887), pp. 1–34, esp. pp. 33–4.

Bokenham (1393–1467?) was an English Augustinian friar who had travelled in Italy where his knowledge of the classics was likely augmented by knowledge of Boccaccio and Petrarch's work. Author of Lyves of the Seyntys (The Legends of Holy Women),[129] *and the* Mappula, *a history of England, Bokenham writes in a Suffolk dialect. He apologizes for his style on the grounds both of upbringing and of custom, linking his "modur-tounge" to the landscape of his early life, suggesting that his learned Latinity is one voice among many he uses. His anxiety is typical of the period and representative of a conventional deprecation of the capacities of English:*

Me semythe[130] that hit is my parte, aftir thes lytylle & shorte treteys drawyn & abstract out of anothur mannys longe & laboryous werke, to preyen and lowly to besechyn[131] yche[132] man that schalle be redere or herere ther-of of III thyngis yn aspecialle. First that they wille vouchesauffe[133] to supporte me, alle be-hit that this seyde tretis be not so convenyently nor so eloquently expressid & spokyn yn englyssh tounge as the excellence of the auctours latyn stile requirithe. For, certenly, the natyff rudnesse of my modur-tounge hathe so inflectyde & cankeryed[134] my speche & my language w[ith] the barbarisme of the soyle the w[hich] I haue be fostryd & brought forthe yn of youthe that y neyther may ner can other thynge vttrryn ne shewyne then hit hathe been vsyd,[135] & acustomyd to. . . . And the olde prouerbe seithe: custome & vse is a nother nature or kynde.

---

126 Equivocal: uncertain, ambiguous.

127 Have many meanings/connotations represented by one word/spelling.

128 May lead easily to peril.

129 *A Legend of Holy Women: Osbern Bokenham, Legends of Holy Women,* Sheila Delay, ed. and trans. (Notre Dame: University of Notre Dame Press, 1992).

130 "It seems to me."

131 Beseech.

132 Each.

133 Graciously deign.

134 Corrupted.

135 With the barbarism of the soil which I have been born to and brought up in since youth that I neither may nor can utter nor bring forth but what I am accustomed to.

1.5 William Caxton, *Prologue to the Aeneid, Prologues and Epilogues of William Caxton*, ed. W. J. B. Crotch, EETS, o. s. 176 (London: Oxford University Press, 1928), pp. 107–9.

William Caxton began his life as a mercer, a merchant who dealt with textiles. His trade took him overseas and brought him into contact with the trade and politics of Flanders and France. He settled in Bruges in the 1460s, becoming the governor of the English nation in Bruges: that is, head of the resident merchant community. During the difficult trading and diplomatic period of the 1460s Caxton undertook negotiations on behalf of English interests. In 1471 he moved to Cologne, a center of early German printing. Evidence suggests that by this time he was already dealing in manuscripts, but while at Cologne it seems he made a decision to deal in printed books. It is no exaggeration to say that decision made him one of the most important figures in fifteenth-century English literature, because of his translations and publications. He returned to England in the mid-1470s and in 1476 established his printing press in the vicinity of Westminster Abbey. He brought with him not only the technology of print, but also a wide acquaintance with Francophone literature that he rightly guessed would appeal to a large English audience. Over time he printed at least a hundred works, and his shop became a site of print and manuscript trade.[136]

Caxton left little to chance, it seems, and so printed his editions with interpretive prologues and epilogues. These ancillary materials provide an extraordinary index to literary tastes in England by the end of the fifteenth century. Carefully attuned to his market, anxious to be accommodating to patrons – both those who bought and those who commissioned – Caxton was also a master apologist for the texts he sponsored, and a reliable witness to the difficulties that arose from the absence of a standard form of English. Working at the end of the fifteenth century, William Caxton describes the difficult choices that confronted him as a translator trying to respond to the desires of his patrons and to the anomalies of the English language.

The prologue to the Aeneid *(Eneydos) translation* of *1490 provides insight into English as a language of learning and literature, yet one still bedeviled in common practice by regional variation and intermittent, as well as unsettling, incomprehension, as the famous anecdote below about confusion over the word for "eggs" illustrates. In its references to Old English the passage shows that English people were aware of the earlier forms of their language, and that some of them, like the Abbot of Westminster, recognized the information contained in "olde englysshe" and saw the value of claiming both the older form of language and the information encoded in it as part of English cultural heritage. This passage, like several others in this section, conflates cultural sophistication and geography, associating archaic and simple forms with "rude vplondyssh" Northern readers, in contrast to the "noble gentylman" who understands love and arms as well as more sophisticated verbal patterns. This passage preserves both the orthography and the punctuation of the original publication.*

---

136 On this market and for more of Caxton's writings see 5.3.

After dyuerse werkes made/ translated and achieued/ hauyng noo werke in hande. I sittyng in my studye where as[137] laye many dyuerse paunflettis[138] and bookys. [It] happened that to my hande cam a lytyl booke in frensche. whiche late was translated oute of latyn by some noble clerke of fraunce whiche booke is named Eneydos/ made in latyn by that noble poete and grete clerke vyrgyle[139]/ whiche booke I sawe ouer and redde therin. [*here Caxton summarizes the story of Aeneas after the fall of Troy and his coming into Italy to found Rome]* . . . In whiche booke I had grete playsyr. by cause of the fayr and honest termes and wordes in frenshe/ Whyche I neuer sawe to fore lyke.[140] ne none so playsaunt ne so wel ordred. whiche booke as me semed sholde be moche requysyte[141] to noble men to see as wel for the eloquence as the historyes/ How wel that many honderd yerys passed was the sayd booke of eneydos wyth other werkes made and lerned dayly in scolis specyally in ytalye and other places/ whiche historye the sayd vyrgyle made in metre[142]/ And whan I had aduysed me in this sayd boke. I delybered[143] and concluded to translate it in to englysshe And forthwyth toke a penne and ynke and wrote a leef or tweyne/ whyche I ouersawe agayn to correcte it/ And whan I sawe the fayr and straunge termes therin/ I doubted[144] that it sholde not please some gentylmen whiche late blamed me sayeng [that] in my translacyons I had ouer curyous terms[145] whiche coude not be vunderstande of comyn peple / and desired me to vse olde and homely[146] termes in my translacyons. and fayne wolde I satysfye euery man/ and so to doo toke an olde boke and redde therein/ and certaynly the englysshe was so rude and brood[147] that I coude not wele vnderstande it. And also my lorde abbot of westmynster ded do shewe to me late certayn euydences wryton in olde englysshe for to reduce[148] it in to our englysshe now vsid/ And certaynly it was wreten in such wyse that it was more lyke to dutche than englysshe/ I coude not reduce ne brynge it to be vnderstonden/ And certaynly our langage now vsed varyeth ferre[149] from that. whiche was vsed and spoken whan I was borne/ For we englysshe men/ ben borne vnder the domynacyon of the mone. whiche is neuer stedfaste/ but euer wauerynge/ wexynge one season/ and waneth and dyscreaseth another

137 Where.
138 Pamphlets.
139 Virgil.
140 The like of which I had never seen before.
141 Requisite, fitting for.
142 Meter, poetry.
143 Deliberated.
144 Feared.
145 Elaborately constructed expressions, or unknown vocabulary.
146 Familiar; homely in the sense of commonly used and simple.
147 Unlearned and inelegant.
148 Translate.
149 Differs greatly.

season/ And that comyn englysshe that is spoken in one shyre varyeth from a nother. In so moche that in my dayes happened that certayne marchauntes were in a shippe in tamyse[150] for to haue sayled ouer the see into zelande/ and for lacke of wynde thei taryed atte forlond.[151] and wente to lande for to refresshe them And one of theym named sheffelde, a mercer,[152] cam in to an hows and axed for mete[153]. and specyally he axyd after eggys And the good wyf answerde that she could speke no frenshe. And the merchaunt was angry. for he also coude speke no frenshe. but wold haue hadde egges/ and she vnderstode hym not/ And thenne at laste a nother sayd that he wold haue eyren/ then the good wyf sayd that she vnderstod hym wel/ Loo what sholde a man in thyse dayes now wryte. egges or eyren/ certaynly it is hard to playse euery man/ by cause of dyuersite and chaunge of langage. For in these dayes euery man that is in ony reputacyon in his cou*n*tre. wyll vtter his commynycacyon[154] and maters in such maners and termes/ that fewe men shall vnderstonde theym. And som honest and grete clerkes haue ben wyth me and desired me to wryte the moste curyous termes that I could fynde/ And thus bytwene playn rude/ and curyous I stand abasshed. but in my Iudgemente/ the comyn termes that be dayli vsed ben lyghter to be vnderstonde[155] than the olde and auncyent englysshe/ And for as moche as this present booke is not for a rude vplondyssh[156] man to laboure therein/ ne rede it/ but onely for a clerke and a noble gentylman that feleth[157] and vnderstondeth in faytes of armes[158] in loue and in noble chyualrye/ Therfor in a meane bytwene bothe I haue reduced and translated this sayd booke in to our englysshe not ouer rude ne curyous but in suche termes as shall be vnderstanden by goddys grace accordynge to my copye.

London Multi-Lingualism: Writing in a Tri-Lingual Culture

While poets and translators worried about phrasing and audience, English flourished as a prose form in a variety of civic discourses in London. The excerpts immediately below, largely from official records of fifteenth-century London, demonstrate several important features of late medieval London English in respect to style and voice: they document awareness of English as a language with its own discourse and idioms; they illustrate the rich narrative exposition that documenting acceptable and unacceptable

150 Thames.
151 At a cape, headland.
152 A merchant who deals in textiles.
153 Came into a house and asked for meat.
154 Communication.
155 Easier to understand.
156 Unsophisticated, unlearned, country person.
157 Comprehends; has experience in.
158 Deeds of arms.

legal, civic, and social practices fostered; they testify to the existence of a high civic style used to address royalty; and they reveal comfort with macaronic[159] *constructions that relied upon specialized discourses drawn from Latin and French.*

1.6 Thomas Usk, from the Prologue to *The Testament of Love*, in *Chaucerian and Other Pieces*, ed. Walter W. Skeat (Oxford: Clarendon Press,1897), pp. 1–2.

Thomas Usk, a London scrivener, was a contemporary of Chaucer's whose best known work, The Testament of Love *(c. 1384–7), a prose inquiry into love, grace and free will, draws on Boethius'* Consolation of Philosophy.

This excerpt from The Testament of Love *indicates that Usk understood London English to offer registers of expression quite distinct from those of French or Latin. The passage is full of metaphors and figures, often communicated through verbs that suggest Usk's wit and sophistication, as well as his ability to shape English to his will. Nevertheless he maintains that English is essentially a plan, simple language.*

Many men there ben that, with eeres openly sprad,[160] so moche swalowen[161] the deliciousnesse of jestes and of ryme,[162] by queynt knittyng coloures,[163] that of the goodnesse or of the badnesse of the sentence[164] take they litel hede or els non.

Soothly, dul wit and a thoughtful soule so sore have myned and graffed[165] in my spirites that suche craft of endytyng[166] wol not ben of myn acqueyntaunce. And, for rude wordes and boystous[167] percen the herte of the herer to the inrest[168] poynte, and planten there the sentence of thinges, so that with litel helpe it is able to springe; this book, that nothyng hath of the greet flode of wit ne of semelich colours,[169] is dolven[170] with rude wordes and boystous, and so drawe[n] togider,[171] to maken the cacchers therof ben the

159 From an adjective that denotes a jumble or mixture; used of language, it denotes a combination of languages in one line or work.
160 Ears "wide open."
161 Metaphorically, to enjoy as if to eat or drink up, to devour.
162 Gests, accounts of deeds and actions, here likely those in romance and ballads; rhymed stories.
163 United by rhetorical devices.
164 Moral substance, ultimate meaning.
165 Dug into and grafted upon.
166 Such a style of writing.
167 Rough, unpolished.
168 Innermost.
169 Attractive verbal ornaments.
170 Dug – a continuation of Usk's digging and farming metaphor; see "plante," "spring".
171 Composed.

more redy to hente sentence.[172] . . . In Latyn and French hath many [English] soverayne wittes had gret delyt to endyte,[173] and have many noble thynges fulfild; but certes, there ben some that speken their poysye-mater in Frenche, of whiche speche the Frenchemen have as good a fantasye[174] as we have in hering of Frenche mennes English. And many terms ther ben in English [of] whiche unneth we Englishmen connen declare the knowleginge.[175] How shulde than a Frenche man born suche termes conne jumpere in his mater, but as the jay chatereth Englyssh?[176] Ryght so, trewly, the understanding of Englishmen wol not strecche to the privy terms in Frenche, what-so-ever we bosten of straunge langage. Let than clerkes endyten in Latyn, for they have the propertee of science, and the knowinge in that facultee; and let Frenchmen in their Frenche also endyten their queynt terms, for it is kyndely to their mouthes; and let us shewe our fantasyes in suche wordes as we lerneden of our dames tonge."[177]

Multi-Lingual London Wills

Wills from the later fourteenth and early fifteenth century in London were commonly written in Latin, French, or English. The first will cited below, written chiefly in Latin, combines Latin, English and French phrases. The second will combines English and French. The wills strongly suggest that ordinary Londoners of the merchant class were comfortable with a kind of macaronic discourse combining legal phrases from Law French and Latin liturgical terms with English.

1.7 Extract from the Will of William Creswyk dated 1405, registered 1407, *A Book of London English 1384–1425*, ed. R. W. Chambers and Marjorie Daunt (Oxford: Clarendon Press, 1931), p. 212.

Orate pro animabus Willelmi Cresewyk & Alicie vxoris sue Henrici & Ricardi Agnetis & Agnetis patrum & matrum ipsorum Willelmi & Alicie Roberti fratris ipsius Willelmi Thome quondam viri ipsius Alicie & pro eis quibus tenentur

172 Apprehend meaning.

173 Compose.

174 Supposition, comprehension.

175 And there are many terms in in English which we Englishmen can scarely recognize.

176 How should then [someone] born a Frenchman know how to put such terms together in his writing, without his English sounding like the chattering of the jay?

177 Right so, truly, the understanding of Englishmen will not stretch to the little-known terms of French, whatever we boast about foreign languages. Let then clerks write in Latin, for they have the wisdom and the knowledge in that subject; and let French men also compose in their strange terms, for French is natural to their mouths; and let us show our imaginations in such words as we learned of our mother's tongue.

& pro omnibus parochianis istius ecclesie & pro omnibus alijs viuis & defunctis.

Et volo quod idem Capellanus qui sic pro tempore fuerit cotidie introeundo ad missam cum vestitus fuerit alba suscipiendo casulam antequam officium incipiat vertens se ad populum dicat in anglicis verbis in hac forma:

For William soule Cresewyk and Alice his wif and for all these paresshins lyues and dedes and for all Cristen soules *pater noster par charyte.*

(Pray for the souls of William Cresewyk and Alice his wife, also Henry and Richard, Agnes and Agnes, the fathers and mothers of William and Alice, Robert, brother to William, Thomas former husband of Alice, and for all the parishioners of this church, and for those who hold them in affectionate regard, and for all the parishioners of this church, and for all others living and dead. And I wish that that same chaplain who was in this position temporarily of daily entering for mass, clothed by taking up the white chausuble, before he begins the service, should, turning to the people, say in English words in this form: For the soul of William Cresewyk and Alice his wife and for all these parishioners living and dead, and for all Christen souls, pray the Our Father, for charity sake.)[178]

1.8 Will of John Pyncheon (1392), *Book of London English*, p. 210.

Ioe volle q*ue* la moneye soit despendu, cestassauoir, to the pore Men that han ben Men before of god conu*er*sacion, some man xx. s, ant som ij Marc, and som xl. s, aftyr that here stat hat ben by-fore, and tha*t* thay be of the same parche, and Of Petris & Cristoforys, or of other next ther by; & wher me[n] may wetyn eny powre lame, ore powre Blynde, in Any plache in the Towne, th*at* thay han Clothys to hele hem fro colde, & Schetys to than th*at* han nede. And to the presonis of newgat, a serteyn A-weke duryng on yere; & to the powre Mesellis a certeyn A-weke during on yere: & tha*t* the hows be ysold, & the Almes yi-do in the worst yere. And wher men may a-spye eny powr man of religion, Monk, Chanon, or Frere, th*at* thay han of my god the gode, And ben powre, eche Man vjs. viijd. th*at* ben prestys.

(I will that the money be distributed, that is to say, to the poor men than have been men, before, of good conversation [speech, well-spoken], some men 20 shillings, and some 2 marks, and some 40 shillings, according to what their estate had previously been, and that they be of the same parish, and of [St] Peter's and [St] Christopher's, or of another next thereby; and where men may know any poor, lame, or poor blind [person] in any place in the town, that they have clothes to heal [protect] them from the

178 We are grateful to our colleagues in Classics, Bruce Arnold and Jeff Sumi, for help with the syntax of this passage.

cold, and sheets to those that are in need. And to the prisoners of Newgate, a fixed [sum of money] weekly during one year; and to the poor lepers a fixed [sum of money] weekly for one year; and that the house be sold, and the alms given in the worst year. And where men may spy any poor man of religion – monk, canon, or friar – that they have of my goods the profit, and if they are poor, each man 6 shillings, 8 pence, who are priests.)

1.9 Writing to the King: "Letter sent to the King by the Mayor and Aldermen," 5 Henry V, A.D. 1417 (Letter-Book I), *Memorials of London and London Life in the XIIIth, XIVth, and XVth Centuries*, ed. Henry Thomas Riley (London: Longmans, 1868), pp. 658–60.

This letter, written by the aldermen of London to Henry V, requests his presence in London in terms both aureate and obsequious. The language is heavily dependent on French courtly terms, and the rhetoric – like the chiasmus of "high excellence and excellent highness" – reflects knowledge of classical rhetorical figures as well as court-ship. Above all the letter is a coded and veiled reproach to the monarch for being absent from the city of London. In its double meaning it is one more text that demonstrates that by the early fifteenth century London English was not a language "rude and boystous," but one that it could be employed in multiple registers of style including those fully adequate to address a monarch with simultaneous flattery and reproach.

Of alle erthely princes our most dred souereigne liege Lord[179] and noblest Kyng, we, youre simple officers, Mair and Aldermen of your trewe Citee of London, with exhibicion of alle maner subiectif reuerence and seruisable lowenesse, that may be hadde in dede, or in mynde conceyued, recommende vs unto your most noble and hye magnificence, and excellent power, bisechyng the Heuenly Kyng, of His noble grace and pitee, that he so wold illumine and extende vpon the trone[180] of yo*ur* kyngly Mageste the radyouse bemys of Hys bounteuous grace,[181] that the begunnen spede[182] by Hys benigne suffraunce and help yn your chiualrouse[183] personne fixed and affermed, mowe so be continued forthe, and determined, so to His plesaunce, your worship, and alle your reumys[184] proffyt, that we and alle yo*ur* other lieges to the desered presence of your most noble and graciouse persone, fro which grete distance of place long tyme hath priued[185] vs, the sonner myght approche and visuelly

179 Having a claim to, and owed service.
180 Throne.
181 Of your kingly majesty the radiant beams of his bountiful grace.
182 Success so far achieved.
183 Chivalrous.
184 Realm's.
185 Deprived.

perceyue, to singuler confort and special joye of vs alle: makyng protestacioun, our most dred soueraigne liege Lord, and noblest Kyng, that be[186] this feruent desire wiche we han[187] to the bodyly sight of your most excellent and noble persone, our entente is noght to move you fro no thing of your hye worship, ne to no thyng that myght be perille to your lond, that ye haue put in obbeissaunce.[188] Our most dred soueraign liege Lord, noblest Kynge, for-as-moche as we trust verryly that the kyngly desyre of your inspired excellence deliteth to here of the welfare of your forsayd cite, which your noble and soueraign Grace with innumerable prerogatifs & liberalle fraunchises hath euer visited and endowed, like it vnto your kyngly Mageste to vnderstonde, that euer syn the tyme of your last departynge it hath stonde,[189] yit doth, and euer shal, by the help of oure Lorde Almyghty, in as gret pees and tranquillite as euer did cite in absence of his most soueraigne and excellent lord. And, forasmoch, most dred souerein liege Lord, and noblest Kyng, as the hertly[190] desire of your forsayd cite ys, as who seith, with an heuenly drynk and infusion so oftetymes gladed and refresshid, as it hereth the soueraign helth and prosperite of your most graciouse & noble personne;[191] therfor we, mekely bowyng our hertes to-for the clernesse of your kyngly Mageste, biseche your highe Excellence and excellent Highnesse, that it lyke, of the roted gentillesse and grounded grace in your nobley,[192] so to visyte vs in assertenyng of your souueragn helth and prosperite, as it is seyd before, that we, in defaute of such visitacioun, languisse not as men from so hie a grace sequestere and exiled. Our most dred soueraign liege Lord and noblest Kyng, we, your symple officers specially beseche vnto alle the holy company of heuenly knyghthode, assembled in the hie blisse wher as is eternal ioye and non euynesse,[193] so be-shyne the noble knyghthode in your cronicable excellence aporeued,[194] that ye mowe in this world vpon vs and alle your other lieges with report of wordly victory longe regne and endure; and after, whan your graciouse erthely personne from your inward spirit ys dessolued,[195] that ye mowe be brought tofor the throne of the hye Kynge, and ther with heuenly ierarchies in eternal glorie perpetuelly duelle and abyde. Wryten at your forsaid Cite of Londone, the xxie day of December. Your humble lieges and simple officers, Richard Merlawe, Mair, and Aldermen of your Cite of London.

186 By.

187 Have.

188 Which owes obedience to you.

189 Stood.

190 Heartfelt, earnest.

191 Is, as if with a heavenly drink and infusion, so many times gladdened and refreshed, as it hears of the sovereign health and prosperity of your most gracious and noble person.

192 Noble nature.

193 Heaviness.

194 Proved.

195 Dissolved, separated.

French of England in London Civic Life

The Guildhall Letter-Books, so named because of the letters written on them for purposes of reference, record the proceedings of the Court of Common Council and the Court of Aldermen in the city of London. The editors of this text describe them this way: "The Letter-books are fifty vellum books of considerable though varying size which take their name from the letters written on the backs . . . the series extends from the reign of Edward I to that of James II" *(p. 92).*

1.10 A false sack of coals: Guildhall Record in *A Book of London English, 1384–1425*, ed. R. W. Chambers and Marjorie Daunt (Oxford: Clarendon Press, 1931), p. 98.

In the case below, from Letter-book I, 1419, the record of a confessed coal merchant who cheated his customers is narrated in a lexicon heavily based on Anglo-French – confession, convict, mayor, deceit, mesure, ensample, false, pillory, for example, are all part of English through Anglo-French. The passage is written in a style of English prose that is succinct, pithy, and highly sophisticated in its use of clauses and phrases.

> For as mych as John Vmbergh, de Shenfeld in Essex, Colier, that here stant,[196] is opu*n*ly co*n*uict,[197] by his *con*fession made afor the Meir & Aldermen, that he, in disceyt[198] of the co*mun*e peple, hath[199] sold coles th*is* same yeer, more th*an* a xij tymes, by ech of thes vij sakkes, th*at* lyen here byside, for sakkis of viij busshels of ful mesure, wher in trouthe thei *con*teyne but v, vi, or vij busshels at moost; th*er*for, in ensa*m*ple th*at* al oth*er* shold be ware in tyme com*yng* of such falsnes & disceyt, The Meir and Aldirme*n* han awardid hym to stonde here on the pilory, & his sakkes to be brent vndur hym.

1.11 Proclamation Against Brokers, Guildhall Record in A Book of London English 1384–1425, p. 97.

Another record from the Guildhall Letter-Books illustrates the French basis of the language of commerce, particularly the wine trade, as it exposes the abuses of Brokours, *or the middlemen of trade whose function, termed* brocage, *was suspect*

---

196 Stands.
197 Openly convicted.
198 Deception.
199 Has.

because it generated money by buying and selling the products others made, without adding value to these products. Their function was associated with usury and overcharging. This text dates from c. 1418–19:

> For as moche as here be-fore the Cite of London hatht [sic] had, ant yet is lykly to haue, but it be the sonner remedied, gret Mischiefs, sclaundres, and harmes thorugh the gret disceyt and falsnesse of Brokours, which for drede of god ne shame of the world, cesen nat, but thaym[200] fro day to day peyne and afforcen vnder colour of Brocage to manteigne the orrible vices of vsure and fals cheuisauns,[201] be which vices is nat oonly this Cite sclaundered, but many worthi men vtterly distroyed, and the good fourme and Cours of Merchaundise poynt[202] to be perisshed for euer, as god for-bede. . . .

1.12 Nusauncis and defautis foundin in the warde of farundon with-out; 1422 record from Guildhall Pleas and Memoranda, in *A Book of London English 1384–1425*, pp. 121–2.

Guildhall records include pleas and memoranda from the proceedings of the Mayor's court. As Chambers and Daunt suggest, as a whole these documents testify to the nuisances and the slow pace of improvement in London civic life. The document below records the unhappy state of affairs in the ward of "Farundon without"(i.e. outside the walls of the City) complained of in a wardemot, a meeting of the citizens of a municipal ward, in 1422. Once again civic documents suggest a lively vernacular register of clear style and concise statements:

> These ben nusauncis and defautis[203] foundin[204] in the warde of farundon with-out, Taken in the wardemot, a-fore Rankyn Barton, Alderman of the same warde, the yere[205] of the kyng aboveseyd [i.e. 9 Henry V].
>
> First, th*at* the mayster of ludgate puttyth out oft tymes dung in the Canell,[206] and stoppit the watir goyng, to grete nusans to all folk ther passyng. Also that a mud wall in the bailly[207] by the hie strete, bytwene the hous of Shelhard habirdassher and hay Sporyer,[208] Fallith doun gobet-mele[209]

200 Them.
201 Lending money; Anglo-Norman, an ill-gotten gain obtained by a loan.
202 On the point of being destroyed forever.
203 Faults.
204 Found.
205 Regnal year.
206 Gutter.
207 Usually a space between two (castle) walls.
208 Spur-maker.
209 Piece wise.

in-to the hi strete, and makith the wey foule, in desese[210] of folk ther passyng and dwelling. . . . Also the pamenits[211] . . . a-fore the dore of harri gras, Barbur, and of Walsshis dore, be diffectif and nedeful to be amendid. Also the commun privey of ludgate is ful diffectif and perlus,[212] and the ordur therof rotith the stone wallys, so that it is like to be a ful grete cost and pereel[213] of tho wallys in tyme comyng, but thei be the sunur[214] amendid. . . .

Uplandisch English: Multi-Lingualism Outside of London

1.13 John Barbour, *The Bruce. Based on The Bruce or The book of the Most Excellent and Noble Prince Robert de Broyss, King of Scots,* ed. Walter W. Skeat, 2 vols (Edinburgh: William Blackwood and Sons, 1894), vol. 1, pp. 1–2.

This poem, written in eastern Scotland during the last quarter of the fourteenth century (c. 1375), tells of Scottish resistance to the attempts of Edward I and Edward II of England to invade Scotland and conquer the Scots, with whom the neighboring English lived in a near constant state of hostility during the fourteenth century. The Scots dialect of this poem is difficult to distinguish from the Northern dialect of Middle English at this period.[215] *The influence of Anglo-French in this poem is likely a result of the Norman presence in Scotland as early as the late eleventh century, and continuing cultural and strategic ties between Scotland and France over the course of the later Middle Ages. This poem shows the influence of French on English language far from the royal court, and far from London. (Key words adapted directly from French in Italics.)*

Incipt liber compositus per magistrum Iohannem Barber, Archidiaconum Abyrdonensem: de gestis, bellis, et virtutibus domini Roberti de Brwyss, regis Scocie illustrissimi, et de conquestu regni Scocie per eundem, et de domino de Douglas Iacobo

(Here begins the book composed by Master John Barber, archdeacon of Aberdeen, which is about the deeds, wars, and virtues of Sir Robert de Bruce, most illustrious king of Scotland, and of his conquest of the kingdom of Scotland, and of Sir James Douglas)

---

210 Discomfort.

211 Pavements.

212 Perilous.

213 Danger.

214 Sooner.

215 Both Scots and Northern English are distinct from other dialects of English in their use of "a" where other Middle English dialects, as well as modern English use "o," as in "sa" (so) and "haly" (wholly) and the -and suffix of the present participle, as in plesand.

Stories to rede ar *delitabill*[216]
Suppos that thai be nocht bot *fabill*;[217]
Than suld[218] *storys* that suthfast[219] wer,
And thai war said on gud *maner*,
Hawe[220] *doubill plesance* in heryng.
The fyrst *plesance* is the carpyng,[221]
And the tothir the suthfastnes,
That schawys[222] the thyng rycht as it wes;[223]
And suth thyngis that ar likand[224]
Tyll mannys heryng ar *plesand*.
Tharfor I wald fayne set my will,
Giff my wyt mycht *suffice* thartill,[225]
To put in wryt a suthfast story,
That it lest[226] ay furth in memory,
Swa that na [lenth of tyme] it let[227]
Na ger it haly be forget.[228]
For aulde *storys* that men redys
Representis to thaim the dedys
Of stalwart folk that lywyt ar,
Rycht as thai than in *presence* war.[229]
And, certis, thai suld weill hawe *prys*
That in that tyme war wycht and wys[230]
And led thar lyff in gret *trawaill*,
And oft in hard *stour*[231] off *bataill*
Wan [richt] gret *price*[232] off *chewalry*,
And war *woydyt*[233] off *cowardy*:

216 Pleasurable.
217 Fable.
218 Should.
219 Truthful.
220 Possess.
221 Reciting.
222 Shows.
223 Right as it was.
224 Agreeable.
225 If my wit might suffice thereto.
226 Last forevermore.
227 So that no length of time should hurt it.
228 Nor cause it to be wholly forgotten.
229 Lived before/Right as if they were present.
230 And certainly they should well have fame/That in that time were valiant and wise.
231 Conflict.
232 Renown.
233 Devoid.

As wes king Robert off Scotland,
That *hardy*[234] wes off hart and hand;
And gud Schyr James off Douglas,
That in his tyme sa worthy was
Thar off hys *price* & hys *bounte*[235]
In fer landis *renownyt* wes he.
Off thaim I thynk this buk to ma;[236]
Now God gyff *grace* that I may swa
Tret it, and bryng it till endyng,
That I say nocht but suthfast thing.

1.14 A York Bidding Prayer c. 1405, in *The Lay Folks Mass-Book: The Manner of Hearing Mass*, Thomas Frederick Simmons, Early English Text Society, o.s. 71 (London, 1879), pp. 64–6.

The documents in this section illustrate the multiple languages a citizen of York in the north of England might be expected to know and use in the later Middle Ages. We begin with a liturgical document, a "bidding" prayer, inviting parishioners to pray for specific needs and desires. The editor of the prayer notes: "The Bidding Prayers, according to the use of York . . . are . . . the only devotions in English which were used publicly in churches before the Reformation" (p. xii). The prayer is written in a Northern dialect of Middle English; note the signature dialect use of "a" where today we use "o".

Ye sal[237] mak your prayers specially till our lord god almighti and til his blessyd moder mary and till all the haly court of heuen for the state and the stabilnes of al halykirk.[238] For the pape of Rome and al his cardinals and for the archebishop of York and for al ercebischops and bischops and for al men and women of religion and for the person of this kirke that has your saules to kepe and for all the prestes and clerkes that has serued or serues in this kirk or in any other. And for al prelates and ordiners and al that halykirk reules and gouerns that god len[239] thaim grace so for to reuel[240] the popil and swilk ensaumpil for to tak or scheu thaim and thaim for to do thare-after, that it may be louing unto god and saluacyon of thaire saules.[241]

---

234 Brave was of heart and action.

235 Excellence.

236 Of them I think this book to make.

237 Shall.

238 Haly, or holy, kirk, a northern form of church in which "ch" is "hardened" to a "k" and "ur" spelled "ir".

239 God give.

240 Govern.

241 And for all prelates and those ordained and all who holy church rules and governs, that God give them grace so to rule the people and such example to show them for them to do thereafter, that it may be pleasing unto God and for the salvation of their souls.

Also ye sal pray specially for the gode state of this reume[242] for the kyng and the quene and for al the peris and the lordes of this lande that God send loue and charite thaim omang and gif thaim grace so for to reule it and gouern it in pes that it be louing to God and the comons un-to profet.[243]

1.15 From *The York Mercers and Merchant Adventurers*, vol. cxxix, Surtees Society (Durham, 1918), pp. 4–5.

The same citizens of York who heard and used the language of the bidding prayer also kept their records using a combination of languages. This excerpt from the account rolls of the York fraternity of the Blessed Mary begins with Anglo-French:

Faite a remembrer des espenses faite . . . les reparacouns des mesouns en Fossgate par J[ohan] Freboyse, mestre du fraternite de nostre dame, lan du regne le roi E, tierz puis le conquist, xxxj (1357).

(Made to record the expenses of repairs of masons in Fossgate by John Freboyse, master of the fraternity of our lady, the regnal year of the king E[dward], third since the conquest, xxj [1357]).

The record continues in French describing the expenses for work done in May: "le simaine procheyn devant le pentecost, lan avantdit" (*The week next before Pentecost* (21May–28 May), *in the year before specified . . . and switches to Latin mixed with English and French, shortly thereafter):* "Die Veneris proximo post festum Corporis Christi (9 June), Item in vj hominibus laborantibus circa meremium apud Sayn Lenerd lendyng, ijs. . . ." *(The Friday next after the feast of Corpus Christi: Likewise for 6 laborers concerning timber near Saint Leonard's landing, 2 shillings.")*

The Language of Love

The influence of French on the language of love and on the expression of love-longing in what became conventional English poetic expression was so pervasive it is hard to over-estimate. The verses below incorporate well-known and familiar conventional expressions of Anglo-French love poetry. They are part of several hundred lines of verse written by one of several scribes who composed a manuscript recording an extended legal dispute about an inheritance (for more on this dispute see 3.10). Titled by their modern editor The Armburgh Papers, *the collection of letters details the*

242 Realm.

243 For the king and the queen, and for all the peers and lords of this land, that God send love and charity among them, and give them grace so to rule it [this kingdom] in peace that it be pleasing to God and profitable to the commons.

contentious dispute over the Brokholes inheritance and the various machinations that attended that dispute.

1.16 A celuy que pluys ayme de mounde, from *The Armburgh Papers: the Brokholes Inheritance in Warwickshire, Hertfordshire and Essex c. 1417–c. 1453*: Chetham's Manuscript Mun. E. 6. 10 (4), ed. Christine Carpenter (Woodbridge, Suffolk: Boydell Press, 1998), pp. 155–6.

Carpenter argues the importance of the correspondence both for what it tells a reader incidentally about gentry life in fifteenth-century England, as well as more specifically because it provides a "graphic account of how members of the gentry went to law. In particular we can see, in both outline and detail, the truth of all the accounts that emphasize the inseparability of private power and private influence from the official public processes and the fact that this was not seen normally as a form of 'corruption', but accepted as part of the way the body politic functioned" (p. 40). The manuscript is a roll containing an epistolary record of the dispute(s); it exists in two separate sections, written by four hands. One of these hands, "Hand 2," inscribed a series of love poems numbering several hundred lines, using spare space on a roll which contains datable entries from the 1420s and 1430s (p. 55), although the copying as well as the inscription of the poems may well have occurred after these dates.

The poems, composed as letters to a beloved, are heavily influenced by French genres and French discourse. Written by a man to a woman, in three different languages, the poems open a window on literacy, language and gender. One can reasonably infer that both writer and implied reader of these were tri-lingual. While the grammar of both the French and Latin is adjusted to accommodate the verse pattern, the author manages to convey a strong sense of sentiment and urgency in this poem which begins the collection:[244]

Aceluy que pluys ayme de mounde
Of all that I haue founde
Carissima
Salutez ad verray amour
With grace joie and honour
Dulcissima.

Sachez bien plessaunce and bele
That I am in good hele
Laus Christo
Mon amour done vous aye
As youre man nygyh[t] and day
Consisto.

244 This is the only one of the poems known to exist outside the Armburgh Papers (Carpenter, p. 155).

Dishore serray joious and fayne
Yf ge will me in certaigne
Amare
Assech serra ioiouz and lele
Ther were nothing that mygth me
Grauare.

Mis tresdouce and tresamez
Euer stedfast that ye will be
Suspiro
Soiez parmaneuant and lele
And in youre hert loue me wel
Requiro.

Jeo vous pray en toute manere
Theise wordys that be writyn here
Tenete
Ore a dieu quc vous garde
And turne youre hert to me ward
Valete.

He that is youre man
I ensure yow to his laste
Sendyth to yow as he can
A rude letre y writen in haste.

Translation:

(To the one that I love best in the world
Of all that I have found
Dearest one
Greetings, with true love
With grace, joy, and honor
Sweetest one.
Know full well, pleasant and beautiful one
That I am in good health
Thanks be to Christ.
I send you my constant love
As your man, night and day,
I am steadfast.
Distant, I will be joyous and happy
If you will me surely
Love
Satisfied, I will be joyous and loyal
There would be nothing that might me
Distress.

My sweet and well-beloved
Ever steadfast that you will be
I hope
Be constant and loyal
And in your heart love me well
I ask.
I pray you in every respect
These words written here,
Hold Fast.
I pray that God keep you
And turn your heart to me.
Farewell.
He that is your man
I assure you to his last [breath]
Sends to you as he can
A simple letter written in haste.)

Further Reading

Cambridge History of the English Language, Richarad M. Hogg, gen. ed. (Cambridge: Cambridge University Press, 1992–2001).

Copeland, Rita, *Rhetoric, Hermeneutics, and Translation in the Middle Ages* (Cambridge: Cambridge University Press, 1991).

Crystal, David, *The Stories of English* (New York: Overlook Press, 2004).

Fisher, John H. *The Emergence of Standard English* (Lexington, KY: University of Kentucky Press, 1996).

Lusignan, Serge, *La langue des rois au Moyen Âge: Le français en France et en Angleterre* (Paris: Presses Universitaires de France, 2004).

Machan, Tim William, *English in the Middle Ages* (New York: Oxford University Press, 2003).

Millward, C. M., *A Biography of the English Language*, 2nd ed. (Fort Worth, TX: Harcourt Brace, 1996).

Oxford History of English, Lynda Mugglestone, ed. (New York: Oxford University Press, 2006.

Trotter, David, *Multilingualism in Later Medieval Britain* (Cambridge: D. S. Brewer, 2000).

Turville-Petre, Thorlac, *England the Nation: Language, Literature and National Identity 1290–1340* (New York: Oxford University Press, 1996).

Wogan-Browne, et al., eds. *The Idea of the Vernacular* (University Park, PA: Pennsylvania State University Press, 1999).

Wogan-Browne, et al., eds. *Language and Culture in Medieval Britain: The French of England, c. 1100–1500* (York: York Medieval Press, 2009).

2

Spiritual Affirmations, Aspirations, and Anxieties

One of the salient characteristics of late medieval English culture was a lively and at times passionate interest in religious doctrine, performance, and institutions. The later fourteenth century witnessed the emergence of a strong mystical tradition, agitation for more direct access to Holy Scripture, and anxiety about the corruption of the Roman Church as well as the institutions and doctrines that opened the way to Paradise. The Papal Schism (1378–1417) gave rise to two popes, one in Avignon, the other in Rome, both claiming the mantle of St Peter. This dispute, exacerbated by the French desire for political reasons to maintain Avignon as the seat of the papacy, exposed the papacy to increased charges of worldliness and opened the way for expressions of dissatisfaction with papal authority.

Medieval English people lived in a world in which the performance of medieval spirituality could take many forms. Most of these forms, which included worship as well as donations of money and additions to the fabric of a church, were localized to the worlds of their parishes. But some performances of devotion, aided by money and status, could take people far beyond familiar boundaries to travel through Europe and to the Holy Land. Because works were closely tied to salvational grace, English people engaged in private devotions, pilgrimage, acts of charity, devotional reading, and withdrawal from the world. All these performances of faith were both popular and doctrinally supported.

While it is hard to know the extent to which individuals accepted the full range of Roman doctrine and to what degree any one person participated in the spectrum of liturgical activities, we do have evidence of the pervasive influence the Church exerted on daily life. The calendar of the Roman Church dominated the calendar of lay record-keeping; the chronology of the year was structured by references to liturgical seasons and saints' days. For the observant, both lay and regular, each day was divided into segments, or "hours" at which specified prayers, psalms and anthems were recited to mark the passing of time and to coordinate it with events in the cycle of the Christian year. Books of Hours, which first appeared as aids to lay devotion at the end of the thirteenth century, grew in popularity, suggesting the imbrication of canonical time and secular time, as people prayed the hours of the day in their private household devotions.

The structure of these prayer books reinforced the connection between medieval time experienced daily and the events of the incarnation of Christ, which happened in historical time and were also endlessly re-created through the daily memorializations and celebrations that constituted the liturgy of worship.

The Church intersected with people's lives in economic terms as well. Ecclesiastical courts exercised jurisdiction over wills, marriage annulments, and immoral behavior, as well as failure to pay expected sums of money, particularly tithes. Individual parishes organized various "stores" or guilds to support the material dimensions of worship, such as candles, and the maintenance of images and shrines, as well as the fabric of the church structure.[1] Giving alms and leaving bequests were encouraged as Christian duty, and as necessary to the functioning of the ecclesiastical system. Over time what began as requests came to be seen as imperative directives, as was the case with the begging friars, whose skill at extracting money in spite of their vow of poverty made them notorious and the subject of a good deal of literary criticism.

The Church held the keys to salvation and taught people to desire and work to achieve salvation. It asserted that Jesus had given the power to bind and to loose to Peter, and that from Peter this power was in turn given to each succeeding Pope. What was at stake for medieval Christians was salvation: eternal bliss in heaven with Mary, the Apostles, and the communion of saints, in the full presence of God. Failure to achieve this bliss – either immediately after death, or after time in Purgatory – meant damnation: eternal torture and submission to the devil and the minions of hell. While doctrinally opposed to the Manichean construction of good and evil, the Church nevertheless employed metaphors of extensive demonic corruption that became part of the culture. Mary was Satan's chief earthly opponent, always victorious. The devil inspired Jews to crucify Jesus. Matter in itself tended to corruption and so posed a constant threat to good Christians. Medieval culture is famous for its misogyny, regarding women as temptresses and seductresses who epitomized the omnipresent attractions and dangers of the material world, a view of women inherited from the Classical world and fostered in monastic scriptoria. Hagiography provided a ready supply of stories of how saints – both men and women – were those who resisted the lure of the material and maintained the kind of physical and spiritual purity that became more and more valued in the secular world, even as it seems to have faded from the world of the regular clergy, who were increasingly charged with venality. Prayer, meditation, and acts of will designed to control the body's "natural inclination" to sin offered ways to purification through self-denial.

Late medieval English spirituality is recorded in works of literature in references to the Mass, to saints' days, to canonical hours, to ecclesiastical corruption and, above all, to the Virgin Mary, celebrated in a rich tradition of lyric poetry.

---

1 For an account of such parish activities on the eve of the Reformation, see Eamon Duffy, *The Voices of Morebath: Reformation and Rebellion in an English Village* (New Haven: Yale University Press, 2001).

Our goal in this chapter is to explore what might be termed the deep culture of late medieval spirituality, a matrix of ideas, words, and deeds that provide the context in which modern readers can understand both "religious" writers like Julian of Norwich and Margery Kempe, as well as omnipresent late medieval literary references, approbatory and critical, to the clergy and functions that constituted the Church. In order to achieve this goal within a limited space, we have selected texts that focus on praxis, on what people heard, did, said – on specific prayers, specific records, popular hagiography, all selected for their exemplary function as representatives of broad classes of material and of devotional performance widely accessible to all classes of people. It would be impossible to represent the full variety of religious expression in the culture, but it is possible to highlight certain elements that appear in English literature, and to suggest some of the rhythms of worship and the templates of prayer for late medieval English people in the decades before the Reformation.

Spiritual Economies

In many respects the medieval Christian Church functioned as a secular bureaucracy in nominal support of spiritual goals. As with most earthly institutions, its life-blood was money. Exchange values came to dominate late medieval Christian theology and practice, producing a cultural anxiety about what we might call the quantification of salvation. The increasing numerization of spiritual rewards, tied to the doctrine of Purgatory, marked the period: manuscript marginalia offered the remittance of thousands of years in Purgatory for reading a prayer. The records of bequests from the later fourteenth and fifteenth centuries accept the interwoven exchange value of money, prayer, and salvation, as the excerpts from the wills of Katherine and John Carpenter illustrate.[2]

2.1 Will of Katherine, widow of John Carpenter, 1458, from *Memoir of the Life and Times of John Carpenter, Town Clerk of London in the Reigns of Henry V and Henry VI, and Founder of the City of London School,* Thomas Brewer (London: Arthur Taylor, 1856), pp. 151–65.[3]

Katherine Carpenter's bequests show how the living negotiate remembrance, a form of community central to medieval Christianity. Money is the medium through which

2 One extra-textual aspect of spiritual exchange that dominates the fifteenth century is the fashion for donating images and windows in churches. On this see Sarah Stanbury, *The Visual Object of Desire in Late Medieval England* (Philadelphia: University of Pennsylvania Press, 2008).

3 This excerpt is from her second will and translated from Latin by her nineteenth-century editor; her first will was in Middle English.

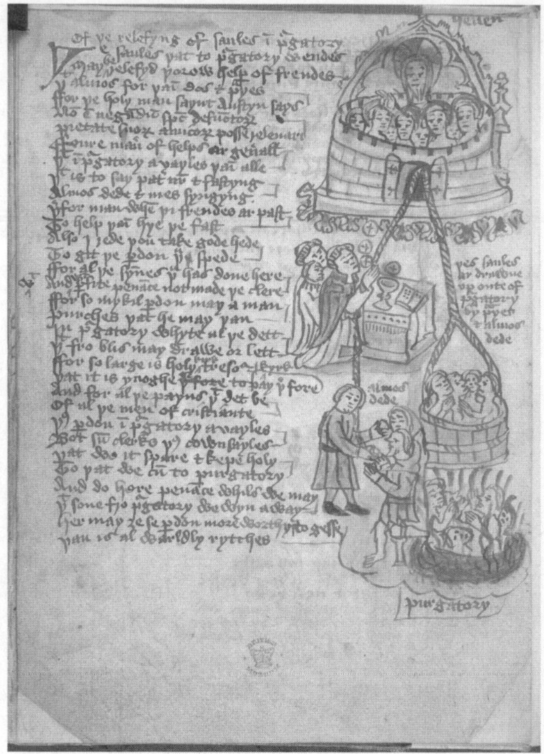

Figure 1 The Power of Prayer: souls being released from Purgatory, a lively if mechanical illustration of the connection between the living and the dead mediated by Church-sanctioned rituals of prayer and by alms-giving. From a book created at Mount Grace Priory (© The British Library Board. Add. MS 37049, f. 24v).

remembrance is established when the living become the dead. It provides the means of ensuring that the wishes of the dead will live, and that the good deeds they endow will add to the positive account of the spiritual reckoning they will offer at the day of judgement. The will begins with a first, conventional bequest of one's soul and body:

> Imprimis: I give and commend my soul to Almighty God my creator and redeemer, and to his mother the blessed Virgin Mary, and to all his saints; and my body to be buried as I have fully declared in another testament of mine concerning my moveable goods previously made.

It goes on to endow the church of St Peter Cornhill, where Katherine Carpenter will be buried alongside her husband, with annual rent from property:

> which I the said Katerine lately held jointly with William Chedworth and Robert Langford (who released to me all their right, interest, and claim

therein by their writing dated the twenty-first day of the month of April, in the twenty-seventh year of the reign of King Henry the Sixth after the Conquest), by the gift, grant, and confirmation of John Gedney late mayor, and of the commonalty of the city of London.

It specifies the terms of an annual service of remembrance as a dramatic event, directing setting, speech, and sound:

under the form & conditions following; to wit, that the said rector and wardens and parishioners and their successors keep and observe ... on the twelfth day of the month of May, if no lawful impediment prevent, or within two days next preceding or following that day . . . solemnly, devoutly, and separately, one anniversary [Mass] by note[4] for the soul of the said John Carpenter my late husband, and for my soul, and for the souls of all the faithful departed, in the form of following, to wit: a certain honest cloth being first placed on the preceding evening before the door of the chancel or choir of the same church, beyond the tomb where the body of the said John my late husband resteth buried, with one suitable wax candle at the head and another at the feet of the same tomb burning, let the rector of the said church, or his *locum tenens*, and all the chaplains and clerks of the same church, devoutly and distinctly chant and sing a *Placebo* and *Dirige*[5] with lauds, and with the full service for the dead used and accustomed on anniversaries of this kind; and on the morrow let them celebrate in the same place one high mass of *Requiem*, by turns, by note reverently and devoutly; and let two of their chaplains separately celebrate two masses without note, and with the special collects and commemorations in the canons of their masses to be made for the aforesaid souls; and let each of the said wardens at the said high mass offer to God, for the aforesaid souls, one penny; but these exequies being finished, let the said rector or his *locum tenens*, the chaplains and clerks, meet round the said tomb, and sing this response, "Libera me Domine," with others used for the dead in such cases, and then let them say the psalm "De Profundis," with the appropriate versicles and prayers for the souls aforesaid; and let them also strike the bell of the same church during the time of the aforesaid exequies, as the custom is in other anniversaries of this kind, that the devotions of those who hear that striking may be more especially and more devoutly excited to pray to God for the souls commemorated.

An important part of the performance of devotion laid out in this testament lies in the distribution of alms. As part of the anniversary observances Katherine Carpenter further instructs the rector and wardens of the Church of St Peter to:

4 I.e. a sung Mass.

5 Placebo and Dirige refer to the offices of Vespers and Matins for the dead.

choose and cause to come thirteen of the more virtuous poor of either sex, namely seven of the parish of St Peter aforesaid, and six of the parish of St Martin Oteswich, London, to be present at the said exequies throughout, and specially to pray for the aforesaid souls; provided always, that no common beggar, nor any other who may have had daily food from any fraternity or mistery[6] of London or elsewhere, be nominated, chosen, or be of the number of these thirteen poor.

Aware of the burden of expense the Church could impose on the poor, she endows the "lights" of the parish of St Peter, on the condition that:

no poor parishioner . . . at the holy paschal season or at any other time whatever, at the Lord's table, shall be kept back, or anyway compelled to pay for any paschal light, commonly called candel silver . . . [on pain of loss of annual rent income] *(from her bequest).*

2.2 *John Carpenter's 1441 will bequeaths considerably larger sums and refers to a range of valuable household possessions to be given to St Peter Cornhill to support the celebration of masses for the repose of his and his family's souls (translated from Latin by the nineteenth-century editor of the* Memoir of the Life and Times of John Carpenter, *Thomas Brewer), pp. 131–44.*[7]

I bequeath for the sustenance and finding of a fit and devout priest to celebrate divine service daily in the same church [St Peter of Cornhill] for my soul, and the souls of my said parents and of all the faithful deceased, during the three years next after my death, twenty pounds.

Also, to the praise and honour of God and of St Martin, and that my soul, and the souls of Katherine my wife and of my said parents, may be the more heartily remembered in the devotions and divine services henceforth to be made within the same church of St Martin, I give and bequeath for the service in the same church my great missale, and my best silver-gilt cup, together with my silver-gilt paxarium, and my two phials or cruets of silver, and my casula[8] of white damask, with all its trimming. Also I will and bequeath that out of fifty marks weight of my silver vessels, which have very often served me for the unreasonable and vain glory of the world, shall be made and provided, according to the discretion of my executors, ecclesiastical vessels and ornaments, for continual service in the said churches of St Peter and St Martin, to the praise and honour of God. In like manner, I will that my furred

6 Craft or trade guild.

7 For John Carpenter's biographical details, see 5.7.

8 An ecclesiastical garment worn during celebration of the Mass.

gowns and other sumptuous vestments, which, God forgive me, I have many times abused in superfluous and useless observances, may be sold, and with their price be purchased, and given out to poor devout persons having need thereof, competent clothing, according to the discretion aforesaid.

There were bequests to various convents and religious houses:

I bequeath to the prior and convent of the Charterhouse of Shene forty shillings. Also I bequeath to the prior and convent of the Charterhouse near London, of which I am an unworthy brother, forty shillings; and to the fraternity of Sixty Priests of London, whereof I am likewise a brother, forty shillings. . . . Also I bequeath to the prioress of Halywell, and to every nun there, under the same form, twenty pence; and in like manner to the prioress of Stratford, and to every nun there, twenty pence.[9]

2.3 Excerpts from Churchwardens' Accounts, St Mary at Hill, from *The Medieval Records of a London City Church: St Mary at Hill, 1420–1559*, ed. Henry Littlehales, EETS, o.s. 128 (London, 1905), pp. 99–101.

Medieval parish churches like that of St Peter, as well as larger foundations like cathedrals, were expensive facilities to run. The generosity of people like Katherine and John Carpenter ensured a stream of income to support maintaining the physical church. The excerpts below illustrate the complex finances of a fifteenth-century London parish church, and show how embedded its finances were with the various trades of the City, including scriveners:

Excerpts from Churchwardens' Accounts, St Mary at Hill, 1479–81:

Thexpensis of the Church.

Rolfe smyth. ffyrste payd to Rolfe Smyth for makynge of diuerse stuffe to the Church, as it apperith by a byll of the same, xiij s iiij d,[10]

Item, to the same Rolfe for diuerse thynges nywe made, and mendyd withyn the churche and othyr places, ij s viij d,

Item, for lowsyng[11] of a lokke in the vestiary, j d,

Item, for mendyng of ij lokkes within the churche, iiij d,

9 Stratford was a town then three miles outside of London; the Priory of Stratford at Bow had connections with prominent London citizens and with royalty in the fourteenth century. On this and Chaucer's Prioress' relation to the same house, see W.Rothwell, "Stratford atte Bowe Re-Visited," *The Chaucer Review*, Vol. 36 (2001), pp. 184–207.

10 "s" stands for "shilling" and "d" for pence.

11 Loosening.

Item, for makynge of ij nywe keys, one to the vestry dore,[12] and the to tothyr to the nywe howse in the churche Rente,[13] ix d,
Item, for a nywe lokke to the longe[14] cheste in the churche, iij d,
A laborer.
Item, payd to John paryse for swepyng of the churche, & ledynge away of the duste, and mendyng of the wyndowse of the churche, and kepyng
clene of the church hawse with othyr diuerse thynges done in the church by the space of this accompte as the boke of parcellis[15] of the same more playnly doth apere. vj s iiij d
Scowryng of the laton.[16]
Item, for scowryng of the latowne, the grete candylstykkes, and the Rode loft with all othyre smale candylstykkys, per idem[17] tempus, &c. iiij s vj d
Item, for Colis[18] to the churche, & frankencence, in wechyng of the sepulcre,[19] & at othyre tymes of the yere by the same space, ii s vj d
ffor swete wyne. Item, for brede, wyne, and ale for prestes and clerkes spent in the church apon dedicacions and othyr festyvall days, as the boke of parcellis of the same more playnly doth appere by the tyme of this accompte, vij s viij d
Ffor flaggis & garlondis:
Item, for flagges and garlondis, and pak thredde for the torchis, apon corpus *christi* day and apon saynt Barnabeys day & othir days. And for vj men to bere the same torchis, as it more playnly shewith by the boke of parcellis, iiij s vij d.
Item, to a mason for settyng of the hokes of the vestry wyndowys with lede, and for mendyng of othyr thynges in the church, vij d
Item, for mendyng of the churche lanterne, vj d,
Item, for beryng of iiij torchis, to bury the portyngaler, ij d,[20]
Item, for the caryyng of ij lode gravell, for the procession
churcheyarde, iij d,
Ffor makynge of a pywe:[21]
Item, payd to Christofer, Carpynter, for the makynge of a nywe pywe in the churche, as it apperith by a bylle, xxj s iij d

12 Door to room where vestments were kept.
13 A dwellingplace for which rent is paid.
14 For storing vestments.
15 Particular items in a list of objects, expenditures, payments received, etc.; listed items in a financial record; also, the itemized list; bille of parceles, a statement of payments; bok of parceles, an itemized account of commercial transactions; etc.; (b) pl. the particulars, the details (OED).
16 Non-precious metal alloy of copper, tin, and other metals.
17 At the same time.
18 Coals.
19 Keeping an Easter vigil, watching the sepulchre.
20 To bury, at the burial of the Portuguese [man].
21 Pew.

Item, in expensis and Costis done in fechynge of the chalis. And for rewardis yevyn to the goldsmyth & othirs, as the boke of parcelis makyth mencion severally, ij s

For candyll:

Item, payd for viij doseyn lb candyll for the churche, as it aperith &c. by this accompte, x s

Item, payd for a table & a payr [of] trestellis to stand in the vestry, to ley the Copis[22] apon in festyvall days, ij s

Item, spent at the Receyvyng of Sir Rafe & Sir Thomas prestes, v d,

Item, for a Shovell to the churche, iiij d,

Wex chaundeler:

Item, payd to the wex chaundeler for makyng of all the wex to tbe churche, by the space of this accompt, &c. xxij s xj d

Item, for vj loode Robyshe to both churchehawis[23], xij d

Item, for haly watyr sprynclys to the church, iiij d

Item, for a stone potte to put in oyle, j d

Item, for a bokyll to hange the clappyr of the lytyll belle

Item, for nayle to amende the whele of the Sanctus bell

Item, for papyr spent in makyng of this accompt & for the parcelse of the same, v s iiij d,

Item, for Bowis[24] and Ivy to the church for ij yere, ij s,

Item, to the cornell Raker[25] for carynge of the

Rubbysshe & duste of the churche at diuerse tymes xij d,

Item, for evys borde[26] to the lityll howse in the churchyarde,

for nayles & makyng, iiij d

Item, for c of ij peny nayle, ij d,

Item, for iij peny nayle, j d.

Mendyng of the Crossis:

Item, payd for mendyng of the crosse that is borne abowte euery day, And for mendyng of the mustenaunce[27] crosse, as it apperith in the boke of parcellis of the same, iij s iiij d

The grete Antiphoner:[28]

Item, payd to a Stacioner for the grete Antyphoner, and for a quayer of clene stuffe sette into the same, & for a Rewarde to the Stacioner, & for berynge of the same boke, as the boke of parcellis more playnly shewith, xxijs ij d

---

22 Copes, ecclesiastical vestments.

23 Churchyards.

24 Boughs.

25 Cornel, front of a house or building; corner, angle.

26 Eave boards.

27 Monstrance.

28 A book containing antiphons, versicles or sentences sung alternately by one group or choir and another.

The Vestyment makere.

Item, for mendyng of iij Rede copis, the grene cope, &, ij blak copis, xvij s j d,
Item, for golde sylke & perle, bokeram[29] & Rebande[30] for the best cope, xiij s,
Item, for mendyng of othyr vestymentes, awbis, chysyblis, copis,[31] & othir diuerse Stuffe boght to the same at diuerse tymes, viij s vij d,
Item, for workemanshyp of the same for the sayd ij yere, xiiij s x d.

Performing Devotions: The Mass

2.4 From "History of the Mass," in *The Golden Legend or Lives of the Saints as Englished by William Caxton*, 7 vols (London: J. M. Dent, 1900), Vol. 7, pp. 243–5.

The central devotion medieval Christians performed was attending the Mass which celebrated the sacrifice of Jesus' body in the Crucifixion and his resurrection. Following His instruction to his Disciples at the Last Supper, that to come together in his name to eat bread and drink wine would be to eat his flesh and drink his blood, the Roman Church's central sacrament, the transubstantiation of the bread and wine into Christ's body and blood, united all Christians in the fellowship and body of Christ. Here the miracle of transubstantiation is explained through a series of analogies as a nine-fold miracle:

The first is that the substance of the bread and of the wine is changed into the substance of the body and precious blood of Christ, and this is showed to us by such a similitude or likeness naturally, that is, that of food of bread and wine, both flesh and blood are engendered in creature, much more stronger our Lord that is sovereign nature, may do by virtue of his words that the bread and the wine is converted into his own body and into his precious blood. The second miracle is, that every day, oft and many times, the bread is converted into the proper and own body of our Lord, and notwithstanding none augmentation or increase is done in God. Ensample of nature. For if I wot[32] a thing secret, I may utter and rehearse in it many and diverse places, and notwithstanding I ne wot it the more ne better than I did tofore. The third is that, every day our Lord is parted and eaten, and hath no diminishing. That is to say that God nor the sacrament is not less therefore. Reason natural. For if I have a candlelight, every one may take of the light of it without it be lessed or diminished therefore. Also, every one may take that holy sacrament without diminishing of it, but who that taketh it unworthily, he diminisheth

29 Buckram.

30 Ribbon, trim.

31 Albs, chausubles and copes, all eccesisastical vestments.

32 Know.

himself. The fourth miracle is that, when the hostie[33] is parted,[34] God is in each part entirely. Ensample of the glass.[35] For when the glass is parted or broken into pieces, in every part of it appeareth the figure of the thing that is presented before in it. The fifth miracle is that, if this precious sacrament be taken of an evil and sinful creature, the sacrament of itself is not fouled therefor. For we see that the beams of the sun pass through and over ordure or filth, and the sun is nothing foul therefor, but rather the ordure or filth is made clean thereof. Thus it is that, sometimes when the creature hath received the body of our Lord unworthily, considering that he hath misdone to have received his Saviour into so great ordure or filth of sin, he conceiveth by bitterness or smarting so great a contrition, that he therefore returneth to grace, and thus he is purged or made clean of his sin. The sixth miracle is, that the body of our Lord Jesu Christ is food of death to the sinners. For S. Paul the Apostle saith that, he that eateth it unworthily, he eateth it to his damnable judgment, for right even so as strong wines or strong meats are unprofitable or letting to sick people, right so is the body of our Lord Jesu Christ nuisable[36] and letting[37] to the sinners. The seventh miracle is, that so great a thing which all the world may not comprehend[38] is contained in so little a hostie, for we see that a great hill may be comprised and perceived with an eye, much more stranger it is that the virtue divine may be by his puissance comprised and contained in a little hostie. The eighth miracle is, that our Lord all entirely in divers places at once is perceived of divers persons. In such manner we see and perceive that the word of a creature is known and perceived in divers places at once of many and divers creatures. The ninth miracle is, when the bread is converted into the precious body of our Lord, the accidents[39] abide, that is to wit, whiteness, roundness, and savour, and not therefore it is no bread, but it is the body of Jesu Christ, the which is given under the likeness of bread, for this, that that might be great horror, a priest to eat raw flesh and also to drink blood.

The documents below are drawn from the late medieval liturgy of the Mass, beginning with the blessing of salt and water which, being purified, would be combined together to make holy water. Both these prayers and the prayers of the priest as he approaches the altar suggest the intense importance of purity in the rituals of the Church. In their focus on purity of heart and freedom from corruption, the prayers below are designed

33 The host, the consecrated bread.

34 Broken into pieces.

35 Mirror, looking-glass.

36 Harmful or noxious.

37 A hindrance.

38 Encircle, encompass.

39 Insubstantial and therefore changeable attributes such as color, size, smell, taste apprehensible by the senses.

to minimize the risk of contagion by sin and the works of the devil whose malign influence was detected in all sorts of evil events. Concern for purity and anxiety about corruption were pervasive elements of late medieval English culture, both clerical and lay:

2.5 Excerpts from *The Sarum Missal in English: Newly Translated by Frederick E. Warren*, ed. Frederick E. Warren, 2 vols (London: De la More Press, 1911).[40] Vol. I, pp. 13–14, 18.

Blessing of salt and water – On all Sundays throughout the year, after prime and the chapter, the blessing of salt and water shall take place, at the step of the quire, by a priest, after the following manner.

I exorcize thee, O creature of salt, by the living + God, by the true + God, by the holy + God, by the God who commanded thee to be cast into the water by Elisha the prophet that the barrenness of the water might be healed, that thou mayest become salt [*Here shall the priest look at the salt*] exorcized for the salvation of them that believe, and that thou mayest be salvation of soul and body to all that take thee; and from that place where thou shalt have been sprinkled, let every delusion and wickedness, of craft of devilish cunning, when adjured, flee and depart. Through him who shall come to judge the quick and the dead and the world by fire.

Collect[41]

Almighty and everlasting God, we humbly implore thy boundless loving-kindness [*Here the priest shall look at the salt*] that of thy goodness thou wouldest deign to ble+ss and sancti+fy this creature of salt, which thou hast given for the use of mankind; that it may be unto all who partake of it health of mind and body; that whatsoever shall have been touched or sprinkled with it may be freed from all uncleanness, and from all assault of spiritual wickedness. Through our Lord Jesus Christ, thy Son, who liveth and reigneth with thee in the unity of the Holy Ghost, God, world without end. Amen.

Here follows the exorcism of the water.

I exorcize thee, O creature of water, in the name of God + the Father Almighty, and in the name of Jesus + Christ his Son our Lord, and in the power of the Holy + Ghost; that thou mayest become water exorcized for

---

40 This edition was based on a printed copy of a 1526 translation of the *Sarum Missal* out of Latin into English.

41 Collect: a short formal prayer that can vary according to usage, usually recited before the Epistle in Christian churches.

putting to flight all power of the enemy; that thou mayest have power to root out and transplant the enemy himself with his apostate angels, by the power of the same Jesus Christ our Lord; who shall come to judge the quick and the dead and the world by fire.

Collect

O God, who for the salvation of mankind has hidden [one of thy] greatest sacraments in the element of water, graciously hearken unto our invocations, and pour upon this element [*Here shall the priest look upon the water*] prepared for divers purifications the power of thy blessing, that this thy creature, serving in thy mysteries, may acquire the effectual power of divine grace for casting out devils, and for driving away diseases; and that on whatsoever in the houses or dwelling places of the faithful this water shall have been sprinkled, it may be freed from all uncleanness, and may be delivered from hurt. Let no pestilential spirit, no corrupting air, linger there. Let all the insidious attacks of the lurking enemy be dissipated; and if there be aught which threatens the safety of the peace of the inhabitants, let it be driven away by the sprinkling of this water, so that saved by the invocation of thy holy name they may be defended from all assaults. Through our Lord Jesus Christ thy Son, who liveth and reigneth with thee in the unity of the Holy Ghost, God, world without end.

From Prayers to be said by the Priest before Mass:

Lord, I am not worthy that thou shouldest come under my roof, but trusting in thy loving kindness I approach thine altar; sick I come to the physician of life, blind to the light of eternal brightness, poor to the lord of heaven and earth, naked to the king of glory, a sheep to the shepherd, a thing formed to him that formed it, desolate to the kind comforter, miserable to the pitiful, guilty to the bestower of pardon, unholy to one that justifieth, hardened to the infuser of grace; imploring the abundance of thy boundless mercy that thou wouldest vouchsafe to heal mine infirmity, to wash my foulness, to enlighten my blindness, to enrich my poverty, to clothe my nakedness, to bring back the wandering, to console the desolate, to reconcile the guilty, to give pardon to the sinner, forgiveness to the wretched, life to the accused, justification to the dead; that I may be deemed worthy to receive thee, the bread of angels, the king of kings, and lord of lords, with such chastity of body and purity of mind, such contrition of heart and flow of tears, such spiritual happiness and heavenly joy, such fear and trembling, such reverence and honour, such faith and humility, such determination and love, such prayer and thanksgiving, as are becoming and thy due, so that I may profitably obtain eternal life, and the remission of all my sins. Amen.

2.6 Special masses for particular occasions: Marriage, Vol. 2, p. 145–8, 155–6.

Masses could be offered for various needs: for protection for travelers, to pray for special needs and people, for the king, or to petition God's help in time of disease. Arguably the most common of these "special" masses – and the one of most interest to students of medieval literature and culture – was the Mass celebrating marriage because of the way it reflects power and gender within a central medieval institution. Medieval marriages were contracted "at church door," celebrated and solemnized at Mass within the church. At the church door the couple exchanged the vows that established the marriage:

> *At the door of the church, in the presence of God, and the priest, and the people. The man should stand on the right hand of the woman, and the woman on the left hand of the man, the reason being that she was formed out of a rib in the left side of Adam . . .*[42]
>
> N. wilt thou have this woman to thy wedded wife, wilt thou love her, and honour her, keep her and guard her, in health and in sickness, as a husband should a wife, and forsaking all others on account of her, keep thee only unto her, so long as ye both shall live?
>
> *The man shall answer,* I will.
>
> Then shall the priest say unto the woman,
>
> *N.* wilt thou take this man to thy wedded husband, wilt thou obey him, and serve him, love, honour, and keep him, in health and in sickness, as a wife should keep a husband, and forsaking all others on account of him, keep thee only unto him, so long as ye both shall live?
>
> *Then the woman shall answer,* I will.
>
> *Then let the woman be given by her father or a friend; if she be a maid, let her have her hand [sic*[43]*] uncovered; if she be a widow, covered; and let the man receive her, to be kept in God's faith and his own, as he hath vowed in the presence of the priest; and let him hold her by her right hand in his right hand. And so let the man give his troth to the woman, by word of mouth, presently, after the priest, saying thus:*[44]
>
> I, *N*, take the[e] *N.* to my weddyd wyf to have et to hold fro this day fawort [for] bettur for wurs for richere for porer: in sikenis se [sic] and in helte tylle deth us departe, if holi chyrche wol it ordeyne: and ther to I plycht the[e] my trouth.[45] (*withdrawing his hand*).

---

42 The vows were to be spoken in the "vulgar tongue" presumably the mother tongue of the couple, rather than the Latin in which the Mass was said, Vol 2, p. 145.

43 "Hand" here may be an error for "Head."

44 The vows were spoken in the vernacular, English, with inflections from French and Latin, as the following passage shows.

45 Troth.

Then shall the woman say, after the priest,

I, *N.* take te [sic] *N.* to my weddyd husbonde, tho [sic] have et to hold from this day for bettur, for wurs, for richere, for porer, in sykenesse and in helthe, to be bonowre et buxum, in bed et atbord, tyll deth vs departe, if holy chirche wol it ordeyne: et ther to I plyche t[h]e[e] my throute (*withdrawing her hand*). . . .

Giving of the ring:

Bless, O Lord, this ring, which we bless in thy holy name; that whosoever she be that shall wear it, may abide in thy peace, and continue in thy will, and live, and increase, and grow old in thy love; and let the length of her days be multiplied. . . .

The man shall take [the ring] in his right hand and with his three principal fingers, holding the right hand of the bride with his left hand, and shall say after the priest,

With thys ryng I the wedde and thys gold and silver I the geue: and wyth my body I the worscype, and wyth all my worldly catell I the honore.

Then shall the bridegroom place the ring upon the thumb of the bride, saying, In the name of the Father; *then upon the second finger, saying, and* of the Son; *and upon the third finger saying,* and of the Holy Ghost; *then upon the fourth finger, saying, Amen, and there let him leave it . . . because in that finger there is a certain vein, which runs from thence as far as the heart; and inward affection, which ought always to be fresh between them, is signified by the true ring of the silver.*

During the Mass of the Trinity which follows inside the church, this prayer is offered by the priest who voices the assumption that it is the man who chooses the wife, and that the wife will benefit from prayer and the implicit exhortation to follow the matriarchs of the Old Testament in their devotion to husband and family. No equivalent prayer is offered for the husband:

O God, by whom woman is joined to man, and the union, instituted in the beginning, is gifted with that bles+sing, which alone has not been taken away either through the punishment of original sin, or through the sentence of the deluge, look graciously, we beseech thee, on this thy handmaiden, who now to be joined in wedlock, seeketh to be guarded by thy protection. May the yoke of love and peace be upon her; may she be a faithful and chaste wife in Christ, and abide a follower of holy matrons. May she be amiable to her husband as Rachel, wise as Rebecca, long-lived as Sara. Let not the father of lies get any advantage over her through her doings; bound to thy faith and thy commandments may she remain united to one man; may she flee all unlawful unions; may she fortify her weakness with the strength of discipline. May she be bashful and grave, reverential and modest, well-instructed in heavenly doctrine. May she be fruitful in child-bearing, innocent and of good report, attaining to a desired old age, seeing her children's children unto the third and fourth generation; and may she attain to the rest of the blessed, and to the kingdom of heaven.

2.7 Sarum Rite: Order of Service for Pilgrims, Excerpts, Vol. 2, pp. 167–73.

In contrast to the marriage service, which is relatively familiar even to modern readers, this Mass for blessing pilgrims may offer an unfamiliar perspective on the act and religious doctrine of pilgrimage, in which the pilgrim becomes the focus of heavenly as well as earthly support and goes forth as a servant-soldier of the cross.

Those who are about to undertake pilgrimage, having made their confession, lie prostrate in front of the Altar, and this order of prayers begins by asking for protection from corruption, disease, and the devil. The service places the pilgrim, who is about to travel away from the world he or she knows, within the communion of saints and the company of heaven symbolized by invocations of angels, the saints, and the Virgin. The elaborate series of prayers offered to sacralize the act of pilgrimage indicates how seriously the Church endorsed, and oversaw the practice:

Collect

O God, who leadest unto life, and guardest with thy fatherly protection them that trust in thee, we beseech thee that thou wouldest grant unto these thy servants *N.* here present, going forth from amongst us, an escort of angels; that they, being protected by thy aid, may be shaken by no fear of evil, nor be depressed by any lingering adversity, nor be troubled by any enemy lying in wait to assail them; but that having prosperously accomplished the course of their appointed journey, they may return unto their own homes; and having been received back in safety, may pay due thanks unto thy name. Through, etc.

and later: Here shall the pilgrims rise from their prostration, and the blessing of the script and staff shall follow, thus*:*

O lord, Jesu Christ, who of thy unspeakable mercy, and at the bidding of the Father, and with the co-operation of the Holy Ghost, didst will to come down from heaven, and to seek the sheep that was lost through the wiles of the devil, and to bear it back on thine own shoulders to the flock of the heavenly country, and didst command the sons of mother Church by prayer to ask, by holy living to seek, and by knocking to persevere, that they may be able to find more quickly the rewards of saving life; we humbly beseech thee that thou wouldest vouchsafe to sanctify and bl+ess these scrips (*or* this scrip), and these staves (*or* this staff); that whosoever, for love of thy name, shall desire to wear the same, like the armour of humility, at his side, or to hang it from his neck, or to carry it in his hands, and so on his pilgrimage to seek the prayers of the saints, with the accompaniment of humble devotion, may be found worthy, through the protecting defence of thy right hand, to attain unto the joys of the everlasting vision, through thee, O Saviour of the world. Who livest, etc. . . .

Blessing of a cross for one on a pilgrimage to Jerusalem

O God of unconquered power, and boundless pity, the entire aid and consolation of pilgrims, who givest to thy servants most invincible armour; we pray thee that thou wouldest vouchsafe to bl+ess this cross, which is humbly dedicated to thee; that the banner of the venerated cross, the figure whereof hath been depicted upon it, may be a most invincible strength to thy servant against the wickedest temptation of the ancient enemy; that it may be a defence by the way, a guard in thy house, and a protection to us everywhere. Through etc. . . .

Collect

May the almighty and everlasting God, who is the way, the truth, and the life, dispose thy (*or* your) journey according to his good pleasure; may he send his angel Raphael to be thy (*or* your) guardian in thy (*or* your) pilgrimage; to conduct thee on thy way, in peace, to the place whither thou wouldest go, and to bring thee back again in safety on thy return to us. May Mary, the blessed mother of God, intervene for thee (*or* you), together with all angels and archangels, and patriarchs, and prophets. May the holy apostles Peter and Paul intercede for thee (*or* you), together with the rest of the apostles, martyrs, confessors, and virgins; and may the saints, whose prayers thou askest (*or* ye ask), together with all the saints, obtain for thee (*or* for you) just desires, and prosperity, and remission of all sins, and life everlasting. Through etc.

Attaining Salvation

Doctrinally and in practice, the celebration of the Mass, the sacrament that commemorates Christ's sacrifice on the cross through the miracle of transubstantiation in which the bread and wine offered at the Mass become for the faithful the body and blood of Christ, lay at the center of medieval Christianity. In private chapels, in parish churches, as well as in monastic establishments and large cathedrals, all Christians would have found essentially the same order and language of celebration, with slight local variances according to custom. Ancillary to this central celebration, a vast body of doctrinal literature circulated in late medieval England aimed at instructing lay persons about how to prepare their own souls for salvation. Items 2.7–2.13 in this section provide several examples of the kind of devotional texts and performances that would have constituted the instructional matrix in which lay people thought about access to heaven.

2.8 "On the Day of Doom and the Last Judgement," from Bk V, *The Pricke of Conscience, a Northumbrian Poem*, ed. Richard Morris, The Philological Society (Berlin, 1863).

Prayer, bequests, alms-giving, attendance at Mass all served to sustain and strengthen an individual Christian's spiritual health. Salvation was the reward of those who lived well, truly repented their sins, and never despaired of Christ's mercy. After a period in Purgatory where they would be purified of their earthly sins, the saved would be received into the company of saints in heaven. Anxiety about who would be saved, and why, appears throughout the period in the paintings and sculpture of Last Judgment scenes, in the popularity of Apocalypse manuscripts that describe the second coming, and in anxiety about the place of Anti-Christ in eschatology. The excerpt below from the mid-fourteenth century Pricke of Conscience, *a northern dialect version of one of the most popular of the devotional manuals of the period, describes the Day of Doom and the Last Judgment, stressing the fact that, as the play* Everyman *shows, humans come before God for judgment with only their good deeds to plead for them:*[46]

Som sal noght be demed[47] that day
That sal wende to helle and swelle thar ay,[48]
Als paens and sarazyns that had na law,
And Iewes that never wald Crist knaw,
Tharfor thai sal ga[49] til payne endeles,
With-outen dome,[50] for thus writen es:
Qui sine lege peccant,
absque lege peribunt.
"Thas that with-outen law uses syn
With-outen law sal perysshe thar-in."
And thar-for at the day of dome namly,
Ilk man sal haf as he es worthy.[51]
A ful hard day men sal that day se,
When alle thyng sal thus discussed be.

46 This text is in a Northern dialect, in which "a" stands for "o" in many spellings.

47 Shall not be judged; throughout the poem "sal" is modern English "shall".

48 Who shall go to hell and swell their number// As pagans and saracens who had no law, i.e., Christian law// And Jews who would not know Christ.

49 Go.

50 Judgment.

51 Deserves.

That day, sal na man be excused
Of nathyng that he wrang here used,[52]
That sounes in ille on any manere,
Of whilk he was never delyverd here.[53]
The synful sal thare na mercy have,
For nathyng may tham than save;
For-whi thai sal than na help gett
Of sergeaunt, ne auturne, ne avoket,[54]
Ne of nan other for tham to plede,
Ne tham to counsayle ne to rede,[55]
Ne na halghe[56] sal for tham pray.
This may be cald a ful harde day,
Forwhi than, als the buke bers witnes,
Sal noght be shewed bot rightwysnes,
And grete reddure, with-outen mercy,[57]
Until alle synful men namely.
Tha that of thair syn here wald noght stynt;[58]
Thay sal that day for ever be tynt[59]
Fra God, with-outen any recoverere,
And delyverd be until the devels powere.
Ful wa[60] sal synful me[n] be that day,
And til helle pyne be put for ay,
And tharfor men may calle that day,
The grete day of delyveraunce,
The day of wreke and of vengeaunce,
The day of wrethe and of wrechednes,
The day of bale[61] and of bitternes,
The day of pleynyng and accusying,
The day of answer and of strait rekkenyng,
The day of iugements and of Iuwys[62]
The day of angre and of angwys,

52 Of none of the wrong he did on earth.

53 Of none of the wrong he committed on earth/ That leads to any kind of ill/ Of which he was not confessed here on earth.

54 No legal counsel will be available, neither sergeant of the law, nor attorney, nor advocate at the final day.

55 Advise.

56 No saint, no holy, or hallowed one.

57 Because, as the book (Bible) bears witness/ Only righteousness shall be shown [exercised] / And great strictness, without mercy.

58 Those who of their sin here would not desist.

59 Separated from.

60 Full of woe.

61 Torment.

62 Doom.

The day of drede and of tremblyng,
The day of gretyng and goulyng,[63]
The day of crying and of duleful dyn,[64]
The day of sorow that never sal blyn,[65]
The day of flaying and of affray,
The day of departyng fra God away,[66]
The day of merryng and of myrknes,[67]
The day that es last and that mast es,[68]
The day when Crist sal make ende of alle;
Thus may nan discryve that day and calle.
Our loverd[69] that all thyng can se and witt
At the dredeful day of dome sal sitt,
Als kyng and rightwyse domesman,[70]
In dome to deme all the werld than,[71]
Opon the setil[72] of his mageste.
That day sal alle men byfor hym be,
Bathe gude and ille, mare and les;
Than sal noght be done bot rightwysnes.
He sal deme al men of ilka degré,[73]
Til ioy or payne that demed sal be,
And rightwyse domes-man and suthefast[74]
And gyf[75] a fynal dome at the last.
Bot how he sale deme I sal shewe,
Als telles the godspelle of Mathewe;
Hys angels than, aftir his wille,
Sal first departe the gude fra the ille,[76]
Als the hird the shepe dus fra the gayte,[77]
That falles to be putt til pastur strayt.
By the shepe understand we may
The gude men that sal be saved that day.

---

63 Weeping and lamentation.
64 Doleful din.
65 End.
66 Being separated from God.
67 Marring, murk.
68 Last and greatest.
69 Lord.
70 Righteous judge.
71 To sit in judgment of all the world then.
72 Seat.
73 Every class.
74 Truthful; truth-fast.
75 Give.
76 Separate.
77 As the shepherd separates the sheep from the goat.

By the gayte understand we may
The ille men, that than dampned[78] sal be.
The gude sal be sette on his right hand,
And the ille on his lefte syde sal stand;
Than sal our loverd say thus that tyde
Til tham that standes on his right syde:
Venite, benedicti patris mei,
possidete paratum notis regnum
a constitucione mundi.
He sal say than, "commes now til me,
My fadir blissed childer fre,
And weldes the kyngdom that til yhow es dight
Fra first that the world was ordaynd right."[79]
For I hungerd and yhe me fedde,
I thrested and at drynk yhe me bedde;
Of herber grete nede I had,
Yhe herberd me with hert glad,[80]
Naked I was, als yhe myght se,
Yhe gaf me clathes and clad me;
Seke I was and in ful wayke state,
Yhe visit me, bathe arly and late;[81]
In prisoun when I was halden stille,[82]
Til me yhe come with ful gude wille.
Than sal the rightwys men that day,
Til our loverd answer thus and say;
'Loverd when saw we the[83] hungry,
And to gyf the mete war we redy;
And when myght we the thresty se,
And gaf the drynk with hert fre;[84]
When saw we the ned of herber have,
And to herber the vouched save;
When saw we the naked and we the cled,
And when saw we the seke and in prison sted,[85]

78 Damned.

79 Come now, to me,/ My father's blessed generous children, / And possess the kingdom that is prepared for you/ From the beginning of the world.

80 I thirsted and you bid me drink/ Of shelter I had great need/ Ye harbored me with a glad heart.

81 Sick I was in a full weak state/ You visited me, both early and late.

82 Closely confine.

83 "the" here and in the next lines, is a form of "thee".

84 With open heart, good will.

85 Enclosed.

And visited the with gude wille,
And comforted the, als was skille?'[86]
Our loverd sal than tham answer thus,
And say, als the godspelle shewes us:
'Suthly I say yhou, swa yhe wroght,
That ilka tyme when yhe did oght
Until ane of the lest that yhe myght se
Of my brether, yhe did til me.'[87]

2.9 Pride and Covetousness: from *Memoriale Credencium: A late Middle English Manual of Theology for Lay People* edited from Bodley MS Tanner 201, ed. J. H. L. Kengen (1979), pp. 52–61, 100.

Of all the seven deadly sins which, unrepented, could prevent a Christian from attaining salvation, pride was regarded as the worst, because centered in regard for oneself rather than others, it was the root from which so many sinful deeds grew, as Chaucer's Parson explains at great length in his Canterbury tale. The two passages below, fifteenth-century descriptions of the sins of pride and its close neighbor covetousness, are designed to instruct a lay person in thinking of sin as action or thought against God and against the community of household and beyond (Translation from Middle English by editors):

Pride is the first and the worst of the seven deadly sins, because it is the head and king of all other sins. And as a king comes not alone, but brings with him many people, so pride, when it comes into a man's heart, brings with it many foul, horrible sins.

Pride is a "highness" in a man's heart. When a man holds himself worth more than any other of his fellow Christians; and pride grows in a man's heart for many reasons: for strength of body, or for good looks, or for hardiness, or for noble blood, and kindred, or for eloquent speech, or for good voice, or quick mindedness, or other kinds of knowing, or for any skill, or for wealth, or for worship, or for intimacy and love of any man or any woman, or for grace and favor of men, or for fair clothing, or for meekness, or for chastity, or of other good deeds, or for a well-shaped body, or limbs, or for fair hair, or lightness, or any virtue of grace that a person may have. Pride has five branches:

The first is disobedience . . . to god's commandments . . . and teachings of Holy Church, or a child to be disobedient to a father and mother, or a servant to his master, or a wife to her husband. . . .

86 Right.

87 Truly, I say to you, as you did/ That very time when you did anything/ Unto one of the least that you might see/ Of my brethren, ye did it for me.

The second branch of pride is boasting or bragging, as when a man blames others for his misfortunes or believes that his own good fortune comes from his own deeds, not God. . . .

The third branch of pride is hypocrisy, that is "pope-holyness" as when a man or a woman pretends to be good, or pretends to be wiser or holier than they are. . . .

The fourth branch of pride is when a man scorns his fellows for any lack, for poverty, or lowly birth, or foulness of body, or for ill-shapen limbs. . . .

The fifth branch of pride is impudence, as when a man is not ashamed of his sin, as a common woman or a common lecher is not ashamed of their lechery, or an open spouse breaker[88] or a monk or friar, or priest, or nun, or any other member of holy church, or any man or woman who give themselves to open sin, be it lechery, drunkenness, manslaughter, or any other open sin and are not ashamed before God and good people. . . .

* * *

Covetousness is an inordinate love of the world's goods, both things and wealth, either through wickedly with-holding, or in falsely getting, as by simony, as do these wicked prelates, or by usury as do merchants and burgesses, or by theft and rapine as do these robbers and thieves, or with false weights as do these young chapmen, or with false measures as do these tapsters and brewers, or by false oaths as do jurymen, or by violence and fear as do these foresters, bailiffs, beadles, purveyors and other ministers of kings and queens and great lords either by extortion as do wicked lords that raise up wicked laws and evil customs that are seldom put down after they are begun. And understand well that they who begin any wicked customs are responsible for the sin of all those men that use the custom after them. . . .

Among the routes to salvation, one popular, if perilous, one was a pilgrimage to Jerusalem. We have seen in the excerpts from the Mass of blessing for pilgrims to the Holy Land, that those who undertook this arduous journey were spiritual Crusaders whose undertaking accrued benefits to themselves and to the communion of saints. Margery Kempe is perhaps the most famous literary pilgrim to Jerusalem, but she was not alone. The excerpt below from Mandeville's Travels, *a mid-fourteenth century text purportedly recounting the travels of Sir John Mandeville, an English knight, shows how spiritually powerful the imagined landscape of the Holy Land was. It was a place where time and space were compressed, a place where one could see visible, physical evidence of Biblical history:*

88 "spousebreche" occurs when a "wedded man takith a nother woman than his wiff other a wedded woman takith a nother man than hir husbande" (p. 139 Memoriale).

2.10 The Holy Land: from *Mandeville's Travels* (mid fourteenth century), ed. Malcolm Letts, 2 vols, Hakluyt Society, second series no. CII (London, 1953), Vol. 2, pp. 444–6.

Besides the citee of Ebron is the citee of Bethleem, where Crist was born. And there is yit the stalle of the oxe and the asse that were atte[89] birthe of Crist, and the pitte that the sterre fille inne, that ledde the three kingis to our lorde Iesu; the wiche were callied Iasp, the ooldest, Melcheor, the mydleste, and Balthasar, the yongeste. Thes three kinges offred to our lorde Iesu Crist golde, mirre, and encens, and alle three they ligge at Coleyn be the watir of the Reene.[90] And wete ye wel[91] that they come neuere thider thorugh ymagenacion of mannes witte, but oonly thorugh the grace of God, that come thider fro so ferre cuntrees in so litil space.[92]

And in the cite of Betheleem is a chirche wher the bonyes of the innocentis arn buriede and leide, that deyde for Cristis sake a litil before the birthe of Crist. And ther is also the sepulcre of seint Ierome, the doctour, and was cardenal of Rome that tyme, and he translatid the Bybille out of Ebrewe into Latyn. And withoute the mynstre[93] is yit the chayer wherinne he satte whenne he translatid the Bybille. Nought ferre[94] fro this chirche in the same cite is anothir chirche, of seint Nicholas, where our lady restid hir aftir the birthe of Crist. And there the [milk] abounded in her pappis that it grevid hir mochel[95], and there she sette hir adoun and mylked hir pappis vpon a ston of marbil that ther laye, and yit the spottis of the milke arn seene vpon the same ston, and eueremore shal be.

* * *

Now wol I telle of the pilgrymage of Ierusalem. Whenne that pilgrymes arn comen vnto Ierusalem, they shalle goo to the chirche were the holy sepulcre is inne. And that is withoute the chirche towarde the north side, but it is enclosid with a walle to the cite. And withinne that ilke chirche is a tabernacle craftely and coryously iwrought, and is igarnysshed[96] with golde, siluere, asure, and with manye othir precyous stones and colours; withinne wiche tabernacle towarde the right side is the holy sepulcre of our lorde Iesu Crist.

89 At the.

90 A reference to the shrine of the Three Kings in Cologne, a triple sarcophagus containing their bones, brought from Milan to Colgne in 1164 in the reign of Frederick Barbarossa the Holy Roman Emperor.

91 Be assured.

92 Who came thither (to Bethlehem) from such far countries in so little time.

93 Outside the church/ minster (where St Jerome is buried).

94 Far.

95 And there the milk in her breasts was so plenteous that it made her uncomfortable.

96 Made and decorated, adorned.

And the lengthe of that tabernacle is viij. foote, and of brede v. foote, and the heighte is xj. foote. And it is noght longe sythenes that pilgrymes myghte come to the sepulcre and seen it openliche,[97] and touche it, and kysse it. But because that some men brak out pecis of it and bare it awey with hem, wherfore the Sowdon hath doo enclose it with a walle aboute, that noo man may neighe it, but on the lift side of the walle[98] And in that tabernacle is a ston stonding vp on the heighte of a man, and that [was a] stoon of the sepulcre, and it is noo more thenne the gretnesse of a foote, and that stoon men kisseth. And also in that same tabernacle arn lawmpis brennynge[99] in wyndowes, but there is oo lawmpe bifore the sepulcre brennynge, the wiche eueremore vpon the Goode ffryday gooth out by the self. And vpon Estre daye hit lighteneth ageyn[100] be the self, atte same tyme that Crist aroos fro deth to liff.

Also withinne that ilke chirche is the mount of Caluerye, where our lorde Iesu Crist was crucified. And ther beside in a rooche, as men seyn, was founden the heede of Adam aftir Noes flode, in tokenynge[101] that Adames synne shulde be bowght ageyn[102] in the same place. And vpon that ilke rooche made Abraham sacrifice vnto God of his sone Isaak, and there the aungel come fro hevene and hilde[103] the swerde of Abraham, with the wiche he wold haue slayn Isaak his sone, thorugh the biddynge of God. And also ther is an awtir[104] bifore the wiche Godfray of Bullion and the Bawdewyne of Surry, and othir that were kingis of Ierusalem liggen buryed there, beside where our lorde Iesu Crist was crucified, and there is wreten of oolde tyme her wordis, "Hire God the lorde bifore that he this worlde wroughte hire in myddes the erthe [sic]."[105] And right vpon the same rooche, where the cros was fastened inne, that Crist was doen vpon,[106] is graven in that rooche thes wordis, *Hoc quod vides est fundamentum tocius fidei huius mundi.*[107] And I doo yow to wite that whenne Crist was crucified he was of age xxxiij. yeer and three monthis. And beside the mount of Caluerye, atte right side of the awtir, is the piler[108] that Crist was bounden too in his flagellacion.

---

97 Openly, clearly.

98 And, until recently pilgrims might come to the sepulchre and see it clearly, touch it, and kiss it. But because some men broke out pieces of it and took them away, therefore the Sultan has had it enclosed with a wall, so that no man may come close to it, except on the left side of the wall.

99 Lamps.

100 It lights again by itself.

101 As a sign.

102 Redeemed.

103 Stopped, deflected.

104 Altar.

105 Here God, before he created the world, created here the middle of the earth.

106 Killed upon.

107 That which you see is the foundation of the faith of this world.

108 Pillar.

Devotional Reading

Reading hagiography, the lives of saints, formed an important element of late medieval spirituality, particularly for women, both lay and cloistered, who were encouraged to model their lives on the virtues female saints manifested in the trials they faced. The biography of St Etheldreda below is a sixteenth-century version of the life of an Anglo-Saxon saint whose hagiography was written in all the languages of England up to the Reformation. The first life appears in Anglo-Saxon in which she bears her original name, Ethelthryth; the second in Anglo-Norman in which she is renamed St Awdry; a third is a Middle English poem, almost a romance, where she is called Etheldreda. In the later Middle Ages St Etheldreda's shrine at Ely attracted numerous pilgrims, including Richard II, who petitioned the saint for the restoration of health to one of his attendants who had been struck by lightning.[109] *Etheldreda was one of the most powerful and important English saints, because she was closely associated with the foundation of Hexham Abbey and Ely Cathedral. Her story, like many stories of women saints, offers instructive lessons for all women, both lay and regular, about female virtue. The life below is from an early sixteenth-century collection; much shorter than either the Anglo-Norman or the Middle English versions of the life, the narrative nevertheless contains the signal and conventional hagiographical elements of her story: her chaste marriage and her determined devotion to Christ, her mortification of her body in life and its incorruptibility in death, as well as her miraculous interventions.*[110]

2.11 Life of St Etheldreda: from *The Kalendre of the Newe Legende of Englande: ed. from Pynson's printed edition, 1516*, ed. Manfred Görlach (Heidelberg: Universitätsverlag C. Winter, 1994), pp. 96–7.

De sancta Etheldreda virgine

Seynt Etheldrede commenly callyd Seynt Awdry was doughter to Anna Kynge of Eest Englonde, and agaynste her wyll she was maryed to Tonbert Kynge of the South Gyrwyes, where is the Ile of Ely. And when she came into the chaumber she commyttyd her virgynyte to our Lorde, and as her husbonde lokyd into the chaumber it was lyke as if all the chaumber had ben on fyre. And so he bad her fere[111] no more for he wolde not touche her, for he sayd our Lorde was hyr defender. And shortlye after he dyed, & she was maryed

109 *Westminster Chronicle* (1381–1394), ed. and trans. L. C. Hector and Barbara F. Harvey (Oxford: Clarendon Press, 1982), p. 43.

110 For a history of this saint's life see Virginia Blanton, *Signs of Devotion: The Cult of St.St Aethelthryth in Medieval England*, 695–1615 (University Park: Pennsylvania State University Press, 2007). .

111 Fear.

ageyne by her frendys[112] to Egfryde Kynge of Northamhumbrorum. & .xii. yerys she was with hym not as a wyfe but as a lady, & for her holynes he worshyppyd[113] her moch & promysyd to the Busshope Wylfryde great gyftys to make her agree to hym in matrymonye; and the busshope contrarye wyse exortyd her to kepe virgynyte. And at laste by assente of the kynge she enteryd into relygyon at Coldyngham[114] vnder Ebba, aunte to the kynge. And when the kynge repentyd hym[115] & wolde haue fet[116] her fro the monasterye, she commyttyd her to our Lorde and with to systers went into a hyll. & there our Lorde brought the see about theym & preseruyd them there beynge in prayers withoute mete or drynke. & when the kynge sawe that he went away & repentyd hym of [h]is presumpcyon. And after [s]he went to Ely that was geuyn to her by her husbonde Tonbert, & there she repayryd[117] a monasterye & gaderyd many susters the yere of our Lord .vi.C.lxxiii. And after that she enteryd into relygyon she neuer ware lynnen,[118] she ete but onys on a day, she was dylygent to vigyllys & prayers. & before her deth she had a great swellynge in her throte & in her cheke, wherin she moche delytyd, & sayde it was a great goodnes of our Lorde if that peyne myghte put away the peyne that she was worthye to haue for her pryde and offencys in werynge golde & precyous stonys aboute her necke when she was yonge. And when a surgeon had cutte the sore place and that easyd her for a tyme, the thyrde day after the peyne came agayne. And she yeldyd her soule to our Lorde the .ix. kalendas of luly after she had ben abbesse .vii. yere. & when she had lyen .xvi. yerys her body & all her clothys were founde vncorrupte, and her necke was hoole & a tokyn apperyd of the cuttynge. & after the monasterye was destroyed by Inguer & Hubba & was renewyd agayne by Seynt Ethelwolde by helpe of the Kynge Edgar. A man that had ben a great vserer & full of synne & was in great syknesse entendyd to serue God in relygyon at Ely the resydew of his lyfe, and the kyngys mynysters prohybytyd it & sayde he was a thyfe & also in the kynges det, wherfore he was had to London & there he was put in prysone. & on a nyght ap[pe]ryd to hym Seynt Benet, Seynt Awdry, & her suster Seynt Sexburghe, and Seynt Benet onlosyd hys irons. & that myracle knowyn he was let goo & so he enteryd into relygyon as he before purposyd.

112 Relatives.

113 Respected.

114 Currently on the Scottish border with Northumberland.

115 Changed his mind.

116 Fetched.

117 Founded/ strengthened an already existing monastery.

118 That is she never wore soft clothing (linen) in order to mortify her flesh.

2.12 Devout Imaginings: from Nicholas Love, *The Mirror of the Blessed Life of Jesus Christ*, ed. Michael G. Sargent (Exeter: University of Exeter Press, 2004), pp. 10–11, 23.

In his introduction, Micheal Sargent describes the Mirror *as "one of the most well-read books in late-medieval England": "Only the Wycliffite Bible translations, the Prick of Conscience . . . and Chaucer's* Canterbury Tales *survive in greater numbers of manuscripts. . . . The* Mirror *identified itself so well with pre-Reformation religious values that since that time, it has nearly disappeared from sight" (p. ix). A Middle English translation of a Latin book of meditations on the life of Christ,* Meditationes Vitae Christi, *written in the early years of the fourteenth century by an Italian Franciscan, the* Mirror *provided devout Christians with a way to enter into the biblical narrative of Christ's life through active imaginative responses to stories, much as Margery Kempe does in her mystical visions when she enters spiritually into the biblical events she recalls.*

Nicholas Love, the translator, served as prior of the Carthusian monastery Mount Grace Priory for some time between the years 1410 and his death in 1424. Mount Grace, founded by Thomas Holland, Duke of Surrey, and nephew of Richard II, was closely aligned with royal and noble patrons in the early years of the fifteenth century.[119] *Love presented a copy of his* Mirror *in 1410 to Archbishop of Canterbury, Lord Thomas Arundel, who "commended and approved it personally, and further decreed and commanded his metropolitan authority that it rather be published universally for the edification of the faithful and the confutation of heretics or lollards" (Sargent,* Mirror, *p. xv).*

The Mirror *encouraged devotional imagination based on scriptural narratives, a mode also encouraged by the images, carvings, and paintings that adorned churches throughout England. Imaginative responses to simple narratives may well have influenced those who produced and staged the mystery cycles, and those who, like Margery Kempe, raised imagination to the level of mystical visions. It is not a coincidence that the single copy we have of the manuscript of* The Book of Margery Kempe *was part of the library of Mount Grace Priory during the fifteenth century.*

From the Proheme of the boke that is clepid the Mirroure of the blissed lyffe of oure lorde Jesu cryste

(The proheme lays out the rationale for imaginative responses to scripture)

. . . a pryncipal & general rewle of diuerse ymaginacions[120] that folowen after in this boke that the discriuyng[121] or speches or dedis of god in heuen & angels or

119 See Sargent, pp. xiii–xiv.

120 Imaginings.

121 Describing.

othere gostly substances bene only wryten in this manere, & to this entent that is to saye as devoute ymaginacions & likenessis styryng[122] symple soules to the loue of god & desire of heuenly thinges for as *Seynt Gregory* seith, Therefore is the kyngdome of heuene likenet[123] to erthly thinges that by tho thinges that bene visible & that man kyndly knoweth[124] he be stirede & rauyshede[125] to loue & desire gostly inuisible thinges, that he kyndly knoweth not.[126] Also seynt Jon seith that alle tho thinges that Jesus dide, bene not writen in the Gospelle. Wherfore we mowen to stiryng of deuotion ymagine & thenk diuerse wordes & dedes of him & other, that we fynde not writen, so that it be not ageyns the byelue,[127] as seynt Gregory & other doctours seyn, that holi writte may be expownet[128] & vndurstande[129] in diuerse maneres, & to diuerse purposes, so that it be not ageyns the byleue[130] or gude maneres.

From Of the Incarnation of Jesu, & the feste of the Annunciacion, & of the gretyng Aue Maria

(This section instructs the reader in how to practice devotional imagining)

Now take hede, & ymagine of gostly thinge as it were bodily,[131] & thenk in thi herte as thou were[132] present in the sight of that blessed lord, with how benyng[133] & glad semblant[134] he speketh these wordes. And on that other side, how Gabriel with a likyng[135] face & glad chere vpon his knen[136] knelyng & with drede reuerently bowyng receueth this message of his lord. And so anone Gabriel risyng vp glad & iocunde,[137] toke his flight fro the hye heuen to erthe, & in a moment he was in mannus liknes before the virgine Marie,[138] that was in hire pryue chaumbure[139] that tyme closed[140] & in hir prayeres, or in hire meditaciones

122 Stirring.
123 Likened.
124 Knows by nature, knows naturally.
125 Transported by ecstasy or delight.
126 That he does not know by his [human] nature.
127 Orthodox doctrines of faith.
128 Explicated, interpreted.
129 Understood.
130 Faith.
131 Imagine spiritual things as if they were material.
132 As if you were.
133 Gracious (benign).
134 Countenance.
135 Pleasant.
136 Knees.
137 Jocund, cheerful.
138 And almost instantaneously he appeared in the likeness of a man before the Virgin Mary.
139 Private chamber.
140 Enclosed, separate.

perauenter[141] redyng the prophecie of ysaie, touchyng the Incarnacion. And yit also swiftly as he flewe, his lord was come before, & there he fonde al the holy Trinite comen or his messagere.[142]

Communal Expressions of Devotion

Throughout late medieval England people joined in various religious confraternities or guilds designed to support both religious and communal purposes. Often these groups were founded to honor a particular saint, or, in the case of the guild whose record appears here, in honor of the Pater Noster, or Lord's Prayer, which Christ specifically directed Christians to pray. The record from 1388–9 illustrates the interwoven devotion, performance, and public recognition that lay behind the guild's regular production of its Pater Noster play in York, usually produced around the time of the feast of Corpus Christi (the body of Christ), in the late spring:

2.13 *The York Pater Noster Guild from Records of Early English Drama: York,* ed. Alexandra F. Johnston and Margaret Rogerson, 2 vols (Toronto: University of Toronto Press, 1979). Vol. 2, p. 693.

First as to the cause of the founding of the said fraternity, it should be known that after a certain play on the usefulness of the Lord's Prayer was composed, in which play, indeed, many vices and sins are reproved and virtues commended, and was played in the city of York, it had such and so great an appeal that very many said: "Would that this play were established in this city for the salvation of souls and the solace of the citizens and neighbours." Wherefore, the whole and complete cause of the foundation and association of the brothers of the same fraternity was that that play be managed at future times for the health and reformation of the souls, both of those in charge of that play and those hearing it. And thus, the principal work of the said fraternity is that the play should be managed to the greater glory of God, the deviser of the said prayer, and for the reproving of sins and vices. . . . Item, they are bound, whenever the play of the said Lord's Prayer is shown in the form of a play in the city of York, to ride with the players of the same through certain principal streets of the city of York and to be dressed in one livery, to give greater ornament to their riding. And some of them are bound to go or ride with those players until the said play be completely finished for the peaceful managing of the said play. . . . Nor do any rents or land, or holdings, or any other chattels, excepting only the apparatus intended for the use of the

141 Perhaps, maybe.

142 And yet, as fast as he flew, his lord was quicker, and there [in Mary's privy chamber] he [Gabriel] found the Trinity come before its messenger.

said play, belong to the said fraternity, which apparatus, indeed, cannot in the least serve any other purpose except only the said play. And there is one wooden chest belonging to the said fraternity to hold the apparatus. . . .

Civic Performance of Devotion: Corpus Christi

In 1311, at the Council of Vienne, Pope Clement V ordered that the Roman Church adopt the feast of Corpus Christi, to be celebrated annually on the Thursday after Trinity Sunday (Corpus Christi is thus a moveable feast that falls between 23 May and 24 June) to honor Christ in the sacrament of the Mass, a celebration that became popular in England in the next decade.

2.14 Corpus Christi Day: From V. A. Kolve, *The Play Called Corpus Christi* (Stanford: Stanford University Press, 1966,) p. 45. (Translation by V. A. Kolve.)

This is the glorious act of remembrance which fills the minds of the faithful with joy at their salvation and brings them tears mingled with a flood of reverent joy. For surely we exult as we recall our deliverance and scarce contain our tears as we commemorate the passion of Our Lord through whiche we were freed . . . because on this occasion we both rejoice amid pious weeping and weep amid reverent rejoicing, joyful in our lamentation and woeful in our jubilations.

It is for this reason that on the same Thursday [after Trinity Sunday] the devout croweds of the faithful should flock eagerly to the churches – in order that clergy and congregation, joining one another in equal rejoicing, may rise in a song of praise, and then, from the hearts and desires, from the mouths and lips of all, there may sound forth hymns of joy at man's salvation.

This feast day was the day on which communal festivals, particularly dramatic cycle pageants of stories from biblical history, were presented in northern English cities like York and Chester. In York, particularly, the feast of Corpus Christi became a civic celebration in which guilds and fraternities rode in livery through the streets through which their pageant wagons moved presenting the plays that comprised the Corpus Christi mystery cycles.

Our Lady of Mercy, Mother of God

The Virgin Mary occupied a central place in late medieval English devotion. The nation of England was termed the Virgin's dower, that is, it was spiritually dedicated to her. Mary's virgin motherhood nicely epitomized the paradoxes central to the Incarnation:

just as Jesus was both perfect God and perfect man, Mary was mother of her son who was also her God. Her earthly perfection sanctified matter, showing that matter could be so pure that it might serve as God's flesh. "Mary" was the site on which medieval Christianity affirmed the body and the world. It is hard to overestimate the intense devotion she inspired. Liturgies, Books of Hours, illustrations, paintings from this period brought her image and the nexus of ideas she symbolized to constant attention. The texts in this section, 2.15–16, provide some sense of the rich verbal adoration that attended the idea of the Virgin as well the incredible power attributed to her as the Mother of God.

2.15 On the Virgin Mary: from *The Writings of Julian of Norwich: A Vision Showed to a Devout Woman and A Revelation of Divine Love,* ed. Nicholas Watson and Jacqueline Jenkins (Philadelphia: University of Pennsylvania Press, 2006), pp. 137–9.

Julian of Norwich celebrates Mary's place in the scheme of salvation, beginning with the fourth chapter of the long text of her visions, A Revelation of Love*:*

> Thus I toke it for that time that our lord Jhesu of his curteys love, would shewe me comfort before the time of my temptation. For me thought it might well be that I should, by the sufferance of God and with his keping, be tempted of fiends before I died. With this sight of his blessed passion, with the godhead that I saw in my understanding, I knew well that it was strength inough to me – ye, and to all creaturs living that should be saved – against all the fiendes of hell and against all ghostely enemies.
>
> In this, he brought our lady Saint Mary to my understanding. I saw her ghostly in bodily likenes, a simple maiden and a meeke, yong of age, a little waxen above a childe, in the stature as she was when she conceivede. Also God shewed me in part the wisdom and the truth of her soule, wherin I understode the reverent beholding that she beheld her God, that is her maker, marvayling with great reverence that he would be borne of her that was a simple creature of his making. For this was her marvayling: that he that was her maker would be borne of her that was made. And this wisdome and truth, knowing the greatnes of her maker and the littlehead of herselfe that is made, made her to say full meekely to Gabriel: "Lo me here, Gods handmaiden." In this sight I did understand sothly that she is more then all that God made beneth her in worthines and in fullhead.[143] For above her is nothing that is made but the blessed manhood of Christ, as to my sight.

143 Fullness.

2.16 Books of Hours: Hours of the Blessed Virgin from *The Prymer or Lay Folks' Prayer Book*, ed. Henry Littlehales, 2 vols, EETS, o.s. 105, 109 (London: 1897). From Vol 2, *Hours of the Blessed Virgin.*

The liturgy devoted to the Virgin, termed the Hours of the Virgin, comprised prayers and psalms to be recited at the canonical hours of each day: Matins, associated with the annunciation; Lauds, the visitation of John the Baptist's mother to Mary; Prime, the birth of Christ; Tierce, the Angels' announcement to the shepherds; Sext, the adoration of the Magi; Vespers, the flight into Egypt/ the Massacre of the Innocents; Compline, the Coronation of the Virgin. Books of hours, which could be elaborately illustrated, like the Tres Riches Heures du Duc de Berry, *typically included the office for the Dead, as well as psalms, and calendars of saints' days. The excerpts below from a fifteenth-century English book of hours represent Marian devotion of this liturgy. Recited in churches, chapels, and private devotions, these prayers expressed the cultural concept of "the Virgin" that pervades spiritual literature throughout this period.*

From the Office of Evensong:

Ant[h]em

Aftir thi child-berynge, thou leftist maide with-outen wem.[144] modir of god, preie for us!

Beata es, virgo.

Blessid art thou, maide marie, that bar oure lord; tho*u* broughtist forth the makere of the world, that made thee; & thou bileuest[145] maide with-outen ende. Thanke we god!

[H]Impnus: Aue maris stella, dei mater!

Hail, sterre of the see, holi modir of god! and thou, euer maide, holi gate of heuene, Takyng tha*t* word "hail" of gabrielis mouth, sette us alle in pees! chaungynge the name of eue,[146] Louse[147] the bondis of gilti men! profere light to blynde men; do awey oure yuelis, & axe alle goodis! Schewe that *thou* art oure modir! take he, bi thee, oure preier,[148] that for us was bore, & suffride to be thi sone! Maide, thou art aloon deboner[149] among us alle! make us vnbounde of synnes, & be chast & deboner! Gyue us clene liyf; make redi a siker weie,[150] so that we, seynge god, be glade euer more! Preisyng be to god

---

144 Spot or stain.

145 Remain(ed).

146 As Eve brought death, so did Mary bring everlasting life for humans.

147 Loose.

148 Asking for Mary's intercession with Christ: take him, by you, our prayer.

149 Kind, gracious, gentle.

150 Make ready a sure way.

the fadir; worschip to the higheste crist, & to the hooli gost; oon worschip to hem thre. amen!

V. Grace is gouun[151] in thi lippis;

[R.] Therfor god hath blessid thee with-outen ende.

Psalm*: Magnificat*

46 Mi soule magnefieth the lord;
47 And my spirit hath gladid in god, myn heelthe;
48 For he hath biholde the mekenesse of [his] hand maidun; for lo, of this alle generaciouns schulen[152] seie that y am blessid.
49 For he that is myghti hath don to me grete thingis; & his name is hooli.
50 And his merci is fro [kynrede into] kynredis to men that dreden him.[153]
51 He made myght in his arme; he scateride proude men with the thought of his herte.
52 He sette doun myghti men fro sete, & enhaunside meke men.[154]
53 He hath fulfillid hungry men with goodis; & he hath lefte riche men voide.
54 He, hauynge mynde of his merci, took up israel, his child.
55 As he hath spekun to oure fadris; to abraham & to his seed in-to the worldis.
Glorie be to the fadir [&c.J.
As it was in the bigynnyng [&c.J.

Ant[h]em*: [Sancta maria, succurre]*

Seynte marie, socoure[155] wrecchis; helpe feerful, and refresche the soreuful! Preie for the puple; bide[156] for the clergie; biseche for deuoute wommanes-kynde!

[V.] Lord, schewe us thi mercy,

[R] And gyue us thin heelthe!

[Orisoun]: concede nos

Graunte us thi seruauntis, lord god, we preien thee, that we moun[157] be ioieful euer more in heelthe of soule & of bodi; & thorour[158] th*e* biseching of

151 Given.
152 Shall.
153 From generation to generation to those who fear him.
154 He has brought down the mighty and raised the low.
155 Help, succour the miserable.
156 Entreat.
157 May.
158 Through.

the glorious euerlastynge maide marie, we moun be delyuerid of this sorewe that we han now, & vse fulliche the ioie with-outen ende, bi oure lord ihesu crist, thi sone, that lyueth & regneth with thee in oonhede[159] of god th*e* hali gost, bi alle worldis of worldis. amen!
Blesse we the lord!
Thanke we god!

From the Hours of the Virgin, Concluding Devotions

[Hora completorii.]

At our of comepelyn
Thei leiden hym in graue,
The noble bodi of ihesu,
That mankynde schal saue.
With spicerie[160] he was biried,
Hooli writ to fulfille.
Thenke we sadli on his deeth;
That schal saue us from helle.
[V] We worschipe thee, crist, & blesse to thee.
[RJ Ffor bi thi deeth thou hast ayenbought th*e* world.

Oracio: *Domine ihesu criste*

Lord ihesu crist, goddis sone of heuene, sette thi passioun, thi cros & thi deeth bitwixe thi iugement and oure soulis, now & in oure of oure deeth; and vouche-saf to gyue to lyuynge men, merci & grace in this liyf here; & to hem that ben deed, forgyuenesse & reste; to the chirche & to the rewme, pees & acord; and to us synful men, liyf & glorie with-outen ende; thou that lyuest & regnest god, bi alle worldis of worldis.
amen!
The glorious passioun of oure lord ihesu crist brynge vs to the ioie of paradis!
amen!
pater noster: Oure fadir [&c.].

*[*Ant[h]em*]: Salue regina!*

Hail, quene, modir of merci, oure liyf, oure swetnesse & oure hope, hail! to thee we crien, exiled, sones of eue[161]; to thee we sighen,[162] gronynge in this

159 Unity .
160 Spices.
161 Eve.
162 Sigh.

valey of teeris; ther-for turne to vsward thi merciful iyen,[163] & schewe to us ihesu, the blessid fruyt of thi wombe, aftir that we ben passid hennes.[164] O, thou deboner, O, thou meke, O, thou swete maide marie, hail!
Hail, marie, ful of grace! the lord is with thee. blessid be thou among wyme[n], & blessid be the fruyt of thi wombe, ihesus!
amen!

[Orisoun]: *Omnipotens sempiterne.*

Almighti endeles god, that art worchinge with the holi gost, wondurfulli thou madist redi the bodi & the soule of the moost blessid modir & [maide] marie, to disserue to be maad a worthi wonyng[165] for thi sone. graunte that we be delyuerid, bi hir meke preier, of yuelis that we han now, and of sudeyn deeth and endeles, bi crist oure lord. amen!

[Ant[h]em]: *Aue regina celorum!*

Hail, quene of heuenes, modir of the king of aungelis! 0 marie, flour of virgines, as the rose or the lilie, make preiers to thi sone, for the helthe of alle cristen men! Hail, marie, ful of grace! [&c.].

Orisoun: *Mer[i]tis & preci[bus].*

Bi the meritis & preieris of his meke modir, blesse us the sone of god the fadir! amen!

Psalm [130]: De profundis.

1 Lord, y criede to thee fro deppis[166]; lord, here *thou* my vois!
2 Thyne eeris be maad ententif in-to the vois of my biseching![167]
3 Lord, if thou kepist wickidnessis, lord, who schal susteyne?[168]
4 For merci is at thee; and, lord, for thi lawe y abode thee.[169]
5 Mi soule susteynede in his word;
[6] My soule hopide in *the* lord. Fro the moruntide keping til to the nyght
[7] Israel, hope in the lord! For whi, merci is at the lord; & plenteuous redempcioun is at him;[170]

163 Eyes, gaze.
164 Our death.
165 Dwelling.
166 The depths.
167 May your ears attend to the voice of my prayer.
168 Lord, if you take note of wickedness, who shall stand?
169 And, Lord, because of your law, I wait on (trust in) you.
170 Because Mercy is in the Lord, and plenteous redemption is in Him.

8 And he schal ayenbie[171] israel fro alle wickidnessis ther-of.
Lord, haue merci of us!
Crist, haue merci of us!
Lord, haue merci of us!
pater *noster:* Oure fadir [&c.J.
[V] And lede us not in-to temptacioun,
[R] But delyuere us from yuel.
[V] Endeles reste, gyue hem, lord;
[R/ And euerlastinge light, lightne to hem![172]
[V] From the gate of helle,
[R/ Lord, delyuere her soulis!
[V] I bileue to se the goodis of the lord
[RJ In *the* lond of lyuynge.
[V] Lord, here my preier,
[R] And my cry come to thee!

[Oracio: Fidelium deus.]

Lord, that art maker & ayenbier[173] of alle feithful men, gyue thou, & graunte, remissioun & forgyuenesse of alle synnes, to the soulis of alle feithful men that ben deed, so that thei mowe[174] haue the forgyuenesse that thei euere desirede; bi crist, oure lord. amen!
[V] Reste pei in pees!
[R] Amen!

Lollard Concerns

In answer to the central question of medieval spirituality, "What must I do to save my soul?", the Church offered itself as the gateway and the path to salvation. Following its injunctions faithfully would lead, by the sacraments, and by virtue of the inexhaustible grace created by Christ's sacrifice, as well as by the faithful witness of the saints, to salvation. But early in the history of the Christian Church, anxieties began to develop. One centered on the role of the clergy, particularly the celebrant of the Mass. What happens if he is a rank sinner? Can such a one actually say a Mass in which the bread and wine become Christ's body? The Church's answer was "yes," the miracle of transubstantiation is God's to perform, not the priest's, and the state of a priest's soul cannot affect this miracle. Nevertheless, anxiety about ecclesisastical corruption persisted. The prayers the priest offers as he prepares to say Mass (*see p. 57 above**),*

171 Redeem.
172 And everlasting light shine upon them.
173 Redeemer.
174 May, might.

suggest the importance of clerical purity and a level of anxiety about that purity. In late medieval England, a body of literature and of thinking critical of ecclesiastical corruption, and suspicious about the spiritual usefulness of pilgrimages, images, and even about the nature of the Eucharistic miracle, began to coalesce into a movement we loosely term Lollardy.[175] *Lollardy is an umbrella term that today covers a wide variety of criticism of the late medieval Roman Church. Fundamental to Lollard religious concerns are the contention of the sufficiency of the Bible and preference for its guidance over the doctrines and policies of the Church; suspicion of the role and place of the "material church" in the true worship of God, particularly criticism of statues and images; anxiety about the purposes and function of pilgrimages and saints' relics in the structure of Christian belief. A frequent Lollard criticism of relics is to term them stocks (stumps of wood) and stones and dead men's bones. Similarly, in questioning the veneration offered to images, Lollards offered the opinion that a living person is the best image of God. Lollard sentiments touched on political issues when they criticized Papal authority and ecclesiasts who held high positions within both the Church and the government. Lollard ideas about the necessity for access to a Bible in the vernacular tongue, and about the centrality of the Word of God in salvation as opposed to the routes offered by the established Church, persisted from the later fourteenth century into the early sixteenth, in spite of official attempts to define them as heretical. They underlay what would become known as the Protestant Reformation.*

2.17 On Monks: From *Regular Life: Monastic, Canonical and Mendicant Rules*, ed. Douglas J. McMillan and Kathryn Smith Fladenmuller (Kalamazoo: Medieval Institute,1997), pp. 60–2.

Chapter 48, Manual Labor:

Idleness is an enemy of the soul. Therefore, the brothers should be occupied according to schedule in either manual labor or holy reading. These may be arranged as follows: from Easter to October, the brothers shall work at manual labor from Prime [first hour prayers] until the fourth hour. From then until the sixth hour they should read. After dinner they should rest (in bed) in silence. However, should anyone desire to read, he should do so without disturbing his brothers.

None [ninth hour prayers] should be chanted at about the middle of the eighth hour. Then everyone shall work as they must until Vespers. If conditions dictate that they labor in the fields (harvesting), they should not be grieved for they are truly monks when they must live by manual labor, as did our fathers and the apostles. Everything should be in moderation, though, for the sake of the timorous.

175 From the Middle English term *loller*, idler, wastrel.

From October first until Lent, the brothers should read until the end of the second hour. Tierce [third hour prayers] will then be said, after which they will work at their appointed tasks until None. At the first signal for None all work shall come to an end. Thus all may be ready as the second signal sounds. After eating they shall read or study the psalms.

During Lent the brothers shall devote themselves to reading until the end of the third hour. Then they will work at their assigned tasks until the end of the tenth hour. Also, during this time, each monk shall receive a book from the library, which he should read carefully cover to cover. These books should be handed out at the beginning of Lent.

It is important that one or two seniors be chosen to oversee the reading periods. They will check that no one is slothful, lazy or gossiping, profiting little himself and disturbing others. If such a brother is discovered, he is to be corrected once or twice. If he does not change his ways, he shall be punished by the Rule (to set an example for others). Nor should brothers meet at odd and unsuitable hours.

All shall read on Saturdays except those with specific tasks. If anyone is so slothful that he will not or cannot read or study, he will be assigned work so as not to be idle.

Sick and frail brothers should be given work that will keep them from idleness but not so oppressive that they will feel compelled to leave the monastery. Their frailty is to be considered by the abbot.

2.18 From *The Middle English Translation of the Rosarium Theologie c. 1386–1420)*, ed. Christina Von Nolcken (Heidelberg: Carl Winter, 1979), pp. 78–9.

Lollard criticism of monastic irregularities reflected a wide and deep sense that the vocation of the monk had degraded and that monks, as well as others with a religious vocation, did not live the lives they had vowed to adopt. This alphabetically arranged text, heavily weighted with citations of authority from the past, provided brief texts on subjects of interest for Lollard preachers to incorporate into their sermons. Individual topics comprising quotations and citations of sources supporting Lollard criticism of current practice structure the text. Rather than being a coherent paragraph, the passage below is an assembly of citations chiefly from the writing of St Jerome (Ieronymus) critical of the laxity of monks' observance of their rule:

> Monke: "Haue he noght the office of a doctour bot of hym that mourneth, wich mourne outher hymself of the worlde, & dredful abide the comyng of our Lorde."[176] *Hec Ieronymus* . . . . *Monachus*: "It hathe plesed to our comon

176 The monk is not like a doctor (teacher) [out in the world], but is one that mourns his own or the world's (failures), and fearfull, abides the coming of the Lord.

consell that none of monkez presume with cursed boldenez for to go out of his abbey for erthily lucre, [ne for to giffe penance,] ne take no childe of baptyme, ne for to baptize, ne for to visite a seke man, ne for to birye a dede man, ne for to passe to a seculer chirch, ne for to intrike or implye[177] hym to another maner bisinez or marchandise. Be he content in his cloystre, for as fisch without water wanteth liffe,[178] so a monke without his abbey. Sitte he forsothe[179] solitarye & be stille, that is ded to the world, & liffeth[180] forsothe to Criste. Knew he his name: *monos* forsothe of Greke is *vnus* of Latine, *achos* on Greke is *tristis* one Latyne, werfor *monachus* is seid, that is *vnus tristis.*[181] Therefor sitte he heuy [and] entent to his office. . . ." *Item Ieronymus in Epistola,* "It is of souerayne fondenez[182] for to renunce or forsake to the worlde, for to leue his contree, for to forsake tovnez or citeez. . . ." *Item Ieronymus ad Pamiachium,* "Wat is it nede to the for to see tho thingis be despising of wich thou began to be a monke?[183] Wom that thou demeth euermore or ofte tyme spekyng to of peynez or monye, out take almous, wich is opone, to al men indiffrently haue thou hym rather a chapman or a marchande than a monk."[184] "The firste vertue of a monk is for to despise the domez of men, and euermore haue mynde of the apostile seyande, "If I plesed yitte to men I war noght the seruant of Criste'."[185] *Item Ieronymus ad Eliodorum, epistola 33.* "Wat dothe a monke in cellez of wymen? Wat wille to tham priue & only speikyngs and eighen[186] flying domismen?[187] Holy lufe hathe nogh inpaciens."[188] *Iterum Ieronymus ad Paulinum, epistola 35.,* "That monke is loued be law or right wiche hath prestez to worchep & bakbiteth noght to the degre be wich he is made a Cristen man."[189] *Item Bernardus in Apologetico,* "A greete abusion the [moste] charge is that the body be clade rewly or religiously, & agaynes the rewle the soule is lefte naked of his clothez. With so mich studie is procured to the body a cote and a coule that to wom thise bene awey he be noght trowed a monke; wy on the same wyse be noght

177 To involve himself in any other kind of business or trade. The passage objects to monks who perform the offices belonging to parish clergy.

178 A fish taken out of water will die, so a monk outside his abbey cannot rightly flourish.

179 Truly.

180 Lives.

181 The sad (sober) one.

182 Trial.

183 Why is it necessary for you to see those things by the despising of which you came to be a monk?

184 Whom you judge (see) always or often speaking of money, except for alms, hold him rather a trader or a merchant than a monk.

185 The first virtue of a monk is to despise the judgements of men, and evermore have in mind the saying of the apostle, "If I pleased men I were not the servant of Christ".

186 Eyes.

187 I.e. secretly, furtively.

188 Holy love is not restless or impatient, not full of earthly desire.

189 That monk is beloved by the law, or the right, who holds priests in worship and does not backbite to the degree that he is a Christian man (acts like a proper monk, or acts like a good Christian).

perueyed pite & mekenes wich forsothe bene gostily clothings to the spirite?"[190] *Item Hugo, De Claustro Anime,* "Monkez maketh tham cloysteris be wich the vtter man may be holden, bot wolde God that thei made cloisterez be wich the inner man schulde ordinately be halden! '[191] *Item Sanctus Ysacc monachus dicit,* "A monke that seketh possession in the erthe is noght a monke," as seith Gregor. . . . 'If thou couaite to be a monke that thou art seid that is alon, wat dothe thou in citez, wich forsothe bene noght duellyng of only men bot of many?"[192]

2.19 On Friars: From *The Regular Life: Monastic, Canonical and Mendicant Rules,* ed. Douglas J. McMillan and Kathryn Smith Fladenmuller, Teams Documents of Practice Series (Kalamazoo, 1997), p. 70.

Similarly, the growing mercenary greed of friars, whose orders were established in the early thirteenth century as a reform movement to bring preaching and charity out of churches and into the market place of daily life, became the object of increasing criticism. Here is an excerpt from St Francis' Rule of 1223 for the Friars Minor, regulating the relationship between monks and money.

Chapter 4. The friars are forbidden to accept money
I strictly forbid all the friars to accept money in any form, either personally or through an intermediary. The ministers and superiors, however, are bound to provide carefully for the needs of the sick and the clothing of the other friars, by having recourse to spritual friends, while taking into account differences of place, season, or severe climate, as seems best to them in the circumstances. This does not dispense them from the prohibition of receiving money in any form.

Chapter 5. The manner of working
The friars to whom God has given the grace of working should work in a spirit of faith and devotion and avoid idleness, which is the enemy of the soul, without however extinguishing the spirit of prayer and devotion, to which every temporal consideration must be subordinate. As wages for their labour they

190 A great abuse the most charged is that the body be clad according to a rule or religiously and the soul is left naked of the (spiritual clothing) of the rule. With so much study (effort) is procured to the body a coat and a cowl that from whom these are absent, he is not believed a monk; why in the same manner be not purveyed pity and meeknes which truly are gostly clothing to the spirit?

191 Monks built for themeselves cloisers by which the outer man is confined, but would God that they made cloisters by which the inner man should be ordinately confined.

192 If you desire to be a monk, whom you say is alone, what do you in cities which truly are not dwellings of solitary men, but of many?

may accept anything necessary for their temporal needs, for themselves or their brethren, except money in any form. And they should accept it humbly as is expected of those who serve God and strive after the highest poverty.

2.20 On Friars: From John Gower, *The Voice of One Crying in the Wilderness (1385), The Major Latin Works of John Gower*, ed. Eric W. Stockton (Seattle: University of Washington Press, 1962), pp. 182–4.

Here is John Gower's criticism of the failings of the "throng of friars" who populated late medieval England:

I grant that the functions of the original order were holy, and that in the beginning its founders were pious. A friar remains blessed who follows after them, who in renouncing the world seeks to reach God, who adopts monastic poverty for himself and bears it voluntarily, and who patiently undertakes the work of his order. Such a man is indeed to be praised for his high merits, for the earth is restored through his prayers. But he who disguises his outer appearance in the order and lacks its true essence, he who preaches outwardly yet inwardly yearns for riches – to such men of the present this book offers its message, since the voice of the people furnished the things for it to say.

The throng of friars overflows the mendicant order; the original rule is dead, inundated by them. These men, who used to bear hardships pleasing to God in accordance with the vow of their order, are becoming soft. . . . They are now acting like people who have no property, yet under a pauper's guise they grab everything. . . .

And so the mendicants are mightier than lords, and from the world they secretly usurp what their order plainly forbids. I would say that these men are not disciples but rather gods: both life and death bring money to them. For a friar demands that he himself bury the dead bodies of those to whom he attached himself as confessor, if they were dignitaries. But if it should be a poor [man's] body, he makes no claim at all, since his piety takes no cognizance of anything unless there is money in it. . . .

A friar's assiduous hypocrisy sows his words in order that his harvest of profit in the world may thrive through them. He thunders out fearful sermons as he publicly damns the practice of sin, like a very servant of God. But like a servant of Satan, he furnishes glosses for them when he comes to sit down for a while in private chambers. His gentle blandishment is soothing to the ear [of] those whom his deep, resounding voice has goaded before. And thus does this sinner cater to sins for others, for by encouraging vice he gets a profit from it. A friar knows well that when sin dies, then his revenue dies for all time. Tell me where a friar will come three times, unless he may take away money.

2.21 *The Lanterne of Light* Based on *The Lanterne of Li3t Edited from MS Harl 2324*, ed. Lilian M. Swinburn, EETS, o.s. 151 (London, 1917), p. 4.

*The passage below gives some indication of Lollard sympathies and the kind of spirituality they looked to, closely associated with scriptural authority and with books. (*The Lantern of Light *(see page 193) was the text John Claydon was charged with owning.) In its focus on the inner spiritual response to the word of God, it reflects strong interest in a kind of spirituality very different from the institutionally mediated salvation offered by Rome and the reliance on images and visions supported in* Love's Mirror *(see above, 2.12). The lantern of light which lights the soul is opposed to corruption and darkness.*

For who that wole not resceyue Crist in peyne of synne he is compellid & constreyned to resceyue anticrist.[193] Therfore in this tyme of hidouse derknes somme seeken the lanterne of light. of the whiche spekith the prophete. Ps. cxviii, "*Lucerna pedibus meis verbum tuum*" that is to seie, Lord thi word is a lanterne to my feet. For as fer as the light of this lanterne schineth, so fer derkness of synne & cloudis of the f[i]endis temptaciouns vanischen awey and moun[194] not abide. And algatis[195] whanne the lanterne lightneth into the hert, it purgeth & clenseith from corrupcioun, it swagith[196] & heelith goostli soris.[197] As the wise man seith, Sap. xvi, "*Neque herba neque malagma sanauit illos sed omnipotens sermo tuus domine qui sanat vniuersa'* That is to seie, Neithir herbe ne plaistir[198] hath helid[199] hem, but Lord thi mighti word that heelith alle thingis. For Lord whanne thou diedist[200] vpon the cros[201] thou puttidist in thi word the spirit of lijf & yauest to it power of quickenyng by thin owene preciouse blood.[202] As thou thi silf seist. Ion. vi, "*verba que ego locutus sum vobis spiritus & vita sunt,*" that is to seie, the wordis that I speke to yow, they ben spirit & lijf."

193 The later Middle Ages expressed anxiety about the coming of Anti-Christ in a variety of ways, perhaps most memorably in English in the Anti-Christ plays of the mystery cycles. The Anti-Christ was expected to come and claim his rule over all the world, deceiving people into thinking he was the Christ, and leading them astray by pretending to divine powers. His rule, however, was one of material sensuality, raw power, and sin. At the root of this expectation lay a fear of mis-placed beliefs in the paths to salvation available. The wrong or uninformed choice could put one on a path to belief in the Anti-Christ and to damnation. For Lollards, the only truth path to salvation was careful study of Christ's words and deeds.

194 May.

195 In every way.

196 Assuages, heals, lessens.

197 Spiritual sores.

198 Poultice.

199 Healed.

200 Died.

201 Cross.

202 You put the spirit of life into your word and gave it the power of life by your own precious blood.

2.22 *From* Remonstrance against Romish Corruptions in the Church Addressed to the People and Parliament of England in 1395, 18 Ric.II, *ed. J. Forshall (London, 1851), pp. 23–4, 28–9.*

A late fourteenth-century text, titled by its nineteenth-century editor the Remonstrance, *documents a series of Lollard anxieties about images, pilgrimages, and the authority of the secular state over ecclesiastical institutions:*

On Images:

Though ymagis maad truli that representen verili the pouerte and the passioun of Jhesu Crist and othere seyntis ben leful,[203] and the bokis of lewid men, bi Gregori and othere doctouris,[204] netheles false ymagis that representen worldli glorie and pride of the world as if Crist and othere seyntis hadden lyuid thus and deseruid blisse bi glorie and pomp of the world, ben fals bokis and worthi to be amendid or to be brent, as bokis of opin errour or of opin eresie[205] agens cristene feith.

On Pilgrimages:

Though it myghte be suffrid that sike men go a pilgrimage in the rewme[206] in visitynge the placis of seyntis to eschewe synnis[207] and to geue godis to nedi men, so that thei sette not hope of helthe in the forseid ymagis, neither leeuen the werkis of merci anentis pore men,[208] which Crist comaundide vndir the peyne of euere lastinge dampnaciouin in the xxv. c^{o}. of Mathu, netheles to gon a[209] pilgrimage and visite suche placis and sette hope of helthe in doumbe idolis[210] or in ymagis maad with mannis handis, in offringe to tho ymagis or to riche men of the world the almes dedis that ben due to pore men bi comaundement of Crist, is vttirli vnleful,[211] and an opin signe of idolatrie, and spoilinge and sleeynge of pore men, and apostasie either goinge abak fro cristene feith.[212]

---

203 Permissible, right, to be allowed.

204 Images were termed the books of ignorant men by St Gregory and other doctors of the Church.

205 Heresy.

206 Realm, kingdom.

207 Avoid sin.

208 So long as they do not set hope of health in the foresaid images, nor leave (forgo) works of mercy in regard to poor men.

209 Go on a.

210 Unspeaking, inanimate idols, i.e. statues of saints.

211 Unjust, unlawful.

212 And an open sign of idolatry, and the destruction and slaying of poor men, and apostasy, or going back from (renouncing) Christian faith.

On Secular Power and the Clergy: (*This passage reveals the political edge of Lollard sentiments, directed at the power of Rome to intervene in national governance, see 7.6.*)

If the bisshop of Rome, or ony othir ante-crist make a decretal othir[213] constitucioun contrarie to this part in endullynge[214] the regalie[215] and power of seculer lordis foundid in holi scripture, holi doctouris, and quik[216] reesoun, alle cristene men and souereynli[217] alle feithful lige men to oure king, owen to[218] despise it as venym disturbinge holi chirche. And whether in Decrees or in Decretals . . . ben ony suche blasfeme[219] constitucionns, kings and seculer lordis shulden make it to be enquirid diligentli bi here feithful clerkis, and if ony such constitucioungs be founde, kingis and seculer lordis shulden make tho to be don awei, and prisone other[220] exile the auctoris and fautouris[221] of tho. Summe constitucioungs in the decretals ben opinli false and contrarie to the kingis regalie. Forwhi, *De foro competenti*, c^o^. ij^o^., the general counseil of wordli clerkis determynith thus, That no iuge presume bi himsilf to distrie[222] or condempne[223] without suffringe[224] of the bisshop, neithir prest neithir dekene, neithir ony clerk neithir the lasse men of the chirche, that is the seruaunt of clerkis. And if he doth, he shal be sequestrid, or departid, fro the chirche, til he knouleche[225] his gilt and amende him. Bi this decretal the king mai neithir streyne[226] neithir condempne ony clerk, though he gilte neuere so moche agens the king,[227] if the bisshop assente not therto. What mai lette[228] thanne bisshopis and clerkis to putte down king and alle lordis, and conquere alle here lordis and godis[229] at here likinge? Therefore alle cristene men crieth out on this false lawe and on the makeris and meyntenouris therof.

213 Or.
214 Dulling, weakening.
215 Sovereignty.
216 Quick, living.
217 Especially.
218 Ought to.
219 Blasphemous.
220 Or.
221 Aiders, abetters, partisans.
222 Destroy.
223 Condemn.
224 Approval, support.
225 Acknowledge.
226 Act to seize his goods.
227 No matter how guilty he may be in respect to the king's law.
228 Hinder, stop.
229 Goods.

2.23 Objections to Drama: from *A Tretise of Miraclis Pleyinge*, ed. Clifford Davidson (Kalamazoo: Medieval Institute, 1993), pp. 93–4.

This early *fifteenth-century treatise against performing (pleyinge) plays condemns the dramatic representation of stories from the Old, and especially the New, Testament, on the grounds that they mock scripture and insult Christ's words and deeds. Clearly a response to the popularity of mystery plays like the* Second Shepherd's Play *and the* York Carpenter's Crucifixion *pageant, with their exuberant, even playful presentations of some of the most spiritually rich moments in the Christian tradition, this treatise treats plays as a form of image whose materiality cannot properly represent the spiritual nature of events they portray. A further anxiety underlies the treatise: the author points out, "of Cristis lawghing we reden never in holy writt, but of his myche penaunse, teris, and scheding of blod, doying us to witen therby that alle our doing heere shulde ben in penaunce, in disciplining of oure fleyssh, and in penaunce of adversite" (p. 95). Religion is no laughing matter. The comparison between the obedient submission an earthly lord can expect from his servant and that which humans owe Christ reflects the interconnected hierarchies of obedience, spiritual and earthly power in late medieval culture.*

Miraclis, therfore, that Crist dude[230] heere in erthe outher in himsilf outher in hise seintis[231] weren so efectuel and in ernest done that to sinful men that erren they broughten forgivenesse of sinne, settinge hem in the weye of right bileve[232]; to doutouse[233] men not stedefast they broughten forgivenesse of sinne, setting hem in the weye of right bileve; to doutouse men not stedefast they broughten in kunning[234] to betere plesen God, and verrey hope in God to been stedefast in him; and to the wery of the weye of God, for the grette penaunce and suffraunce of the tribulacion that men moten have therinne, they broughten in love of brynninge charite to the whiche alle thing is light, yhe to suffere dethe, the whiche men most dreden, for the everlastinge lif and joye that men most loven and disiren of the whiche thing verry hope puttith awey all werinesse heere in the weye of God.[235]

Thanne, sithen[236] miraclis of Crist and of hise seintis weren thus efectuel, as by oure bileve we ben in certein, no man shulde usen in bourde[237] and

230 Performed.

231 Either by himself or by his saints.

232 Belief, faith.

233 Doubtful.

234 Knowledge, understanding.

235 And to those weary of the way of God, because of the great penance and suffering of tribuation that men must have therin, they brought the love of burning charity to which all things are light, yea, even to suffer death, which thing men dread most, for the everlasting life and joy that men most love and desire, the very hope of which banishes all weariness here in the way of God.

236 Since.

237 Jest.

pleye the miraclis and werkis that Crist so ernystfully wroughte to oure helthe. For whoevere so doth, he errith in the byleve, reversith[238] Crist, and scornyth God. He errith in the bileve, for in that he takith the most precious werkis of God in pley and bourde, and so takith his name in idil[239] and so misusith oure byleve. A, Lord, sithen an erthely servaunt dar not takun in pley and in bourde that that his erthely lord takith in ernest, myche more we shulden not maken oure pleye and bourde of tho miraclis and werkis that God so ernestfully wrought to us. For sothely whan we so doun, drede to sinne is takun awey, as a servaunt, whan he bourdith with his maister, leesith his drede to offendyn him, namely whanne he bourdith with his maister in that that his maister takith in ernest. And right as a nail smiten in holdith two thingis togidere, so drede smiten to Godward holdith and susteineith oure bileve to him.[240]

Further Reading

Aers, David, *Sanctifying Signs: Making Christian Tradition in Late Medieval England* (Notre Dame, Ind.: University of Notre Dame Press, 2004).

Beckwith, Sarah, *Signifying God: Social Relation and Symbolic Act in the York Corpus Christi Plays* (Chicago: University of Chicago Press, 2001).

Brantley, Jessica, *Reading in the Wilderness: Private Devotion and Public Performance in Late Medieval England* (Chicago: University of Chicago Press, 2007).

Bryan, Jennifer, *Looking Inward: Devotional Reading and the Private Self in Late Medieval England* (Philadelphia: University of Pennsylvania Press, 2008).

Camille, Michael, *The Gothic Idol: Ideology and Image-Making in Medieval Art* (Cambridge: Cambridge University Press, 1989).

Coletti, Theresa, *Mary Magdalene and the Drama of Saints: Theatre, Gender, and Religion in Late Medieval England* (Philadelphia: University of Pennsylvania Press, 2004).

Dove, Mary, *The First English Bible: The Text and Context of the Wycliffite Versions* (Cambridge: Cambridge University Press, 2007).

Duffy, Eamon, *Stripping of the Altars* (New Haven: Yale University Press, 1992).

French, Katherine, et al., (eds), *The Parish in English Life 1400–1600* (Manchester: Manchester University Press, 1997).

Gibson, Gail McMurray, *Theater of Devotion: East Anglian Drama and Society in the Late Middle Ages* (Chicago: University of Chicago Press, 1989).

238 Overthrows, overturns, casts down.

239 Vain.

240 Ah, Lord, since an earthly servant dares not take in play and jest that which his earthly lord takes in earnest, much more should we not make our play and jest of those miracles and works that God so seriously [ardently] wrought for us. For truly, when we so do, fear of sin is taken away, as a servant, when he jests with his master, loses his fear to offend him, particularly when he jests with his master about that which his master takes seriously. And just as a nail hammered in holds two things together, so dread hammered of God holds and sustains our belief in him.

Heffernan, Thomas J. and E. Ann Matter, (eds), *The Liturgy of the Medieval Church* (Kalamazoo, MI: Medieval Institute Publications, 2001).

Rubin, Miri, *Corpus Christi: the Eucharist in Late Medieval Culture* (Cambridge: Cambridge University Press, 1991.

Rubin, Miri, *Mother of God: A History of the Virgin Mary* (New Haven: Yale University Press, 2009).

Sanok, Catherine, *Her Life Historical: Exemplarity, and Female Saints' Lives in Late Medieval England* (Philadelphia: University of Pennsylvania Press, 2007).

Wogan-Browne, Jocelyn, *Saints Lives and Women's Literary Culture c. 1150–1300: Virginity and its Authorizations* (Oxford: Oxford University Press, 2001).

Zieman, Katherine. *Singing the New Song: Literacy and Liturgy in Late Medieval England* (Philadelphia: University of Pennsylvania Press, 2008).

3

Violence and the Work of Chivalry

No image of the Middle Ages is more familiar to people today, at least those in the "modern" West, than that of a knight, armored and armed, with lance, sword and shield, mounted on a horse, also richly – or expensively – appareled. Whether the image originates in movies ostensibly about episodes or individuals from the Middle Ages, or in books for children and adults loosely based on the works of Chaucer, Malory, or anonymous creators of late medieval romances, it is an image so deeply embedded that it informs critical judgments we sometimes make about people in our own world: how often, that is, do we wish for – or more rarely, applaud – "a knight in shining armor" who has come to our rescue in one of our moments of desperation?

With some justice, present readers of late medieval literature take for granted the centrality and importance of the knight and chivalric values to understanding the world in which authors then wrote and their audiences heard, or read, what we now engage as the literary achievements of that era. Chaucer, after all, did not randomly select a knight to begin a description of his Canterbury pilgrims, and William Caxton published Thomas Malory's stories about King Arthur's knights in confidence that they would find an interested audience among his late fifteenth-century contemporaries. Knights *were* important in the late Middle Ages, and we should take them, and the social relationships and political structures within which they lived, seriously. But in taking the image of the armed knight seriously, we need also to engage it critically. Linking literature that celebrated chivalry with documents recording the actions of knights and those close to knights in late medieval England, we may find that they faced a complex and fascinating array of choices and decisions, choices and decisions for which our modern imaginings of knights in shining armor have prepared us so poorly to understand.

Documents in this chapter focus on the social and political elite of the era, and on the values that were supposed to inform their conduct, values that shaped their own self images and also figured centrally in the vision of social harmony and political unity they, and those who wrote for and to them, took for granted were shared by all English men. These ideals and aspirations for harmony and unity, however, were fundamentally compromised by the violent force that was not only necessary for performance of their self-assigned function as warriors/governors, but that was part of the ideal itself. The sources presented below reveal an aristocracy, including both titled nobles and gentry, that justified itself conceptually and defended itself practically through violent force, even as the military importance of the aristocracy became less prominent and feudal lordship was losing its practical significance during these centuries.

Whatever the persistence of knighthood and chivalry over the late Middle Ages and into subsequent centuries, the sources here are chosen to emphasize not only the ambiguities and complexities of an elite identified by the right to bear and use arms – in the pursuit of harmony and concord – but also the flexibility and creativity of those who defended their place in, or aspired to join, the highest ranks of late medieval society. Preserving and celebrating chivalry, they also were changing it.[1]

3.1 A Model of Chivalry, c.1385, from *Life of the Black Prince by the Herald of Sir John Chandos*, ed. and trans. from the Manuscript in Worcester College by Mildred K. Pope and Eleanor C. Lodge (Oxford at the Clarendon Press, 1910), pp. 135–8 and 170[2] [Anglo-French].

There is, of course relatively little description of peasant lives, or that of artisans and craftsmen, outside the records that they left of their actions, in court records, and the archives preserved by their social and political superiors. For the aristocracy, on the other hand, we have abundant material, although much of it is may represent fantasy more than the reality of their lives – although even the latter worked its way into the evidence that survives for us, in chronicles and "biographies" (of the Black Prince, for example). We start here with brief excerpts from an account that introduces us to the images of heroism and valor that made the life of Edward III's oldest son a source for modern as well as medieval dreams of chivalry. Yet these heroic images, illustrated here by descriptions of grand battles, are accompanied in this very long poem of 4,000 lines by lengthy descriptions of negotiations with both allies and enemies, preparations for battle, movements of troops, and other "business" necessary for the rare moments when this prince and his aristocratic supporters engaged each other in combat. This account, then, introduces us to a culture in which the temporal elite identified themselves, and were recognized no doubt by many of their social inferiors, as warriors whose job was

1 Much has been written about knighthood, chivalry, and changes within both during the late Middle Ages, but a recent, brief and provocative introduction can be found in an essay by Peter Coss, "An Age of Deference," in *A Social History of England, 1200–1500*, ed. by Rosemary Horrox and W. Mark Ormrod (Cambridge: Cambridge University Press, 2006), pp. 31–73.

2 This prose translation is also available online at http://elfinspell.com/ChandosTitle.html. For another translation of the Chandos Herald's *Life* and other accounts of his military and chivalric exploits, see Richard Barber, ed. and trans., the *Life and Campaigns of the Black Prince* from contemporary letters, diaries and chronicles, including Chandos Herald's *Life of the Black Prince* (1979, repr. Woodbridge: Boydell Press, 1986, 1997).

violent combat with each other; but it is also a culture in which such organized violence, however central to self-definitions and social status, was in practice erratic and, in comparison with the work necessary for exercising that violence, occupied a relatively small part of their time. Although only the beginning and end of Prince Edward's life is covered by the passages below, they make clear the centrality of violence in justifying the Chandos Herald's celebration of the Prince's life, the importance of loyalty along with courage as an attribute of knights, and the ease with which chivalric violence could be joined to Christian piety and devotion.

In times of yore it was seen that they who fashioned fair poems were in sooth esteemed as authors or in some sort recorders to show knowledge of the good, in order to draw remembrance of good from their hearts and to receive honour (?). But it is said, and truly, that there is naught that does not dry up, and that there is no tree that does not wither, excepting one only, the tree of life: and this tree, moreover, buds and flowers in this life in all parts. On this I will dwell no longer, for although such writers are held of no account, and a chatterer, a liar, a juggler, or a buffoon who, to raise a laugh, would grimace and make antics, is more esteemed than one who had skill to indite – for without gainsaying, such a one is ill received at court nowadays – but albeit they who set forth the good are held in no estimation, yet ought men not to refrain from making and remembering fair poems – all such as have skill thereto; rather they should enter them in a book, that after their death true records may be kept; for to relate the good is verily alms and charity, for good was never lost without return at some time. Wherefore, incited by my desire, I wish to set my intent on making and recording fair poems of present and past times.

Now it is high time to begin my matter and address myself to the purpose, which I am minded to fulfil. Now, may God let me attain to it, for I wish to set my intent on writing and recording the life of the most valiant prince of this world, throughout its compass, that ever was since the days of Claris, Julius Caesar, or Arthur, as you shall hear, if so be that you listen with good will: it is of a noble Prince of Aquitaine, who was son of the noble and valorous King Edward and of Queen Philippa, who was the perfect root of all honour and nobleness, of wisdom, valour, and bounty.

This noble Prince of whom I speak, from the day of his birth cherished no thought but loyalty, nobleness, valour, and goodness, and was endued with prowess. Of such nobleness was the Prince that he wished all the days of his life to set his whole intent on maintaining justice and right, and therein was he nurtured from his childhood up; from his generous and noble disposition he drew the doctrine of bounty, for gaiety and nobleness were in his heart perfectly from the first beginnings of his life and youth. Now, is it full time that I address myself to carrying forward my matter, how he was so noble, bold, and valiant, so courteous and so sage, and how he loved so well the holy Church with his whole heart, and, above all, the most lofty Trinity; its festival and solemnity he began to celebrate from the first days of his youth and upheld it all his life zealously, without evil thought.

Now I have wished to record his youth, and now it is right that I should relate to you that which all should hold in esteem – that is, chivalry: this was upheld in his person, in whom it held sway thirty years (?). Nobly he spent his life (?), for I would dare to say this, that since the time that God was born there was none more valiant than he, as you shall hear in my records if you will hearken and give ear to the matter to which I am coming.

You know well that the noble King his father, with very great array, of his high and noble puissance made war on the realm of France, saying that he ought to have the crown; wherefore, in maintaining the quarrel, he kept up right cruel war which lasted long. Now it befell that just at this time he crossed the sea to Normandy. With right noble following, barons, bannerets, and earls . . . he landed in the Cotentin. There was many a good and true knight, the noble Earl of Warwick of high esteem, and the right noble Earl of Northampton, the Earl of Suffolk, and the Earl of Stafford, of the stout and bold heart, and the Earls of Salisbury and Oxford; and John de Beauchamp was there, the valiant Reginald de Cobham, Sir Bartholomew de Burghersh, bold in deed, the good Guy de Brian, the good Richard de la Vache, and the good Richard Talbot of great prowess. And Chandos and Audeley were there, who smote mightily with the sword, and the good Thomas de Holland, of great prowess, and a great number of others, whose names I cannot tell.

The English army arrived, and when he was about to disembark the King knighted the Prince, the Earl of March also, and the Earl of Salisbury, John of Montagu, his brother, and others, more than I could tell you. And know well, the Marshal Bertrand, who was of great valour and hardihood, was there, and thought right easily to keep them from landing. But the English power landed by force. There were achieved so many feats of arms that one might have compared Roland, and Oliver, and the very courteous Ogier the Dane. There might one behold men of prowess, valour, and hardihood. There was the fair and noble Prince, who made a right goodly beginning. All the Cotentin he overrode and wholly burnt and laid waste, La Hogue, Barfleur, Carentan, Saint-Lô, Bayeux, and up to Caen, where they conquered the bridge; and there they fought mightily; by force they took the town, and the Count of Tancarville and the Count of Eu were taken there. There the noble Prince gained renown, for he was eager to acquit himself well, and was but eighteen years old. And the Marshal rode away, nor stopped before Paris; he told the King the news that was in no wise pleasing to him. Such marvel he had that scarcely could he believe it, for he thought not that such folk would have had such hardihood. Then he assembled his power; throughout France there remained neither duke nor earl of account, nor baron, banneret, nor squire, that he did not cause to assemble.

He sent to the King of Bohemia, whom he heartily loved, who brought in his company his son, who was King of Germany, and the good John de

Beaumont of Hainault, of high renown. Well did he think to defend his land against the English king, and very little did he esteem him, and right sorely did he threaten him. But afterwards, meseems, the King and the Prince together rode through Normandy, and laid waste all the country. Many a great affray did they have, and many a good and valiant man did they take, and they came to the bridge of Poissy; but the story says that the bridge there was broken, yet they did so much that with great logs they remade the bridge by force, whereat the French marvelled, and crossed one morning. They took their way through Caux, burning, laying waste, harrying; whereat the French were sore grieved and cried aloud: "Where is Philip our king?"

He was at Paris, to speak the truth, for at this time he made ready and collected his great power. And there he assembled his men and said that he would esteem himself but little if he did not take great vengeance, for he thought to have shut in the English, as I think, between the Seine and the Somme, and right there he thought lightly to give them battle. But the English to disport themselves put everything to fire and flame. There they made many a widowed lady and many a poor child orphan. They rode, day and night, until they came to the water of the Somme; on the other side was many a man, for there were the forces of the communes of Picardy and also Sir Godemar du Fay. Very wide was the river, swift and fierce with the tide, wherefore the English marvelled sore how they should cross over. But the Prince made choice of a hundred knights, of the best of his vanguard, and sent them to see how they might pass. And they who were worthy of praise rode abroad until they found a fellow who showed them the passage of the Somme, and all the hundred with one accord dashed into the water on their chargers, lance couched – very valiant knights were they – and the Prince came after, keeping ever close behind them. Sore strife was there at the passage of the Somme, and stoutly did the knights fight; and there on both sides they were at pains to shoot and cast; but the men of Picardy were speedily scattered and put to flight, together with Messire Godemar, and with the help of God all passed in due time.

When King Philip heard the tidings he was sore grieved and angry at heart, and said: "By St Paul, the valiant, I mistrust me of treason;" but nevertheless he hasted greatly. He passed through Abbeville, very rich was his array, for he was there with three other kings: the Kings of Majorca and Bohemia and the King of Germany; there were many dukes and earls, so that it was a goodly number. They rode on until they pitched their camp right near Cressy, in Ponthieu. There King Edward was camped, and the Prince, who that day led the vanguard. There they had made but brief stay, when on either side they were told that both were so close that each one could see the array and the order of the other. Then they raised a loud cry and began to order and draw up their divisions.

That day was there battle so horrible that never was there man so bold that would not be abashed thereby. Whoso saw coming the puissance and power of the King of France, great marvel would he have to relate! Inflamed with ill-will and anger they set forth to encounter together, bearing themselves in such true knightly fashion that never since Christ's coming did one behold fiercer battle. There was seen many a banner embroidered in fine gold and silk, and there the English were all afoot like men ready and eager to fight. There was the good Prince who led the vanguard; so valiantly he bore himself that it was a marvel to behold. Hardly did he suffer any one to attack, however bold or strong he might be. They fought that day until the English had the advantage. And there was slain the noble and courteous King of Bohemia, and the good Duke of Lorraine, who was a very noble leader, and the noble and renowned Count of Flanders and the good Count of Alençon, brother to King Philip, the Counts of Joii and Harcourt. What should I say in brief word? One king, one duke, and seven counts, and, as the account says, more than sixty bannerets were there stark dead, and three kings who left the field, and divers others fled, of whom I know not the number, nor is it right that I should enumerate them. But well I know that that day the brave and noble Prince led the vanguard of the army, as one should take note, for by him and his courage was the field gained and won.

* * *

Now if I have set forth in rhyme to you the whole life of the Prince; pardon me if I have passed over it a little briefly, but I must make dispatch to bring it to an end. For one could make a book of it as big as of Arthur, Alexander, or Claris, merely to bring to remembrance and knowledge his deeds and his right lofty prowess, and his very noble largesse, and also his valour, how he was all his life a valiant man, loyal and catholic, and zealous for the common weal, and how he made a very noble end, confessing with loyal heart his God and his true creator, and said to his household: "Fair lords, behold, for God, we are not lords here on earth; all will have to pass this way. No man may scape; therefore I beseech you right humbly that you will pray for me."

Then he had his room opened and made all his men come who had served him in his life and still gladly served him. "Sirs," says he, "pardon me, for, by the faith that I owe you, you have loyally served me; nor can I of myself give to each his guerdon, but God, by His most holy name will render it you in the holy heaven." Then each one sobbed heartily and wept very tenderly, all those who were present, earls, barons, and bachelors. And he said to all, loud and clear: "I commend to you my son, who is very young and little, and pray you, as you have served me, to serve him loyally."

Then he called the King, his father, and the Duke of Lancaster, his brother; he commended to them his wife and his son, whom he greatly loved and besought them right then that each one should help him. Each one swore it on the book and promised him without reserve to support his child and maintain him in his right; all the princes and all the barons standing round swore it; and the noble and renowned Prince gave them a hundred thousand thanks. But never, so God help me, was such sore grief beheld as there was at his departing. The lovely and noble Princess felt such grief at heart that her heart was nigh breaking. Of lamentation and sighing, of crying aloud and sorrowing, there was so great a noise that there was no man living in the world, if he had beheld the grief, but would have had pity at heart.

There was so noble a repentance that God of His mighty power will have mercy on his soul; for he prayed to God for mercy and pardon for all those misdeeds that he had committed in this mortal world. And then the Prince passed from this world and departed, in the year one thousand three hundred and seventy-six, in the fiftieth of his father's reign, in London, the noble city, on the festival of the Trinity, of which he kept the feast all his life, gladly, with melody. Now let us pray God, the King of kings, who died for us on the cross, that He will have pardon on his soul and grant him of His gift the glory of His paradise. Amen. And here finishes the poem of the most noble Prince Edward, who never turned craven. This hath the Herald of Chandos related, who gladly made record.

3.2 A Knight's Ideal Knight, c. 1350, from *The Book of Chivalry of Geoffroi de Charny*, ed. and trans. Richard W. Kaeuper and Elspeth Kennedy (Philadelphia: University of Pennsylvania Press, 1996), pp. 87, 89, 91, and 95. [French, translated into modern English by Kennedy.]

Richard Kaeuper has made a compelling case that violence was not incidental to aristocratic identity in the late Middle Ages, not something to be controlled and "civilized," but a very definition of what constituted "civilized" behavior for knights and others among the landed elite. Supporting his case is the kind of instruction and guidance provided by, for example, Charny, whose manual for knights Kaeuper has edited, and which we include here, for the analysis of the violent deeds required of knights, and honored by those who acknowledged them as cultural and political superiors. Charny, himself on the French side of the early conflicts of the Hundred Years' War, was a contemporary of the Black Prince. In the excerpts here, among a survey of the various circumstances and settings in which men-at-arms might demonstrate their prowess – in tournaments, for example, or on long journeys and pilgrimages, or for rewards – we find a strong celebration of war, not only for wars initiated by princes but also those fought on behalf of their kinsmen and lords. War is, of course, men's business and men's work; but Charny acknowledges that women, or at least ladies, have a role to play, in encouraging and guiding naïve young men towards military prowess, valor, renown, and thus honor.

Deeds of Arms in Local Wars

After speaking of the above-mentioned peacetime activities in the practice of arms, I should now turn to another category of men-at-arms, those involved in war, for many aim to make their reputations in this calling in a number of different ways. I shall therefore speak first of those who seek out and participate in the wars in their own locality without going into distant regions and who deserve praise for their great exploits and undertakings which they have achieved and are achieving by their good sense, their physical strength and dexterity as those who have to wage war on their own behalf in order to defend their honor and inheritance, or those who want to wage war to assist in the defense of the honor and inheritance of their kinsmen, or like those who stay to serve in the wars to defend the honor and inheritance of their rightful lord who maintains them, for the faith and loyalty which they owe to their lord cannot be better demonstrated than by serving him and assisting him loyally in such urgent need as that of war which is so grave as to put person, land and resources all at risk.

Deeds of Arms in Local Wars [sic]

There are others still who want to serve their friends or kinsmen, when they are at war, and there are some who have not the means to leave their own locality. And when God by his grace grants that such people as are mentioned above perform great exploits, fight well and distinguish themselves in several successful days of combat which they may have, such people should be valued and honored who have conducted themselves so well within their own region. It seems indeed that they would also have done well elsewhere. And I am prepared to say that all men-at-arms who have done well in this art of war and who have often been successful, even if it were only in their own district, should be honored among all men in their own locality as one should honor good men-at-arms and as is appropriate in relation to such a very noble activity as the practice of arms in war, which surpasses all other except the service of God.

Deeds of Arms in War Are the Most Honorable

We have spoken of those men, and of the men-at-arms who in their own region, perform deeds of arms in the way which seems best to them; indeed no one should speak except in favorable and honorable terms, especially in relation to armed exploits in war, in whatever region, provided that they are performed without reproach. But it seems to me that in the practice of arms in war it is possible to perform in one day all the three different kinds of military art, that is jousting, tourneying, and waging war, for war requires jousting with the point of the lance and striking with the edge of the sword as in a tournament, and attacking with the swordthrust and other weapons, as war demands. Therefore one should value and honor men-at-arms engaged in war more highly than any other men-at-arms; for in the practice of arms in jousts some are pleased enough with what they do without undertaking any other deeds of arms. The same is true in relation to tournaments, for some are satisfied with taking part just in them and not in any other use of arms. And these two uses of arms are both to be found in armed combat in war. It is therefore a great and honorable thing that these uses of arms, of which some feel they have achieved enough by performing just one, should all be carried out together by men-at-arms engaged in war each day they have to fight on the battlefield. For this reason you should love, value, praise, and honor all those whom God by his grace has granted several good days on the battlefield, when they win great credit and renown for their exploits; for it is from good battles that great honors arise and are increased, for good fighting men prove themselves in good battles, where they show their worth in their own locality without traveling outside it. We have now dealt with those good men-at-arms who have fought well in their own region and have found good battles to take part in.

* * *

Deeds Undertaken for Love of a Lady

There is another category of men-at-arms who when they begin are so naive that they are unaware of the great honor that they could win through deeds of arms; nevertheless they succeed so well because they put their hearts into winning the love of a lady. And they are so fortunate that their ladies themselves, from the great honor and superb qualities that reside in them, do not want to let them tarry nor delay in any way the winning of that honor to be achieved by deeds of arms, and advise them on this and then command them to set out and put all their efforts into winning renown and great honor where it is to be sought by valiant men; these ladies urge them on to reach beyond any of their earlier aspirations. Such naive men-at-arms may nevertheless be so fortunate as to encounter such good adventures that their deeds of prowess and achievements in a number of places and fields of battle are held to be of great account. And they should be praised and honored, and so also should the noble ladies who have inspired them and through whom they have made their name. And one should indeed honor, serve, and truly love these noble ladies and others whom I hold to be ladies who inspire men to great achievement, and it is thanks to such ladies that men become good knights and men-at-arms. Hence all good men-at-arms are rightly bound to protect and defend the honor of all ladies against all those who would threaten it by word or deed. But I must now return to the kind of men-at-arms who act in the way described above. And again I say: he who does best is most worthy in feats of arms in peace and in feats of arms in war where great honor wins recognition. Thus your ladies will and should be more greatly honored when they have made a good knight or man-at-arms of you. And when one could say that a good knight or a good man-at-arms loves a certain lady, where it might be possible for this to be known, greater honor would indeed come to the lady who might have such a love than to those who might choose to waste their time on a paltry wretch, unwilling to take up arms, neither for deeds of arms in peace nor even for deeds of arms in war, when he would have had the physical strength and skill to perform them. And those who love thus and want to love, what honor do they confer on their ladies when it could be said that each one of these loves a miserable wretch?

3.3 A Knight's Office, from *The Book of the Ordre of Chyualry*, trans. and printed by William Caxton [1484], from a French version of Ramon Lull, Le Libre del Orde de Cauayleria, ed. Alfred T. P. Byles, EETS (1926), pp. 24–33, 37–41.

It is worth comparing Charny's fourteenth century treatise with William Caxton's version of a work that circulated much more widely in the late Middle Ages, a thirteenth-century Catalan treatise translated into French and from the French version translated and published by Caxton in the late fifteenth cenury. Excepts below are chosen to underscore the close connection between chivalric valor and governmental responsibility, as well the emphasis given a partnership between knights and clerks.

Of thoffice that apperteyneth to a knyght

Offyce of a knyght is thende and the begynnynge / wherfore began the ordre of chyualrye / Thenne yf a knyght vse not his offyce / he is contrarye to his ordre / & to the begynnyng of chyualrye to fore sayd: By the whiche contraryete he is not a very knyght / how be hit that he bere the name / For suche a knyght is more vyle than the smythe or the carpenter / that done their office after that they owe to doo & haue lerned / The office of a knyght is to mayntene and deffende the holy feyth catholyque / by the whiche god the fader sente his sone in to the world to take flesshe humayne in the glory-ous vyrgyn oure lady saynt Mary / And for to honoure & multyplye the feythe suffryd in this world many trauaylles / despytes / & anguysshous deth / Thene in lyke wyse as our lord god hath chosen the clerkes for to mayntene the holy faith catholike with scripture & resons ayest the mescreaunts[3] and not

3 Pagans, the unfaithful, skeptics, traitors.

bileuyng / In lyke wise god of glory hath chosen knyghtes / by cause that by force of armes they vaynquysshe the mescreauntes, which daily laboure for to destroye holy chirche / & suche knyghtes god holdeth them for his frendes honoured in this world / & in that other when they kepe & mayntene the feith by the whiche we entende[4] to be saued / The knyght that hath no feythe / and vseth no feyth / & is contrarye to them that mayntene it / is as thentendement[5] of a man / to whome god hath gyuen reason and vseth the contrary / Thenne he that hath feithe / and is contrary to feythe / and will be saued / he doth ageynst hym self / For his wylle accordeth to mescreaunce / whiche is contrary to feith and to the sauacion[6] / By the whiche mescreaunce a man is Iuged to torments infynytes & perdurable[7] / Many there ben / that haue offyces whiche god hath gyuen to them in this world / to thende / that of hym he shold be serued / & honoured / but the most noble & the most honourable offyces that ben / ben thoffyces of clerkes & of knyghtes / And therfor the grettest amytye that shold be in this world / ought to be bitwene the knyghtes & clerkes / Thenne thus as clerkes be not ordeyned of their clergy that they be ayenst thordre of chyualry / Also knyghtes maintene not by thordre of chyualry them that be contrary to the clerkes which ben bounden to loue & mayntene thordre of chyualry / Thordre is not gyuen to a man for that he shold loue his ordre only / but he ought to loue the other ordres For to loue one ordre / and to hate another / is nothynge to loue ordre / For god hath gyuen none ordre that is contrarye to other ordre / Thenne thus as the relygyous that loueth not soo moche his owne ordre / that he is enemy of an other ordre / he foloweth not ne ensieweth the rule of thordre / Thus a knyght loueth not thoffyce of a knyght that so moche loueth and preyseth his owen ordre / that he myspryseth and hateth other ordre / For yf a knyght loued the ordre of Chyualry / and destroyed somme other ordre / hit shold seme that the ordre shold be contrary to god / the whiche thyng may not be / syth he hath establysshed ordre /

So moche noble is cheualrye / that every knight oughte to be gouvernour of a grete countre or loud / But there soo many knyghtes / that the lond maye not suffyse to sygnefye that one ought to be lord of al thynges / Themperour ought to be a knyght & lord of a knyghtes / but by cause that themperour may not by him self gouerne al knightes hym behoueth that he haue vnder hym kynges that ben knyghtes / to thende / that they ayde & helpe to mayntene thordre of Chyualry / And the kynges oughte to haue vnder them / dukes / Erles / vycountes and other lordes / And vnder the barons ought to be knyghtes / whiche ought to gouerne hem after the ordynaunce of the barons / whiche ben in the hyhe degree of chyualry to fore named / for to shewe

4 Understand.

5 The mind; judgment, intellect, understanding.

6 Salvation.

7 Permanent, enduring.

thexcellence / seygnorye[8] / power and wysedome of oure lord god gloryous whiche is one only god in Trynyte / and can and may gouerne alle thynges wherfore hit is not thyng couenable[9] / that a knyght allone shold by hym self gouerne alle the people of thys world / For yf one knyght allone myght so do / the seygnorye / the power & wysedom of god shold not be so wel sygnefyed / And therfore for to gouerne alle the peples that ben in the world / god wyl / that ther be many knyghtes / of whome he is gouernour only / lyke as it is sayd atte begynnyng / And thene kynges & prynces which make prouostes & baillyes of other persones than of knyghtes done ayenst thoffyce of chyualry / for the knyght is more worthy to haue the seygnorye ouer the peple / than ony other man & by thouour of his offyce ought be done to hym more gretter honour / than ony other man that hath not so an honourable offye & by thonour that he receyueth of his ordre / he hath noblesse of herte / & by noblesse of courage he is the lasse[10] enclyned to doo a vylaynous fait[11] or dede than another man

Thoffyce of a knyght is to mayntene and deffende / his lord worldly or terryen[12] / for a kyng ne no hyhe[13] baron hath no power to mayntene ryghtwysnes[14] in his men without ayde & helpe / Thenne yf ony man do ageynst the commadement of his kyng or prynce / it behoueth that the knyghtes ayde their lord whiche is but a man only as another is / & therfor the euyl knyght whiche sooner helpeth another man that wold put doun his lord fro the seignory that he ought to haue vpon him he foloweth not thoffyce by which he is called a knyght / By the knyghtes ought to be mayntened & kept iustyce / for in lyke wyse as the juges haue thoffyce to juge / in lyke wyse haue the knyghtes thoffyce for to kepe them fro violence / in exercysyng the fayt of iustyce yf it myght be that chyualry & clergy assembled them to gyder in such manner that knyghtes shold be lerned / so that by science they were suffysaunt to be juges / none office sholde be so couenable to be a juge as chyualry for he that by justice may best be holden is more couenable[15] to be a juge than ony other

Knightes ought to take coursers to juste[16] & to go to tornoyes[17] / to holde open table / to hunte at hertes[18] / at bores[19] & other wyld bestes / For in

8 Seigneury, lordship.
9 Convenient, feasible.
10 Less.
11 Action, deed.
12 Temporal, earthly.
13 Nor no high.
14 Righteousness.
15 Appropriate, suitable.
16 Joust.
17 Tournaments.
18 Deer.
19 Boars.

doynge these theynges the knyghtes exercise them to armes / for to mayntene thordre of knighthode Thene to mesprise[20] & to leue the custom of that which the knyght is most apparailled[21] to vse his office is but despising of thordre / & thus as al these thynges afore said apperteyne the soule to a knyght as touching his body lyke wise justice / wysedom / charite loyalte / verite / humylite / strength hope swiftues & al other vertues semblable apperteyne to a knyght as touchyng his soule / & therfor the knyght that vseth the thynges that apperteyne to thordre of chyualry as touchyng his body / & hath none of these vertues that apperteyne to chyualry touchyng his soule is not the frende of thordre of knygthode. For yf hit were thus / that he made separacion of the vertues aboue sayd / sayenge that they apperteyne not to the soule / and to thordre of chyualrye to gyder /jt shold signefye that the body & chyualrye / were bothe two to gyder contrarye to the soule and to these vertues / and that is fals / Thoffyce of a knight is to mayntene the londe / for by cause that the drede of the comyn people haue of the knyghtes / they laboure & cultyue[22] the erthe / for fere / leste / they shld be destroyed / And by the drede of the knyghtes / they redoubte[23] the kynges / prynces and lordes / by whome they haue theyr power / But the wicked knight that aydeth not his erthely lord and naturel countrey / ageynst another prynce / is a knight withoute office / And is lyke vnto faith withoue werkes and lyke vnto mysbyleue / which is ayenst the feyth.

* * *

Therefore a noble knyghte that loueth Chyualrye / how moche lasse he hath ayde of his felawes / and lasse of armes and lasse to deffende /So moche more hym behoueth tenforce hym self to haue thoffyce of a knyght by hardynesse of a stronge courage / and of noble appareuce ageynste them that ben contrarye to chyualry / And yf he deye[24] for to mayntene cheualry thenne he acquyreth chyvalrye in that / in whiche he maye the better loue and serue hit / For chyvalry abydeth not soo agreably / in no place as in noblesse of courage / And no man may more honoure and loue Chyualrye / ne more for hym maye not be do / than that deyeth for loue & for to honoure the ordre of chyualrve / Chyualrye and hardynesse may not accorde without wytte and discrescion /And yf hit were thus that folye and ygnoraunce accorded therto / wytte and discrescion shold be contrary to the ordre of chyualrye And that is thynge Impossyble / by whiche is openly sygnefyed to the knyght / that thow hast grete loue to the ordre of chyualrye / That al in lyke wyse as Chyualrye by noblesse of courage hath made the to haue hardynesse / so that

20 Disparage.
21 Furnished, equipped, accoutered.
22 Cultivate?
23 Fear, honor.
24 Die.

thow doubtest no peril ne deth / by cause thaw myghtest honoure chyualry / In lyke wyse hit behoueth that thordre of chyualry make the to loue wysedom by whiche thow mayst loue and honoure the ordre of chyualrye / ageynst the disordynauce and deffaulte that is in them that wene[25] to ensiewe and folowe the ordre of Chyualry by folye and ygnoraunce / and withoute entendement / Thoffyce of a knyght is to mayntene and deffende wymmen / wydowes and orphanes / and men dyseased[26] and not puyssaunt[27] ne stronge / For lyke as customme and reason is / that the grettest and moost mighty helpe the ffeble and lasse[28] / and that they haue recours to the grete / Ryght soo is thordre of chyualry by cause she is grete / honourable and mighty / be in socoure and in ayde to them that ben under hym / and lasse myghty and lasse honoured than he is Thenne as it is soo that for to doo wrong and force to wymmen wydowes that haue nede of ayde / And orphelyns[29] that haue nede of gouernaunce / And to robbe and destroye the feble that haue nede of strengthe And to take awey fro them that is gyuen to them / These thynges may not accorde to thordre of chyualry / For this is wyckednesse cruelty & tyranny / & the knyght that in stede of these vyces is ful of vertues / he is dygne[30] & worthy to haue thordre of chyualry / And al in lyke wyse as god hath gyuen eyen[31] to the werk man for to see to werke / Ryght so he hath gyuen eyen to a synnar to thende that he bywepe[32] his synnes / And lyke as god hath gyuen to hym an herte / to thende that he be hardy by his noblesse / So ought he to haue in his herte / mercy / And that his courage be enclyned to the werkes of myserycorde[33] and of pyte That is to wete / to helpe and ayde them that al wepynge requyre of the knyghtes ayde and mercy /and that in them haue their hope / Thenne knyghtes that haue none eyen / by whiche they may see the feble & not strong ne haue not the herte ne myght by whiche they maye recorde the nedes of the myschaunt[34] and nedy peple ben not worthy to he in thordre of Chyualry / yf chyualrye / whiche is so moche an honourable offyce / were to robbe aud to destroye the poure peple and not myghty / and tengyne[35] and doo wronge to good wymnen / wydowes / that haue nothynge to defffende them / That office thenne were not virtuous / but it shold be vycious

Thoffyce of a knight is to haue a castel and horse for to kepe the wayes / and for to deffende them that labouren the londes and the erthe / and they ought.

25 Think (erroneously).
26 Diseased.
27 Powerful.
28 Young woman, or female infant or child.
29 Orphans.
30 Noble, worshipful.
31 Eyes.
32 Weep for, bewail.
33 Mercy.
34 Unfortunate.
35 Entice, seduce (a woman), inveigle.

to haue townes and Cytees for to holde ryght to the peple /And for to assemhle in a place men of many dyuerse craftes / whiche ben moche necessarye to the ordenaunce of this world to kepe and mayntene the lyf of man and of woman.

3.4 A Gentleman's Paternal Advice, c.1445–1450, from *Peter Idley's Instructions to his Son*, ed. Charlotte D'Evelyn, Modern Language Association of America Monograph series, Vol. VI (Boston: D. C. Heath and Company, 1935), pp. 81–105.

That military valor and the skillful use of arms were central to the "work" of chivalry, and by extension to the landed aristocracy, seems clear; but also evident in what contemporaries wrote, and read, about their "profession" of chivalry was a conviction that the exercise of force accompanied their work as governors and rulers, howbeit in service to the monarch, and in aid of those who depended on their superiors for justice.[36] *The latter – the work of governance – may have become a more important and more valued attribute of aristocratic conduct in the later part of the period covered here, as the poem written for his son by Peter Idley*[37] *suggests, where the virtues of civil life are more emphatically presented than preparation for a life in arms. Idley took for granted that his son would bear arms, but his advice centers on matters of friendship, on the importance of good counsel, the pursuit and handling of wealth, and, not a minor matter, the profession of law, which he urges upon his son in explicit terms; not least important as an indication of priorities is the space he devotes to his son's relations with his wife, one of the more significant "counselors" surveyed by the father/poet.*

In the begynnyng of this litell werke
I pray to God my penne he leede;
ffor in makyng I am as a yonge Clerke
That lerneth first: Cristis Crosse me spede!
But that nature dryueth me to this dede,
As y can to teche the, my childe,
That art yet yonge and somdele wylde.

[On respecting one's superiors]
ffirst God and thy kyng thou loue and drede;
Aboue all thyng thou this preserue.

36 See, for examples, not only the preceding selection but also Christine de Pisan, *The Book of Fayltes of Armes and of Chyvalry*, trans. and printed William Caxton, ed. A. T. P. Byles, EETS (1932; Kraus Reprint, 1988) pp. 5–11.

37 The editor of his letter, Charlotte D'Evelyn, identified Idley as a landed gentlemen – formally, an "esquire" – whose estates included Drayton, in Oxfordshire; among other offices, he served as bailiff for the Honour of Wallingford and of St Valery, part of the duchy of Cornwall, and Controller of the King's Works throughout England. (Peter Idley's *Instructions*, pp. 5–19).

ffaile not this for no maner nede,
Thoughe thow therfore shold perissh and sterue.
A man ony tyme fro his trowthe to swerve
Hymsilf and his kynne doith grete shame;
Therfore euer kepe the fro suche maner blame.
Allso thy fadre and modre thow honoure
As thou wolde thy sone shold to the;
And euery man after riche and pouere,
As euer thow wilt haue Loue of me;
And in Rewarde it is geve vnto the
The blessyng of thy fadre and modre:
Goode soone, that thou deserue noon other.

* * *

What man thou serue, loke thou hym drede;
His goode as thyn thou kepe and spare
Lete neuer thy will thy witte ouerlede;
Be lowly in seruice and love his welfare;
And if thou wilt be out of drede and care,
Restreyne and kepe well thy tonge:
Thus, childre, lerne while ye be yonge:
Be true in worde, werke, and dede,
And flee doublenes in all wyse;
Throghe all the worlde in lengthe and brede
Gretter vertues can no man devise,
And sonnest to worshippe causeth man to rise;
Be not autour also of tales newe,
ffor callyng to rehersaill lest thou it rewe.

* * *

[On the study of law]
I conceyve thy witte bothe goode and able,
To the lawe, therfore, now haue I ment
To set the, if thou wilt be stable
And spende thy witt that God hath sent
In vertu with goode entent;
Than shall I helpe the as y can
With my goode till thou be a man.
And if thou do the contrarie, trust me well,
I woll put fro the without nay
Londe and goodis eueri deell
And all that euer I goodly may;

Therfore that thou laboure nyght and day
God and man hoolly to please,
Thy fadre and modre to hertis ease.
To grete worshippe hath the lawe
Brought forth many a pouere man
That wolde flee vices and to vertu drawe,
Many a thousande sith the world beganne.
Greate miserie haue they that no goode canne;
Therefore learne besily while youthe last,
And murielie[38] in age to leeve be not agast.
And if to worshippe thou happe to rise
By fortune of connyng for tattayne[39]
fforgete not thysilf in noo maner wyse;
fro proudnesse of herte thou the refreyne.
Lete mekenes euer be thy Rayne,
And remembre that many in this world wyde
Haue be cast adoun for theire grete pride.

* * *

Now of whom thou shalt counceill Resceyve,
This must thou wele vndirstonde;
And whos counceill thou shalt weyve,[40]
How to examyne counceill in euery lande,
How and whenne counceill is to be take on honde,
And whan thou shalt chaunge counseill and promise,
I woll shewe the after my symple aduyse.

* * *

And if thou wilt by counceill vnclose
To put thysilf in suerte and peas,
To a preved true frende thou it vnclose:
It woll turne thy matere to good encrees.
God hymsilf oure lady chies[39]
ffor a true frende and a feithfull maide.
She kept in cloos al that the aungel saide.

* * *

38 Joyfully, cheerfully.
39 To attain.
40 Decline, eschew.
41 Chose.

De Laude mulierum[42]
The counceill of a woman y woll not dispise,
Though poetis write of straunge will
That womans counceill in many wyse
Ys ouer good or passyng ille.
I pray you sey well or be stille;
Disclaundre not of women the name –
Remembre tendirly who was youre dame.
I sey womans counceill is good and reasonable –
As by scripture is proved in many a place –
ffull sure, full sadde, and right aggreable,
With short avisement and in litell space.
God hath sent hem suche a grace,
To be redy of answere and tendre of mynde,
They beith so pure and of noble kynde.

* * *

Also by God woman was first named
Whan Adam was made to his likenes,
Of a Rybbe full clene was she framed,
Put in hir a spirite of mekenes,
And called hir an helper to man in distresse;
So without helpe of woman which is sure,
This worlde in no wyse might long endure.
I reporte me to you that be maried:
Wher is ther ony so glorius a lyffe!
All thyng is wele and no thyng myscaried;
No defaute is founde in the good wyffe.
Betwene wedded folk is neuer striffe,
But "ye" and "nay," ther is non other
They lieve in rest as shippe without Rother.[43]

* * *

[On rewarding counsellors]
Then rewarde thy counceill for her besynesse,
In suche as they holde hem pleased,
ffor her grete diligence and avisenesse;
Lete hem departe in no wyse displeased:
A Carte goith more easily whan he is greesed.

---

42 In praise of women.
43 Rudder.

In olde prouerbe it is saide, whiche is sure,
With empty hande men may no hawkes lure.

* * *

Richesse in hymsilf y wote is no synne,
Thoughe all Regions be ruled by his mediacion;
ffor euery creature of God that man may mynne[44]
Ys good of hymsilff after his first creation;
And like as a body of euery nation
Without soule may not of lyffe be sure,
So without goodis temporall may not longe endure.
By vetaille and vesture mannes lyffe is ladde;
Who wanteth this, his lyffe may not laste;
Without goodis temporall this may not be hadde;
Also honour, worship, and frendship is past.
ffor as a shippe in the see without rother or mast
Ys ouerthrow and turned with waves and flodes,
So is a man for lak of temporall goodis.

* * *

Iff a man of hye degree and grete astate,
Mighty of possession and riche of goode,
If he perseuer in weer,[45] striff, and debate,
It woll make hym weere[46] a threedbare hoode:
A low ebbe cometh after an hyee floode.
Be debate is loste right, title, goodis, and lyffe:
This is thende of werre, debate, and stryffe.
Comite not thysilf to werre in ony wyse;
If thou be pouere, thow art cast to grounde,
Perauenture neuer after of power to arise,
In nede and miserie euer after to be bounde;
And if in Richesse thou grettely habounde,
The gretter weight in costis thou bere shall,
And if you be ouerthrowe the gretter is thy fall.

* * *

44 Call to mind, think of.
45 War.
46 Wear.

Also for thy kyng and for the Reawmes right
To put thy body with due diligence,
With alle thy power and thy hooll myght,
Looke in the be founde noo necligence
To stande with thy kynge in the Reawmes defence,
And neuer to flee in no maner kynde
But uttirly abide to the last ende.
Also for thy person to make sauffegarde
It is leefull to have wapon in hande,
Manly to fight and not to flee as a cowarde,
Thyn enemys malice to withstande,
Be stronge in herte, bow not as a wande,
Or as a dormoyse that al day slepeth:
A good castell saueth he that his body kepeth.

* * *

Thy wyffe thou loue in perfit wyse
In thought and dede, as hertely as thou can,
With gentill speche the best thou can deuyse;
This shall make hir a good woman,
And also to loue the best of ony man,
Thy goodis kepe, noither waste ne spende.
And if thou be croked and crabbed of speche,
Lordly of countenauns and comberous to please,
Cast at hir suche as thou may reche –
This shal cause grete vnhertis-ease,[47]
And al hir loue hoolly thou shalt leese;
What wold growe more I telle not all,
That thou were lothest peraventure myght falle.
She is part of thy body, remembre this,
And to dispise thy flesshe you were to blame,
Or hurt it in ony maner kynde I-wysse;
Defoule you neuer thyn owne name,
Vse not unclenly wordis, fy for shame!
To lieve in quyete it is a blesfull lyffe:
Euer a good man maketh a good wyffe.
God hymsilf gaue hir a name,
Called her an helper and a soker[48] vnto man,
And toke a ribbe from the side of Adam
And made Eve therof, thus he beganne;

47 Anxiety, uneasiness.
48 Help, support, comfort.

Also God commaundeth we shold for woman
Leeve fadre and modre and kepe hir for euere,
Till deth the lyfes from vs dessever.
Thappostole to the Ephesyos[49] said alsoo
In his epistell, whooso lust[50] to loke,
"Ye men to love youre wyffis ye ought to doo,
As Crist hys churche," thus seith the booke.
God hymsilf in wedlok tooke
His birthe, that sacrament to honoure
And vs to Redeme as oure sauyoure.
House and lande and all goodis temporall
Ys yeuen by fadre and modre and othir frendis,
But thy wyffe is yeven by thy Lorde eternall
To lieve with aungellis in Ioye wher non ende is;
And wher love is stable God euer sendeth
Prosperite and welthe and good encrese;
Therfore lerne, sone, to lieue in peas.
And if thou fynde a defaute with thy wyffe
That shold displease the in ony maner kynde,
With an ease spirite and in noo stryffe
Remembre and also haue in mynde
That non erthly thyng shalt thou fynde
But somtyme woll faile moche or lite:
Sauffe God aloone nothyng is perfite.
Seneca aboue all erthly thyng commendeth
A benyngne wyffe and a softe of speche;
Whom that oure Lorde suche oon sendeth,
She is vnto hym a verri hertis leche.
But yet oo thyng the wyse man doith teche,
ffor ony loue yeve hir not the maistrie;
And if thou doo, thou shalt fynde hir contrarie.
Thus saith the philosofre, blame not me!
I wold in no wyse women displease;
ffor I am bounde and may not flee.
Women beith goode, whoso can hem please.
Well y woote sufferaunce doth ease.
I sey no thyng but as myn auctor techeth:
Euer the yonge cok croweth as the olde precheth.

* * *

49 Ephesians 5.25.
50 Wishes.

Thi seruantis and othir hired men alsoo
Whiche be to the true, feithfull, and kynde,
Hem you loue and cherisshe euermoo;
To thy power haue hem in mynde,
So that they perceuere vnto the last ende
And to the be sure as tresoure in cofre:
This is the counceill of the wyse philosofre.
Be not in thy hous as a lyon wylde
Or as a tiraunt to hem that thy seruauntis be,
But meke and gentill as a mayde childe,
And of thy worde bountevous and free;
To all maner of seruise than woll they aggree,
Loove and worshippe the and also drede;
This holde I best, therfore take hede.
He that is cruel and wrathfull in herte
To his subiectis that be hym vndree
Is ofte cause of his owne smerte;
Thoughe he not thryve it is noo wondir,
ffor the good willis of them be parted asondree
That shold cause is profite and welfare alsoo;
Therfore cherisshe a good seruaunt whereuer thou goo.
And wher a good maister is and a lorde,
All be in reste that dwelle hym amonge,
Of an hoole mynde and of a good accorde;
Who doith the contrarie, doth hymsilf wronge;
The loue of his seruauntes woll not last long.
And if thou kepe ony seruaunt ayenst his wylle,
Thow kepest thyn enemye with the stille.

* * *

Remembre that this worlde woll not ay laste;
He that loueth hym most, shall sonnest departe;
All erthly thyng shall wane and waste
Whenne deth cometh with his darte;
There is noo connynge, crafte ne arte
That may availle ageyn the stroke of dethe:
All thyng vndre heuene he striketh and sleith.

* * *

And he that doith well and is vndefiled
Shall haue the blisse that will not sease
And resseyued in heuene as Goddis owne childe,
ffro troble and sorow to lyve in peas,
And ther to abide in Ioye endles:

To that blis most glorious he vs brynge
That is oure brother, oure fadre, oure kyng.
This is thende of my litell frame,
Roughly hewe and without ony square;
That shold be sharppe is dulle and lame,
My wytt, I meane – I pray you to spare;
I haue non vtteraunce for this cheffare
Sauffe oonly nature whiche doith me leede
ffor the, my childe, to this symple dede.
Deo gracias
Here endith the first booke and soo foloweth the sceconde as ye may after see.

3.5 A Lament for the Decline of Chivalry, 1475, from William Worcester, *The Boke of Noblesse addressed to King Edward the Fourth on His Invasion of France in 1475*, ed. J. G. Nichols (Roxburghe Club, 1860; reprint, New York: Burt Franklin, 1972), pp. 76–8.

We may detect in William Worcester's "Lament" *awareness that the distinguishing marks of aristocratic superiority may have been undergoing a subtle transformation, from the exercise of violence as a central obligation of aristocrats, to the exercise of authority as agents of the state. We should not, however, exaggerate the turn from violent force to judicial or executive action on the part of either the greater or lesser aristocracy of the fifteenth century; even Idley acknowledges that his son should be prepared to use arms in defense of his king, and William Worcester's Lament for the Decline of Chivalry below illustrates anxiety among some observers that chivalry and the practice of arms might well be in decline. Worth noting is that, throughout the period of this book, and beyond, the use of arms in defense of property rights of the aristocracy remained legitimate, as sources included in Chapter 6 below make clear.*

How lordis sonnes and noble men of birthe, for the defense of her londe, shulde exercise hem in armes lernyng.

And also moreover for the grettir defens of youre roiaumes,[51] and saufe garde of youre contreis in tyme of necessite, also to the avauncement and encrece[52] of chevalrie and worship in armes, comaunde and doo found, establisshe, and ordeyne that the sonnes of princes, of lordis, and for the most part of alle tho that ben comen and descended of noble bloode, as of auncien knightis, esquires, and other auncient gentile men, that while they ben of grene age[53] ben drawen forthe, norisshed, and exercised in disciplines,

51 Realms.

52 Increase.

53 Green age, i.e., young and inexperienced.

doctrine, and usage of scole of armes, as using justis,[54] to can[55] renne with speer,[56] handle with ax, sworde, dagger, and alle other defensible wepyn,[57] to wrestling, to skeping,[58] leping,[59] and rennyng, to make hem hardie, deliver,[60] and wele brethed,[61] so as when ye and youre roiaume in suche tyme of need to have theire service in enterprises of dedis of armes, they may of experience be apt and more enabled to doo you service honourable in what region they become,[62] and not to be [unkonnyng,[63]] abashed, ne astonied,[64] forto take enterprises,[65] to answere or deliver a gentilman that desire in worship to doo armes in liestis[66] to the utteruance, or to certain pointis, or in a quarell rightfulle to fight, and in cas of necessite you and your roiaume forto warde,[67] kepe, and defende from youre adversaries in tyme of were. And this was the custom in the daies of youre noble auncestries, bothe of kingis of Fraunce as of Englande. In example wherof, king Edwarde .iij[de] that exercised his noble son Edwarde the prince in righte grene age, and all his noble sonnes, in suche maiestries,[68] wherby they were more apt in haunting[69] of armes. And, [as myne autor seyd[70] me,] the chivalrous knight [fyrst] Henry duke of Lancastre, which is named a chief auctour and foundour in law of armes, had sent to hym frome princes and lordis of straunge regions, as out of Spayne, Aragon, Protingale, Naverre, and out of Fraunce, her children, yong knightis, to be doctrined,[71] lerned, and broughte up in his noble court in scole of armes and for to see noblesse, curtesie, and worship. Wherthoroughe here honoure spradde and encresid in renomme[72] in all londis they came unto. And after hym, in youre antecessour daies, other noble princes and lordis of gret birthe accustomed to excersise maistries appropred[73] to defense of armes and gentilnes to them longing.[74] But now of late

54 Jousts.
55 Learn.
56 To run with a spear.
57 Defensible weapons.
58 Skipping.
59 Leaping.
60 Free, liberal.
61 Well-bred.
62 Enter, come to, find themselves.
63 Ignorant, lit. unknowing.
64 Astonished, amazed.
65 Show initiative.
66 Lists (at tournaments).
67 Guard.
68 Matters to be mastered.
69 Practicing (addictively).
70 Informed.
71 Taught, indoctrinated.
72 Renown.
73 Appropriate.
74 Belonging.

daies, the grettir pite is, many one that ben descended of noble bloode and borne to armes, as knightis sonnes, esquires, and of other gentile bloode, set hem silfe to singuler practik, straunge[75] [faculteez] frome that fet,[76] as to lerne the practique of law or custom of lande, or of civile matier, and so wastyn gretlie theire tyme in suche nedelese besinesse, as to occupie courtis halding,[77] to kepe and bere out a proude countenaunce at sessions[78] and shiris halding[79], also there to embrace[80] and rule among youre pore and simple comyns[81] of bestialle[82] contenuance that lust[83] to lyve in rest. And who can be a reuler and put hym forthe in suche matieris, he is, as the worlde goithe now, among alle astatis[84] more set of[85] than he that hathe despendid .xxx. or .xl. yeris of his daies in gret jubardies[86] in youre [antecessourys] conquestis and werris. So wolde Jhesus they so wolle welle lerned theym to be as good men of armes, chieveteins,[87] or capetains in the feelde that befallithe for hem where worship and manhode shulde be shewed, moche bettir rather then as they have lerned and can be a captaine or a ruler at a sessions or a shire day, to endite[88] or amercie[89] your pore bestialle peple, to theire [enpoveryshyng,] and to enriche hem silfe or to be magnified the more, but only they shulde maynteyn your justices and your officers using the goode custom of youre lawes. And than ye shulde have righte litille need to have thoughte, anguisshe or besinesse for to conquere and wyn ayen youre rightfulle enheritaunce, or to defende your roiaume from your ennemies. And that suche singuler practik shulde [not] be accustomed and occupied [undewly] with suche men that be come of noble birthe, [but he be the yonger brother, having not whereof to lyve honestly.] And if the vaillaunt romayns[90] had suffred theire sonnes to mysspende theire tyme in suche singuler practik, using oppressing by colours [of custum of the law, they had not conquered twyes[91] Cartage ayenst alle the Affricans.

75 Alien, foreign.
76 Conduct; i.e., they are adopting conduct foreign to practices of chivalry praised above.
77 Holding courts.
78 Sessions of the Peace.
79 The sheriff's court for the county.
80 Influence illegally or bribe jurors.
81 Commons.
82 Bestial.
83 Wish.
84 Estates.
85 Esteemed.
86 Jeopardy.
87 Chiefs.
88 Indict (accuse of criminal conduct).
89 Impose a monetary penalty or fine.
90 Romans.
91 Twice.

3.6 Liveries, Loyalties and Service: Sir Roger Leche v. William Vernon et al., 1410, from TNA KB 27/596, m.76, in *Select Cases in the Court of King's Bench*, Vol. 7: Richard II, Henry IV, and Henry V, ed. G. O. Sayles, Selden Society Publications 88 (London, 1971), pp. 192–4 [Latin].

Historians continue to argue about the level of violence during the fifteenth century, although few would any longer insist on a decline into near-anarchy, once labeled, pejoratively, as "bastard feudalism." Whatever the verdict of historians on the degree of violence characteristic of politics in England during the late Middle Ages, contemporaries fretted repeatedly over "livery and retaining,"[92] and both the king and the lesser aristocracy, even as they themselves engaged in the practice, at the very least used it as a scapegoat for unjustified violence and corruption of justice in the realm. But it may in any case be a mistake to cast the debate in terms of a warrior aristocracy versus an administrative elite who defined themselves primarily in terms of their obligations (and privileges) as governors; and no less may be it be a mistake to contrast law with disorder. After all, in defending their estates, whether as governors acting on behalf of themselves or their families, or as wielders of military force suppressing challenges to their family interests, they were sustaining the "natural" order of society. Violence and the preservation of a just social order might well be understood by fifteenth century landed aristocrats as both sensible and necessary correlates. Whether violence and force in defense of claims to property were interpreted as a regrettable but necessary resort to drastic action on behalf of justice, or a blatant disregard for law and justice, would depend on the perspective of those using such violence and force. Illegitimate use of violence, and abuse of judicial procedures, were not easily distinguished from legitimate self-defense and justified manipulation of legal institutions to preserve one's rightful interests, if one's own interests were understood as beneficial to the social hierarchy and conducive to its preservation.

Derbyshire

William son of Sir Richard Vernon of Harlaston, esquire, John North of Bubbenhall the younger and John Brown of Tideswell were attached, together with John Amot of Monyash, John de More of Matlock, Richard Smithson of

92 The term refers to the practice, condemned frequently in statutes of the late fourteenth and fifteenth centuries, by which aristocrats, greater and lesser, sought service and loyalty in return for liveries (clothing, hoods, or badges) and other benefits, among which protection and support even in legal cases figured prominently. For a contemporary discussion of the practice and its implications for royal authority, see the selection from Fortescue in Chapter 7, or see the Statute on Livery and Maintenance, 1390 (SR ii. 74–75), translation of which can be found in *English Historical Documents* IV: 1327–1485, ed. A. R. Myers (London: Eyre & Spottiswoode, 1969), pp. 1169–70. In the same collection of documents is Edward IV's denunciation of livery and maintenance, 1472, p. 1132.

Youlgreave, Robert of Sheffield of Bakewell, William of Bradbury, John Clifford of Bakewell, John Wright of Ashford, Richard Johnson of Wardlow, Henry Johnson of Wardlow, John Stafford of Eyam the younger, William Blanchard of Wardlow, Henry of Stafford, Henry of Heath of Tideswell, Robert Swallow of Tideswell, John of Buxton of Tideswell, Richard Wayn of Hartington Soke, John Wayn of Hartington Soke, Roger Henryson of Hartington Soke, Richard Taylor of Norton near Twycross, William Maddock of Tideswell and Henry of Poynton, to answer Sir Roger Leche on this plea: whereas it was ordained among other things in the statute promulgated in the king's parliament held at Westminster in the first year of his reign[93] that no archbishop, bishop, abbot or prior or any other ecclesiastic or layman, no matter what his estate or position may be, within the said realm of the king of England is to give any livery of cloth to anyone, save only to members of his household and to officials and those ecclesiastics and laymen, learned in one or the other law, who are of his counsel, under penalty of making fine and ransom at the king's pleasure, and it was afterwards ordained and enacted in the present king's parliament, held in the seventh year of his reign[94] that the said statute as well as the statute concerning hats[95] made in the time of the late king Richard of England, second after the Conquest, are to be firmly held and kept and duly implemented, adding to the same that, if any knight or any other person of lesser estate should give any such livery of cloth or cloths in breach of the terms of the aforesaid statutes, he is to incur the penalty of a hundred shillings for each such livery of cloth or cloths, to be paid to the king as often as he contravenes the aforesaid statutes and ordinances, and that he who receives any such livery of cloth or cloths is likewise to incur a penalty of forty shillings, to be paid to the king as aforesaid, and he who wishes to prosecute in this case is to have a half of such penalties for his pains, and that the aforesaid penalties may not in any way be remitted, as is more fully set out in the aforesaid statutes and ordinances, why did the aforesaid William son of Richard give a certain livery of cloths at Nether Haddon to the aforesaid John [et al.], who are not members of the aforesaid William son of Richard's household or his officials or those, learned in one or the other law, who are of his counsel, in breach of the terms of the aforesaid statutes and ordinances, and the said John [et al.] received such livery there from the aforesaid William son of Richard, in contempt of the present king and in breach of the terms of the aforesaid statutes and ordinances. And the said Roger Leche, who sues in his own person on behalf of the king as well as himself, complains thereof that the aforesaid William son of Richard, on Monday before the Feast of St Luke the Evangelist in the eleventh year of the

93 1 Henry IV, c. 7, SR ii.113–14.

94 7 Henry IV, c. 14, SR ii.155–6.

95 1 Richard II, c. 7, SR ii. 3, confirmed by 20 Richard II, c. 2, SR II 93.

reign of king Henry, fourth after the Conquest[96] at the aforesaid Nether Haddon gave a certain livery of cloths, that is to say, three yards of green cloth to each of the aforesaid John [et al.] who are not members of the aforesaid William son of Richard's household or his officials or those, learned in one or the other law, who are of his counsel, in breach of the terms of the aforesaid statutes and ordinances, and the said John [et al.] received such livery from the aforesaid William son of Richard at the aforesaid day, year and place, in contempt of the present king and in breach of the terms of the aforesaid statutes and ordinances. And he produces suit thereof on behalf of the king as well as of himself etc.

And the aforesaid William son of Richard Vernon, John North the younger, and John Brown came in their own persons and severally denied all contempt and whatever etc. And the aforesaid William son of Richard Vernon, while protesting that he does not acknowledge that he gave any livery to the aforesaid John North and John Brown or to the aforesaid John Amot, John del More, John de Clifford and Henry Heath, as alleged above, says as his entire plea that the said John North, John Brown, John Amot, John del More, John Clifford and Henry of Heath, on and before the aforesaid Monday on which the aforesaid Roger Leche pretends that the said William son of Richard Vernon had given the aforesaid livery in the aforesaid manner, were the said William's servants and lawfully retained continuously in his service and do him service every day. And he is ready to prove this. Therefore he does not believe that the aforesaid Roger Leche can assign to him any tort in this case etc.

And the aforesaid John North and John Brown, while protesting that they received no livery from the aforesaid William son of Richard Vernon, as alleged above, also say that they were the aforesaid William son of Richard Vernon's servants and retained continuously in his service and do him service every day in the way in which the said William alleged above in pleading. And they are likewise ready to prove this etc., wherefore they do not believe that the aforesaid Roger Leche can assign to them any tort in this case etc.

And as for the aforesaid Richard Smithson and all the others mentioned in the aforesaid writ and count, the aforesaid William son of Richard Vernon says that he gave and delivered no livery to them or to any one of them in breach of the terms of the aforesaid statutes and ordinances, as the aforesaid Roger Leche alleges above by his writ and count. And as to this he puts himself on the country etc. And the aforesaid Roger Leche does likewise etc.

And as regards the aforesaid John North, John Brown, John Amot, John del More, John Clifford and Henry Heath the aforesaid Roger Leche says that the said John North, John Brown, John Amot, John del More, John Clifford and Henry, at the time when the aforesaid livery was given and delivered by the aforesaid William son of Richard Vernon in the aforesaid manner, were resident

96 14 October 1409.

in their own and separate houses and they resided there to attend to their own affairs save when the said William son of Richard Vernon sent for them or ordered them to ride with him to market towns and elsewhere to maintain him in his pleas under colour of negotiating and of holding love-days in the said pleas, without the said John North and John Brown being the said William son of Richard Vernon's servants on the said Monday and retained continuously in his service and doing him service every day in the way in which the said William, John North and John Brown alleged above in pleading, and without the aforesaid John Amot, John del More, John de Clifford and Henry Heath being the said William's servants at that time or retained continuously in his service in the way in which the said William son of Richard Vernon alleged above in pleading. And as to this he puts himself on the country etc. And the aforesaid William son of Richard Vernon, John North and John Brown do likewise etc. Therefore let a jury thereon come before the king at a Fortnight after Trinity wherever etc., and by whom etc., and who neither etc., to make recognition etc. Because as well etc. The same day is given to the aforesaid parties, the present plaintiffs etc.

3.7 Lords, Their Wives or Mothers, and Local Warfare: Margaret Paston to John Paston II,[97] 1469, from *The Paston Letters. A Selection in Modern Spelling*, ed. Norman Davis (London: Oxford University Press, 1963), pp. 184–6 [English].

Correspondence among members and servants of the Norfolk family of Paston has long been exploited by historians and used by students of fifteenth-century England to gain an unusually rich and vivid view of both public and family life from the perspective of lower aristocrats who had acquired a place among the landed elite by way of the legal profession. But whatever their indebtedness to law and its practice for their status by the middle of the century – and their continuing entanglement in legal proceedings is amply documented throughout these letters – they clearly regarded force and violence as legitimate in the struggle to maintain their status. The letter below also makes clear that aristocratic women on occasion threw themselves energetically into the fray, readily accepting responsibility for forceful defense of the lands – in this case, Caister – threatened by social superiors – again in this case, the Duke of Norfolk.

Not included here, but readily accessible,[98] *is another letter by Margaret to her son, also written during the period of conflict over Caister, in which she describes her*

97 John II was the eldest son of Margaret and her late husband, John Paston I. John II had a younger brother, also named John.

98 Pp. 181–3, dated 1469, 10 September, in the Davis edition with modernized spelling. In addition to many other printed editions, most notably those of Colin Richmond, ready access to the correspondence of the Paston family is available online: Paston letters and papers of the fifteenth century, Part I, Electronic Text Center, University of Virginia Library [a machine-readable transcription], at http://etext.lib.virginia.edu/toc/modeng/public/PasLett.html.

strenuous efforts to invalidate the marriage of her daughter, Margery, to Richard Calle, the family's bailiff, and a correspondent whose letters are part of the collection. Juxtaposing the two letters illuminates the political and social centrality of the family to a culture that celebrated the individual knight; such juxtaposition also highlights the role of women in managing political and social affairs within a culture that frequently depicted women in a passive position. The very richness and unusual bulk of this late medieval correspondence, of course, urges caution in generalizing too hastily from the Pastons' experience to that of other English aristocratic families, but engaging their correspondence is to engage some of the fundamental features – and contradictions – of late medieval England.

I greet you well, letting you weet that your brother and his fellowship stand in great jeopardy at Caister, and lack victual; and Daubeney and Berney[99] be dead, and divers other greatly hurt, and they fail gunpowder and arrows, and the place sore broken with guns of the tother part; so that, but they have hasty help, they be like to lose both their lives and the place, to the greatest rebuke to you that ever came to any gentleman, for every man in this country marvelleth greatly that ye suffer them to be so long in so great jeopardy without help or other remedy.

The Duke hath be more fervently set thereupon, and more cruel, sith that Writtle,[100] my Lord of Clarence man, was there than he was before, and he hath sent for all his tenants from every place, and other, to be there at Caister on Thursday next coming, that there is then like to be the greatest multitude of people that came there yet. And they purpose then to make a great assault, for they have sent for guns to Lynn and other place by the sea's side, that with their great multitude of guns, with other shoot and ordnance, there shall no man dare appear in the place. They shall hold them so busy with their great people that it shall not lie in their power within to hold it again them, without God help them or [they] have hasty succour from you. Therefore, as ye will have my blessing, I charge you and require you that ye see your brother be holpen in haste. And if ye can have none mean, rather desire writing fro my Lord of Clarence, if he be at London, or ell of my Lord Archbishop of York, to the Duke of Norfolk that he will grant them that be in the place their lives and their goods[101]; and in eschewing of insurrections, with other inconvenience that be like to grow within the shire of Norfolk, this troublous

99 Osbern Berney, a cousin of Margaret Paston. This report was false; he was not killed at Caister, and lived for many years after. Margaret left him a legacy in her will.

100 Walter Writtle, gentleman, of White Roding, Essex, in this year sheriff of Essex and Hertfordshire. He was in the service of George, Duke of Clarence, through whom John Paston II was seeking to come to terms with the Duke of Norfolk. He was a clerk of the Exchequer from 1455 to 1472, often J.P. and M.P., and sheriff again in 1471. He died in 1475.

101 When Norfolk finally took Caister he issued a safe-conduct, on 26 September 1469, for John Paston III and the other defenders, saying in the preamble that he did so at the instance of the Archbishop of Canterbury, the Duke of Clarence, and others.

world, because of such conventides and gatherings within the said shire for cause of the said place, they shall suffer him to enter upon such appointment, or other like taken by the advice of your counsel there at London, if ye think this be not good, till the law hath determined otherwise; and let him write another letter to your brother to deliver the place upon the same appointment. And if ye think, as I can suppose, that the Duke of Norfolk will not agree to this, because he granted this aforn and they in the place would not accept it, then I would the said messenger should with the said letters bring fro the said Lord of Clarence, or ell my Lord Archbishop, to my Lord of Oxford[102] other letters, to rescue them forthwith, though the said Earl of Oxford should have the place during his life for his labour. Spare not this to be done in haste, if ye will have their lives and be set by in Norfolk, though ye should lose the best manor of all for the rescue. I had liefer ye lost the livelode than their lives. Ye must get a messenger of the lords or some other notable man to bring these letters.

Do your devoir now, and let me send you no more messengers for these matters; but send me by the bearer hereof more certain comfort than ye have do by all other that I have sent before. In any wise, let the letters that shall come to the Earl of Oxford comen with the letters that shall comen to the Duke of Norfolk, that if he will not agree to the tone that ye may have ready your rescue, that it need no more to send therefor.

God keep you. Written the Tuesday next before Holy Rood Day[103] in haste.

By your mother

3.8 Commanding Tenants and Exercising Lordship: Two Letters to a Northern Knight, late fifteenth century, from *The Plumpton Letters and Papers*, ed. Joan Kirby, Royal Historical Society Publications, Camden Fifth Series 8 (Cambridge: Cambridge University Press, 1996), pp. 106–7 and 144–5.

Throughout the fifteenth century, formal condemnations of livery and retaining as a source of disorder demonstrate the persistence of the practices, even if they exaggerate the disorder consequent on such practices, difficult at best to separate from the acceptable, even necessary, exercise of patronage that was, in some deep sense, the very heart of effective governance in the late Middle Ages. In light of debates over the transition to

---

102 John de Vere, thirteenth Earl of Oxford (1442–1513), a prominent Lancastrian. He was imprisoned in the Tower for a time in 1468, took a leading part in the temporary restoration of Henry VI in 1470–1, and after it went into exile. He seized St Michael's Mount in September 1473 and held it for some months, but was forced to surrender and was imprisoned for ten years. In Henry VII's time John Paston III became a member of his council and William Paston III was in his service.

103 14 September.

capitalism from feudal relations,[104] *the most noteworthy violence exercised more or less routinely by aristocrats may not be force against rivals for estates and power, but coercion directed towards the tenants on whose work the aristocracy depended. On the one hand, tenants were themselves a source of military force available to aristocrats and their sovereign; on the other, violence may have been a not uncommon tactic for preserving lordship over tenants. The search for a balance between wooing the loyalty of tenants and exploiting them may well have been the most important task facing a landlord, the most crucial work to be done by aristocrats, greater and lesser. The Plumpton family's correspondence below gives us some insight into how members of one family in the lesser aristocracy sought such a balance. Whatever Sir Robert Plumpton's personal valor and courage, fulfillment of his duties to his sovereign depended, as Henry VII's letter illustrates, on a capacity to summon servants and tenants on his estates to suppress disorder and unrest. And whether he needed the loyalty of servants and tenants for his own interests or those of his king, Sir Robert could not afford to manage his affairs from a distance*

Henry VII to Sir Robert Plumpton, 28 May 1492

Trusty & welbeliued wee greete you well, & as soone for the good & agreable seruice yee did vnto vs in this last commotion of our subjects in our county of Yorke,[105] wee can giue you our full speciall thanks, & shall not forgite the good disposition yee haue been of in that behalfe. And in as much as diuerse & many such commotions & insurrections haue beene heretofore committed in our said county, to thutter destruction of greate number of our subjects therein cause, wee would haue executed the just course of our lawes. We therefore, intendinge to prouide for the tyme to come & to haue the same our county in a restfullnes, both for the duty amongst God & vs, & alsoe for theire owne profites, will & desyre you that forthwith & by as wyse wayes as yee can, yee put your selfe in a surety of your meniall seruants & tenants, & to knowe assuredly how many of them will take your parte in

104 Robert Brenner, in the essay "Agrarian class structure and economic development in pre-industrial Europe," *Past and Present* 70, pp. 30–75, touched off a vigorous debate over the origins of a transformation that would not only make lordship and manors an anachronism, certainly in economic productivity, but also confirm the nation state as the dominant political reality of the modern era. The first stages of the debate may be found in a subsequent issue of the journal, *Past and Present* 97 (1982); but historians, and not only economic historians, continue to argue the issues that Brenner addressed: see, for example, S. R. Epstein, *Capitalism and Growth. The Rise of States and markets in Europe, 1300–1750* (London: Routledge, 2000), pp. 3–7. An elegant appreciation and criticism of Brenner may be found in Ellen Meiksins Wood, *The Origin of Capitalism: A Longer View* (London: Verso, 2002), especially pp. 34–49. Relevant to "the transition from feudal relations to capitalism" is the letter to the President of Magdalen College below, 6.7.

105 A reference to a skirmish at Ackworth, against northern rebels protesting the levying of a benevolence.

seruinge vs accordinge to your & theire duties foresaid. When yee shall haue demeaned the matter in this wise, which wee would yee did, as aboue, with all diligence, then wee pray you to certify our couzen the earle of Surrey of the number of such assured men as yee will bringe with you, to the intent hee may ascertayne vs by his wrytinge of the same.[106] Giuen vnder our signet at our manor of Shene the 28th day of May the seuenth yeare of our reigne.

Endorsed: To our trustie & wellbeloued knight Sir Robart Plompton

Robert Plumpton and others to Sir Robert Plumpton [1501][107]

After most lowly & all due recomendations, we lowly recomend us vnto your good mastership, certyfying you that as fare as we can vnderstand or know, John Rocliffe & John Sotell[108] ar come to Knyreston Place[109] & ther purpose to tary & abyde to such tyme as they thinke tyme convenient for to enter into your liflods[110] in this country, & toke distor;[111] & we have bene at dyverse places of your liflods & finds your tenants well disposed toward you, & sithen the most part of gentlemen in this country, & especyally the Eyres,[112] so that ye wold come yourselfe & be sene amongst your tenants & frynds, the which were to them a singler pleasure & comforth, & to yourselfe a great strength; & to bring with you not ouer the number of xx horse at the most, & such as may have your aduise & counsell to take derection, the which may be to the suerty of your lyflod & tenants; & if ye can gett Master Mydleton[113] & bryng him with you, or Richard Grene, or some other, & come to Hassop, for we haue deseuered us & some departed tham; & with the grace of Jesu, & ye come betwixt this & Tuesday, that all things shalbe to your harts comforth in tyme to come. But Sir, they haue bene here diuerse tymes doing for your wele & pleasure, & thinkes ye will or dar not put you in iopartie[114] for your owne. For & ye come they will put them in deuer to do any thing that may be to the well of your liflod & tenants; &, Sir, bryng with you money convenient for

106 Appended: this was for his service against the rebels that killed the earle of Northumberland at Thriske in the 4 yeare of H. the 7 for yt was the last rebvellion afore 7 H. 7 & 29th of May.

107 Robert Plumpton was Sir Robert's illegitimate half-brother.

108 Sir John Sotehill, husband of Elizabeth Plumpton, having died in 1494 the writers are in error. The legal estate was by now vested in Robert Bubwith and Richard Burgh.

109 Kinston Place, home of the Babingtons.

110 Property, land, rent, or income

111 The tenants of lands in contention were in an unenviable position.

112 Kirby, p. 312 of *The Plumpton Letters and Papers*, describes the Eyres as a knightly family between 1430 and 1509 with lands in the northern uplands of Derbyshire, who "made themselves useful to landowners like the Plumptons with estates in the county by their expertise in estate management."

113 The lawyer Thomas Middleton.

114 Jeopardy.

your expenses, for as yet [blank] here be now rent teyned. Now ouer to you at this tyme, who the holy Trenety haue you in his keping.

By your servant Robinit Plompton with other moe

Endorsed: To our right worshipfull master Sir Robart Plompton kt be this letter deliuered in hast

3.9 Critics of a Knight's Misbehavior: Petition of the King's Tenants at Banstead, Surrey [between 1413–1419], TNA SC 8 /92/4576, in *A Book of London English 1384–1425*, ed. C. W. Chambers and Marjorie Daunt (Oxford: Oxford University Press, 1993), pp. 224–7.

Whether commanded by the king to aid in maintenance of local order, or begged by family and servants to exercise personally lordship of tenants, knights and other members of the landed elite in late medieval England, not surprisingly, had trouble distinguishing self and family interest from their public duties. We know much more about how their peers and superiors understood the duties – and rights – of landed knights than about how their peasant tenants judged their performance as knights; but critics of Sir Richard Arundel, a knight rewarded by Henry IV with lands and offices in southern England, left an account of behavior which, in their judgement, unmistakably crossed the line between reasonable defense of seigneurial self-interest and unjust exploitation of a knight's authority and a landlord's rights. The petition from tenants on the manor of Banstead, now included among petitions to king and parliament in the National Archives, may, to be sure, exaggerate the force and threats of force directed against them; but it also provides an exceptionally vivid description of how peasant tenants may have perceived their submission to seigneurial authority, and seigneurial claims on their time and energy. Their appeal to custom should be read in the context of the two customaries included in this volume, 6.1 below.

These ben the Wronges Iniuries Damages Diseases Losses and Greuaunces, which that Sir Richard Arru[ndell and those officers of the kyng] that occupien for hym there han do to the kynges tenantes of Banestede, in the Counte of Surre, [which maner was graunted to him by] the worthi kyng Henri the fourthe, whiche god assoille, as hit is more pleyneli shewid and wreten [herin, and that will be foreuere undoing] of the kynges lordship there, And also of his tenantes, but if [hit] be the rathur holpe and remedied, and [justice done by the ordenances made] there vpon in olde tyme bi the kynges noble prog[e]nitours. First the forsaid Sir Richard and his Officers wrongisly chargen the forsaid tenantes with newe charges and [ordenances ageynst her olde customes], as it is shewid and to shewe bi hire olde Custumarie, of olde auncient tyme made bi the kynges of England, [and bi hem grauntid and confer]med, which that woll be vndoyng of the forsaid kynges lordship & eke of his tenantes there. And for this [cause mani of the worthiest te]nantz of the forsaid lordship haue left lond & tenement, and left & forsake the forsaid lordship, and other many mo [bene in purpos to avoide] the forsaid lordship for euere, but if hit be the rathur holpen.

Also John Colcok, Richard Colcok, John wythemere, John Clerk and other mo tenantes of the forsaid lordship, in especiele for that thei woll no[t gree hem & assen]te to newe ordenances and newe custumes late made ageyns her olde Custumarie, The Officers of the forsaid Sir Richard greteli th[retnen hem] that thei shult lese her landes; And thogh thei sowe hem, the forsaide officers wolle repe hem, and haue hem aftirward for euere [more to] vndoyng of the forsaide tenantes.

Also all the forsaid tenantes pleyneth hem of the forsaid Sir Richard, and of his Officers, in that the same Officers amercied the forsaid tenantes in ix marcs, For that thei wolde nat gree hem[115] to the newe custumes and vsages late made ageyns hir olde Custumarie; And of that somme aforsaide there was arerid xxvj s viij d of John White, tenant there, And that same John White, in the forsaid Sir Richard Arrundell In, was holde in prison in london tille he had founde surete to paie it hym.

Also the forsaide Sir Richard take Robert atte Mere, Petre atte Mere, and enprisoned hem and stokkid hem withinne the forsaid lordship, forto haue had hem his bonde men,[116] there that thei and alle tenantz of the same lordship aren fre, and euere haue be, and all hire auncestrie sithen tyme oute of mynde. And, for as moche that thei nolde nat assente to hym, he amercied hem excessiflich fro court to court to the somme of xi s. And for that same amercimentes he destreined hem bi here Bestes and catell, to vtre destruccion of hem, but if thei ben holpen.

Also the forsaid Sir Richard and his Officers claymed and toke oon Julian Lampit, that was fre tenant of the kynges there, to be his bondewomman, and helde hire in prisoune tille he had raunsommed her to an c s, whiche that had be fre tenant withinne the same lordship lx yere & more.

Also the forsaide Sir Richard and his officers, agayns the tenure of hire holdyng of the same manere of Banestede, makis hem Bedelles[117], and aftirward woll yeve hem none acquytance, but claymeth hem for his bonde men, and alwey fro tyme to tyme putteth hem to fyne & raunsomme, ageyns her olde auncien custumes and vsages of olde tyme made.

Also for these causes aforsaid, John Taillour, Richard Colcok and John Clerc, which that were most sufficeaunt and olde tenantes of the foresaide lordship, aren avoided and go oute of the forsaid lordship for euere more, and

115 Agree, or conform themselves.

116 Arundel tried to reduce them to the status of villeins.

117 A beadle was a minor judicial officer, capable of holding a court, and responsible for executing all attachments and other legal processes as the lord or steward of the lord's court may direct to him. Sir Richard made the tenants beadles, then charged them with withholding money for which their office made them accountable.

many mo bene in purpos to avoide & go oute of the forsaid lordship for euer-emore, to vndoyng of the forsaid lordship for euere, but if it be remedied.

Also the forsaid tenantes of Banstede aren destreyned by the kyngges Baillife from terme to terme for the rerages of the countes of the same Sir Richard, for dyuerse writtes that rennyth a-yens hym yn the Cheker for the same Maner of Banstede, Wawton, and Cherwode, yn the Coounte of Surre, whiche he hath for terme of lyf of the yeft of the kyng, yn recompensacion of 80 mark, accountyng for the surpluys yn the Chekyr, as it schewith by his patentes ther-of to hym y-grauntyd, In gret hyndryng and lettyng of theyre labour, and also in vexacion by diuerses tymes to the Marchalsie by cause that the distresse were nat redy atte comyng thedir of the Bailly; In gret destruction and anientisyng of hem, but it be holpyn and remedy don ther-to the sonner by your graciouse help.

3.10 Patronage and Betrayal: Joan Armburgh to John Horell of Essex 1429/30, in *The Armburgh Papers. The Brokholes Inheritance in Warwickshire, Hertfordshire and Essex c.1417–c.1453*, ed. by Christine Carpenter (Woodbridge: Boydell Press, 1998), pp. 120–3.

Loyalty was fundamental to the work of knights, whether the particular work was warfare on behalf of a lord or seeing justice done; but loyalty itself was, of course, a complex commitment, as the debate over livery and retaining illustrates. When did loyalty represent the truest, deepest ideals of the chivalric order, and when did it become a justification and source of abusive behavior, an excuse for ganging up on a rival or opponent, in law courts and elsewhere? A fascinating example of the ambiguities inherent in medieval ideals of loyalty is found in the words of a woman, Joan Armburgh, below, who gave vivid expression to the ideal, even as she invoked it in defense of her and her family's landed interests.[118] *Betrayal surely has not often been more powerfully castigated. Joan Armburgh's prose points to the importance of medieval bestiaries, whose imagery provides her a powerful weapon against a former dependant now siding with rivals for the family's property; more importantly, it underscores the vigor and initiative with which women of gentry and noble families asserted their rights and responsibilities for the well-being of their families and dependants – and their willingness to insist that dependants should be grateful for their dependence.*

---

118 Among her notes to this letter, Carpenter explains that the recipient, John Horell, had taken "a lease of the parsonage of Radwinter with Joan and Robert Armburgh in May 1422, when he was said to be of Great Sampford. From the letter, he was clearly intimately connected to Joan's family. He is probably the tax commissioner for Essex in 1463, although given the time-lag between this date and the probable date of this letter, the commissioner could be another member of the family, perhaps a son."

To John Horelle [in margin] Bare [sic] frende in suche maner wise as thu hast deseruyd I grete the, for as moche as yt is not vnknowen to the and oopynly knowen in all the centre that thi chef makyng hath be thorough the maner of Radewynter, first be my lady my modres day[119] and sithern in my tyme and notwithstondyng that thu, as a kukkowysbird devouryng the heysogge whan she hath bred hym vp and as an vnkynd bird that foulyth his owne nest,[120] hast labouryd fro that tyme in to this with myn aduersarie John Sumpter and with hem that haue weddyd his tweyne bastard doughters, noising hem all aboute the cuntre for mulirers and right heires, there as thu knowst wele the contrarie is soth, so fer forth that thu as the develes child, fadre of falshode, whos kynde[121] is alwey to do evil a yenst good, hast forsworn the diuerse tymes before chetours[122] and justices to yeue the cuntres[123] fals enformacion that shuld passe betwene vs in disherityng of me and of myn heires of the moyte of the modres enheritance in al that ever in the is, the which with the grace of God shal neuer ly in thi power nor in no javelys[124] that han weddid thoo fals bastardes. And beside this thu hast steryd myn aduersariis to do stripe and wage with yn my ground and to throwe donn myn hegges and my wodes and specially the tymbre that growith aboute in the gardyn, the whiche grevith me more than all the wronges that thei han do to me in to this tyme, and conseillest hem not to levyn so moche stondyng as peretrees nor appiltrees nor no maner trees that berith frut and hast a reioisyng in thyn hert to se the place at the vtmost devouryd and stroyd.[125] In so moche that whan thu sittiste in tauernys[126] among thi felowys thu hast a comyn byword in matter as a fals prophete, sayng that thu hopist to se the day to do an hare stirtyn vpon the herth stone[127] of of [sic] Radewynter halle, but I trust to God, or that maner that hath ben an habitation and a dwellyng place for many a worthi man of myn antiseters[128] from the conquest in to this tyme and long tyme before be so desolat as thu desirest, that thu shalt se be leue of myn husband a peire galweys[129] set vp with yn the same ffraunchise[130] for thi nekke, for thou tho currys,[131] the

119 Ellen Brokehole.

120 Heysogge is the hedge-sparrow, one of the three most common hosts for the cuckoo in England.

121 Nature.

122 Escheators, royal officers responsible for investigating the king's feudal rights.

123 Jurors convened to provide information to royal escheators or justices.

124 Worthless fellows.

125 Destroyed.

126 Taverns.

127 The image of the hare on the hearthstone as a symbol of devastation was a traditional one in medieval literature. It is used to striking effect, for example, by John Rous in his polemic against enclosures; see J. Rous, *Historia Regum Angliae*, ed. T. Hearne, Oxford, 1716, p. 130.

128 Ancestors.

129 Gallows.

130 A reference to the right of infangenthef, to hang a thief caught red-handed on one's lordship.

131 Currish, mean.

whiche be more able to dewelle vpon a bonde tenement as here kyn askyth, non vpon a lordship rial[132] the whiche shewyth wel be the destruccion that thei doon in the seid maner, levyn not a stykke stondyng vpon the ground, I thanke God I am strong y nogh to by tymbre for a peyre galwys to hange the vpon, and that thu hast wel deseruyd by the same tokne that thu robbest tweyn women of Sampford, the whiche is wel knowyn, of the whiche oon of hem thu settyst vpon a tre and that other thu laiest by a yenst here will in the porters hous with yn the maner of Radewynter, for she shuld discuuere[133] the. Wherfore I trust to God that he wol vouchesaf to yeve me pouer to serue ye as the egle seruyth his birdys whiche he fynt vnkynde and that wol smyte the damme with the bylle and contrarie to his owne kynde, for whan the egle hath kept vp his birdys til thei ben sumwhat myghty of hem self, he dressith here hedys evene ayenst the sunne whan yt shyneth most bright and suche as hath founde kynde to the damme and that loke werily in the sunne with oute eny twynklyng or blenchyng[134] of her ie[135] as here kynde askyth, he bredyth[136] hem vp til thei be myghty i nogh of hem self to fle[137] where hem lust.[138] And such as he hath foundyn vnkynd[139] to the damme and that mowe not lokyn a yenst the sunne with oute twynklng of here ye, as here kynd wold, he drawyth hem owt of his nest and drowith[140] hem down a yenst the ground and brekyth here nekkys. This egle in holy writ is lykned to Crist the whiche is fadre and modre to all cristyn peple. Hes birdys ar lyknyd to the peple here on erthe, the which ought to be alle his childryn, the sunne is lykned to rightwosnesse and trouthe and, lyke as the egle seruyth his vnkynde birdys in maner and forme as yt is before rehersid, ryght so the good lord shal serue the vnkynde childryn of this world that wol not loke in the sunne of rightwysnesse ne goon in the wey of his comaundementes but robbyn and revyn[141] and doo extortions and benym[142] men here goodes, here lyflodys and here lyves with fals forsweryng, he shal shortyn here dayes and drawe hem out of here nest that thei haue be brought vp yn, that is for to say out of this world and drowe hem in to the pytte of helle.[143] And therfore by leve of that good lord I takyn example at the egle and for as moche as thou lyk to the eglys birde

132 A contrast of bond or villain land with "real property," that is immoveable property, but in this case, implying also freely held land with lordship.

133 Discover.

134 Winking or blinking.

135 Eye.

136 Breeds.

137 Fly.

138 Like.

139 Unnatural.

140 Throw.

141 Plunder.

142 Deprive, despoil.

143 The image of an eagle and its young was a commonplace of medieval bestiaries.

that may not behold in the sunne of rightwysnesse, that is for to sayn hast made thi self blynd as thorough briberie and mede that thu hast takyn of myn aduersariis and woll not knowe the trouthe, but as an vnkynd birde hast defoulyd thi nest that thu were bred vp yn of a knave of a nought, that is for to seyn thu hast conceillyd myn aduersariis to streyn the maner[144] of Radewynter as with ynne rehersid, the whiche maner was cause of thi trist,[145] and as a fals kukhowys birde hast labouryd to devoure thi damme, that is to say my lady my modre and me, the whiche haue be modres of thi trist and thi bryngers vp. For a none after the deces of my modre thu stalyst awey he [sic] mevible[146] goodys fro Radewynter, that is to say nete and shepe and sweyn and hostilmentes[147] of houshold that shuld haue be sold be here executours and doon for here soule, and afterward thu haddyst the gouernance of Radewynter and Thykho[148] and haddyst as moche of my good as drew to the value of xl markes and feyndist falsly a general acquitance vnder my husbondes seel[149] and woldest neuer sesyn[150] from that tyme in to this with thi fals recordys, in hope to haue disheryt me of my lyflode. And therfore I sure[151] the my trouthe, yt shal not be longe, though yt shuld cost me xl li,[152] but that I shal gete me a juge to syttyn vnder commyssion as ney[153] the ffraunchise of Radewynter as I may and, yf lawe wol serue, with the grace of God thu shalt be pullyd out of that nest that thu hast gotyn yn thi trist and labouryd so sore to stroy yt and made to brekyn thi nekke on a peire of galwys. I can no more at this tyme but I pray God send the that thu hast deseruyd, that is to say a rope and a ladder.

3.11 Ideals of Loyalty and Dangers from Confederacies: Rex v. John Berwald *et al*, TNA KB 27/528, 1393, m.37d (crown), in *Select Cases in the Court of King's Bench*, Vol. 7: Richard II, Henry IV, and Henry V, ed. G. O. Sayles, Selden Society Publications 88 (London, 1971), pp. 83–5 [Latin; the rhyme appeared in the record in Middle English, here re-phrased in modern English].

Aristocrats throughout the period struggled with the ambiguities of loyalty; but they probably did not recognize as examples of the loyalty they celebrated the ties among

144 Manor.

145 Position, post.

146 Moveable.

147 Utensils, implements.

148 Thicko in Ashdon, Essex.

149 Seal.

150 Cease.

151 Assure.

152 Pounds.

153 Near.

their social inferiors, ties they could easily condemn as "confederacies" justifying the full force of the law. The confederacy in Yorkshire blamed on John Berwald and others, prosecuted before the Court of King's Bench in 1393, illustrates the difficulties faced by both crown and aristocracy, not only in resolving ambiguities within their own ranks over loyalty, but in maintaining a monopoly over the ideal of loyalty. The rhyme which constituted the principal evidence against these Yorkshiremen invokes neighborly cooperation to justify their conduct – conduct that for the king represented interference with one of his most important local officers, the escheator, responsible for conducting inquests on the holdings of the king's own tenants at the death of an occupant. As the "rebels" in this case point out, such a confederacy could indeed be harmful, as they point a critical finger at friars willing to "cover" for each other; but clearly, they are proud of their own willingness to provide mutual support against any challenges, however great.

Yorkshire

Again, they present that John Berwald the younger of Cottingham, Thomas Rawlinson of Cottingham, Edmund Howden of the same, John Slater of the same, John Tyndale, formerly the servant of Robert Bulmer of the same, Andrew Crauncewick of the same, Robert Green of Cottingham, farrier, William Barker of Hessle, William Marshall of Cottingham, Stephen Thomson of the same, Richard Johnson of the same, John Berwald the elder of the same, John Watson of Dunswell, William Brotelby of the same, William Steven the elder of the same, William Mageson of Newland, John Webster of the same, John Ricall of the same, Patrick Gesede of the same, Thomas Rayner of the same, John of Skidby, flesher, of the same, Thomas son of Richard of Holme, Richard Johnson of Cottingham, Thomas Cartwright of the same, John Navendyke, flesher, of the same, Robert son of Steven Malynson of the same, Simon son of Steven Malynson of the same, John Rayner the younger of Newland, Thomas King of Hullbank, John King son of the said Thomas, and Robert Stevenson of Hullbank, together with other malefactors of their covin to the number of eighty, whose names they do not know, were dressed for the last six years in one livery of a single company by corrupt allegiance and confederacy, each of them in maintaining the other in all plaints, true or false, against whosoever should wish to complain against them or any one of them, in breach of the terms of the statutes,[154] etc. And they were dressed and assembled in such aforesaid livery of a single company in various places in the county of York, namely, at Beverley and Benningholme, on Saturday after the Feast of the Nativity of St John the Baptist in the tenth year of the reign of king Richard, second after the Conquest.[155] And they assaulted William, a

154 13 Richard II, stat. 3, SR II. 74–5.

155 30 June 1386.

former servant of John of Garton, at Beverley with force and arms, namely, with swords etc., and there they beat, wounded and ill-treated him so that his life was despaired of, in breach of the king's peace. And they say that no sheriff of the county of York, escheator or any other royal minister of whatsoever rank he is can at any time do anything that it is his duty to do within the domain of Cottingham, and that Robert Bulmer of Buttercrambe and William, his son, are the chief maintainers and leaders of all the aforesaid malefactors, in breach of the terms of the statute promulgated thereon and in breach of the peace etc.

And they say that the aforesaid John Berwald the younger of Cottingham and the others made a certain rhyme in English and had the said rhyme publicly recited at Beverley on Sunday before the Feast of St James the Apostle[156] and at Hull on the Sunday immediately following[157] and at various other places within the county of York on various occasions in the sixteenth year of the reign of king Richard, second after the Conquest. And the rhyme follows in these words:

In the country we heard that wicked men would be coming into our district to see that everything is carried out.
It is true as regards the friars and many more orders, whether they are sleeping or awake,
that each of them will cover up for the other and support him as his brother, both in wrong and right.
And we too will maintain our neighbours through thick and thin with all our might.
Every man may come and go, just as he likes, among us, I tell you for sure.
But we will suffer no mocking, neither of Tom, Dick or Harry] no matter who he be.
For we would be unnatural if we suffered any wicked mockery from great or small [men].
But we would be paid back double if we should consent and fully agree to tolerate our chastisement.
And on this purpose yet we stand: that if a man wrongs us in one quarter, where-ever it be,
He might, as surely as I live and breathe, have done it against us all.
Therefore the sheriff was told not to fail in making them come to answer etc.

And now, that is to say, on Wednesday after the Feast of the Ascension of the Lord in this same term[158] [the aforesaid defendants] came before the king at York. And they are asked separately how they wish to clear themselves of the

156 21 July 1392.
157 28 July 1392.
158 21 May 1393.

aforegoing charges against them. They say separately that the present king of his special grace has pardoned them the suit of his peace, which pertains to him for the aforesaid wrongdoings and misprisions, by his letters patent, which they put forward here in court.

Pardon, dated 19 March 1393 at Westminster, to Robert Bulmer of Buttercrambe, one of the tenants of the earl of Kent's manor of Cottingham in Yorkshire, for wrongdoings: inter alia for interfering with William Holme, the late escheator in Yorkshire, when performing his duties.

Similar pardons, dated the same day, to William Barker of Hessle and William son of Robert Bulmer of Buttercrambe.

3.12 Founding Families, Abducting Women: Kebell v. Vernon, 1502, TNA STAC 2/10/71, in *Select Cases Before the King's Council in the Star Chamber 1477–1509*, ed. I. S. Leadam, Selden Society Publications 16 (London, 1908), pp. 130–7.

The work of the aristocracy included warfare on the one hand, governance on the other. But both were closely tied to preservation of their families, and neither warfare nor governance in late medieval England can be sharply distinguished as "public" responsibilities from "private" interests, or "domestic" interests. Nor could violence be excluded from the conduct of domestic affairs, given the critical importance of achieving and preserving the interests of an aristocrat's family. Retaining and livery provoked significant legislative responses during the late Middle Ages; but also on the political agenda was the "abduction of women," a problem also arising from the struggles by landed aristocrats to preserve the basis of their power, in land and control of tenants, through marriage. To conclude this chapter on the aristocracy of the late Middle Ages with an account of a woman's forcible abduction may, we admit, exaggerate the frequency with which domestic and intimate relations were characterized by violence against women; but it leaves unmistakably clear that force and violence on the part of a nominally "warrior" elite, even in the construction of marriages, not only occurred, but could be imagined as one way to found a family. Does this mean that women were treated simply as objects? If so, it also suggests that they were extremely valuable objects – and objects capable of using the legal system itself to their advantage.

Sir Henry Vernon's many royal offices – and the several occasions on which he was accused of using unlawful force to achieve his ends – are summarized by Leadam in his notes to this case; his notes also provide extensive information about Thomas Kebell, an important serjeant at law in the reign of Henry VII, whose widow, Margaret, was the object of William Vernon's alleged abduction.[159]

159 For an illuminating discussion of this case in an essay devoted to the origins and significance of the Statute of 3 Henry VII, c.2, Agaynst taking awaye of Women, see E. W. Ives, "'Against the taking away of women': the inception and operation of the Abduction Act of 1487," in Eric William Ives et al., eds, *Wealth and Power in Tudor England: Essays Presented to S. T. Bindoff* (1978),

To prove Wyllyam Vernon brodur to sir Henry Vernon knyght gylty off felous[160] takyng & Rauishement of margaret Kebell Wedow & off the felous reseyuyng by the seyd Wyllyam Vernon off Roger Vernon. & dyuers odur partiez previe to the rauishement.

First, the seyd margaret seyth that she was broght by Roger Vernon[161] & dyuers odor[162] Contrarie to her mynd & good wyll from blore in the Countee off derby[163] to Henry columbell ys[164] place in the same Countee[165] & on Candylmas day last past [2 February 1502] sche was broght by the seyd Roger & dyuers odor to a manor place off sir Henry Vernon callyd Sheyll in the Countee off leycester[166] where in duellyth on Wyllyam Vernon brodur to the seyd sir Henry & the seyd Wyllyam Vernon with owt the dore resceyuyd the seyd Roger Vernon margaret Kebell & odor dyuers partiez preve[167] to the felous takyng a wey off the seyd margaret & Wyllyam Vernon & Roger toke the seyd margaret by the armez & broght her to a chamber where in was a feyr fyre redy made a fore the Cummyng off the seyd margarett & by cause the fyre brend[168] not clere the seyd wyllyam Vernon was very angry.

Item the seyd margaret seyth that when the seyd Roger Vernon & Wyllyam had broght the seyd margaret to her chamber they departyd & walkyd down in gret Counsell. Whydur[169] they walkyd the seyd margaret can not tell and immediatly aftur ther departyng Came the Wyff off the seyd Wyllyam Vernon to the seyd margaret & askyd off the seyd margaret what thyng shuld cause the seyd margaret to be so sad & hevy and furtheremore sche askyd off the seyd Margaret whedur[170] Roger Vernon had takyn her Contrarie to her mynd & good wyll & the seyd margaret seyth that sche seyd that Roger Vernon had takyn the seyd margaret contrarie to here mynd & wyll & that he schuld repent yff euer the seyd margaret Cam to her libertee furthermore the seyd margaret seyth that the Wyff off Wyllyam Vernon desyryd the seyd

21–45; but see an alternative view of royal policy regarding women's abduction and forcible marriage, as well as documents from another case of alleged abduction, in an essay by Alan Cameron, "Complaint and Reform in Henry VII's Reign: the Origins of the Statute of 3 Henry VII, c.2," *Historical Research* Vol. 51, No. 123 (May 1978) pp. 83–9.

160 Felonious.

161 A son of Sir Henry Vernon.

162 Various others.

163 Now in N.E. Staffordshire, less than a mile from the borders of Derbyshire; according to Leadam, the manor appears to have been held by the family of Bassett or Basset.

164 His.

165 Lord of the manor of Darley, about five miles S.E. of Bakewell, Derbyshire, and about 12 miles N.N.E. of Blore.

166 Now Seale. The Vernons, according to Leadam, had held land in the manor of Over Seale since the time of John, and acquired that manor in 1427.

167 Privy.

168 Burnt.

169 Wither.

170 Whether.

margaret to haue pite and Compassion on the seyd Roger & not to vndo hym for euer.

Item the seyd margaret seyth that the Wyff of Wyllyam Vernon departyd from the seyd margaret & went to the seyd Roger Vernon & Wyllyam & seyd to them that hyt was pitee that the seyd Roger Vernon levyd by cause that the seyd Roger toke a wey any good Gentylwoman as the seyd margaret ys contrarie to her mynd & wyll.

Item the seyd margaret seyth that the Wyff off Wyllyam Vernon Came to her & schewyd what sche had seyd to Roger Vernon & Wyllyam her husbond and inmediatly aftur Cam the seyd Roger Vernon in to the chamber to the seyd margaret & seyd Alas mastres Wyl hyt be no bettur yit I mervell gretly that ye wyll schew yowr mynd to suche a strong strumpett & a hore as sche ys for sche Can kepe no Councell & al that ye doo ys to vndoo me for euer & with that the seyd margarett seyth that the seyd Roger wept very fast and the seyd margaret seyth that sche seyd sche wold do so en eny place where so euer sche Came & wold not let for no man.

Item the seyd margaret seyth that on the moroo next aftur Candylmas dey last past[171] yerly[172] in the mornyng the seyd Roger Vernon & Wyllyam causyd a preest to syng masse in the chamber a fore the seyd margaret & the seyd Roger Vernon and Wyllyam Came in to the chamber where as the seyd margaret was knelyng & wept & made gret lamentation & sorow & that the seyd Roger Vernon & Wyllyam see & hard[173] the wepyng and lamentacion made & there they hard masse & when masse was endyd the seyd Roger Vernon & Wyllyam went to gedur to a wyndow & there they talkyd to gedur the space off an owr[174] in gret Concell what hyt was the seyd margaret Can not tell but as sche supposyth hyt was for her takyng a wey for inmediatly the seyd Roger Vernon and Wyllyam send vppe to london on Jhon Alsoppe to dyuers off the fryndys off the seyd Roger Vernon for to labur for hym in the mater & the seyd margaret seyth at that tyme the seyd Wyllyam Vernon was redy to ryde & the seyd Roger Vernon shewyd to the seyd margaret that the seyd Wyllyam Vernon schuld goo to Haddon to hys[175] fadur & then the sayd Roger Vernon & Wyllyam toke the seyd margaret by the armez & broght her to her hors the whyche be causes sufficient to prove the seyd Wyllyam gylty off the premissez. And the seyd margaret besekyth yowr good lordsehyppes that the seyd Wyllyam may be put to Answere to the premissez & that the seyd sir Henry Vernon bryng in the seyd Wyllyam Vernon for he ys continualy with the seyd sir Henry Vernon and he aydyth Confortyth & resceuyth the seyd Wyllyam the whych ys felonye in hyt selff.

171 I.e., 3 February, Festival of St Blasius.

172 Early.

173 Heard.

174 Hour.

175 I.e., Roger's father.

Indorsed. This bill my lord Chaunceller deliuered to me W. Stodham in the sterre chambre vpon Wednysday the xvij'h day of Juyn

Termino Trinitatis Anne regni regis xvij° [1502]
Margareta Keble vidua contra Henricum Vernon & alias.

Further Reading

Britnell, R. H. and A. J. Pollard, eds, *The McFarlane Legacy* (Stroud: Sutton, 1995).

Carpenter, Christine, *Locality and Polity: A Study of Warwickshire Landed Society, c.1401–1499* (Cambridge: Cambridge University Press, 1992).

Coss, P. C., *The Knight in Medieval England 1000–1400* (Stroud: Sutton, 1993).

Davies, R. R., *Lords and Lordship in the British Isles in the Late Middle Ages*, ed. Brendan Smith (Oxford: Oxford University Press, 2009).

Given-Wilson, Christopher, *The English Nobility in the Late Middle Ages: The Fourteenth-Century Political Community* (London: Routledge, 1996).

Kaeuper, Richard W., *Chivalry and Violence in Medieval Europe* (Oxford: Oxford University Press, 1999).

Keen, Maurice, *Chivalry* (New Haven, CT, and London: Yale University Press, 1985).

Given-Wilson, Christopher, *The English Nobility in the Late Middle Ages* (London: Routledge, 1987).

Mertes, K., *The English Noble Household 1250–1600: Good Governance and Politic Rule* (Oxford: Basil Blackwell, 1988).

Meyerson, Mark D., Daniel Thiery, and Oren Falk, eds, *"A Great Effusion of Blood"? Interpreting Medieval Violence* (Toronto: University of Toronto Press, 2004).

Moreton, C. E., *The Townshends and their World: Gentry, Law, and Land in Norfolk c.1450–1551* (Oxford: Oxford University Press, 1992).

Payling, S. J., *Political Society in Lancastrian England: The Greater Gentry of Nottinghamshire* (Oxford: Oxford University Press, 1991).

Pryce, Huw and Watts, John Lovett, eds, *Power and Identity in the Middle Ages: Essays in Memory of Rees Davies* (Oxford: Oxford University Press, 2007).

Rawcliffe, C., *The Staffords, Earls of Stafford and Dukes of Buckingham 1394–1521* (Cambridge: Cambridge University Press, 1978).

Richmond, Colin, *The Paston Family in the Fifteenth Century: The First Phase* (Cambridge: Cambridge University Press, 1990).

Richmond, Colin, *The Paston Family in the Fifteenth Century: Fastolf's Will* (Cambridge: Cambridge University Press, 1996).

Richmond, Colin, *The Paston Family in the Fifteenth Century: Endings* (Manchester: Manchester University Press, 2000).

Woolgar, C., *The Great Household in Late Medieval England* (New Haven, CT: Yale University Press, 1999).

4
Scientia: Knowledge, Practical, Theoretical, and Historical

Medieval culture inherited and actively built on the learning of the classical past and of Arabic science. In many respects the later European Middle Ages was a time of technological development and scientific inquiry, a time that fostered the development of sophisticated theories of vision, of architecture and of mechanical technology that included improved design of water wheels, the invention of the escapement mechanism central to the mechanical clock, and optical technology that explored the properties of lenses and prisms. During the later fourteenth century a group of mathematicians at Merton College, Oxford, known as the "Oxford Calculators," used mathematics and logics to solve philosophical problems in ways that anticipate modern formulae for kinematics and exponential growth.[1]

Medieval people constructed an elaborate network of theories to account for natural phenomena in the heavens, on earth, and in the human body. For modern readers these theories may at best look like a series of familiar concepts viewed through a distorting lens, at worst, like a series of imaginative speculations. But different as medieval knowledge systems were from ours, they developed out of two rational principles: authority, and its lesser partner, observation. Observed experience, what would become the basis for the scientific method, coexisted with respect for authority at every turn. Exceptional awareness of the night sky, the movement of planets and stars marked the highly sophisticated astronomy of the period. But this observation served inherited and powerful theories of astrology in which astral and planetary influence were thought to shape individual lives and precipitate natural events. A basic system of observing symptoms underlay knowledge of the human body, particularly in illness; we have documents that describe plague symptoms and signs of imminent death in great detail. But this proto-scientific approach was joined to authoritative humoral explanations of disease that understood illness as imbalance among the four major humors of the human body. Medieval theories of optics developed a

1 Thomas Bradwardine, William Heytesbury, Richard Swineshead and John Dumbleton. On this group and their connection to Walter Burley see Edith Dudley Sylla, *The Oxford Calculators and the Mathematics of Motion, 1320–1350: Physics and Measurement by Latitudes* (New York: Garland, 1991).

highly-sophisticated geometry of vision based on experimentation[2] but relied on essentially mechanical classical models of human psychology that underwent continual refinement in an attempt to to account for what we know today as neurological and chemical processes. Nowhere was the influence of received authority more clearly preferred to observation than in theories of human gender and sexuality. Maleness was accepted as the natural human norm. Women, according to Aristotelian tradition, were lesser men whose bodies were not able to achieve male perfection either physically or mentally; female sex organs were regarded as incompletely expressed versions of male genitalia. In matters of conception women's wombs were thought to provide the site in which the fully complete embryo, introduced by male semen, grew to birth.

In addition to contributing to what we might term "the roots" of "modern science," medieval culture preserved and transmitted a vast body of knowledge about the natural world and about humans' place in that world. The practical "common knowledge" of the period – knowledge of husbandry, estate management, hunting – constituted a body of knowledge that enabled people to run well-functioning households, complex organizations in which a variety of people served in a variety of modes for mutual benefit. The bureaucratic sophistication of medieval life on all levels is an aspect of the culture that rarely appears in contemporary studies, although the skills required to administer complex webs of production, consumption and exchange were not negligible.[3] Similarly, knowledge of how to use land and the crops and livestock nourished on that land in prudent and profitable ways was crucial to supporting the wider network of labor and exchange as well as the smooth running of the household.

The documents below are selected to represent late medieval thinking about a variety of subjects that appear in the literature of the period: households, lordship, astrology, alchemy, magic, vision and psychology, history, "natural history," human sexuality. The knowledge represented in this chapter is a fluid body of thinking, tradition, and experimentation that defies modern categories: alchemy morphs into medicine, vision into psychology, and household arrangements into "natural" hierarchies. Our sources are arranged in part in the manner of medieval encyclopedias, beginning with the heavens and time, moving on to astrology, alchemy, medicine, and focusing on the human body in its relation to the created world, its senses, capacities. We move then to the systems of knowledge that late medieval English people relied on and generated

2 See David C. Lindberg, *Theories of Vision from Al-kindi to Kepler* (Chicago: University of Chicago Press, 1976) and *John Pecham and the Science of Optics: Perspectiva Communis* (Madison, WI: University of Wisconsin Press, 1970).

3 T. F. Tout's magisterial six-volume work *Chapters in the Administrative History of Mediaeval England; the Wardrobe, the Chamber and the Small Seals* (London, New York: Longmans, Green & Co., 1920–33) is an early standard example of such research.

– received wisdom about household and estate management, concluding with some examples of how late medieval English people thought about and received information about the historical past.

Time, the Heavens and the Seasons

4.1 Concerning the Solar Year: Translated from *On the Properties of Things*: John Trevisa's Translation of *De Proprietatibus Rerum*, 3 vols (Oxford: Clarendon Press, 1975), Vol. I, pp. 519–24 (Translation from Middle English by the editors).

The passages below come from a medieval encyclopedia of knowledge about the created world. Arranged hierarchically to represent a chain of being, the work begins with the properties of God, angels, and humans, and moves down an imaginary ladder of natural hierarchy, dealing at last with a series of definitions and explanations of accidents – color, taste, and putrefaction, the most ephemeral and unstable aspects of matter. It concludes with discussions of numbers, arithmetical computations, measure, and weight. Between beginning and end, the work considers the heavens, the earth, plants, animals, stones, and gems. Discussions and definitions rely heavily on cited authority and often read as though they are an accumulation of juxtaposed facts interspersed with doubtful etymologies. Yet, as the first excerpt below shows, a good deal of precise knowledge was enclosed within what seems at first to be a chaotic system of organization. Here are two passages that indicates the precision with which the culture reckoned the time in a solar year and characterized the seasons. Both passages cite etymological and historical precedents to authorize their information. (Translated from the original Middle English by the authors.)

Concerning the Solar Year, Book 9, Chapter 3

As Isidore[4] says, a year is the full course and passing and winding about of the sun, that returns to his own place in three hundred three score days and five and a quadrant, that is six hours. And a year is called *annus, and* has that name because it comes about as the months come about therin, and therefore a year has the name *annus* of *an*, that is "aboute", as it were a circle that comes again into itself and is renewed. Therefore among the Egyptians before letters were discovered the year was betokened by a dragon painted biting its own tail and coming again into itself, as Isidore says.

4 Isidore of Seville, 560–636, ecclesiast and encyclopedist, devoted much of his energies to preserving ancient classical knowledge.

Concerning Spring Time, from Book 9, Chapter 5

This section provides a glimpse into the many reasons why spring time is a prominent and recurrent season in medieval literature. The stress on the temperate nature of the season reflects Aristotelian ideals of the mean and reflects the importance of balance, even in a season of burgeoning life:

> And spring time is between hot and cold most temperate, between winter and summer mean in quality and shares with either in quality, for then blood begins to multiply in bodies of beasts, and humors that were bound and made thick in winter begin to move and to be dissolved by heat in spring time. Also spring time is in [its] qualities temperate and most healthful time and least grievous and sickly as Constantyn says and Galen also. For in these two qualities nature has pleasure, for heat is the cause effective of nourishing and increasing, and moisture is the cause material. And therefore in spring time blood is most created that is most nedeful to nourishing of body. If spring time exceeds its own nature [is intemperate], that breeds many sicknesses and evils.
>
> * * *
>
> Also, spring time opens the earth that is long closed and bound with cold and brings forth . . . roots and herbs that were hidden in the earth, and hides the earth and renews it with flowers and herbs and excites birds and fowls to chittering and love, and clothes and hides al the outer part of the earth with a wonderful fairness. Therefore spring time is called *ver*, and has that name of *viror* or of *vigor*, that is to mean greenness or of vertu, for then herbs and trees begin to spring and to wax green with blossoms and sprigs. Spring time is the time of gladness and of love, for in spring time everything seems glad, for the earth waxes green, trees blossom and spread, meadows bring forth flowers, heaven shines, the sea rests and is quiet, fowls sing and make their nests, and all things that seem dead in winter and fallow, are renewed in spring time. Therefore Macrobius calls the clearness of the air of spring tyme "Iupiteris laughynge'.

4.2 *A Zodiacal Lunary for Medical Professionals*, Irma Taavitsainen, in *Popular and Practical Science of Medieval England*, ed. Lister M. Matheson (East Lansing: Colleagues Press, 1994), pp. 283–300. From BL MS Egerton 2572, the Guild-Book of the Barber Surgeons of York (293–7).

In her introduction to this late-fifteenth-century text Irma Taavitsainen observes, "Zodiacal lunaries are explicitly based on the contemporary science. The philosophical basis lies in the belief in the correspondence between the macrocosm of the universe and the microcosm of man. The states of the heavens were thought to be projected down to the earth where they influenced everything" (p. 289).

The zodiac is a narrow band in the sky in which the movements of the major planets, the sun, and moon take place; it is divided into 12 sections that are named for major constellations (see below). As the moon moves across the sky during the course of a year, it occupies various sites whose aspects are more or less favorable for a wide but defined variety of activities that include personal commitments, trade, dealings with lords, contracts, land, benefices, medicine, agriculture, and imprisonment. The fifteenth-century zodiacal lunary that follows appears in the Guild Book of the Barber-Surgeons of York *advises when it is and is not appropriate to consult with popes and monarchs, a fact which suggests the universal utility of such documents, rather than specific application.*[5] *The recurrent observations that being imprisoned is a "perilous" activity in each sign, and the advice in each sign that it is best not to begin something that one wants soon done, raise the question of how seriously this text might have been taken. The editor discusses the possibility that it may have been designed to be a humorous version of the class of advice literature it represents.*[6] *Even if that is the case, however, it serves a useful double purpose in this text, indicating the kind of astrological advice that was routinely available, and the degree of skepticism that attended the reception of such advice.*

When the Mone is in **Aries**,[7] yt ys gude to speke wythe grete lordis of myghty men, as kynges, erlis, barons, knyghtes, popis, princes, and such other gret lordis and noble men and myghty, and for to gange[8] *to* fyght in batell aganys thy foys,[9] and for to take vyages[10] into the estward, for this is an esterne signe and in the est he standis.

Also, yt ys gude for to make marchandysse[11] and to deyll wyth golde, and to wyrke all maner of werkes that ys wroght wyth ffyer, for this [ys J a signe that mekyll[12] hath of the ffyer, and for to do all maner of werkes that thowe walde haue hastely done, for this is a hasty signe.[13]

Bot yt ys yll and perilus to do oght tyll[14] a manys hede,[15] as to wesche or to keme[16] yt or to schaue, or to do ony medicyne therto, or arise ony blode[17]

5 For a critique of the generic nature of such guides, see Oresme, 4.3 below.

6 Taavitsainen concludes her introduction by considering the question of just how seriously a lunary such as this was taken; see p. 292.

7 Aries is the first sign or house of the zodiac, represented by a ram.

8 Go; a Northern dialect in which "a" occurs where modern spelling uses "o".

9 Foes.

10 Voyages.

11 Have to do with trade.

12 Has much to do with.

13 Those that you would do quickly, for this is a sign that supports haste.

14 Anything to.

15 Head.

16 Wash or comb.

17 Cause blood to flow.

that be any maner of wyse, or to blede at the nesse,[18] or for to be lettyne outte of prisone, and for to warech[19] of sekenese, and for to receue ony purgacione.[20] And so it ys in all maner of suche that chewen codes,[21] as ys ilke selfe tupe[22] and the bule and the Iyone and the gotte and the latter part of the Archeys, for he ys afixyde.[23]

Whene the Mone ys in the **Bull (Taurus)**, yt ys gude to make feleschype and to trete of connauntes[24] and pese betwene enmys, and for to founde houses, and to lowge[25] and to bylde, and to entir into possessions and castelles, and for to receue lordschyppes of strynght, and for to teyll[26] the erthe and wynyerdes[27] and vynes, and for to sawe for to plante, and for to wede wives, and for to do all maner of thyngys that shulde last longe.

Bot ytt ys yll and perilus to begyne any longe viage, or any batell or any plee,[28] and to be pute into a prisone, and for to fall in sekenese, and to come before any lorde or domysmane[29] to sve[30] for any grace. And for to do ony medicyne in the neke or in the throte, or to be hurte in any of thys places, or for to do ony thynge that thowe walde haue sone done.[31]

When the Mone ys in **Gemine**, yt ys gude to begynne vyage, and to speke wyth myghty men and wyth ffaders and moders and wyth other kynysmen and fryndys, and wyth all maner of persones, and for to trouthplyghte[32] women bot not to wede thame, and for to make felischype and newe counaundes[33] and merchandisse.

Bot yt ys yll and perilus to be lattyne blade[34] on the armys that the Gemine made, ffor th[o]ugh a mane be stekyne neuer so oft on the armes, he ne shall not blede bot the arme shall swell hugely and fall in gret perell or dye therof, or ellis be manyde.[35] For a mans blade[36] then ys so serfetus[37] and so thike

18 Nose.
19 Cure.
20 Purgatives; purgation.
21 Cuds.
22 Ram.
23 Associated with stability or permanence.
24 Covenants.
25 Dwell.
26 Till.
27 Vineyards.
28 Plea, judicial proceeding.
29 Judge.
30 Sue, plead.
31 Anything you would like to have quickly done.
32 Become engaged to.
33 Covenants.
34 To be bled, literally to be let blood.
35 Maimed.
36 Blood.
37 In such surfeit.

thore[38] kynde of that signe and the Mone that er be the watir that the blade may not of the vayne.[39]

And also yt ys yll to gange or to be delyueryd out of prisone, and to entre into religione, and for to warysse[40] of sekenes, and for to do any thynge that long shulde laste.

Whene the Mone ys in the **Crabe,**[41] yt ys gude to travell be watters, as on the see and other viage, and for to do any thynge [that J be watters or on watters er wroght. And yt ys gude to reccue[42] purgacions and to make marchandysse and to entermette or chaunge wyth mony and syluer,[43] and to do all maner of thynge that thowe walde haue sone done.

Bot yt ys yll and perilus for to founde houses, and entir into newe possessiones and castelles, and to make any contraccione[44] of matrimone, and to entre into religione, and to wende out of prisone, and for to wariche of sekenes, and for to do ony thynge that lange shulde last.

Whene the Mone ys in the **Lione,**[45] yt ys gude to speke wyth kyngys and wyth nobyll men, and to wyrke wyth golde and to change yt, and to make marchandysse, and to make all maner of werkes that ys mayde wyth fier, and to take lordschype of thynge, and for to by horse and for to by catell.

Bot yt ys yll and perilus for to clethe[46] a mane in newe clothes in that tyme, for he myght lyghtly be stykede[47] or drownede, brent, or hangyd at that tyme.

Also, yt ys yll to begyne batell or plee, or to begyne a longe vyage, and for to be put in prisone, and for to fall in sekenes. . . .

[*here follows a discussion of the Canyclere Days, or Dog days of July and August.*]

Whene the Mone ys in the **Mayden,**[48] yt ys gude to tyll the erthe, and to sawe[49] and to plante and to sette trees and vynes, and to begyne schort vyage bot noght lange vyage, and yt ys gude to by bestes that er not to ryde,[50] os kowe and other recher[51] or schepe, bot nother horse, ne mayre, ne mole,[52] ne

38 Through, on account of.
39 The blood will not flow out of the vein.
40 Heal, cure.
41 Cancer.
42 Receive.
43 Become involved with and to change money and silver.
44 Contract.
45 Lion, Leo.
46 Clothe.
47 Carelessly, accidentally stabbed.
48 Virgo.
49 Sow.
50 Ridden or driven far.
51 Horned animal, or cud-chewing animal; *os* or *as*.
52 Mule.

asse, ne suche as men ridis one. And yt ys gude to make connaundes and marchandisse.[53]

Bot it ys yll to be put in prisone, and to wax seke, and to wede madens,[54] for thane thay shulde be barayne[55] or shall haue bot fewe chy[l]dir.[56]

Whene the Mone ys in **Libra**, yt ys gude to make marchandisse, and to delue and to teyll[57] the erthe, and to do all maner of thynge that thow wolde haue sone done.

Bot it ys yll and perilus to begyne a longe iornay,[58] and to contrary matrimone, and to do ony thynge that longe shulde last, and to warysse of sekenese and to entir into religione.

Whene the Mone ys in the **Scorpione**,[59] yt is best to make purgacione and to by.

Bot yt ys full yll then to begyne other plee or batell or to do ony thynge that thowe wolde haue done.

Whene the Mone ys in **Sagittarius**, yt ys gude to begyne iornays towarde the est, and to take medicyne to saue man in his gret nede. Also, yt ys gude to make marchandisse and to chaunge, and to make all thynge that er mayde wyth fyre, and to entir into religione and benyfesse[60] of holy kyrke, and to go in pilgramage, and sende furthe letters and messagers into fere countres.

Bot yt ys yll and perilus to clyme vpwarde, os into hillys, by ladris,[61] or on trees, or on ony thynge ellis that vpwarde is for brekynge of his lymes. Also, yt ys perilus to do ony medicynes tyll[62] man this tyme, or for to do ony thynge that fallithe to wattir.[63]

Whene the Mone ys in **Capricornus**, yt ys gude to teyll the erthe, and to sawe, and to sette, to plante trees and vynes, and to make all maner of thynges that er mayde wythe fyer, and to make marchandise, and to speke with myghty men and all maner of domysmen,[64] and for to entre into lordschype and into serues[65] of lordis.

Bot yt ys yll and perilus to make ony purgacione, and to do ony thynge that ys wroght wyth fyer.[66]

---

53 Contracts and trade.
54 Maidens.
55 Barren.
56 Children.
57 Delve, dig in; till.
58 Journey.
59 Scorpio.
60 Benefices; interestingly this direction pertains particularly to clergy.
61 Ladders.
62 To.
63 Has to do with water.
64 Judges.
65 Service.
66 A seeming contradiction to the advice in the preceding paragraph.

Whene the Mone ys in the **Watirwarde**, that ys callyde **Aquarius**, yt ys gude to wake on the watters[67] and to deyll[68] wyth them, and to speke wyth frendis and to aske them of helpe and of counsell, and for to wede [f. 61] wyues,[69] and to enture into religione, and for to founde houses, and for to by aritages,[70] and for to enture into lordschyppes and newe possessions and gret lordys seruys.

Bot yt ys yll and perilus for to begyne longe iornay and batelle and plees, for thay er not likely to provale.[71]

Whene the Mone ys in **Pissis**,[72] yt ys gude to receue purgaciones of sekenes and yll humores wythin a man. Also, yt ys gude to enture into a couente,[73] dignites and prebendes of holy kyrke newly gettyne,[74] and to by horses, and to trauell on the see, and to make matrimone

Thes er the twelue of the firmament that makes and fourmes a chylde in his m[o]dir wombe

The fyrst signe, that ys, the Aries, makes the chyldes heede. And Taurus makes the neke and the throte. Gemine makes the armes, the handes, and schulders. Cancer makes the brest and the herte. Leo makes the stomake. Virgo makes the womebe to the navyll. Libra makes fro the navyll to the granynges.[75] Scorpio makes the pyntill[76] and the stones wythe the codes.[77] Sagittarius makes the thees.[78] Capricornus makes the knees and the hames.[79] Aquarius makes the legges. Pissis[80] makes the fette.[81]

4.3 An Attack upon Astrology: from *Nicole Oresme and the Astrologers: A Study of His Livre de Divinacions* (1361–5), ed. and trans. G. W. Coopland (Cambridge, MA: Harvard University Press, 1952), pp. 51–7.

The French scholar Nicole Oresme, born in 1323 (d.1382), studied at the University of Paris where he was taught by the philosopher Jean Buridan. He was counselor and

67 Be active or alert on the waters.
68 Deal.
69 Wed wives.
70 Buy inheritable property.
71 Prevail.
72 Pisces.
73 Convent.
74 Gotten.
75 Groins.
76 Penis.
77 Testicles and scrotum.
78 Thighs.
79 Muscles adjoining the knees.
80 Pisces.
81 Feet.

adviser to the French king Charles V and tutor to Charles VI. In addition to holding several ecclesiastical offices (including Dean of the Cathedral of Rouen and Bishop of Lisieux), he was a learned mathematician, philosopher, and translator who wrote on topics as varied as natural magic, mathematics, astronomy, judicial astrology and the nature of money supply. He was famous for his skepticism about astrological divination, nevertheless he did not reject all elements of astrology.

Here begins Master Nicole Oresme's Book against Divination.

It is my aim, with God's help, to show in this little book, from experience, from human reason, and from authority, that it is foolish, wicked, and dangerous even in this life, to set one's mind to know or search out hidden matters or the hazards and fortunes of the future, whether by astrology, geomancy, nigromancy, or any other such arts, if they can correctly be called arts; and, further, that such things are most dangerous to those of high estate, such as princes and lords to whom appertains the government of the commonwealth.

Hence I have written this little book in French so that laymen may understand it for I have heard that many of them are overmuch given to such stupidities. At a former time I wrote in Latin on this matter and if any man wishes to attack what I shall say let him do it openly and with set argument, not in mere slander, and let him write against it and I shall reply so far as I am able, for in such wise we may arrive at truth. In any case what I say is submitted to the correction of those whom it concerns. And I beg that I may be excused for my rough manner of expression because I have never learned or been used to set forth or write anything in French.[82]

Chapter I

There are many arts or sciences by means of which men are accustomed to enquire into the future or into things occult, secret, and hidden, or which can be applied to such uses. One of these is astrology which appears to me to have six principal parts. The first of these has to do chiefly with the movements, the signs, and the measurements of the heavenly bodies, so that by means of tables, constellations, eclipses and suchlike things in the future can be known. The second is concerned with the qualities, the influences, and physical powers of the stars, with the signs of the zodiac, with degrees, with the heavenly signs, and so on; as, for instance, that a star in one quarter of the

82 See Chapter 1 on the growing importance of French vernacular in this period. In spite of his invocation of the modesty topos, Oresme's French exposition was sophisticated and learned.

sky signifies or has power to cause heat or cold, dryness or moisture, and similarly with other physical effects. This part of astrology is introductory to the making of predictions. The third part deals with the revolutions of the stars and with the conjunctions of the planets, and is applied to three kinds of predictions; first, that we may know from the major conjunctions the great events of the world, as plagues, mortalities, famine, floods, great wars, the rise and fall of kingdoms, the appearance of prophets, new religions, and similar changes; next, that we may know the state of the atmosphere, the changes in the weather, from hot to cold, from dry to wet, winds, storms, and such movements in nature; third, that we may judge as to the humors of the body and as to taking medicine and so on.

The fourth part has to do with nativities, and especially with decisions as to a man's fortune, from the constellation which is in the heavens at the moment of his birth.

The fifth deals with interrogations, that is, decides and answers a question according to the constellation which is in the heavens at the time when the question is asked.

The sixth is of elections by which the time to start a journey or to undertake a task is ascertained and in this part is included the branch which teaches how to make images, carettes,[83] rings, and such things.

The other sciences are geomancy, hydromancy, and similar devices, palmistry, experiments, and such auspices as sneezing, encounters, arguments drawn from the song or flight of birds, from the members[84] of dead animals, magic art, nigromancy, interpretation of dreams, and many other vanities which are not sciences properly speaking.

The Second Chapter

The first part of astrology is speculative and mathematical, a very noble and excellent science and set forth in the books very subtly, and this part can be adequately known but it cannot be known precisely and with punctual exactness, as I have shown in my treatise on the Measurement of the Movements of the Heavens and have proved by reason founded on mathematical demonstration.

The second part is a part of natural science and is a great science and it too can be known so far as its nature is concerned but we know too little about it and in particular the rules in the books are false, as Averroes says, and have either slight proof or none. And some of them which were fulfilled in the place or at the time when they were laid down, are false in other places or at

83 Coopland is unsure of the meaning of this term, unless it is a variant of charroi, a "letter written in magical characters that made the bearer invulnerable" (p. 195).

84 Alternative ms reading, nombres/numbers.

the present time: for the fixed stars which according to the ancients have great influence are not now in the position they were in then and these same positions are used in making predictions.

And of the three subdivisions of the third part of astrology the first, which is concerned with the great events of the world, can be and is sufficiently well known but only in general terms. Especially we cannot know in what country, in what month, through what persons, or under what conditions, such things will happen, or the other particular circumstances. Secondly, as regards change in the weather, this part by its nature permits of knowledge being acquired therein but it is very difficult and is not now, nor has it ever been to anyone who has studied it, more than worthless, for the rules of the second part are mostly false as I have said, and are assumed in this branch. And, similarly, the detailed rules bearing on this part are false, so that we see every day that sailors and husbandmen can prophesy changes in the weather better than the astronomers. In the third place, so far as medicine is concerned, we can know a certain amount as regards the effects which ensue from the course of the sun and moon but beyond this little or nothing. All this third part of astrology has to do chiefly with physical effects; the parts which follow, with the effects of fortune.

The fourth part, of nativities, is not in itself beyond knowledge, so far as the complexion and inclination of the person born at a given time are in question, but cannot be known when it comes to fortune and things which can be hindered by the human will, and this section has to do with those things rather than with physical effects. And one often sees in practice that two people are born at intervals of time so minute as cannot be recorded and yet their fortunes are quite different, so I say that this part of astrology cannot be known and the rules written down on it are not true.

Humoral Explanations of the Human Body

4.4 Humoral Theory: from *John Trevisa, On the Properties of Things*, 3 vols (Oxford: Clarendon Press, 1975), Vol. I, Book IV, Chapter 6, pp. 147–9.

Trevisa describes the classical humoral theory of the Middle Ages, and explains its sources in diet and bodily metabolism. At least as old as Greek thought, and fundamental to Roman and Arabic medicine, the humoral theory of human health dominated medieval thinking about the health and temperament of the human body. In referring to "colerick" humor, Trevisa deviates slightly from the classical description of the four humors as blood (associated with sanguine personalities), yellow bile (associated with choleric personalities), black bile (associated with melancholic personalities), and phlegm (associated with phlegmatic personalities). The proper balance of humors within a body underlaid health; imbalance led to disease, both physical and mental. (Translation from Middle English by the editors.)

For humor is the first principal material of bodies that have feeling and a chief help in their working, and that because of nourishing and of feeding. Constantine says that the humors are called the children of the elements [earth, air, fire, and water], because each of the humors comes from a quality of the elements. And there are four humors: blood, phlegm, choler[a], and melancholia. . . .

These four humors, if they are in even proportion in quantity and quality, feed all bodies that have blood and make them perfect and preserve them in life and a state of health; in contrast, if they are uneven in proportion and infected, then they breed evil. These humors are necessary to the making of the body and to the ruling and keping thereof, and also to restore what is lost [corrupted] in the body [in the processes of living].

These four humors are bred in this manere. When meat is taken into the . . . stomach, first the more subtle part and fleeting that physicians call *pthisinaria*[85] is drawn by certain veynes to the liver, and there by working of natural heat it is changed into the four humors. The breeding of them begins in the liver, but it does not fully end there. First, by working, heat turns what is cold and moist into what is by nature phlegm, and then what is hot and moist into the nature of blood, and then what is hot and dry into the nature of choler, and then what is cold and dry into the nature of melancholia. . . . And so such is the order, as Avicenna says: the breeding of elements is straight and reciprocal, for air is born of fire, and fire of aire, and every element of the other.

. . . in the humors is one part that is light and comes upward, and that is choler; another is as were lees[86] and goes downward, and that is melancolia; the third is as it were unrefined, unfiltered, that is phlegm; the fourth is blood, purified and cleansed of other humors. And therefore by mixing of other humors, blood changes nature and color; for by mixing of choler it seems red, and by malencolia it seems black, and by phlegm it seems watery and foamy.

Vision and the Human Mind

4.5 Medieval Faculty Psychology: From John Trevisa, *On the Properties of Things*, 3 vols (Oxford: Clarendon Press, 1975). Vol. I, Book V, Chapter 2, pp. 168–74, 178 .

The excerpts below outline the major elements of medieval thinking about the primacy of the head among the members of the body, a primacy which underlies a great deal of metaphor in discussion of household and state relations during this period. They also

85 Meaning not found.

86 Dregs.

outline the basic elements of faculty psychology[87] *in relationship to the brain, its structure and separate functions, as well as indicating the primacy of the eyes in cognition and thinking. All these elements contribute to the disease of lovesickness that impels the plots of so many romances and tales. (Translation from the original Middle English by the authors.)*

Among the principal members of a man, we shall first begin to treat of the properties of the head, for the head is the first principal part of a man. And among all the external members of the body, in respect to place and office, the head is the principal. . . . In the head all the wits are seen. Therefore in a manner the head presents the "person" of the soul that counsels and rules the body. Then, as Isidore says, the head is the place and seat of the wits, *principium* and beginning and the proper dwelling place of the virtue of feeling, and the instruments of all the wits. And the head gives and sends feeling and moving to the nether members, and has seven holes that are the instruments of wits and correspond to the seven spheres of planets, as some men say. Also the head is worthier and more noble than all the other members, for he is governor and ruler of all the body. . . .

And the head is distinguished by three cells or ventricles, for the brain has three hollow places that physicians call ventriculos, "small wombs." In the foremost cell *imagination*[88] is conformed and made; in the middle, reason; in the hindmost, recording and remembering . . . In these three cells and wombs are three principal workings, for in the first is shaped the likeness of things that are felt and gathered in the *fantasie*[89] and in the *imagination*. Then the shape and likeness is sent to the middle cell, and there is judgment [about them] made. And at the last, after the judgment of reason, that shape and likeness is sent . . . to the memory.

Among all the wits the eyes are next to the soul [in importance and essential quality], for in the eyes is the token of the soul. For in the eyes is known and seen all the judgment of mind, disturbance and gladness of the soul, and also love and anger and other passions.

4.6 Constantine the African and Gerard of Berry on Lovesickness or *Amor Hereos*: From *Lovesickness in the Middle Ages: The Viaticum and Its Commentaries*, ed. and trans. Mary Frances Wack (University of Pennsylvania, 1990), pp. 187–91, 199–202.

Amor Hereos, *or lovesickness that reaches a morbid, melancholic state modern medicine would term depression, afflicts a great number of men in medieval English literature –*

87 The phrase "faculty psychology" refers to the psychology of the faculties of the human mind, the senses, the estimative faculties, and the capacity for memory.

88 Imagination here denotes the images introduced into the mind primarily by sight.

89 In medieval psychology *fantasie* refers primarily to the image impressed on the mind by a sensual apprehension of a material object.

perhaps most famously Chaucer's Troilus, and Palamon and Arcite in The Knight's Tale. *It afflicts some women, too, notably Elaine of Astolat in Malory's* Works, *and Dorigen in Chaucer's* Franklin's Tale. *The extent to which it was a recognized disease in living humans rather than fictional ones is not entirely clear. What is certain, however, is that its sources and its progression reflect assumptions basic to medieval medicine, especially that the role of medicine is to restore disrupted balance and harmony among the elements that comprise the body and the mind. Above all lovesickness is described as excess, an imbalance that needs urgent correction, often through sensual and sexual means.*

The concept of lovesickness entered Europe in the eleventh century, as Wack observes: "It was not until a North African named Constantine (d. 1087) brought a cargo of Arabic medical texts to southern Italy in the late eleventh century that the disease of love became an important part of medieval culture" (p. xiii). By 1200, along with law and theology, medicine emerged as one of the advanced faculties at European universities, and Constantine's Viaticum, *a title Wack tells us that denoted a handbook for travelers who had no access to medical care (p. xiii), became a major text, preserved in over 100 manuscripts, and in four print editions between 1505 and 1536 (p. 179). We begin with a selection from Constantine's chapter on love from the* Viaticum, *and follow it with a late-twelfth-century Parisian commentary that expands on the original material:*

> The love that is also called "eros" is a disease touching the brain. For it is a great longing with intense sexual desire and affliction of the thoughts. Whence certain philosophers say: Eros is a word signyfying the greatest pleasure. For just as loyalty is the ultimate form of affection, so also eros is a certain extreme form of pleasure.
>
> Sometimes the cause of this love is an intense natural need to expel a great excess of humors. Whence Rufus says: "Intercourse is seen to benefit those in whom black bile and frenzy reign. Feeling is returned to him and the burden of eros is removed, even if he has intercourse with those he does not love." Sometimes the cause of eros is also the contemplation of beauty. For if the soul observes a form similar to itself it goes mad, as it were, over it in order to achieve the fulfillment of its pleasure.
>
> Since this illness has more serious consequences for the soul, that is, excessive thoughts, their eyes always become hollow [and] move quickly because of the soul's thoughts [and] worries to find and possess what they desire. Their eyelids are heavy [and their] color yellowish; this is from the motion of heat which follows upon sleeplessness. Their pulse grows hard and does not dilate naturally, nor does it keep the beat it should. If the patient sinks into thoughts, the action of the soul and body is damaged, since the body follows the soul in its action, and the soul accompanies the body in its passion. "The power of the soul," Galen says, "follows the complexion of the body." Thus if erotic lovers are not helped so that their thought is lifted and their spirit lightened, they inevitably fall into a melancholic disease. And just as they fall

into a troublesome disease from excessive bodily labor, so also [they fall] into melancholy from labor of the soul.

What better helps erotic lovers so that they do not sink into excessive thoughts: temperate and fragrant wine is to be given; listening to music; conversing with dearest friends; recitation of poetry; looking at bright, sweet-smelling and fruitful gardens having clear running water; walking or amusing themselves with good-looking women or men.

From Gerard of Berry, Glosses on the Viaticum (c. 1190–1220)

Love that is called Heros. This disease is called a melancholic worry by medical authors. It is indeed very similar to melancholy, because the entire attention and thought, aided by desire, is fixed on the beauty of some form or figure.

It is difficult to understand what the cause of this disease is, by which the faculties are hindered. The cause, then, of this disease is a malfunction of the estimative faculty [of the brain], which is misled by sensed intentions into apprehending non-sensed accidents[90] that perhaps are not in the person. Thus it believes some woman to be better and more noble and more desirable than all others. Thus it is, for sometimes some sensed object appears very pleasing and acceptable to the soul, so that it judges other sense objects to be dissimilar [i.e. not pleasing]. Any unfitting sensations are, as a consequence, obscured by the non-sensed intentions [i.e. that the person is more noble, better, etc.] deeply fixed in the soul. The estimative [faculty], then, which is the nobler judge among the perceptions on the part of the sensible soul,[91] orders the imagination to fix its gaze on such a person. The imaginative [faculty orders] the concupiscible, in fact, so that the concupiscible desires this one alone, for just as the concupiscible [faculty] obeys the imaginative, so the imaginative [obeys] the estimative, at whose command the others are inclined toward the person whom the estimative judges to be fitting, though this may not be so . . .

Now, some of the signs of this disease are drawn from the soul's part, some from the body's part. From the soul's part are depressed thoughts and worries, so that if someone talks about something, [the patient] scarcely understands; if, however, he speaks of the beloved, he is immediately moved. From the body's part are the signs: sunken eyes, since they follow the *spiritus* racing to the place of the estimative [faculty]; also, dryness of the eyes and lack of tears unless weeping occurs on account of the desired object. There is a continual motion of the eyelids, so that he laughs easily and is easily changed from tears

90 Detecting non-existing qualities; "non-sensed" in the sense of not subject to sensory proof.

91 Sense, appetite, judgment, breath, and awareness of motion.

to laughter. But nevertheless he weeps when he hears love songs and especially if mention is made of rejection and separation of beloved objects. All his members dry out. His pulse is disordered, for sometimes it is frequent and swift when he recalls something similar to the beloved object.

This disease cannot be perfectly cured without intercourse and the permission of law and faith. For then the faculties and the body return to their natural disposition. Before it is established, therefore, consider whether there may be burning of humor; if there is, purge it. Then administer lengthy sleep, humectation, and good nourishment, and freshwater baths. Occupy the patients with various things, so that they are distracted from what they love. In this, moreover, the counsel of old women is very useful, who may relate many disparagements and the stinking dispositions of the desired thing. Also useful is consorting with and embracing girls, sleeping with them repeatedly, and switching various ones. Hunting and various types of games also help.

Illusions of the Human Mind

4.7 From *Forbidden Rites: A Necromancer's Manual of the Fifteenth Century*, Richard Kieckhefer (Sutton Publishing: 1997), pp. 51–3.

Medieval magic encompassed a broad spectrum of beliefs and actions. A fifteenth-century commonplace book created by Richard Reynes (see 5.1) includes a direction for divination from the fingers of a child, an unremarked and unremarkable entry among a number of bits of useful knowledge. Romance stories abound with magic, from the illusory world of Sir Gawain and the Green Knight, *to the popular romance tales of Melusine, to the adventures of King Arthur's court in Malory's works. Chaucer uses magic as well as astrology in his* Franklin's Tale, *as does Gower in* Confessio Amantis, *notably in the story of Alexander the Great's mother Olympia and Nectanabus the Egyptian magus. In medieval literature magic appears most frequently in the form of illusions. Part of a category of magic called necromancy, the conjuring of illusions requires the summoning of demonic spirits. This was achieved through incantations, and through tracing magical figures and symbols, chief among them the circle whose shape was thought to have the power to contain the spirits summoned by the black arts. The directions below from a fifteenth-century Latin book of necromancy written on the continent, provide instruction in creating an illusory castle which is well defended – a chimera that recurs in medieval romance.*

Richard Kieckhefer introduces this "experiment," with these words: "The following experiment (no. 7) is designed to obtain an illusory castle, with defenders. It is introduced in grandiose manner, as a 'splendid experiment' by which the magician can convoke spirits to produce an elegant castle with armed men . . . there are two phases, first the summoning of spirits and then having them work the illusion."[92] *(Translation from the Latin by Kieckhefer.)*

An Illusory Castle

Here follows another experiment for invoking spirits so that a man can make a fine and well fortified castle appear, or for summoning countless legions of armed men, which can easily be done, and among other things is deemed most beautiful.

First, go out on the tenth [day of] the moon, under a clear sky, outside of town to some remote and secret place, taking milk and honey with you, some of which you must sprinkle in the air. And with bare feet and head, kneeling, read this while facing west: "O Usyr, Salaul, Silitor, Demar, Zanno, Syrtroy, Risbel, Cutroy, Lytay, Onor, Moloy, Pumotor, Tami, Oor and Ym, squire spirits, whose function it is to bear arms and deceive human senses wherever you wish, I, so-and-so, conjure and exorcize and invoke you . . . that, indissolubly bound to my power, you should come to me without delay, in a form that will not frighten me, subject and prepared to do and reveal for me all that I wish, and to do this willingly, by all things that are in heaven and on earth." Having read this once facing west, do so again facing south, east, and north.

And from far off you will see a band of armed men coming toward you, who will send ahead a squire to say that those you summoned are coming to you. You should tell him, "Go to them and tell them to come to me in such a state that they frighten no one, but I may abide safely with them." When you have said this, he will return at once to them.

After a short interval they will come to you. When you see them, show them at once this circle, which has great power to terrify those fifteen demons; they will see it and say, "Ask whatever you wish in safety, and it will all come to pass for you through us." You should then tell them to consecrate their circle so that whenever you gaze on it and invoke them they must come to you quickly and do that which is natural to them, namely make fortifications and castles and moats and a multitude of armed men appear. They will say they are willing to do so. You should extend a book to them, and you will see one of them place his hand on the book and speak certain words, which you will not understand. When this is done, they will restore it to you.

Then they will ask you to permit them to leave, because they cannot depart from you except with permission. You should say to them, "Make a castle here, so that I may see your power." Immediately they will make a castle around you, with many other things, and you will see yourself in the middle of the castle, and a great multitude of knights will be present. But

92 On the proper attitude toward such illusions, see Sidrak and Bokkus, 4.13 below.

these fifteen will not be able to depart from you. After the space of an hour they will ask you that they may depart, and you should say, "Be ready whenever I gaze on this circle and invoke you to return at once." They will swear to come immediately. Then tell them to depart wherever they wish. And the entire spectacle *[ludus]* will be destroyed, and no one will remain there.

When all this is done, return home, guarding well the book in which all power is found. And when you wish to work this fine art, gaze at the circle, reading the names, beginning from the east, saying, "O Usyr, Salaul, Silitol, Denior, Zaimo, Syrtroy, Ristel, Cutroy, Lytoy, Onor, Moloy, Pumiotor, Tamy, Dor, [and] Ym, I summon you to come here, by the consecration of this circle, in which your signs are inscribed, and to make a well fortified castle appear for me, with a deep moat, and a plenteous company of knights and footsoldiers." And suddenly a splendid castle, with all that is necessary, will appear there. If you wish to enter it, you can, for a knight will at once stand by you, to whom you may command that all you wish should appear, and he will have it done. Once when I [wished to test] this art I exercised it with the emperor, when many nobles were accompanying him on a hunting expedition through some dark forest. This is how I proceeded. First I gazed at the circle, calling the aforesaid demons with a clear voice. And at once a handsome knight came to me, whom no one but I could see, and who said to me, "I am one of the spirits you have invoked; I am named Salaul, and the others have sent me. Command what you will, and it will be done." I said to him, "I want you to have a legion of armed men appear, whom the emperor and his companions will take to be rebels." He said, "It is done." And then all the counts and the emperor himself turned and looked to the north, and from far off they saw coming to them an innumerable multitude of knights and soldiers. One of them dismounted, and before an hour's time *[ante magne hore spacium]* came to the emperor and said, trembling, "Lord emperor, behold, an innumerable horde is coming toward us, swearing to put us and all your counts to death and to kill you pitilessly." On hearing this, the emperor and the counts did not know what to do. Meanwhile, the spirits approached. Seeing and hearing them, and their terrifying weapons, they began to flee, but the others followed them, shooting arrows, and cried with one voice, "You cannot escape your death today!" Then I said, "O Salaul, make a wondrous castle before the emperor and his men, so that the emperor and the others can enter it." And it was done. A perfectly safe castle was made for the counts, with towers and moat, and the drawbridge down. It seemed excellently constructed and filled with mercenaries, who were crying out, "O lord emperor, enter quickly with your companions!" They entered, and it seemed that servants and many friends of the emperor were in it; he supposed he had come upon people who would defend him manfully. When they had entered, they raised the drawbridge and began to defend themselves. Then the spirits with their war machines attacked the castle with wondrous power, so that the emperor and the others feared all the more. Then Salaul said to me, "We do not have the power to remain here longer than a quarter of the day, so we must now withdraw." Then the castle disappeared, and the attackers, and everything else. The emperor and the others then looked around and found themselves in some marsh, which left them greatly astonished. I said to them, "This episode has been quite an adventure!" And after this experiment I made a dinner for them.[93]

Remember that this art cannot last longer than a quarter of a day, unless it lasts one quarter one time [and is then renewed for another quarter day], etc.

Perfecting Matter: Alchemy

Medieval alchemy comprised two distinct branches: one was the world of so-called "puffers," those who vainly sought the secret of transmuting baser metals into gold, often resorting to trickery and deception to fool the public into supporting their attempts. The other was the world of philosophic alchemy, an intellectual and spiritual search that depended on preparing the senses and training the mind to understand the deep cosmic secrets at play in purifying corrupt matter. The goal of medieval alchemy was to purify matter, freeing it to attain the natural state of perfection it strives for. In the later Middle Ages alchemy was regarded as having the potential to reveal the hidden unity of all matter, and its practice was compared to the mystery of the Mass where bread and wine became the body and blood of Christ. Langland, Gower, Lydgate, Chaucer, and Thomas Norton all touch upon the vexed subject of alchemy in their works. None of them actually repudiates the "science" as it was termed, although all acknowledge that it is a deep mystery.[94] The excerpts below reflect the spread of thinking about alchemy in the later Middle Ages; the first two represent the affirmative tradition, the third the critical tradition articulated by the Church.

4.8 Jean de Meun, from *The Romance of the Rose*, trans. Frances Horgan (Oxford: Oxford University Press, 1994).), ll. 16053–118.

In this passage Jean de Meun argues that it is possible to change the essential nature of matter (the species or category of things to which any object belongs), as well as outward, visible form, in individual instances. He argues by analogy, a commonly used tool in constructing arguments in medieval science.

93 This conclusion bears a curious resemblance to a moment in Chaucer's Franklin's Tale, ll. 1209–12 (*The Riverside Chaucer*, 3rd ed., ed. Larry D. Benson (Boston: Houghten Mifflin,1987), when the magician in this tale creates an illusion that concludes with an invitation to dinner.

94 For examples of these writers' interest in alchemy see Carolyn P. Collette and Vincent DiMarco, "The Canon's Yeoman's Tale," in *Sources and Analogues of the Canterbury Tales*, 2 vols (Woodbridge, Suffolk: D. S. Brewer, 2005), vol. 2, pp. 715–47.

It is worthy of note, nevertheless, that alchemy is a true art, and that anyone who worked at it seriously would discover great marvels. Whatever may be true of species,[95] individuals at least, when subjected to the operations of the intellect, can be changed into so many different forms, and their complexions so altered by various transformations, that this change can rob them of their original species and put them into a different one. Have we not seen how those who are expert in glass-making can, through a simple process of purification, use ferns to produce both ash and glass? Yet glass is not fern, nor fern glass. And when we have thunder and lightning, we often see stones fall from the clouds, although they did not rise as stones. Experts may know what causes matter to be changed into different species. And thus species are transformed, or rather their individuals are alienated from them in substance[96] and appearance, by Art in the case of glass and by Nature in the case of the stones.

The same could be done with metals, if one could manage to do it, by removing impurities from the impure metals and refining them into a pure state; they are of similar complexion and have great affinities with one another, for they are all of one substance, no matter how Nature may modify it. Books tell us that they were all born in different ways, in mines down in the earth, from sulphur and quicksilver. And so, if anyone had the skill to prepare spirits in such a way that they had the power to enter bodies but were unable to fly away once they had entered, provided they found the bodies to be well purified, and provided the sulphur, whether white or red, did not burn, a man with such knowledge might do what he liked with metals. The masters of alchemy produce pure gold from pure silver, using things that cost almost nothing to add weight and colour to them; with pure gold they make precious stones, bright and desirable, and they strip other metals of their forms, using potions that are white and penetrating and pure to transform them into pure silver. But such things will never be achieved by those who indulge in trickery: even if they labour all their lives, they will never catch up with Nature.

4.9 Defense of Alchemy: From *The Opus Majus* of Roger Bacon (1287), trans. Robert Belle Burke, 2 vols (Philadelphia: University of Pennsylvania Press, 1928), Vol. 2, pp. 626–7.

Bacon connects the work of alchemy to the perfection of humans through analogy: if it is possible to purify metals so that they reach their apogee, it should be possible to rid human bodies of corruption, the weight of matter that medieval religion, medicine and

95 Outward, visible form whose resemblances constitute a group or category.

96 In their essential nature.

science viewed as the sign of sin after the Fall. What Bacon imagines is a world redeemed from these signs of sin. Thus his alchemic vision is ultimately Edenic.

> There have always been a few who during their life have known this secret of alchemy; and this science does not go beyond that. But experimental science by means of Aristotle's *Secret of Secrets*[97] knows how to produce gold not only of twenty-four degrees but of thirty and forty degrees and of as many degrees as we desire. For this reason Aristotle said to Alexander: "I wish to disclose the greatest secret"; and it really is the greatest secret, for not only would it procure an advantage for the state and for every one his desire because of the sufficiency of gold, but what is infinitely more, would prolong life. For that medicine which would remove all the impurities and corruptions of a baser metal, so that it should become silver and purest gold, is thought by scientists to be able to remove the corruptions of the human body to such an extent that it would prolong life for many ages.

The Alchemy of Death

References to death and dying are universal in late medieval English literature. In religious texts, romances, and in drama the imminence of death and its destruction of the body appears repeatedly. The fifteenth-century morality play Everyman *is a spare and haunting reminder of the end that awaits all life. It might be said, though, that death is a kind of natural alchemy working to release the human soul from the "foul contagion" of matter, freeing it to ascend through the refining fires of Purgatory, ultimately to heaven. Medieval knowledge of death was intimate and precise. We include a passage from a fourteenth-century medical text that offers guidance on how to recognize impending death, a matter of great importance in a religious culture where last rites could aid the soul after death.*

4.10 From *Johannes de Mirfeld of St Bartholomew's, Smithfield: His Life and Works*, ed. and trans. Percival Horton-Smith Hartley and Harold Richard Aldridge (Cambridge: Cambridge University Press, 1936), pp. 55–7.

The editors of Mirifeld's texts note that he came of a "powerful" family in Yorkshire and that he was associated with St Bartholomew's Hospital in London where he resided within the walls of the Priory, and that, having access to the priory library, he wrote two books. "The first of these, the Breviarium Bartholomei, *is a purely medical work*

97 A spurious text assigned to Aristotle in the Middle Ages, the "Secreta Secretorum" (Secret of Secrets) was believed to have been a letter written by Aristotle to Alexander the Great, his former pupil.

composed probably between 1380 and 1395, and the second, the Florarium Bartholomei, *a theological treatise containing one medical chapter. . . . In these two compilations, named after the House in which he lived, he laboriously gathered together everything that he believed would be conducive to both the physical and spiritual health of mankind, and dedicated it to the service of suffering humanity" (p. 25).*

Mirfeld's work reflects the role of observation in medieval medicine, particularly the careful attention to the body as producing a series of visible signs keyed to its state of health or disease. The physician's job is to interpret this web of signs correctly. Imminent death is a matter of somatic decay detected by various signs whose presence betokens a coming change before which the doctor retires. Theologically the death of the human body released the soul, previously trapped by the material and sensual which it sloughs off in a kind of alchemy of transformation. (Translated from the Latin by Hartley and Aldridge.)

Concerning the Signs of Evil Portent Appearing in Feverish and Other Types of Patients

When you visit your patient, you must bear in mind first of all the matters to which you should give heed, such as paying due regard to his countenance, and opening the mouth and looking at his tongue; moreover, his eyes and nails must be inspected, and consideration given to many other matters connected with him which will be set forth below. Wherefore, indeed, it should be known that of those signs of evil portent which manifest themselves in the eyes and features of the sick, some appear within the three first days of the onset of the disease, and others appear later.

Of such evil symptoms, those which sometimes appear within the first three days are these: the eyes are hollowed, the temples sunken, the forehead dry and tense; the nostrils pinched; the ears cold, with the lobes turned outward and contracted; the colour livid, greenish or black, or something similar.

If these symptoms appear at the commencement of the disease, and by reason of the virulence of the malady itself, then death is signified, especially if the stools be very loose and the urine oily: but this is not the case if they appear later. If however, the appearance of these signs in the opening stages is due, not to the severity of the disease itself, but rather to its accidents, such as sleeplessness, or frequency of stools, lack of food, and the like, then evil is not thus portended. Moreover, if all these aforesaid symptoms appear after the first three days, and result from the disease itself, or if they develop a good deal later during its course, then they are not of ill omen; because if they do not make an appearance until after a considerable lapse of time, then this is a matter neither of wonderment nor of concern. It must, however, be understood, that if such symptoms do appear after the commencement of the disease and accompanied by pronounced weakness, death may thus be signified, although not so effectually as when the appearance occurs at the beginning: for it is reasonable to assume that the body of the patient has been wasted away owing to the process of time; and it would, indeed, be a bad sign if such were not the case.

Of those signs of evil import, which appear in the features of the patient, there are some which show themselves later than the outset of the disease, such as on the fourth day or afterwards. They are as follows: The patient cannot bear to gaze upon a lighted candle and he sheds involuntary tears, whilst the eyes appear to squint, and one seems smaller than the other: or the whites of the eyes appear bloodshot, and the veins black, swarthy, or sallow, the eyes inflamed, and the eyeballs protruding or sunken, whilst the whole aspect of the face is unsightly and horrible to look upon. These symptoms, I say, all signify death in most cases, and they are of worse import than those mentioned in the first place; they can also appear at the outset; but this, however, rarely happens.

We may therefore, it would seem, conclude that whenever and wherever, at the outset or later, all these last-mentioned symptoms appear on account of the fury of the disease and the weakness of the constitution, then most assuredly death is betokened. And to the aforesaid we may add some other indications of death; namely, if the whites of the patient's eyes appear during sleep, without his being able to see anything; if he has lost all his sense of taste and is totally unable to discern those things, which he was once accustomed to perceive; and if he can smell nothing; and if the teeth also, as well as the tongue, appear dry. These and similar tokens portend not merely an approaching death, but death within the doors [sic]. With such cases therefore do not meddle. Let your prognosis be given, and then retire.

Household Knowledge

4.11 From the *Rules of Robert Grosseteste the Good Bishop of Lincoln Made for the Countess of Lincoln, on How to Guard and Govern Lands and Household* in Excerpts on Household and Manor Management from *Walter of Henley and Other Treatises on Estate Management and Accounting,* Dorothea Oschinsky (Oxford: Clarendon Press, 1971), pp. 399–407.

Good husbandry of land and livestock ensured food and laid the basis for exchange beyond the boundaries of one's estate. The seasonal matrix in which humans lived gave rise to seasonal activities that sustained life. Among these the rituals of household and estate management were central. Running an estate and a household required varied kinds of knowledge about weather, land, and seasons, as well numeracy and literacy. Robert Grosseteste's advice to the Countess of Lincoln (c. 1235–53) on how to be a good steward of the land and people put under her care shows that such stewardship requires familiarity with the law, the central government, and with arithmetic. Concern for the principles of the temperate and appropriate that characterize so much of late medieval English writing on household and nature appear below as well. Grosseteste begins by asserting that, "He who will keep to the rules will live well and comfortably off his demesne and keep himself and his people" (p. 389), moving on to a series of specific injunctions designed to provide means for truthful accounting and a range of prudential behaviors including careful monitoring of sources of income such as rents, customs, and fees, surveying and recording all possessions, and managing one's stewards and bailiff. Reading between the lines tells us a great deal about tensions and patterns within the medieval aristocratic household.

The history of English literature is full of poetic celebrations of well-run households whose abundant largesse and open hospitality symbolize the fertility of the land and the virtue of its management. Good management of a household meant careful attention to creating a unified and loyal community and to ensuring a high moral and ethical standard governed all actions. Attention to both the food and the customs of the hall helped construct such unity. Hospitality was regularly extended to unanticipated travelers as well as to invited guests. From within its walls the household extended beyond the boundaries of the physical house. Chaucer's Franklin stands at the beginning of this tradition which is arguably most famously expressed in Ben Jonson's poem celebrating the Sidney estate at Penshurst.[98] *(Translated from Anglo-French by Oschinsky.)*

> The (eighth) rule teaches you the general instruction which you ought to give, often, to your household:
>
> Admonish all your household often that all those who serve you should endeavour to serve God and to serve you loyally and diligently and in order to do the will of God they ought to do your will and pleasure in all things; in all things, that is, that are not against God.[99]
>
> The (ninth) rule teaches you what you ought to say often to high and low of your household that they shall all obey your orders:
>
> Tell high and low, and this do often, that they ought to execute all your orders that are not against God, fully, quickly, and willingly and without grumbling or contradiction.
>
> The (tenth) rule teaches you the special order that you ought to give to the marshal of your house:
>
> Order those who are in charge of your house, in the presence of your entire household, that they keep a careful watch that all your household, within and without, be faithful, diligent, chaste, clean, honest and useful.

98 Rules for household governance are one kind of knowledge about running complex hierarchical organizations. On the general subject of governance, see Chapter 7.

99 Obedience could be commanded only in so far as what was asked did not involve sin, or placing human concerns above religious ones.

The (eleventh) rule teaches you who ought to be accepted as part of your household in and out of doors:

Order that no one be accepted or retained as part of your household in or out of doors, without good reason for believing them to be faithful, knowledgeable, diligent in the work for which they have been engaged, and, above all, honest and of good character.

The (twelfth) rule teaches you what enquiry about your household ought often to be made by your order:

Order that an enquiry is made, often and carefully, whether there are any servants who are disloyal, ignorant, vile, indecent, habitually drunk, and not useful. And those who are found to be such, or are reputed to be such ought to be turned out of your household.

The (thirteenth) rule teaches you how by your orders peace shall be kept in your house:

Order that there are on no account men among your household who create strife, discord, or disagreement in the house but all ought to be of one accord and of one will, as one heart and one soul. Order that all your household officers are obedient, and quick to serve those who are over them, in matters pertaining to their work.

The (fourteenth) rule teaches you how your alms, by your order, ought to be faithfully guarded and collected and wisely spent among the poor:

Order that your alms be faithfully guarded and collected and not sent from the table to the men servants, nor carried out of the dining hall, nor wasted in suppers or dinners for the menservants but freely, wisely and moderately, without dispute and strife, distributed among the poor, sick, and beggars.

The (fifteenth) rule teaches you how your guests ought to be received:

Order emphatically that all your guests, secular and religious, are received by porters, ushers, marshals promptly, courteously, frankly, and with good cheer. And that they are to be courteously addressed by seneschals and all, and are in the same way lodged and served.

The (sixteenth) rule teaches you in what clothing your men ought to wait on you at table:

Order your knights and your gentlemen who wear your livery that they ought to put on that same livery every day, and especially at your table and in your presence to uphold your honour, and not old surcoats, and soiled cloaks, and cut-off coats.

The (seventeenth) rule teaches you how you ought to seat people at meals in your house:

Let your freemen and guests be seated at tables on either side together, as far as possible, not here four there three and when the free household are seated all the grooms shall enter, be seated, and rise together. Strictly forbid that there is loud noise during mealtime and you yourself be seated at all times in the middle of the high table, that your presence as lord or lady is made manifest to all and that you may see plainly on either side all the service and all the faults. And take care that you have every day at mealtime two men to supervise your household while you are at table and be sure that this will earn you great fear and reverence.

The (eighteenth) rule teaches you the points about giving leave to household officers who wish to visit their homes:

Allow your household officers as little leave as possible to visit their homes and when you give leave allow them only a short time until their return if they wish to serve you. And if any of them complain or grumble, say that you intend to be lord or lady and that you intend that they serve you according to your will and your pleasure. Those who are not willing to do so ought to tell you and you can find others who wish to serve you after your wish, of whom you will find enough to your liking.

The (nineteenth) rule teaches how your household ought to be served at mealtime:

Order that your baker with the bread and your butler with the cup come step by step into your presence at table before grace and that three valets be assigned by the marshal every day to serve the high table and the two side tables with drink. And no vessel of ale ought to be placed on the table but under the table. And the wine ought to be placed (on the table) on the side tables only. But at the table there where you are wine and ale ought to be under the table except only before your place where wine and ale ought to be on the table.

Order that your marshal take care to supervise your household in person and especially in the hall to see that your household conduct themselves indoors and out of doors respectably, without dispute or noise or bad words. At each meal he ought to name the servers who are to go to the kitchen; he himself ought to go all the way before your steward as far as your place until your meal is served you and then he ought to go and be at the far end of the hall in the middle aisle and see that the servants go orderly and without noise with the dishes to all parts of the hall to the officers who have been appointed to divide out the food so that this is not – because of favouritism – placed or served out of order. Concerning this you yourself ought to keep an eye on the serving until the dishes are placed in the hall and then attend to your own meal.

And order that your dish be so refilled and heaped up, especially with the light courses, that you may courteously give from your dish to right and left to all at high table and to whom else it pleases you that they have of the same as you had in front of you.

The (twentieth) rule teaches you how to follow the example of serving dinner and supper in the house of a wise man:

And if you know the establishment of the house of the bishop of Lincoln you will know that each quarter of corn renders 180 white and brown loaves of bread together, that is loaves of the weight of five marks. And that the household is served at dinner with two dishes, large and full, to increase the alms, and with two light courses, also in generous helpings, for the freemen; and at supper with one dish of a lighter nature and also a second course and afterwards cheese. And if strangers should come for supper they are served according to their need.

The (twenty-first) rule teaches you how your people ought to behave towards your special friends in your presence and in your absence:

Order that your knights, and chaplains, your household officers and your gentlemen receive and honour, everywhere and in your presence or absence, with good manners, hearty cheer, and good service all those whom they perceive – by your word or mien – to be specially welcome and whom you would wish to have specially honoured. And by such behaviour your household can in particular prove that your wishes are theirs. Make special efforts to eat as far as possible except for reason of sickness and fatigue, in the dining hall before your people because you may be sure that from it great benefit and honour will come to you.[100]

The (twenty-third) rule teaches you about the forbidding of dinners and suppers outside the dining-hall:

Forbid dinners and suppers outside the hall in hiding-places and in chambers because much waste results from this and no honour to lord or lady.

4.12 *The Master of Game by Edward, Second Duke of York: The Oldest English Book on Hunting*, ed. W. A. Baillie-Grohman and F. N. Baillie-Grohman (New York: Duffield & Co., 1909), pp. 1–2, 4–8.

This work is a translation of part Livre de la chasse, *written between 1387 and 1389 in France by Gaston Phébus, Count of Foix. Phébus' work was immediately popular in England where Edward, Duke of York translated approximately 30 chapters from the*

100 Over the course of the later Middle Ages lords withdrew from public feasting in hall, often preferring to dine in private quarters; Grosseteste's concern with maintaining the dining hall as a central place in household life for all members reflects the importance he places on community.

beginning of Livre de la chasse *sometime between 1406 and 1413 (he died at Agincourt in 1415).*[101]

The excerpt below moves beyond the world of the household and the hall, to explicate the aristocratic pastime of hunting, a sport that recurs in medieval literature. The text places explicit emphasis on the supposed moral and spiritual benefits of hunting; implicitly, however, it recommends hunting as a form of exercise to take up the energies of knights and lords who might otherwise find hostile or disruptive outlets for those energies. The passage also suggests the extensive knowledge and customary tradition that underlay the sport of hunting as an appropriate aristocratic pastime. The conclusion to the Prologue links the subject and the audience, as well as the author, directly to literature and the place of reading in the aristocratic life of the time, as it invokes Chaucer's words at the beginning of the Prologue *to the* Legend of Good Women, *that books are the key to remembrance. (Translation from Middle English by W. A. and F. N. Baillie-Grohman.)*

The Prologue and Chapter I

To the honour and reverence of you my right worshipful and dread Lord Henry by the grace of God eldest son and heir unto the high excellent and Christian Prince Henry IV, by the aforesaid grace King of England and of France, Prince of Wales, Duke of Guienne of Lancaster and of Cornwall, and Earl of Chester.

I your own in every humble wise have me ventured to make this little simple book which I recommend and submit to your noble and wise correction, which book if it pleaseth your aforesaid Lordship shall be named and called MASTER OF GAME. And for this cause: for the matter that this book treateth of what in every season of the year is most durable, and to my thinking to every gentle heart most disportful of all games, that is to say hunting. For though it be that hawking with gentle hounds and hawks for the heron and the river be noble and commendable, it lasteth seldom at the most more than half a year. For though men find from May unto Lammas [1 August] game enough to hawk at, no one will find hawks to hawk with.[102] But as of hunting there is no season of all the year, that game may not be found in every good country, also hounds ready to chase it. And since this book shall be all of hunting, which is so noble a game, and lasting through all the year of divers beasts that grow according to the season for the gladdening of man, I think I may well call it MASTER OF GAME. And though it be so my dear Lord, that many could better have meddled with this matter and also more ably than I, yet there be two things

101 *The Hunting Book of Gaston Phébus: Manuscrit français 616 Paris, Bibliothèque nationale,* ed. Marcel Thomas, et al. (London: Harvey Miller Publishers, 1998), p. 5.

102 The hawks would be mewing and unfit to fly.

that have principally emboldened and caused me to take this work in hand. The first is trust of your noble correction, to which as before is said, I submit this little and simple book. The second is that though I be unworthy, I am Master of this Game with that noble prince your Father our all dear sovereign and liege Lord aforesaid. And as I would not that his hunters nor yours that now be or that should come hereafter did not know the perfection of this art, I shall leave for these this simple memorial, for as Chaucer saith in his prologue of "The 25 Good Women": "By writing have men mind of things passed, for writing is the key of all good remembrance."

* * *

Furthermore I will prove by sundry reasons in this little prologue, that the life of no man that useth gentle game and disport be less displeasable unto God than the life of a perfect and skilful hunter, or from which more good cometh. The first reason is that hunting causeth a man to eschew the seven deadly sins. Secondly men are better when riding, more just and more understanding, and more alert and more at ease and more undertaking, and better knowing of all countries and all passages; in short and long all good customs and manners cometh thereof, and the health of man and of his soul. For he that fleeth the seven deadly sins as we believe, he shall be saved, therefore a good hunter shall be saved, and in this world have joy enough and of gladness and of solace, so that he keep himself from two things. One is that he leave not the knowledge nor the service of God, from whom all good cometh, for his hunting. The second that he lose not the service of his master for his hunting, nor his own duties which might profit him most. Now shall I prove how a hunter may not fall into any of the seven deadly sins. When a man is idle and reckless without work, and be not occupied in doing some thing, he abides in his bed or in his chamber, a thing which draweth men to imaginations of fleshly lust and pleasure. For such men have no wish but always to abide in one place, and think in pride, or in avarice, or in wrath, or in sloth, or in gluttony, or in lechery, or in envy. For the imagination of men rather turns to evil than to good, for the three enemies which mankind hath, are the devil, the world and the flesh, and this is proved enough. Nevertheless there be many other reasons which are too long to tell, and also every man that hath good reason knoweth well that idleness is the foundation of all evil imaginations. Now shall I prove how imagination is lord and master of all works, good or evil, that man's body or his limbs do. You know well, good or evil works small or great never were done but that beforehand they were imagined or thought of. Now shall you prove how imagination is the mistress of all deeds, for imagination biddeth a man do good or evil works, whichever it be, as before is said. And if a man notwithstanding that he were wise should imagine always that he were a fool, or that he hath other sickness, it would be so, for since he would think steadfastly that he were a fool, he would do foolish deeds as his imagination would command, and he would believe it steadfastly. Wherefore methinks I have proved enough of imagination, notwithstanding that there be many other reasons the which I leave to avoid long writing. Every man that hath good sense knoweth well that this is the truth.

Now I will prove how a good hunter may not be idle, and in dreaming may not have any evil imaginations nor afterwards any evil works. For the day before he goes out to his office, the night before he shall lay him down in his bed, and shall not think but for to sleep, and do his office well and busily, as a good hunter should. And he shall have nothing to do, but think about all that which he has been ordered to do. And he is not idle, for he has enough to do to think about rising early and to do his office without thinking of sins or of evil deeds. And early in the dawning of the day he must be up for to go unto his quest, *that in English is called searching,* well and busily, for as I shall say more explicitly hereafter, when I shall speak of how men shall quest and search to harbour the hart. And in so doing he shall not be idle, for he is always busy. And when he shall come again to the assembly or meet, then he hath most to do, for he must order his finders and relays for to move the hart, and uncouple his hounds. With that he cannot be idle, for he need think of nothing but to do his office, and when he hath uncoupled, yet is he less idle, and he should think less of any sins, for he hath enough to do to ride *or to foot it well* with his hounds and to be always near them and to hue or rout well, and blow well, and to look whereafter he hunteth, and which hounds are *vanchasers and parfiters,*[103] and redress and bring his hounds on the right line again when they are at fault[104] or hunting rascal.[105] And when the hart is dead or what other chase he was hunting, then is he less idle, for he hath enough to do to think how to undo the hart in his manner and to raise that which appertaineth to him, and well to do his curee.[106] And he should look how many of his hounds are missing of those that he brought to the wood in the morning, and he should search for them, and couple them up. And when he has come home, should he less think to do evil, for he hath enough to do to think of his supper, and to ease himself and his horse, and to sleep, and to take his rest, for he is weary, and to dry himself of the dew or peradventure of the rain. And therefore I say that all the time of the hunter is without idleness and without evil thoughts, and without evil works of sin, for as I have said idleness is the foundation of all vices and sins. And the hunter may not be idle if he would fill his office aright, and also he can have no other thoughts, for he has

---

103 Hounds that came in the first relay (vanchasers), or group of hounds to give chase to a newly-discoverd hart, and those in the third or last relay (parfiters).

104 Diverted off line.

105 Chasing small deer.

106 Ceremony of giving the hounds their reward on the skin of the animal they chased; cf. *Sir Gawain and the Green Knight* hunting scenes.

enough to do to think and imagine of his office, the which is no little charge, for whoso will do it well and busily, especially if they love hounds and their office.

Wherefore I say that such an hunter is not idle, he can have no evil thoughts, nor can he do evil works, wherefore he must go into paradise. For by many other reasons which are too long to write can I prove these things, but it sufficeth that every man that hath good sense knoweth well that I speak the real truth.

4.13 Medieval Compendia of Knowledge: From *Sidrak and Bokkus: A Parallel-text Edition from Bodleian Library, MS Laud Misc. 559 and British Library, MS Lansdowne 793*, ed. T. L. Burton, et al., 2 vols, EETS, o.s. 311–312 (Oxford: Oxford University Press, 1998).

Burton begins his introduction to this new edition of a virtually forgotten medieval text by noting its immense popularity in late medieval Europe:

> *Sidrak and Bokkus* is a Middle English verse adaptation of an Old French prose book of knowledge, cast in question-and-answer form, enclosed within a framing adventure story. Its astonishing contemporary popularity is shown by the number and distribution of surviving manuscripts: several dozen in French; seven in English, excluding fragments; others in Italian, Danish, and Dutch . . . the subtitle found in many of the French versions, "La fontaine de toutes sciences," bears witness to its alleged authority (p. xxi).

Burton's edition is based on two manuscripts from the second half of the fifteenth century, Bodleian MS Laud 559 (B), and British Library MS Landsdowne 793 (L); the excerpts here are taken from Landsdowne (L). The selections we have chosen represent the encyclopedic nature of this work – Burton says that it "covers just about everything from the invisibility of the Deity and the power of devils to the cause of leprosy and the copulation of dogs." Our selections also represent the seemingly random structure of the whole which moves abruptly from subject to subject. The questions and answers in this text are designed for an audience less clerical and less learned than those who might have read Trevisa's On the Properties of Things. *For that reason this text, as its editor remarks, provides a very useful index to popular knowledge and thought. This is the sort of text that would have found a home in a literate merchant, gentry, or aristocratic household. Various questions – about sexual desire, the mechanisms of human vision, and the reality of illusions – present popularized versions of subjects that also appear in more academic texts cited throughout this volume.*

From the Landsdowne Manuscript, Vol. I

Question 51:
'Now I preie that thou telle me:
Gentilnesse, what may it be?'[107]
'Gentilnesse thanne is powere
And richesse that a man hath here
Of londes, of rentis, and of fee,
And is ycome out of antiquite;[108]
And in coostes hath to defende
That him of malys wolde shende.[109]
And some ben riche men of good
And ben cherles bi kynde of blood:[110]
A riche man men clepen hym oon
But gentilman is he noon.
And he that is riche wondirly
And noble man of his body,
Curteis and wijs and holden fre,[111]
A ful greet gentilman is he.[112]
And thogh he be a pore man,
And he among men hym bere can
As of norture in boure and halle,
A gentilman men shal him calle;
For of pouer[113] men alle we cam,
As of Eue and oure fader Adam.'

Question 117:
'Is ther any other folk than we
That haue of the sunne cleerte?'[114]
'Other folk the worlde beeth ynne
And fer from vs thei ben atwynne[115]

---

107 This question, which is central to Chaucer's *Wife of Bath's Tale*, is one often raised and answered in later medieval writing. At issue is the source of gentility: is it an innate quality that appears in individuals of any class, or is it tied to social status?

108 Of old time, inherited.

109 And who, by virtue of his status, must defend himself and his people in various regions against people who wish him/them destruction.

110 Some are rich, but are by nature of blood cherls who may call themselves gentlemen but are not.

111 Courteous, wise and regarded as generous.

112 The true gentilman is possessed of wealth and health, is courteous, wise, generous; even if he is poor, if he can move within bower [private chambers] and hall [i.e.has the right manners and deportment], he shall be called a gentleman if he performs gentle deeds.

113 Poor.

114 Clarity, light.

115 Separated.

And vndre vs thanne ben tho
That her feet ageinst oures go.[116]
And whoso al the world might see,
In oone sunne bothe we be
But alweie whanne here is night
Thanne haue thei the sunnelight,
And here to vs shyneth the sunne
Whanne that thei noon se kunne;[117]
For whanne the sonne gooth to reste thore,
Half prime it is to vs and more;[118]
And the roundenesse, ywisse,
Of the world maketh al thisse.
Oure somer and oure wynter also
Is bothe in vs and in hem to[o]
But aftir the sunne hath his gate,[119]
Whanne here is erly, there is late;
And also in other stedes mo[120]
Of the world it fareth so:
Some han somer resonably hoote
And some winter colde and woote.[121]
And God hath of the sunne, ywis,
Made the weie that maketh al this.

Question 130:
'Wherof euer may it be,
The lightning that we as fire see?'
'Clowdis that somtime on the sky
Renneth togidre vp an hy
With so greet ire and so kene[122]
That fire lightneth[123] hem bitwene,
And that is that we lightnyng calle.
And somtime it wole doun falle;
And somtime it slaketh[124] alofte
In the clowde, and that is ofte.

116 Under us, i.e. on the other side of the earth, there are people whose feet are "opposed" to ours.
117 Can.
118 Halfway between prime (c. 6 am) and tierce (c. 9 am).
119 But as the sun follows his path.
120 In many other places.
121 Wet.
122 Such great and keen anger.
123 Makes light.
124 Slakes, dies down.

Question 138:
'Mighte any man on drie loud wel
Go aboute the world euerydel?'
'No man in *erthe* might goo
Aboute the world to ne fro
For he shulde finde many letting[125]
And that of many skynnes[126] thing.
He shulde fynde waste[127] cuntrees grete
Wherynne were neither drinke ne mete
But wilde bestes many one
For to tere in sonder[128] euery bone.
Weren an hundred men wroght
On oone and that him lette noght,
The opene erthe shulde letting be,
That swoloweth the rage of the see;[129]
For whanne the see bigynneth to flowe,
Be it hie, be it lowe,
The erthe swoloweth it agein[130]
And makeþ the see lowe and plein.
Yit ben there many lettinges moo,[131]
If he eest or west wolde goo;
And if he goo north or south,
Other lettinge there ben many couth.
For thre yles he shal finde
There no man may lyue ynne bi kinde:[132]
Oone is hote and colde beth two;
May no lyuing thing be in tho.
And Goddis wille it is also
That no man be mighti therto.

Question 168:
'Telle me now if that a man
Shal delite him oght with a womman.'

125 Many hindrances.

126 Kinds of.

127 Waste, uninhabited.

128 Tear apart.

129 Were the strength of a hundred men wroght into one (?) and that stopped him not, the open earth should be a hindrance itself.

130 The editor points out that the original line is not clear here.

131 Many additional hindrances.

132 For three isles he shall find/Where no man may live naturally (i.e. where it is impossible for a human to survive).

Delite with womman ther beeth tweie
And whiche thei beeth I wole you seie.
That oon is goostly with chast lyf
As a man with his owne wyf:
Fleisshely knowe hir wel he may
Children to gete to Goddis pay;[133]
And fro that same time that he
Wote[134] that she with childe be
He shal from hir absteine truly
Til it be bore of hir body – [135]
This is delite of chastite,
That worthi and honest ought to be.
Bodily delite ther is also
That no time hath reward to[136]
But euery time he wole take
His flesshely lust and not forsake,
And that is pure lyf of beest
That is nouther good ne honest;
And suche delite with womman
No man shulde haue that good can.[137]

Question 199:
'Telle me now, withouten mys:
Whiche is the derkest thing that is?'
Derker thing may noon be
Than wicked man in his pouste[138]
And the soule that is in him
So is bothe derke and dym.
And if a wicked man might
Se him withynne fully aright[139]
Hou derke his soule is for synne,
I trowe of synne he wolde blynne:[140]
A foule thing he shulde se it
Wherthorgh he lightly might lese his witt[141]:

133 Glory.
134 Knows.
135 Til the child be born of her body.
136 Bodily delight that takes no heed, nor has any restraint.
137 Knows what is right and good.
138 Power, strength.
139 See inside himself clearly.
140 Cease, turn away.
141 Seeing how foul his soul is, he might easily lose his wits/mind.

Therfore there is no derknesse
Ageinst a man in his wickidnesse.'[142]

From Volume II, Landsdowne MS:

Question 225:
'Enchauntementz and sorcerie,
Availe thei oght or be folie?'[143]
The body may thei somdel availe
But the soule thei doo greet trauaile;
And he that hem worche shal,[144]
Thre thinges he muste haue withal:
First behoueth[145] him to knowe aright
The houres and the pointes of day and night
For if he doo oght theragein,[146]
Al his werke is in vein.
That other is that he moste nede
Geue greet trist[147] to his dede
And haue stedfast in his thoght
That the deuel shal faile him noght.
Yit bihoueth him to kunne[148] astronomye
For that must helpe him the most partie;
And faile him any of these thre,
Al his werke is but vanite.

Question 241:
'Whan a man seeth a thing,
Wheper yeuep the [eye] out in seing
Or it resceiueth inward therto
The shappe that it seeth so?'[149]
'Nothing may come out owhere
But there it yede in bifore,[150]
For ye may nothing geue outward
But it haue firste ytake inward.[151]

142 To compare with [against] his wickedness.
143 See 4.7.
144 And he who works them.
145 Behooves.
146 If he works in opposition to rather than with nature.
147 Trust.
148 Know.
149 This question represents the popular dimension of debate about intromission and extramission in sight. On vision, see 4.5.
150 Nothing may come out of anything unless it went in before.
151 You may give nothing out except you have first taken it in.

Therfore vndirstande aright
Thre thinges goon to the sight:
First the thing that thou shalt see;
The secounde that it ycoloured be –
For alle of thinges is seen nothing
But only the colourynge;
The thridde ben beemes of the sight[152]
That vpon that thing shal alight
That be seen shal. And after this
The moisture that in the yghen is
Draweth to him the shaping
And the facioun[153] of that thing
And that shap yildeth it the beam to
And the beam to the herte also:[154]
The herte resceiueth it him at the laste
And memorie it holdeth faste;
And for that wole the herte
Thenke another time als smerte[155]
Of thing that the yghen had somwhore[156]
Seyne somtime therbifore.

Question 316:
'Dremes that men dremen anight,
Wherof cometh it to mannes sight?'
'Some cometh from God oure king
Forto shewe to man somthing;
And of the deuel thei come some throwe
To begile hem that on hem trowe;[157]
And somtyme of humors stering[158]
Aboute the herte of man sleping;
Somtime wole ful wombe it make,
Oueremiche mete and drinke to take;[159]

152 Rays of sight from the eyes.

153 Fashion.

154 Accepting the extramission theory of vision, this passage talks about the shape of the object of vision "yielding" to sight, and the vision so produced being sent to the heart which receives it, and memory holds it fast; the memory in the heart comes forcefully to the mind, even though it is divorced from the time and place of its creation.

155 Vigorously.

156 Somewhere – on the effect of sight in creating lovesickness, see 4.6.

157 Believe.

158 Stirring.

159 Dreams may arise from over-eating.

Somtime whan thei seen oon deie
And can [nat] lightly putte it aweie[160]
Or thing that he hath of grete thoght,
In sleep it is bifore him broght.
Thus is man broght ofte in tourment
Thorgh diuerse sightes here present
That annoyen him ofte in the night
And ofte maketh him sore aflight.[161]

Question 328:
'Why haue wommen al the woo
Of this world and the ioye also?'
'Lightly woo and lightly wele
Han thise wymmen ech dele:[162]
Ful lightly take thei ioye hem to
And ful lightly eke woo also.
Lightnesse of the brayn maketh this,
There no sadnesse ynne ne is:[163]
Lesse thei ben than man of witt,[164]
Therfore her thoght wole lightly flitt.
Thei fare as leef vpon a tree
That tourneth there the wynde wole be.
Were her wit sad as of a man,
Men shulde of hem, for that thei can,[165]
Domesmen[166] and iustices make;
But no lawe wole it now hem to take.[167]
Lightly thei trowen that men hem saye[168]
And as smertly[169] it is awaye;
And for thei now trowe[170] and now lat go
Thei haue the sonner wel and woo.

160 And cannot easily forget the sight.
161 Afraid, disturbed.
162 Lightly woe and lightly well have women in each portion: i.e. women experience both woe and weal in the same way.
163 Women feel such emotions so "lightly" because there is no constancy in them.
164 Women possess less wit than men, therefore their thoughts flit lightly.
165 Because they are able.
166 Judges.
167 No legal system now will allow them.
168 They easily believe what men tell them.
169 Quickly.
170 Believe.

Reading the Past

The accumulated wisdom of generations, preserved in stories and in natural history, was a cherished element of medieval culture. As we have seen, citation of past authors in matters of science created an intellectual imprimatur that underlay the authority of medieval writing. Chaucer's short lyric titled "The Former Age" exemplifies conventional medieval thinking about the past: it was a golden, pastoral age of knowledge, peace and of human contentment. In contrast, the current age is one of of "Doublenesse, and tresoun, and envye/ Poyson, manslawhtre, and mordre in sondry wyse" ("The Former Age," *ll.61–3, in Benson,* Riverside Chaucer*).*

Although the past was not like the present, neither was it entirely separate from the present. Manor court cases, and cases in Common Law, as well, depended on the past in the form of custom and precedent. Lydgate begins his Troy Book *by invoking the "verray knighthod. . . . The Worthynes . . . And the prowesse of olde chivalrie," implying contemporary decline from past ideals and standards, a major topos in the literature of the period.*[171] *Richard of Maidstone, chaplain to Richard II, emphasizes in his* Concordia, *a poem about the reconciliation of the City of London to Richard II in 1392, that London is Troy Novant, the new Troy, founded by Brutus after the fall of the original Troy, and therefore linked directly to the heroes of the past.*[172] *His analogy likens the city aldermen to Roman senators.*[173] *Medieval hagiography, too, is structured on narratives of the past, designed to encourage virtuous living in the present to provide future salvation. As John Trevisa says in* De Proprietatibus Rerum, *all time is past, present, and future (Vol. I, p. 518).*

Increasingly, over the course of the fifteenth century, as humanism influenced English literary culture, stories from the past began to reflect ethical, classical values and virtues that, while consonant with Christian values and virtues, introduced classical heroes and heroines whose deeds provided exemplary patterns of behavior not just for the noble, and certainly not for the clerical, but increasingly for town gentry and country aristocrats. As Chaucer said, books held the "key of remembrance" about this past world and offered it ever anew to contemporary readers for their ethical benefit as individuals, as members of households, and as citizens.

4.14 The Golden Age: from Guillaume de Lorris and Jean de Meun, *The Romance of the Rose* (c. 1230/c.1275), ed. and trans. Frances Horgan (Oxford: Oxford University Press, 1994), ll. 8319–424.

The Romance of the Rose, *a contentious and highly influential allegory of love written in France during the thirteenth century, contains a broad range of medieval learning and*

171 John Lydgate, *Troy Book: Selections*, ed. Robert R. Edwards, TEAMS Middle English Texts Series (Kalamazoo, MI, 1998), Prologue, ll. 76–8.

172 Richard of Maidstone, *Concordia: the Reconciliation of Richard II with London*, trans. A. G. Rigg, ed. David R. Carlson, TEAMS Middle English Texts Series (Kalamazoo, MI, 2003); see ll. 39,123.

173 L. 73.

science, including this classic statement about the Golden Age of the past. As in Chaucer's lyric above, the past here appears as a pastoral dream of plenty and peace, a semi-paradise of fertility. This conventional pastoral ideal, rooted in Roman thought, expressed a medieval ideal of harmony and pleasure while also providing a critique of contemporary failure to live up to the standard of the past.

The Present Age Contrasted to the Golden Age

Formerly, in the days of our first fathers and our first mothers, according to the evidence of the literature through which we learn of these matters, love was loyal and true, free from covetousness and rapine, and the world was a very simple place. Men were not so fastidious in the matter of food and dress. Instead of bread, meat, and fish, they gathered acorns in the woods and searched through the thickets, valleys, plains, and mountains for apples, pears, nuts, and chestnuts, rose-hips, mulberries, and sloes, raspberries, strawberries, and haws, beans and peas, and such things as fruit, roots, and plants. And they rubbed the grain from the ears of corn and gathered grapes in the vineyards without putting them in presses or vats. They sustained themselves abundantly with the honey that ran down the oak trees and drank pure water, without asking for spiced or aromatic wine, nor did they ever drink wine that had been decanted.

At that time the earth was not ploughed but was just as God had prepared it and bore of its own accord the things with which each man fortified himself. They did not look for salmon or pike but wore shaggy skins and made garments from wool just as it came from the animals, without dyeing it with plants or seeds. Their huts and villages were covered with broom plants, leaves, and branches, and they made ditches in the earth. When they feared the stormy air of some approaching tempest, they took refuge among the rocks or the great trunks of full-grown oaks where they had fled for safety. And when at night they wanted to sleep, they brought piles and bundles of leaves or moss or grasses into their huts instead of feather beds.

And when the air was calm, the weather mild and fine, and the breeze soft and pleasant, as if in an eternal springtime, and every morning the birds were at pains to greet the dawn, which stirred all their hearts, in their own language, then Zephyrus, with Flora, his wife, who is goddess and lady of the flowers, would spread out their quilts of flowers for men. (These two bring the flowers to birth and the flowers know no other master, for he and she go throughout the world together, sowing flowers; they give them their shape, and colour them with the colours which the flowers use to honour maidens and favoured young men with lovely, gay chaplets. They do this for the sake of true lovers, who are very dear to them.) These flowers shone with such splendour in the pastures, meadows, and woods that you would have thought that the earth wanted to compete and contend with the sky as to which had the better stars, so proud was she in her flowers.

On such couches as I have described, those who enjoyed the games of love embraced and kissed each other, free from greed and rapaciousness. In these woods, the green trees spread the tents and curtains of their branches over them in order to protect them from the sun. There, these simple, secure folk would have their dances, games, and gentle amusements, free from every care except to enjoy their loyal and loving pleasures. No king or prince had as yet committed the crime of robbing or stealing from others. All were accustomed to be equal and did not want to have anything of their own. They well knew the saying, which is neither false nor foolish, that love and lordship never bore each other company nor dwelt together: the one which dominates always separates them.

4.15 "That, though we love more the works of the ancients, yet we have not condemned the studies of the moderns," from Richard de Bury, *Philobiblon*, ed. and trans. Archer Taylor (Berkeley: University of California Press, 1948), pp. 57–8.

Born in Leicestershire and educated at Oxford, Richard de Bury (1287–1345) was tutor to the young prince who would be King Edward III, whom he subsequently served in a variety of administrative posts. He also held a number of benefices in the gift of the crown including the bishopric of Durham. He travelled on various diplomatic missions for the crown to the papal court at Avignon where he met Petrarch. He became treasurer of the exchequer and ultimately chancellor of the realm from 1334 to 1335. His household in Durham and the London inn of the bishops of Durham included at various periods Thomas Bradwardine, mathematician and theologian; Walter Burley, logician; and Robert Holcot, theologian and biblical scholar – an impressive group of diverse scholars in de Bury's affinity. A collector as well as lover of books, Bury composed Philobiblon *to express his own love of books as part of a plan to bequeath his library to Oxford University. Unfortunately his wish was not fulfilled, for as W. J. Courtenay, explains, "While his episcopal income was substantial, his consecration as bishop in 1333 required him to give up his benefices and canonical prebends, and his lifestyle as prelate, royal envoy, and patron of learning exceeded his familial and episcopal revenues. His books, filling more than five large carts, were sold by the executors of his estate."*[174]

Richard de Bury praises the ancients for their subtle minds and for a greater devotion to the love of learning than he finds in his contemporaries. He dwells on the failings of the moderns who give in to temptations of the flesh, skim through their studies, and live for wealth, not philosophy. Although it is a conventional trope, this critique may also stem from his recognition that the inexorable movement of learning through the world meant that Western scholarship was becoming the custodian of a venerable

174 Biographical details from Oxford DNB online.

tradition of learning. It now bore the responsibility of preserving and of passing on the learning of the past.

Though the novelties of the moderns have never been distasteful to us, who have cherished with ever grateful affection those who had leisure for study and added to the opinions of our own forefathers whatever they could of subtlety or use, yet with more reckless eagerness have we desired to search through the perfected labors of the ancients. For, whether they flourished by nature with a subtler kind of mind or chanced to indulge in more instant study, or whether they made their way supported by the help of both, this one thing we have found to be evident, that their successors scarce suffice to discuss the attainments of those that went before them or to receive even through a compend of their doctrine what the ancients produced by prolonged investigation. And just as we have read that they surpassed in excellence of body what modern times are known to exhibit, so it is in no wise absurd to think that many of the ancients were eminent for greater brightness of mind, since their works prove each of these alike unattainable by posterity. Hence Phocas writes in the prologue of his grammar:

> The Ancients all things in their books explore.
> Say much in little then: thou canst no more.

And if our discourse turn upon fervor of learning and zeal for study, then it is they who devoted their entire life to philosophy. But our contemporaries in these times, glowing for a few years of fervid youth, in turn devote themselves slothfully to the allurements of vice; and when their passions are allayed and they have reached the height of discernment for judging between conflicting truths, being entangled in external affairs, they soon withdraw and bid farewell to the schools of philosophy. They pour out the cloudy must of their youthful minds on the difficulties of philosophy and bestow on anxiety concerning the affairs of this world the wine which clears with age. Yet more, as Ovid justly complains in the first book of his *De Vetula*:

> All turn aside to things that make for gain.
> Few learn; but after wealth all strive amain.
> O Virgin Science! they defile thee so:
> They shame thee who shouldst chaste embraces know;
> Not seeking thee thyself; but gain through thee,
> They live for riches, not philosophy.

And again below:

> The Love of Wisdom banished,
> The Love of Money reigns.

And this, it is clear, is the most violent poison of learning.

4.16 From Giovanni Boccaccio, Preface to *De Mulieribus Cleris* (1361–2), in *Famous Women*, ed. and trans. Virginia Brown (Harvard, 2001), pp. 9–13.

In his preface Boccaccio outlines an apology for telling classical tales of powerful, notorious, and virtuous women from the past. He constructs this group in distinction to Christian heroines whose virtues, while similarly courageous, were different. Moreover, he maintains that both Christian and classical narratives can be read for moral benefit. His work is notable for a number of reasons, including his deliberate construction of the category of good women which appears in both Christine de Pizan's City of Ladies, *and Chaucer's* Legend of Good Women. *The lives and deeds of classical heroines appear in English literature from the late fourteenth century throughout the early modern period. (Translated from the original Latin by Brown.)*

Long ago there were a few ancient authors who composed biographies of famous men in the form of compendia, and in our day that renowned man and great poet, my teacher Petrarch, is writing a similar work that will be even fuller and more carefully done. This is fitting. For those who gave all their zeal, their fortunes, and (when the occasion required it) their blood and their lives in order to surpass other men in illustrious deeds have certainly earned the right to have their names remembered forever by posterity. What surprises me is how little attention women have attracted from writers of this genre, and the absence of any work devoted especially to their memory, even though lengthier histories show clearly that some women have performed acts requiring vigor and courage.

If we grant that men deserve praise whenever they perform great deeds with the strength bestowed upon them, how much more should women be extolled – almost all of whom are endowed by nature with soft, frail bodies and sluggish minds – when they take on a manly spirit, show remarkable intelligence and bravery, and dare to execute deeds that would be extremely difficult even for men!

Lest, therefore, such women be cheated of their just due, I had the idea of honoring their glory by assembling in a single volume the biographies of women whose memory is still green. To these I have added some lives from among the many women who are notable for their boldness, intellectual powers, and perseverance, or for their natural endowments, or for fortune's favor or enmity. I have also included a few women who, although they performed no action worthy of remembrance, were nonetheless causal agents in the performance of mighty deeds.

Furthermore, I do not want readers to think it strange if they find such chaste matrons as Penelope, Lucretia, and Sulpicia in company with Medea, Flora and Sempronia or others like them, who had strong but, as it happened, destructive characters. It is not in fact my intention to interpret the word "famous" in such a strict sense that it will always appear to mean "virtuous".

Instead, with the kind permission of my readers, I will adopt a wider meaning and consider as famous those women whom I know to have gained a reputation throughout the world for any deed whatsoever. Indeed, in the case of illustrious men I remember having read not only about the Leonidases, the Scipios, the Catos, and the Fabricii, but also about the turbulent Gracchi, sly Hannibal, and treacherous Jugurtha; about Sulla and Marius, stained with the blood of civil war; about Crassus, as avaricious as he was rich; and others of similar bent.

An account that praises deeds worthy of commemoration and sometimes heaps reproaches upon crimes will not only drive the noble towards glory and to some degree restrain villains from their wicked acts; it will also restore to this little book the attractiveness lost as a result of the shameful exploits of certain of its heroines. Hence I have decided to insert at various places in these stories some pleasant exhortations to virtue and to add incentives for avoiding and detesting wickedness. Thus holy profit will mix with entertainment and so steal insensibly into my readers' minds.

To avoid the time-honored custom of dwelling only superficially on events, I think it will be useful and appropriate to deal with the stories at somewhat greater length, learning where I can from trustworthy authors. It is my belief that the accomplishments of these ladies will please women no less than men. Moreover, since women are generally unacquainted with history, they require and enjoy a more extended account.

Nevertheless, it seemed advisable, as I want to make plain, not to mix these women, nearly all of them pagan, with Hebrew and Christian women (except for Eve). The two groups do not harmonize very well with each other, and they appear to proceed in different ways.

Following the commands and example of their holy Teacher, Hebrew and Christian women commonly steeled themselves for the sake of true and everlasting glory to an endurance often at odds with human nature. Pagan women, however, reached their goal, admittedly with remarkable strength of character, either through some natural gift or instinct or, as seems more likely, through a keen desire for the fleeting glory of this world; sometimes they endured grievous troubles in the face of Fortune's assaults.

Besides, Christian women, resplendent in the true and unfailing light, live gloriously in their deserved immortality; we know too that their virginity, purity, holiness, and invincible firmness in overcoming carnal desire and the punishments of tyrants have been described in individual works, as their merits required, by pious men outstanding for their knowledge of sacred literature and revered for their dignity. The merits of pagan women, on the other hand, have not been published in any work designed especially for this purpose and have not been set forth by anyone, as I have already pointed out. That is why I began to write this work: it was a way of giving them some kind of reward.

May God, the Father of all things, assist me in this pious endeavour; may He lavish his favor on what I shall write and grant that I write it to his true glory.

4.17 From the Preface, *Caxton's Mirrour of the World* (1481), ed. Oliver H. Prior, EETS, e.s. 110 (London: 1913), pp. 5–6, 19, 24, 25.

In the beginning of this encyclopedic work about salvation, the world, and the cosmos, Caxton offers a survey of the progress of philosophia, or love of knowledge, combined with a critique of contemporary intellectual sloth, and an exhortation to his audience of gentlemen and gentlewomen to gain ethical instruction by reading the words of the ancients. His theme is the industry, devotion, and selflessness the ancients demonstrated in the pursuit of knowledge.

Consideryng that wordes ben perisshyng, vayne & forgeteful, and writynges dwelle & abide permanent, as I rede *Vox audita perit, littera scripta manet,*[175] thise thinges haue caused that the faites[176] and dedes of Anncyent menn ben sette by declaracion in fair and Aourned[177] volumes, to thende[178] that science and Artes lerned and founden of things passed myght be had in perpetuel memorye and remembraunce; ffor the hertes of nobles in eschewying of ydlenes at suche tyme as they haue none other vertuouse ocupacion on hande ought texcersise[179] them in redyng, studyng & visytyng the noble faytes and dedes of the sage and wysemen somtyme[180] travaillyng in prouffytable vertues; of whom it happeth ofte that sommen ben enclyned to visyte the bookes treatyng of sciences particuler, and other to rede & visyte bookes spekyng of faytes of armes, of loue, or of other mervaillous histories. And emonge alle other this present booke, whiche is called the ymage or myrrour of the world, ought to be visyted, redde & knowen, by cause it treateth of the world and of the wondreful dyuision therof. In whiche book a man resonable may see and vndrrstande [sic] more clerer, by the visytyng and seeyng of it and the figures therin, the situacion and moeuyng of the firmament, and how the vnyuersal[181] erthe hangeth in the myddle of the same, as the chapitres here folowyng shal more clerly shewe and declare to you. Whiche said book was translated out of latyn in to

175 The voice perishes, the written word remains.

176 Deeds; here, and throughout this preface Caxton uses "doublets," two words, often one French, the other English or thoroughly anglicized originally French.

177 Adorned.

178 The end.

179 To exercise.

180 In the sense of "at some time" in the past.

181 Entire.

ffrensshe by the ordynaunce[182] of the noble duc Johan of Berry and Auuergne, the yere of Our Lord. M.CC.xlv. and now at this tyme rudely translated out of ffrensshe in to Englissh by me symple persone William Caxton, at the request, desire, coste and dispense of the honourable & worschipful man Hugh Bryce, Alderman and Cytezeyn[183] of London, entendyng to present the same vnto the vertuous, noble and puissaunt lord, Wylliam lord Hastynges, lord Chamberlayn vnto the most Crysten kynge, kynge Edward the fourthe, kynge of England and of Ffraunce, etc., and lietenaunt for the same of the toun of Calais and marches there, whom he humbly besecheth to resseyue in gree[184] and thanke.

* * *

Wherefor and how the vii Artes liberal were founden and of their order. capitulo v.

Now declareth this book whiche is drawen out of Astronomye how somtyme the notable and wyse philosophres wold enquere of the maner of the world, and how hit had ben created and made of God, wherof moche peple meruaylled.

And thenne whan the world was made and compassed, ther was peple ynowhe of which many behelde the firmament that torned round about the world and meuyd. They had grete meruaylle how it myght be made, and they waked and studyed many nyghtes and many dayes. Thenne began they to beholde the sterres that roos in the eest, and meued aboute ouer their hedes.

Certaynly thise philosophres apetyted not[185] these grete mangeries[186] ne delicyuous wynes, ne for to fille their belyes as don beestis that seche nothinge but their pasture, like as this day doo they that retche[187] of nothinge but to fylle their paunche with good wynes and good vitailles and after to haue a fair bedde, white shetes and softe, and there to slepe as the swyne. But those were wakyng and studyeng many nyghtes, and it greued[188] them not; but they were embelisshid[189] moche of that they sawe the firmament thus torne[190] and so nobly to holde his cours and termes.

* * *

182 Decree, direction.
183 Citizen.
184 Favor and good will.
185 Did not have appetite for.
186 Banquets.
187 Care about.
188 Grieved.
189 Cheered.
190 Turn.

And somoche trauaylled and studyed that they knewe, by the helpe of Our Lord of whom alle science groweth and haboundeth, grete partye of that it is. But this was not in lytel tyme, ffor they were longe in studye and vnderstode moche. And they that were first, alle that they vnderstode and knewe, they put it in wrytyng the best wise they coude, to thende that they that shold come after them and wold entremete[191] in connyng,[192] myght haue their wrytyngis and trauaylle alway in the science, as they had don byfore. Alle that they fonde and sawe, they sette in compilacions. And did so moche, eche in his tyme, that they were more than .ii.M. and .CCCC. yere ere they, by their labours and continuel studyes, had goten the vii Artes or sciences liberal and put to gydre.

But they helde their labour wel employed, and the payne that they put therto; ffor they knew, by their witte and by their clergye,[193] alle that was come on erthe by nature, whan they wold sette their cure[194] theron. And also were not abasshed whan a merueyllous caas happed on heuen or on erthe; ffor they could wel enquere the reson wherfore it was, and sith that it happed by nature. And so loued God moche the more, whan they saw such meruayllous werkis.

* * *

So were ther suche philosophres that by their witte and vnderstandyng prophecyed the holy tyme of the comyng of Ihesu Cryste; lyke as Virgyle saide whiche was in the tyme of Cezar[195] at Rome, by whiche plente of peple haue ben better syth than they were bifore; ffor he saide that a newe lignage was enioyed fro heuen on hygh, that shold do vertues in erthe, by whom the deuyl shold be ouercome.

4.18 From *The Brut or The Chronicles of England*, ed. Friedrich W. D. Brie, 3 vols, Vol. 1, EETS, o.s. 131, 136 (London, 1906), pp. 1–4, 11–12.

The passages below, from a manuscript dated c.1400, tell the two major foundation stories of the British Isles; one, the story of Brutus, is familar, the other, the story of Albina, seems to have been neglected by most modern editors. The story of Albina was, however, well known to Anglo-Norman writers whose work often refers to the giants who inhabited England and to the demons who exercised power there. This foundation myth provides background for medieval romances in which England is Logres, a land

191 Become involved in; have dealings with.

192 Study or learning.

193 Study, scholarship.

194 Care.

195 Caesar.

of mystery and magic, a conception likely fostered by the inclusion of the Albina narrative in the Anglo-Norman, Latin, and subsequent Middle English versions of the Brut, or history of Britain, which constituted one of the most popular histories of the Middle Ages. Here is the foundation story that accounts for the name Albion:

How King Dioclisian wedded his 33 Daughters to 33 Kings whom they afterwards murderd; and how these Widows came to England, & had children by the Giants of the land

In the noble land of Surrye[196] ther was a noble kyng and mighty, & a man of grete renoun, that men called Dyoclician, that wel and worthily hym governed, & rewlede[197] thurgh his noble chiualrye, so that he conquered alle the landes abowte hym, so that almoste all the kynges of the world to hym were entendaunt.[198]

Hyt befell thus, that this Dioclician spousede a gentyl damysele that was wondyr fayr, that was hys Eemys[199] doughter, Labana; & sche loued hym as reson wolde, so that he gate upon here xxxiij doughtres, of the which the eldest me[n] called Albyne. And these Damysels, whan they comyn in-to Age, bycomen so fayre that it was wondyr.

Wherfore this Dioclician anon lete make A sompnyng,[200] & comaundid by his lettres that Alle the kyngys that heldyn of hym schulde come at A certayn day . . . to make A ryal fest . . .[201]

And hit befelle[202] thus, that this Dioclician thoughte maryen[203] his Doughtres among all tho knyghtys that tho were at that solempnite, and so they speken & dede,[204] that Albbyne, his eldest doughter, & alle her sustres, richely were maryed unto xxxiij kynges that wer lordes of gret honour, & Also power, at this solempnite. . . .

And hit byfelle thus aftyrward that this dame Albyne bycome so stoute[205] & so sterne,[206] that sche told litel prys of her lord,[207] And of hym hadde scorne and dyspite,[208] and wolde not done his wylle, but wolde haue her

196 Syria.
197 Ruled.
198 Attendant, obedient.
199 Uncle's.
200 Summoned or summoning.
201 To attend a royal feast.
202 It happened.
203 Thought to marry.
204 Did.
205 Proud, arrogant.
206 Inflexible.
207 Had little respect for, little valued.
208 Contempt.

owne wyll in diuerses maners. And all her other sustres, eche on bere hem so euel a-yens here lordes that it was wonder to wete.[209]

[*In spite of fair speech, gifts and kind words, the kings were not to regain the "loue and frenschipe" of their wives. Desperate, Albina's husband wrote to her father for help. Dioclician summoned his daughters and their husbands to his court, to settle the matter. He told his daughters that if they did not change their behavior they would lose his love for evermore.*]

And whanne the ladyes herd al this, they becomen abasshed & gretly a-schamed; & to here fadir they seyd that they wolde make al amendes; & so they departed out from her fadres chambre. and Dame Albyne that was the eldest suster, lad[210] hem all into her chamber, & tho made voide al that were therin,[211] so that no lyf was among hem but sche & here sustres y-fere.[212] Tho[213] said this Albyne, "My fair sustres, ful weel ye knowith that the kyng oure fadir, vs hath reprouyd, schamed & dispised, for encheson[214] to make vs obedient vn-to oure housbandes; but certes that schal y nevere, whiles that I lyve, seth that I am come of a more hyere kynges blode than my housband is'[215] & whan sche had so seyd, all here sustres seyd the same."

And tho seyd Albyne: "ful wel y wot,[216] fayr sustres, that our housbandes haue playned[217] unto owre fadir vpon vs, wherfore he hath thus vs foul reproued & dispised. wherfore, sustres, my counseil is that, this nyght, when owre housbandes ben abed, all we with on[e] assent cutten here throtes, & than we mow be in pees of hem,[218] & better we mowe do this thing vndir our fadres power than elles-where." & anon All the ladyes consentid and graunted vnto this counceil.

And what nyght was comyn, the lordes & ladies wente to bedde, & anon as here lordes were in slepe, thei cutte all here housbandes throtes, & so they slowen[219] hem all.

[*Dioclician was so angry he would have had them all burned, but his barons and lords counseled him not to do so, rather to banish them forever from his land instead.*

209 And all her other sisters, each one bore herself so ill toward their lords that it was wonder to see (know of).

210 Led.

211 Ordered everyone previously in that chamber to leave.

212 Together.

213 Then.

214 In order

215 A higher king's blood line, of greater worship than my husband's, i.e. her father's blood line is more worthy and noble.

216 You know full well.

217 Complained.

218 And then we will be in peace from (free of) them.

219 Slew.

Agreeing, he commanded them to go on board a ship which he provisioned with food for half a year, and so they sailed forth in the sea, putting their trust in "Appolyn[220] *that was her god."*]

And so long they sailled in the see, til at the laste thei come & aryved in an yle that was all wyldernes.

And when dame Albyne was come to that land, & all her sustres, this Albyne went ferst[221] owt of the shipe, & sayde to here other sustres: "for-as-mich,"[222] quod sche, "as I am the eldest suster of all this cumpanye, & ferst this land haue takyn, & for-as-meche as myn name is Albyne, y[223] wil that this land be called Albyon, after myn owne name;" & anon all here Sustren her graunted with a good wylle.

Tho wenten owt all the Sustres of the Shippe,[224] & tokyn the lond Albyon, as her Suster called hit; & there they wente up and doun, and founde neither man ne woman ne child, but wylde bestes of divers kyndes.

And whan here vitaill were dispended,[225] & hem faylled, they fedde hem with erbes & frutes in seson of the yeer, & so they lyved as they best myght. And after that, they tokyn flessh of divers beestys, and bycomen wondir fatte,[226] and so they desirid mannes cumpanye and mannys kynde that hem faylled[227]; and for hete they woxen wondir coraious[228] of kynde that hem faylled,[229] so that they desirid more mannys cumpanye than eny other solas or merthe.

Whan the Devyll that perceyued and wente by divers contres, & nome[230] bodyes of the eyre & likyng natures shad [sic; shap?]of men, & come in-to the land of Albyon and lay by the wymmen, and schad tho natures upon hem,[231] & they conceiued, and after thei broughten forth Geauntes,[232] of the which on me[n] called Gogmagog, and another Laugherigan, & so they were nompned[233] by diuers names; & in this manere they comen forth, and weren boren horrible Geauntes in Albion; & they dwellyd in Cavys & in hulles[234] at here

220 Apollo.

221 First.

222 For as much, see also "for-as-meche" below.

223 I.

224 Then all the sisters left the ship.

225 When their food had been used up.

226 Became very fat.

227 They desired men's company and men's nature which they lacked.

228 Desirous, eager.

229 Of sex; male semen that they lacked.

230 Took bodies of the air, and in the form of men.

231 And shed those natures upon them, i.e. seeming to be men, had sex with the women, impregnating them with inhuman embryos.

232 Giants.

233 Named.

234 Hills.

will,[235] & had the lond of Albyon as hem liked, unto the tyme that Brut Arryved & come to Tottenesse, that was in the Ile of Albyon. and there this Brut conqueryd & scomfyted[236] these geauntes aboueseyd.

In contrast to the unbridled will and wild ways of Albina and her sisters, which ultimately result in a race of monsters in Britain, the later story of the re-founding of the island's culture shows the central importance of harmony, organization, and deliberation. This second narrative provides the topos of New Troy which appears in Sir Gawain and the Green Knight. *The two foundation stories together suggest anxieties as well as the affirmations about the relationships that underlie both household and polity.*

How Brut made London, & Called this land Brytaigne, & Scotland Albyne, & Wales Camber

Brut and his men wenten[237] forth & sought aboute in divers places wher they myghte fynde a good place & a couenable[238] that they mighte [make] in a Cytee for hym and for his folk, so at the laste they come by a fayr Ryuer that is called the Tamyse;[239] & ther Brut be-gan a fayre Cyte for hym & for his folk; & lete calle[240] it "the new Troye," in mynde & remembraunce of the gret Troye, fram which place all her lynage was comen.

And this Brut let felle adoun wodes,[241] & lete erye & sowe londes,[242] & done mow medes[243] for sustinaunce of hym & of his peple. & he departed the land to hem,[244] so that eche of hem had a certayn place for to dwelle upon. And Brut lete Calle al this land Britaigne, after his owne name, & his folk he lete calle Britouns.

And this Brut had geten on his wyf[245] Gennogen iij sones that were worthy of dedes[246]: the first me callyd Lotryn, the secounde Albanac & the thryd kambyr.

And Brut bare Crowne in the Cyte of new Troye xx yeer after tyme the Cyte was made; & ther he made the lawes that the Britouns holdeth: & this Brut

235 As they pleased.
236 Grieved.
237 Went.
238 Suitable.
239 Thames.
240 Named it
241 Caused woods to be cut down.
242 Plow and sow lands.
243 Ordered that meadows be mowed.
244 Divided the land among them.
245 Begotten on his wife.
246 Who did noble deeds which gained worship.

was wondirly weel byloved among all men; & Brutes Sones also loueden wonderly wel to-gydere.

Further Reading

Akbari, Suzanne Conklin, *Seeing Through the Veil: Optical Theory and Medieval Allegory* (Toronto: University of Toronto Press, 2004).

Albertus, Magnus, Saint, *On Animals: A Medieval Summa Zoologica*, translated and annotated by Kenneth F. Kitchell, Jr., & Irven Michael Resnick (Baltimore: Johns Hopkins University Press, 1999).

Bartlett, Robert, *The Natural and the Supernatural in the Middle Ages: the Wiles Lectures Given at the Queen's University of Belfast, 2006* (Cambridge: Cambridge University Press, 2008).

Biernoff, Suzannah, *Sight and Embodiment in the Middle Ages* (New York: Palgrave Macmillan, 2002).

Carey, Hilary M., *Courting Disaster: Astrology at the English Court and University in the Later Middle Ages* (New York: St Martin's Press, 1992).

Chance, Jane, *Medieval Mythography* (Gainesville: University Press of Florida, 1994).

Collette, Carolyn P., *Species, Phantasms, and Images: Vision and Medieval Psychology in* The Canterbury Tales (Ann Arbor: University of Michigan Press, 2001).

Copeland, Rita, *Pedagogy, Intellectuals, and Dissent in the Later Middle Ages: Lollardy and Ideas of Learning* (Cambridge: Cambridge University Press, 2001).

Courtenay, William J., *Schools and Scholars in Fourteenth-Century England* (Princeton, NJ: Princeton University Press, 1987).

Edson, Evelyn, *Mapping Time and Space: How Medieval Mapmakers Viewed their World* (London: British Library, 1997)

Edson, E. and E. Savage-Smith, *Medieval Views of the Cosmos: Picturing the Universe in the Christian and Islamic Middle Ages* (Oxford: Bodleian Library, 2004).

Fleming, John, *Classical Imitation and Interpretation in Chaucer's Troilus* (Lincoln, NB: University of Nebraska Press, 1990).

Freudenthal, Gad, *Science in the Medieval Hebrew and Arabic Traditions* (Burlington, VT: Ashgate, 2005).

Frugoni, Chiara, *Books, Banks, Buttons, and Other Inventions from the Middle Ages*, trans. William McCuaig (New York: Columbia University Press, 2003).

Givens, Jean E. et al., eds. *Visualizing Medieval Medicine and Natural History, 1200–1550* (Burlington, VT: Ashgate, 2006).

Grant, Edward, *The Foundations of Modern Science in the Middle Ages: Their Religious, Institutional, and Intellectual Contexts* (Cambridge: Cambridge University Press, 1996).

Green, Monica Helen, *Women's Healthcare in the Medieval West: Texts and Contexts* (Burlington, VT: Ashgate/Variorum, 2000).

Harvey, P. D. A., *Medieval Maps* (London: British Library, 1991).

Hughes, Jonathan, *Arthurian Myths and Alchemy: The Kingship of Edward IV* (Sutton: Stroud, 2002)

Kaye, Joel, *Economy and Nature in the Fourteenth Century: Money, Market Exchange, and the Emergence of Scientific Thought* (Cambridge: Cambridge University Press, 1998).

Langermann, Y. Tzvi, *The Jews and the Sciences in the Middle Ages* (Brookfield, VT: Ashgate/Variorum, 1999).

Lindberg, David C., *The Beginnings of Western Science: The European Scientific Tradition in Philosophical, Religious, and Institutional Context, Prehistory to A.D. 1450* (Chicago: University of Chicago Press, 2007).

Linden, Stanton J., *Darke hierogliphicks: Alchemy in English Literature from Chaucer to the Restoration* (Lexington: University Press of Kentucky, 1996).

Matheson, Lister M., *Popular and Practical Science of Medieval England* (East Lansing: Colleagues Press, 1994).

Nolan, Barbara, *Chaucer and the Tradition of the Roman Antique* (Cambridge: Cambridge University Press, 1992).

North, John David, *Chaucer's Universe* (Oxford: Clarendon Press, 1988).

North, John David, *Stars, Minds, and Fate: Essays in Ancient and Medieval Cosmology* (Ronceverte, WV: Hambledon Press, 1989).

Nicole Oresme and The Marvels of Nature: A Study of his De causis mirabilium with Critical Edition, Translation, and Commentary by Bert Hansen (Toronto: Pontifical Institute of Mediaeval Studies, 1985).

Orme, Nicholas, *Medieval Schools: from Roman Britain to Renaissance England* (New Haven, CT: Yale University Press, 2006).

Park, Katharine, *Secrets of Women: Gender, Generation, and the Origins of Human Dissection* (New York: Zone Books, Distributed by the MIT Press, 2006).

Petrina, Alessandra, *Cultural Politics in Fifteenth-Century England: The Case of Humphrey, Duke of Gloucester* (Leiden: Brill, 2004).

Saliba, George, *Islamic Science and the Making of the European Renaissance* (Cambridge, MA: MIT Press, 2007).

Sherman, Claire Richter, *Imaging Aristotle: Visual and Verbal Representation in Fourteenth-Century France* (Berkeley: University of California Press, 1995).

Voigts, Linda E. and Patricia Deery Kurtz, *Scientific and Medical Writings in Old and Middle English* (Ann Arbor: University of Michigan Press, 2000).

Wakelin, Daniel, *Humanism, Reading, and English literature, 1430–1530* (Oxford: Oxford University Press, 2007).

5

Book Production: The World of Manuscripts, Patrons, and Readers

Book production in England increased rapidly over the course of the fourteenth and fifteenth centuries. Surviving records in London tell us that in the early years of the fourteenth century the number of book artisans in London totaled fewer than ten; in the decade 1390–1400, 34 book artisans are documented; from 1400 to 1409, 44. For most of the fifteenth century the number of documented book artisans – a class of trade that included stationers, bookbinders, text writers and manuscript artists – fluctuated between 35 and 50.[1]

In part the expansion of production, as well as the consumption and technology that accompanied it, built on systems already in place. The book trade near universities flourished well before the fifteenth century, and for centuries monastic libraries had copied, stored, and circulated texts. During the later Middle Ages they continued to do so, keeping what are now regarded as the major chronicles of events of the period. Higden's Polychronicon, *Thomas Walsingham's St Alban's chronicles, and Henry Knighton's chronicle, written at St Mary's Abbey, Leicester, are outstanding examples of this category of texts. The resources of monastic scriptoria were also enlisted in the early fifteenth century in disseminating works like Nicholas Love's* Mirror of the Blessed Life of Jesus Christ, *an extremely popular text endorsed by the Archbishop of Canterbury as worthy to be made available in order to refute Lollard errors.*[2]

As Ann Hudson has shown, Lollard authors, with their signature regard for the written word of God, were aware of the power of textual dissemination. Despite government

1 See C. Paul Christianson, *A Directory of London Staioners and Book Artisans 1300–1500* (New York: Bibliographical Society of America, 1990), p. 14. See, too, Christianson, "Evidence for the Study of London's Late Medieval Manuscript-Book Trade," in *Book Production and Publishing in Britain, 1375–1475*, ed. Jeremy Griffiths and Derek Pearsall (Cambridge: Cambridge University Press, 1989), pp. 87–108. On distinctions among stationers, scriveners and text-writers, and the development of the London book trade see Graham Pollard, "The Company of Stationers before 1557," *The Library*, 4th series, Vol. XVIII, No. 1, June, 1937, pp. 1–38.

2 On the authorization of religious words for dissemination beyond monastic walls in the early fifteenth century, see A. I. Doyle, "Publication by Members of Religious Orders," in Griffith and Pearsall, pp. 109–23, 115–17. The fact that Nicholas Love was the first prior of Mountgrace, the Carathusian house closely tied to Lancastrian nobility, suggests some of the intersections of polity and doctrine in the period. On Love, see, too, 2.12.

attempts to suppress them, a large number of Lollard texts survive from the period: "more copies of the Wyliffite Bible than of any other medieval work in English, more copies of the standard sermon cycle than of any single version of Piers Plowman, and nearly twice as many as of Troilus and Criseyde.*"*[3] *Judging by the records of the 1415 trial of John Claydon, an apparently illiterate London skinner, the Lollard desire for books could be termed almost fetishistic. The records suggest that a commitment to book-ownership, as much as his own beliefs, served to condemn him. Claydon confessed to "complete sympathy" (Hudson, p. 126) with the ideas expressed in* Lanterne of Light (see 2.21)*, a heterodox text of the period that bewailed the pervasive corruption of society, its falling away from virtue to follow the anti-Christ, and extolled the role of scripture, particularly the gospels, as a lantern of light to those who sought the true way. Claydon was intimately involved in the production of his own copy of the* Lanterne of Light *as the trial records show:*

> [his copy of] the *Lanterne* was said to be covered in red leather, well bound and written on vellum in a good English hand. The volume had been made to Claydon's specifications by John Gryme; Gryme had brought the loose quires to Claydon's house in St Martin's Lane, where he and one of Claydon's servants, John Fuller, had read the material to Claydon, himself illiterate . . . after which Claydon had expressed himself well pleased with the book. Its binding presumably followed also at Claydon's expense. (Hudson, 126)

The details of the case open a window on the entrepreneurial and somewhat ad hoc dimensions of book production in London, a trade that grew rapidly over the course of the fifteenth century, driven by increased literacy, and, if Claydon is any example, desire simply to own a book, an object of vertu.

Central to the book trade was the role of "audience" – the people who would desire to own and presumably to read books. The role of patronage was crucial in the creation of manuscripts, which were largely bespoke productions, reflecting the buyer's tastes and desires, and either copied to order, or created by binding already copied texts together into a volume.[4] *The book trade operated both on a system of bespoke ordering – asking for a copy of a specific text, or combination of texts – and a system supported by the stockists of exemplar texts. One could ask for a book that combined a number of already prepared texts, bound together in a unique volume made to individual specifications. None of these elements was an innovation, but all flourished and changed over*

3 Ann Hudson, "Lollard Book Production" in Griffiths and Pearsall, pp. 125–42, p. 137. For a further discussion of Lollard ideas, see Chapter 2.17–23.

4 See Kate Harris, "Patrons, Buyers and Owners: the Evidence for Ownership and the Role of Book Owners in Book Production and the Book Trade," in Griffith and Pearsall, pp. 163–99, and Carol M. Meale on Chaucer's grand-daughter, Alice Chaucer and her connection especially to the works of Christine de Pizan in "Reading Women's Culture in Fifteenth-Century England: the Case of Alice Chaucer," in *Mediaevalitis: Reading the Middle Ages: the J. A. W. Bennet Memorial Lectures*, Ninth Series, ed. Piero Boitani and Anna Torti (Perugia, 1996), pp. 81–101.

the course of the century. It is hard not to look at the changes from a teleological perspective and come to the conclusion that the two major technological achievements of the period – increased paper production and the printing press[5] *– responded to the increased demand of the market, and the changed nature of the literate population of England: no longer essentially clerical, that population now included country gentry and city merchants who had both money and a desire for access to the knowledge of fact and of imagination available in books.*[6]

The documents assembled here highlight some of the major elements of the manuscript book trade as they affect understanding of literary production in the later fourteenth and fifteenth centuries. We begin with the physical fact of books – the materials of which they were composed – because medieval books were literally labor-intensive artifacts whose production entailed physical labor over an extended period of time. The next group of texts provides a contemporary description of what was available for purchase from scriveners, stationers, and parchment makers in the later Middle Ages. The following class of documents illustrates some of the forces at play in book production – patronage, economics, taste, and cultural anxiety. Excerpts from Richard de Bury's Philobiblon *provide a series of rhapsodic and critical reflections about the almost transcendent nature of books and the number of ways such precious vessels might be abused by careless readers (see 5.5). Wills are a useful, if imperfect, means of access to book ownership and circulation. They can tell us about the range of literature available to and valued by English men and women in the fourteenth and fifteenth centuries; for this reason we include some of the inventories and descriptions of books bequeathed in wills. Finally, this chapter concludes with several documents that indicate the power of books for moral instruction as well as the lure of the imagination that made them objects of improper desire from some perspectives.*

5.1 Recipe for Ink from *The Commonplace Book of Robert Reynes of Acle: an Edition of Tanner MS 407*, ed. Cameron Louis (New York: Garland, 1980), item #30 (Receipts for Ink, Glue and Tempering), pp 170–3.

We start with the more tangible, tactile aspects of book creation and of the book trade, as a reminder to those of us who live in a world of virtual texts that late medieval books

5 For an introduction to William Caxton, England's first printer, see 1.5.

6 Modern scholarship has revealed that the late medieval book trade was a protean, dynamic system of exchanges that flourished all over England. In the Sandars Lectures of 1959, Graham Pollard laid out a description of how the book trade in England, and especially the London trade, was part of a system of insular and continental exchanges in which individual stationers, and later printers, could buy and sell book stock. His work suggests the importance of the provincial book fairs where London and European book dealers brought already bound books for sale and resale. These fairs were held throughout the country, generally outside of large towns, in a space where stalls and booths could be set up to trade a variety of goods including book manuscripts. Graham Pollard, "The English Market for Printed Books: The Sandars Lectures, 1959," *Publishing History*, 4 (1978), 9–48; see esp. pp. 11–14.

were artifacts made through laborious processes dependent on a whole chain of agricultural and mercantile interactions. A book was both an expensive and a very real "natural" object.

This recipe for ink reveals a need for a combination of local and exotic ingredients that presupposes a market in which to obtain them. It was recorded by Robert Reynes (c.1450–1505/12?), son of a village carpenter, who served as a churchwarden and reeve on behalf of Tintern Abbey, which held the manor of Acle in Norfolk where he lived. Reynes performed a number of administrative activities for the Abbey, including keeping accounting records, supervising agricultural work, recording taxes, and meeting with the Abbot of Tintern. He created a manuscript in his own hand, referred to today as his "commonplace book." A miscellaneous collection of various records – the French words for numbers, various law codes, charms for divining the future, astrology, Marian devotions – it is one of a class of miscellany manuscripts increasingly common in the fifteenth century. Louis, his most recent editor, suggests that Reynes may have been educated to read and write documents such as charters and conveyances, and that through this education he used his literacy to expand his knowledge. His book certainly reflects a broad range of interests. In contrast to many late medieval receipts, his directions include fairly precise measurements of quantity, and an interesting indication of time-measure through a familiar recitation. As a scribe of his own manuscript, Reynes was likely very familiar with the processes and ingredients needed to make ink in order to be able to write. (Biographical details and quoted material from DNB *online.)*

To Make Ink

Ffor to make blak ynke, take gallys[7] coporose[8] and gumme of rabyk,[9] of iche aleke mekyll be wyte.[10] And make powder of thi gallys and of thy coporose, of eyther be hemselff.[11] And ley thi gumme in watir to stepe[12] al a nyght. And on the morwen take thi gumme-water and thi pouuder of gallys, and put hem togeder, and sette hem ouer the fyer, and let hem sethen[13] the space of this psalme seying, "Miserere mei, Deus."[14] And than cast thi powder of coporose therin, and steret[15] well togeder, and than take it don.[16] And if thu wylt make

7 Oak gall.

8 Vitriol.

9 Gum of Arabic; gum from certain species of Acadia.

10 Take an equal amount of each by weight.

11 Make a powder of each of these separately.

12 Soak in water.

13 Boil.

14 That is, for as long as it takes to say this psalm, which is Psalm 50, a penitential psalm which takes about three minutes to read (see Louis, p. 388).

15 Stir it well together.

16 Off the fire.

inke for ony book of grete prys[17], take as mekell[18] coporose as gumme and gallys. And to iii vncis[19] take a quarte of reyn water, for that is best therfor. And than it is good inke, sekerly. And stere it well euery day. Gumme, i quart, gall, i quart, coporose, i quart: iiii d.[20]

Ffor to make reed ynke, take vermelyon,[21] and grynit with gleyer,[22] and temperit. Ffor to make gleyer, take the whyte of an egge, and brayet[23] in a dissch with a sponge tyl it is as schort[24] as ony water, and than it is good gleyer to gryne and temperyn[25] with vermelyon for reed inkke. If it burbelyt[26] whan ye gryne it, take sape[27] of youre eere, and grynit "therwith", and that schal don away alle tho burbelys.

Ffor to make blew inkke, take byse[28] and temperyt with gumme-water, and steryt well, and than it is good blew inkke. Ffor to make gumme-water, take gumme of arabyk as moche as aboue, and put it in a sauser[29] ful of clene water a day or a nyght tyl it is turned alle to water. And than it is good to temperyn with byse for blew hynk.[30]

5.2 Making Parchment and Paper: from *Pen to Press: Illustrated Manuscripts and Printed Books in the First Century of Printing*, Sandra Hindman and James Douglas Farquhar (Baltimore: Johns Hopkins, 1977), pp. 12, 16.

Most medieval manuscripts were written on a form of animal hide called parchment. The hides to be prepared were usually taken from sheep or goats, often from cows. The most prized hides were those of lambs, kids and calves, and, as the brief description below indicates, those prized above all for smoothness and quality were the skins of aborted fetuses of these animals. The preparation of parchment and vellum required soaking skins in a lime solution in order to loosen hair which was then discarded. The skin was then stretched on a frame and scraped repeatedly with a special, curve-bladed knife over a period of days during which time the skin was stretched under increasing

17 Value.
18 Much.
19 Ounces.
20 The price: 4 pennies.
21 Vermilion.
22 Grind it, in the sense of crushing, with an egg white.
23 Crush.
24 Thin, not viscous.
25 Mix with.
26 Bubbles.
27 Ear wax.
28 A pigment of gray.
29 Saucer.
30 Ink.

tension to yield a smooth writing surface. Hindman and Farquhar note the confusion surrounding the terms parchment and vellum, variously applied to the skins of born and unborn goats, pigs, calves, and sheep. They include this definition of both terms, taken from a 1519 text:

> That stouffe that we wrytte vpon: and is made of beestis skynnes: is sometyme called parchement/ somtyme velem/ somtyme abortyue/ somtyme membraan. Parchement of the cyte: where it was first made [Pergamum]. Velem/ bycause it is made of a caluys skynne. Abortyue/ because the beest was scante perfecte. Mambraan/ bycause it was pulled of by hyldynge[31] fro the besstis lymmes. (William Horman, *Vulgaria* [London: 1519, fol. 80v–81], reprinted in facsimile, Amsterdam, 1975, cited Hindman, Farquhar, p. 12)

Paper

Parchment and vellum, which are so closely associated with animal bodies, link the world of thought directly to the world of corrupt matter. Paper production dealt with textiles, rather than animals, but it, too, involved a lengthy process of decomposition and transformation. Paper was not uncommon in Europe after the thirteenth century, but it became much less expensive and much more available during the fifteenth century. It was usually made from linen rags which were soaked to a pulp to the extent that the texture of the cloth dissolved into fibers which were placed into a large vat full of warm water. This watery pulp mixture was kept warm and moving to provide consistent suspension of the fiber particles. From this vat the pulp was scooped into flat screened paper moulds from which the water ran away. The fibers were dried, and then sealed with a solution made from a boiled mixture of parchment and leather bits, in order to produce a surface on which the ink would neither run nor seep into the paper. Here is Horman's description of paper whose origins, like parchment's, are traced to the Middle East.

> Papyr fyrste was made of certeyne stuffe like the pythe of a bulrusshe in Aegypt: and syth it is made of lynnen clothe soked in water stampte or grunde pressed and smothed. (Horman, fol. 80, in Hindman, Farquhar, p. 16)

5.3 The Book Trade from *William Caxton's Dialogues in French and English*, ed. Henry Bradley, EETS, e.s., Vol. 79 (London, 1900), pp. 36–9, 47.

The excerpt below is from a 1480 print publication by William Caxton. It is from the English translation of a series of French dialogues designed to help speakers learn the

---

31 Flaying, stripping off the skin.

vocabulary and some of the idioms of both languages. Like a modern phrase book that tourists might carry to a country where the language is unfamiliar to them, this series of dialogues offers help with the lexicon of a wide variety of subjects – house, household, time, seasons, trade, ecclesiastical and noble titles. Written originally in Bruges in 1367, and titled Livre des Metiers, *it proved useful a hundred years later when it was translated by an English merchant and published by Caxton.*[32] *It contains descriptions of the world of manuscript production and dissemination, of scriveners, book sellers, and parchment makers' work. Not coincidentally this early printed book affords a lively perspective on book-related trades in the late fourteenth and fifteenth centuries – including the difficulties one might encounter with an improperly prepared parchment skin.*

Geruays the scriuener	(writer, scribe)
Can well write chartres,	(deeds conveying property or title)
Preuyleges, instrumentis,[33]	(rights)
Dettes, receyttes,	(debts)
Testamentis, copies.	(wills)
He can wel rekene	
And yelde rekenynges	(accounts)
Of all rentes,	(income)
Be they of rente for lyf,	
Or rent heritable,	(inherited income)
Of all fermes.	(rents, annual payments)
He is well proufitable	
In a good seruise;	
That whiche he writeth	
Abydeth secrete.	
Hit is the most noble craft	
That is in the world;	
For ther is none so hye	
Ne so noble	
That may hym shame	
For to lerne ne for to doo.	
Yf it wer not [for] the scripture	(fr. *Escriture,*writing)
The law and faith shold perisshe,	
And all the holy scripture	
Shall not be put in forgeting.[34]	

32 C. Paul Christianson, "A Century of the Manuscript-Book Trade in Late Medieval London," *Medievalia et Humanistica*, 12 (1984), pp. 143–65, p. 160. Bradley notes the strong Flemish influence of lexicon and idiom and assumes Caxton was the translator who also added references to English fairs, towns and bishoprics (p. vi–vii).

33 A written document by which formal expression is given to a legal act, contract, title deed.

34 Shall not be forgotten; because of writing, we can remember and have Holy Scripture.

Therfore euery true cristen man
Ought for to do lerne
To his children and frendes;
And them selfe owe it to knowe,
Or othirwyse, without faulte,
God shall demande them
And shall take of vengeaunce;
For ignorance
Shall nothyng excuse hem.
Euery man so acquite hym
As he wylle ansuere!

George the booke sellar
Hath moo bookes
Than all they of the toune.
He byeth them all
Suche as they ben,
Be they stolen or enprinted, (with a mark of ownership?)
Or othirwyse pourchaced.
He hath doctrinals, catons, (grammars; works of Cato)
Oures of our lady,
Donettis, partis, accidents,[35]
Sawters well enlumined,
Bounden with claspes of siluer,
Bookes of physike,[36]
Seuen salmes, kalenders,
Ynke and perchemyn,
Pennes of swannes, (pens of swan feather)
Pennes of ghees, (pens of goose feather)
Good portoses, (breviaries)
Which ben worth good money.

IOSSE the parchemyn maker
Solde me a skyn of parchemyn
That alle flued, (made the ink run)
And a coueryng of franchyn (a sort of parchment)
Shauen on the one syde,
Whiche nought was worth,
That I myght not write vpon.

---

35 Hours of Our Lady (see below, p. xxx); Donatus' grammar, books of parts of speech; books of accidents.

36 Psalters, books of psalms well illumined, bound with clasps of silver, books of medicine.

Goo fecche a pomyce (to scrape off, erase)
And of the best papier,
My penknyf, my sheris. (scissors)
I shall write a letter of loue,
And shall sende it to my loue.

5.4 How Books circulate: John Shirley's Book Lists: From *The Chaucer Tradition*, Aage Brusendorff (London: Oxford University Press, 1925).

This excerpt is from the book lists of John Shirley (c.1366–1456), a London book seller who had been in the service of Richard Beauchamp, earl of Warwick, before moving to London where he is thought to have operated a scriptorium and a circulating library patronized by gentry and aristocracy in shops in Doke Lane (c.1438–56). A close friend of the poet John Lydgate, Shirley's network of connections embodies the close affiliations among authors, scribes, and book sellers of later medieval London. His versified tables of contents illustrate the eclectic nature of manuscript compendia, and the broad range of reading matter of interest to his possible patrons.[37] *In the verses below Shirley shows his admiration for Chaucer (ll. 26–34), as well as for his contemporary, John Lydgate (l. 80–1).*[38] *(Punctuation added by the editors.)*

The prologe of the Kalundare of this litell booke

If that you list for to entende
Of this booke to here legende[39]
Suche as is right vertuous,
Of maner of mirthe nought vicious,
As wryten haue thees olde clerkis
That been appreued in alle hir werkis
By oure eldris here to fore
(Remembraunce ellyswere forlore),
Ther fore, dere sire, I you beseche
That ye disdeyne not with my speche
ffor affter the symplesse of my wit
So as feblesse wolde suffice hit
This litell booke with myn hande
Wryten I haue, ye shal vnderstande,

37 Biographical details from Oxford DNB online.
38 On the relationship between Shirley and Lydgate see Brusendorff, pp. 460f.
39 Narrative, usually of a saint's live, but also a narrative of an event.

And sought the copie in many a place
To haue the more thank of youre grace
And doon hit bynde in this volume,
That bothe the gret and the comune
May ther on looke and eke hit reede.
Theyres beo the thanke and the meede[40]
That first hit studyed and owt founde;
Nowe beon they dolven[41] deep in the grounde.
Beseche I god he gyf hem grace
In hevens b!isse to haue a place.
And for to put hit in youre mynde.
ffirst thus by ordre shul ye fynde
Of Boece the hole translacyoun
And phylosofyes consolacyoun
Laboured by Geffrey Chaucier
whiche in oure wolgare[42] hade neuer his pere
Of eloquencyale Retorryke.
In Englisshe was neuer noon him Iyke.
Gyff him þe prys and seythe ther hoo
for neuer knewe ye suche na moo.[43]
The passyoun thanne of Nichodeme[44]
fful wel translated shul ye seen.
The whiche of Berkeley lord Thomas
(Whome god assoyle for his grace)[45]
Lete[46] oute of latyn hit translate
By Johan Trevysa that hit made,
A maystre in Theologye,
Approued clerk for the maistrye.[47]
Thankethe the lord and the clerk
That caused first that holy werk.
Thanne filowethe nexst as in writing
The notablest story of huntyng
That euer was made to fore this day.
Redethe and proue hit by assaye.

40 Reward.

41 Buried.

42 Vernacular, vulgar tongue.

43 He deserves the commendation, for his equal has ever been known.

44 An apocryphal New Testament gospel.

45 Whose sins God forgive, by His grace.

46 Commanded.

47 “for the maistrye,” an idiomatic expression to suggest exceptionalism to a high degree.

Maystre of the game men hit calle;
I prey to god feyre mot him falle
Duk of york the last *Edwarde*
That dyed in the vauntwarde[48]
Of the bataylle In picardye
At Agincourt this is no lye.[49]
ffor as of huntyng here to fore
Was neuer taught so truwe lore.
To alle that beon gentyl of kynde[50]
Beon bounde to haue his soule in mynde
And namelych of this oure Regyoun
Whiche was cleped Albyoun
That now is cleped Engeland.
Thanne shul ye wit and vnderstand
Of an Abstrait made in latyne
Al in proose eke lyne by lyne
Grounded vpon holy writte
Regula sacerdotalis is men clepen hit.
God helpe me so as that I not
Who first hit made ne hit wrot.
Ther fore noon Auctour I allegge.

Drynkethe to my lady and I hir plegge:
Lest some folk wolde me mysse construwe,
Thanne, and ye wol the wryting suwe,[51]
Shul ye fynde wryten of a knyght
That serued his souueraine lady bright
As done thees loueres amorous
Whos lyff is offt seen parillous,
Askethe of hem that haue hit vsed.[52]

A dieux Ioenesse, I am refused
Whos complaynt is al in balade
That daun *Johan* of Bury made –
Lydegate the Munk clothed in blacke –
In his makyng ther is no lacke.

48 Fore.

49 On this text and Duke Edward its English translator, see 4.12. Agincourt, the famous English victory in France, on St Crispin's Day, 1415.

50 For all who are born gentle by nature/family.

51 If you will read on.

52 Ask them who have lived such a life.

And thankethe daun Johan for his peyne
That to plese gentyles is right feyne,
Bothe with his laboure and his goode.
God wolde of nobles he hade ful his hoode.[53]
And other balades moo ther beon.
Right godely looke and ye may seon.
And whane ye haue this booke ouerloked
The right kynde with the crooked,[54]
And the sentence vnderstonden,[55]
With Inne youre mynde hit fast ebounden.[56]
Thankethe the Auctoures that these storyes
Renoueld haue to youre memoryes;[57]
And the wryter for his distresse,[58]
Whiche besechithe youre gentylesse
That ye sende this booke ageyne
Hoome to *Shirley* that is right feyne
If hit hathe beon to yowe plesaunce,
As in the Reedyng of the Romaunce
And alle that beon in this companye
God sende hem loye of hir ladye
And euery womman of hir loue
Prey I to god that sittethe abouc.
Explicit.

5.5 Richard de Bury, *The Philobiblon,* on valuing and sharing books: "That the Treasure of Wisdom Lieth Especially in Books" and from "Of the Manner of Distributing Our Books to All Students" (c. 1340–5), Archer Taylor (University of California Press, 1948), pp. 10–11, 93–7, 103–5.

Richard de Bury[59] *was an unabashed bibliophile whose writing about books ranges from rhapsodic description of the wisdom they contain to biting criticism of those too ignorant or too lazy to accord books the honor they deserve. The value of books, measured by money, by their attractiveness even to children, and their fundamental*

53 God willing, he ought have a hood full of nobles (coins).

54 And when you have finished looking through this book, looking at the edifying and less edifying material.

55 The edifying meaning.

56 Hold it bound fast.

57 Thank the authors who have written these stories anew for your memory.

58 And the writer of this kalendar for his trouble.

59 For Bury, see, too, 4.15.

association with the Christian faith, underlies his exposition, as does his distress at the fact that while they are powerful artifacts, books are essentially powerless in the hands of their users.

From "That the Treasure of Wisdom Lieth Especially in Books"

Finally, consider what delightful teaching there is in books. How easily, how secretly, how safely in books do we make bare without shame the poverty of human ignorance! These are the masters that instruct us without rod and ferrule, without words of anger, without payment of money or clothing. Should ye approach them, they are not asleep; if ye seek to question them, they do not hide themselves; should ye err, they do not chide; and should ye show ignorance, they know not how to laugh. O Books! ye alone are free and liberal. Ye give to all that seek, and yet set free all that serve you zealously. By what thousands of things are ye figuratively recommended to learned men in the Scripture given us by Divine inspiration! Ye are the mines of deepest wisdom unto which the wise man, in the second chapter of Proverbs, sends his son thence to dig treasure. Ye are the wells of living water which father Abraham digged at first, Isaac cleared, and which the Philistines strove to fill again (the twenty-sixth chapter of Genesis). Ye are, in truth, most delightful ears filled with corn, to be rubbed by apostolic hands alone, that the sweetest food may drop forth for hungering souls.[60] Ye are the golden pots in which is stored the manna, rocks that flow with honey, yea, also honeycombs, udders streaming with the milk of life, storehouses ever full. Ye are the tree of life and the fourfold stream of Paradise, by which the human mind is fed and the arid intellect is moistened and watered.

The circulation and distribution of books, as Shirley's poetic list-advertisement (5.4) shows, was a continual concern. Here de Bury explains university practices of sharing books.

From "Of the Manner of Distributing Our Books to All Students"

Five of the scholars dwelling in the aforesaid hall are to be appointed by the master of that hall and to them the keeping of all the books is to be deputed. Of these five, three, and in no case fewer, shall have power to lend out a book or books solely for inspection and use in study; but for copying and transcribing we allow no book to pass beyond the walls of the house [college]. Therefore, when any scholar secular or religious, whom we reckon as on equal

60 See Matthew 12.

footing in our present favor, shall ask for the loan of any book, let the keepers carefully consider whether they have the book in duplicate. If so, let them lend him the book, after taking a security the value of which in their judgement is greater than that of the book lent, and make out at once a written entry concerning the security and the book lent, with the names of those who have delivered the book, and of him who has received it, together with the day of the year of our Lord when the loan was made. But if the keepers find that the book required is not in duplicate, let them in no wise lend that book to any one out of the company of the scholars of the said hall, except it be for inspection within the walls of the house or hall aforesaid, but not for removal beyond them. But any book may be lent by three of the aforesaid keepers to any scholar of the said hall, his name and the day in which he receives the book being first noted down. He may not, however, lend to another the book that has been delivered to him, except on leave of three of the above-mentioned keepers, and then let the name of the first borrower be erased and the name of the second, with the time of delivery, be written in its place.

All the keepers shall bind themselves to observe all these rules when the custody of the books is committed to them, and those who receive a book or books shall swear in like manner that they will use the books for no other purpose than inspection and study and will neither take them nor suffer them to be taken beyond the city of Oxford with its suburbs. . . .

But this we must add, that each and every one who has received a book as a loan shall bring it once in the year to the keepers and, if he like, see his security. Furthermore, if any books should happen to be lost through death, theft, fraud, or carelessness, let him who has lost it, or his administrator or executor, pay the price of the book and receive the security; but if profit should in any way accrue to the keepers themselves, it is to be devoted to none other purpose than the repair and maintenance of books.

Of Showing Honorable Respect in the Care of Books:

Not only do we offer a service to God in preparing new volumes, but we practice a duty of sacred piety if we handle them without injury and commit them when returned to their proper places to an inviolable custody, that they may rejoice in their purity while held in our hands and rest in security when laid away in their own couches. No doubt, next after the vestments and vessels dedicated to the body of the Lord, sacred books deserve honorable handling from the clergy; for an injury is done so often as an unclean hand presumes to touch them. Wherefore, we think it expedient to exhort our students regarding various negligences, which might always be easily avoided and which do marvelous harm to books.

First, then, let there be considerate moderation in the opening and shutting of books, that they be not opened in headlong haste nor, when our inspection is ended, be thrown away without being duly closed. For we ought to care far more diligently for a book than for a boot. But the race of scholars is commonly educated badly and, unless it be curbed by the rules of its elders, becomes accustomed to endless childishness. They are moved by petulance; they swell with presumptuousness; they give judgment as though certain of everything, whereas they are expert in nothing.

You shall chance to see some stiff-necked youth sluggishly seating himself for study, and while the frost is sharp in the winter time, his nose, all watery with the biting cold, begins to drip. Nor does he deign to wipe it with his cloth until he has wet the books spread out before him with the vile dew. Would that such a one were given in place of a book a cobbler's apron! He has a nail almost as black as jet and reeking with foul filth, and with this he marks the place of any matter that pleaseth him. He sorts out innumerable straws which he sets in divers places, evidently that the mark may bring back to him what his memory cannot hold. These straws, because the stomach of the book does not digest them and no one takes them out, at first distend it beyond its wonted place of closing and at length, being quite overlooked, begin to rot. He halts not at eating fruits and cheese over the open page and, in a slovenly way, shifts his cup hither and thither. And because he has not his alms bag[61] at hand, he casts the residue of the fragments into the book. With endless chattering he ceases not to rail against his companions and, while adducing a multitude of reasons void of all sensible meaning, wets the books spread out in his lap with the sputtering of his spittle. And what shall I say more? Soon doubling his elbows, he reclines upon the book and by his short study invites a long sleep and, by spreading out the wrinkles, bends the margins of the leaves, doing no small harm to the volume.

And now the rain is over and gone, and the flowers have appeared on the earth. Then the scholar whom we are describing, a neglecter rather than an inspector of books, will stuff his book with the violet, the primrose and the rose, yea, also with the quatrefoil. Then he will apply his watery hands, all damp with sweat, to turning over the volumes. Then will he pound on the white parchment with his dusty gloves, and line by line hunt over the page with a fusty leather finger. Then, at the nip of the biting flea the holy book is flung aside, and scarcely being shut within a month's time, becomes so swollen with the dust that has fallen in it that it cannot obey the effort of one who would close it.

Especially, moreover, must we restrain impudent youths from handling books – those youths who, when they have learned to draw the shapes of letters, soon begin, if opportunity be granted them, to be uncouth scribblers on the best volumes and, where they see some larger margin about the text, make a show with monstrous letters; and if any other triviality whatsoever

61 Pouch for collecting items (of food, esp.) to be given to the poor.

occurs to their imagination, their unchastened pen hastens at once to draw it out. There the Latinist and the sophister and every unlearned scribe proves the goodness of his pen, a practice which we have seen to be too often injurious to the best of books, both as concerns their usefulness and their price.

There are also certain thieves who make terrible havoc by cutting off the margins for paper on which to write their letters, leaving only the written text; or they turn to various abuses the flyleaves which are bound in for the protection of the book. This sort of sacrilege ought to be prohibited under pain of anathema.

Patronage and the Making of Books

5.6 "Balade to my gracious Lord of York" (Edward, 2nd Duke of York, 1402–15, translator of *Master of Game*, see 4.12) from *Hoccleve's Works: the Minor Poems*, ed. Frederick J. Furnivall and I. Gollancz, rev. by Jerome Mitchell and A. I. Doyle, EETS, e.s. 61, 73 (London, 1970).

Thomas Hoccleve (c.1367–1426) was a poet and a clerk of the privy seal in the royal Chancery, as well as a close associate of both Geoffrey Chaucer and his son Thomas Chaucer. From his own words in his most famous work, Regiment of Princes, *addressed to the future Henry V, and surviving in 43 manuscripts, we know that he joined the privy seal office c.1387 and remained there for 38 years. His dual career is typical of a cadre of civil servants, of whom Chaucer was one, who served the crown in various administrative functions and who also wrote poetry. Because he was a man of limited means, he sought patronage from great men. The poem below demonstrates both the flattery and the dependency central to achieving the patronage that supported literary production in the medieval and early modern periods.*[62]

Go, little pamfilet, and streight thee [ad]dresse
Vn-to the noble rootid gentillesse
Of the myghty Prince of famous honour,
My gracious lord of york/ to whos noblesse
Me recommande with hertes humblesse,[63]
As he that haue his grace & his fauour
Fownden alway/ for which I am dettour
For him to preye/ & so shal my symplesse
Hertily do/ vn-to my dethes hour.[64]

---

62 Biographical details from Oxford DNB online.

63 Humility.

64 Recommend me with humility/ as he who has his grace and his favor always found,/ for which I am in debt to pray for him,/ and so I shall in my unworthiness, willingly do until the hour of my death.

2.
Remembre his worthynesse, I charge thee,
How ones at London, desired he,
Of me that am his seruant/ & shal ay,
To haue of my balades swich plentee
As ther weren remeynynge vn-to me;[65]
And for nat wole I/ to his wil seyn nay,
But fulfille it/ as ferfoorth as I may,
Be thow an owter of my nycetee[66]
For my good lordes luste,[67] and game, & pleye.

* * *

6.
If that I in my wrytynge foleye,[68]
As I do ofte, (I can it nat withseye,[69])
Meetrynge amis/ or speke vnfittyngly,
Or nat by iust peys/ my sentences weye,[70]
And nat to the ordre of endytyng obeye,[71]
And my colours[72] sette ofte sythe awry;
With al my herte wole I buxumly,[73]
It to amende and to correcte, him preye;
For vndir his correccioun stande y.[74]

7.
Thow foul book, vn-to my lord seye also,
That pryde is vn-to me so greet a fo[e],
That the spectacle,[75] forbedith he me,
And hath y-doon of tyme yore ago;
And for my sighte bluye hastith[76] me fro,
And lakkith that that sholde his confort be,
No wonder thogh thow haue no beautee.
Out vp-on pryde/ causer of my wo!
My sighte is hurt thurgh hir aduersitee.

65 How once he asked for as many of my balades as I possessed.
66 Expression of my simple wit.
67 Pleasure.
68 Make mistakes.
69 Contradict.
70 Or if I do not construct my sentences in a balanced fashion.
71 And do not obey the rules of writing verse.
72 Rhetorical figures.
73 Obediently.
74 I pray him to correct my errors, for I stand subject to his correction [and superior wit].
75 Eyeglasses; forbids.
76 Quickly hastens.

Book Owners and Readers: Tastes and Connections

5.7 Based on *A Study of Books Privately Owned in England 1300–1450*, ed. Susan H. Cavanaugh, PhD Thesis, University of Pennsylvania, 1980, unpub.

Book ownership in late medieval England was highly fluid – and not always recorded. Wills, as some of the brief notices below show, can provide some information about book ownership, literacy, and the circulation of texts as subjects of interest and indices to social bonds and affinity. The entries here are designed to suggest lines of patronage and the breadth of books available to the nobility as well as the gentry during the later fourteenth and fifteenth centuries. They record the wide variety of reading material available, details of borrowing and transmission, and the catholic tastes of English book owners of the period, men and women.[77]

Joan Neville, Countess of Westmorland (c.1379–1440)

Daughter of John of Gaunt and Katherine Swynford, Joan Neville's second husband was Ralph Neville of Raby, first earl of Westmorland. The children of this marriage in turn married into a number of noble houses over the course of the fifteenth century. Her will, which is printed in John Nichols, A Collection of all the Wills, Now Known to be Extant, of the Kings and Queens of England . . . *(London, 1780) p. 176, mentions no books, but she is linked to books through a number of personal connections. At the time of his death Henry V had in his possession two chronicles of the Crusades which he had borrowed from her. A 1424 letter she sent to Humphrey, Duke of Gloucester, protector of the realm after Henry's death (printed by Thomas Rymer,* Foedera, Conventiones, Litterae, et Cujuscunque Generis Acta Publica, Inter Reges Angliae, etc., *2nd ed, George Holmes, 10 [London, 1727], p. 317), requests their return: "pur faire deliverance a la Countesse de Westmerland d'un Livere (contenant les Cronikels de Jerusalem, & le Viage de Godfray Boylion)."*

Her meeting with Margery Kempe in 1413 is central to a charge levied against Kempe during her interrogation by the suffragan bishop of the Archbishop of York, a charge of interfering in the marriage of Lady Westmorland's daughter, Lady Greystoke, urging that woman to leave her husband, a counsel she is told, "j-now [enough] to be brent for."[78] *Hoccleve addresses her directly at the end of his "Tale of Jonathas and Fellicula":*

---

77 Because of space considerations, one aspect of book ownership that does not appear among these excerpts is the consistently large collections of books owned by ecclesiasts of all ranks, including monks.

78 *The Book of Margery Kempe*, ed. Sanford Meech and H. E. Allen, EETS, o.s. 212 (1940), 133–4.

Go smal book/ to the noble excellence
Of my lady/ of Westmerland/ and seye,
Her humble seruant/ with al reuerence
Him recommandith vn-to hir nobleye . . .[79]

John Carpenter, Town Clerk of London (w. 1442)

In 1417 John Carpenter, the notable bibliophile and citizen of fifteenth-century London (see 2.2), was elected Town (or Common) Clerk of the city of London, a position in which he became the city's archivist, guarding the city's records and organizing them in his Liber Albus, *a compendium of London governance procedures and rules. Closely tied to various guilds and merchant constituencies in the City, he was an executor of Richard Whittington's will. In addition to collecting a sizeable library of his own books, he substantially supported the Guildhall Library.*[80] *Carpenter's bequests are expressed in an informal and allusive style that indicates the dynamic interest in books in his circle, a world of secular merchant-clerks. It also suggests that books form a natural and vital element in the bonds of friendship within that circle; note the categories of bequests that structure this account of books as elements of social and political ties:*

> . . . I give and bequeath to Master John Carpynter, warden of the hospital of St Anthony, as a memorial of me, that book on architecture which Master William Cleve gave to me; and in like manner I give and bequeath to Sir John Neell, master of St Thomas de Acon, that book "cum Secretis Aristotelis,'[81] and "De miseria conditionis humanae,"[82] and other notable things, which my master Marchaunt [his predecessor as Common/ Town Clerk of London] gave to me. . . . Also I give and bequeath to Master William Byngham, as a memorial of me, that book which Master Roger Dymok made, "contra duodecim errores et hereses Lollardorum,"[83] and gave to King Richard, and which book John Wilok gave to me. Also I give and bequeath to Sire William Taillour, chaplain dwelling with me, as a memorial of me, my book "de meditationibus et orationibus Sancti Anselmi,"[84] beginning "Meditationes quae me consolatur," etc., so that he may bestow that book after his decease upon some devout person to pray for our souls. Also I give and bequeath to Sir David Fyvian, rector of the church of St Benet Fink, as a memorial to think of my soul, that book "Bibliae abbreviatae, " and with the

79 For biographical details see Oxford DNB online; information based on Cavanagh, pp. 605–6.
80 See Thomas Brewer, *Memoir of the Life and Times of John Carpenter, Town Clerk of London* (London, 1856), for a translation of Carpenter's will and enumeration of his books, pp. 131–44.
81 *The Secrets of Aristotle*; a handbook for princes' rule.
82 On the misery of the human condition.
83 Against twelve errors and heresies of the Lollards.
84 About the meditations and prayers of St Anselm; beginning "meditations which have consoled me."

"Historiae provinciarum"[85] at the end, which John Sudbury gave to me. . . . Also I bequeath to Robert Langford, late my clerk, as a memorial of me, that book of mine called "Speculum morale regium,"[86] made for a sometime king of France; and to John Crouton, late my clerk, as a like memorial of me, my little book containing "Alanus de planctu,"[87] with other notable things. . . . Also I bequeath to John Brown, late my clerk, as a like memorial of me, all my book in French which belonged to Sir Thomas Pykworth chivaler, containing in the beginning the ten commandments, the twelve articles of faith, the seven theological virtues. . . . Also in like manner I give and bequeath to Richard Lovell, late my clerk, the little book "De corpore pollecie,"[88] in French. Also I give and bequeath in like manner to Robert Blount, late my clerk, my little book "de Parabolis Solamonis,"[89] "Ecclesiasticus," "Seneca ad Callionem," "De remediis utriusque fortunae,"[90] and "De Quatuor virtutibus cardinalibus," together with "Sententiae diversorum prophetarum," translated from Greek into Latin by Master Peter de Alphense, and "Liber de regimine dominorum," otherwise called "Secreta secretorum Aristotelis"[91]./ Also I will that the same Robert may have for the whole of his life, if he will, the use of all my little books or quartos of the modes of entry and engrossing of the acts and records as well according to the common law of the realm as the custom of the city of London, so that, after the decease of the same Robert, they may remain to the chamber of the Guildhall of London, for the information of the clerks there. Also I bequeath to Nicholas Mason and John Elys, my clerks, five marks sterling, to be shared equally between them, and so many of my little books or quartos . . . as shall seem fit to be done by the discretion of my executors. . . . And the residue of all my goods and chattels not bequeathed in my present will, after payment of my debts if any there be, I give and bequeath to my executors within written, to dispose of them in works of piety and mercy. . . . Provided always, that if any good or rare books shall be found amongst the said residue of my goods, which, by the discretion of the aforesaid Master William Lichfeld and Reginald Pecok, may seem necessary to the common library at Guildhall, for the profit of the students there, and those discoursing to the common people, then I will and bequeath that those books be placed by my executors and chained in that library, under such form that the visitors and students thereof may be the sooner admonished to pray for my soul.

---

85 A history text.

86 A mirror of morality for princes

87 Alanus de Insulis, *The Plaint of Nature*.

88 The body politic.

89 The Proverbs of Solomon; Ecclesiasticus from the Bible.

90 Petrarch, *Remedies for Fortune, Good and Bad*. Two works by Seneca: *To Callionem* and *Concerning the Four Cardinal Virtues*.

91 *Thoughts of Various Philosophers: A Handbook for Princes*.

Margaret Courtenay, Countess of Devon (w. 1391)

The 1391 will of Margaret Courtenay, Countess of Devon, granddaughter of Edward I, through her mother Elizabeth, indicates something of the tastes of later fourteenth-century English noble women. Her will, written in French, is excerpted here from Cavanaugh, pp. 213–4.

> Item ieo deuise a William moun fitz Erceuesque de Canterbirs . . . et moun messall que iauoye du Seigneure William Weston. . . . Item a ma fille luttrell* . . . et mon liure appelle Tristram. Item a ma fille Dangayne . . . et mes deux primers et un liure appelle Artur de Britaigne. . . . Item ieo deuise a Anneys Chambnoy . . . et un liure de medycynys et de marchasye et un autre liure appelle vyces et vertues et un liure appelle merlyn. . . . Item a Sire John Dodyngton . . . et mon rouge messall.

[*Also, I bequeath to William my son, Archbishop of Canterbury, my missal, which I had from Sir William Weston; also to my daughter Luttrell, my book titled Tristrem; also to my daughter Dangayne my two primers and a book called Arthur of Britain; also I bequeath to Agnes Chambnoy a book of medicine and skill in caring for horses [?] and another book titled vices and virtues and a book titled Merlyn; also to Sir John Dodyngton, my red missal. Translation by the editors.*]

Robert Thornton (fl. 1440)

Sometime around 1440 Robert Thornton of East Newton, Yorkshire, compiled what is today one of the most famous of the manuscript miscellanies of the fifteenth century, a period noted for the creation of such compendious collections (as in the case of Acle, see 5.1). The miscellany exists in two principal manuscripts, Lincoln Cathedral MS A.i.17, known as The Thornton Miscellany, and BL Additional MS. 31042. The contents of the Lincoln manuscript printed here from a Camden Society edition of the Miscellany, The Thornton Romances, *ed. James O. Halliwell (London, 1844), reflect the encyclopedic nature of these late medieval miscellanies, combining romance and spirituality with a heavy dose of practical knowledge.*[92] *The largely bi-lingual titles generally use Latin for works of spirituality, and English for secular works. (Translations below by the editors.)*

92 On the compilation of the Lincoln Thornton manuscript see John J. Thompson, "The Compiler in Action: Robert Thornton and the 'Thornton Romances' in Lincoln Cathedral MS 91," in Derek Pearsall, *Manuscripts and Readers in Fifteenth-Century England; the Literary Implications of Manuscript Study* (Cambridge: D. S. Brewer, 1983), pp. 113–24.

Excerpted contents of Lincoln Cathedral Ms. A.i.17

Life of Alexander the Great, in prose
Prognostications for each month of the year in which thunder falls
The lamentation of a sinner in purgatory, entitled Lamentacio Peccatoris
Morte Arthure, at the end of which is written "Here endes Morte Arthure, writene by Robert of Thorntone"
Romance of Octovyane
Romance off syr Ysambrace
Romance off Dyoclicyane the emperour and the erle Berade of Tholous, and of the emprice Beaulilione
Vita Sancti Christofori, at the end of which is written: "Explicit vita sancti Christofori. Thorntone." (Life of St Christoper; here ends the life of St Chrsitopher)
Eglamour of Artasse
De miraculo Beate Marie (Miracles of Blessed Mary)
Lyarde[93]
Thomas of Ersseldoune
Awentyrs of Arthure at the Terne-Wathelyne
Romance off Syr Percyvelle of Gales
A charm for the tooth-ache
A similar charm
A charm for the tooth-ache, in Latin prose

Epistola Sancti Salvatoris (Letter of Saint Salvatore)
A Latin orison (prayer), with a proeme in English
A preyere *off* the ffyve joyes of owre Lady (in) Ynglys, and of the ffyve sorowes
Psalmus, *Voce mea ad Dominum clamavi* (My voice cries unto the Lord, ps. 130)
Five Latin prayers
Short prayer entitled *Oracion in Ynglys*
A cole[c]tt to owre lady Saynt Marye, in Latin
Oracio in modo collecte, pro amico (a prayer in the form of a collect, for a friend)
Antiphona sancti Leonardi cum collecta (antiphon for St Leonard with a collect)
Previte off the Passioune of owre Lorde Jhesu
Tractatus Willelmi Nassyngtone, quondam advocati curiae Eboraci, de Trinitate et Unitate, cum declaracione operum Dei, et de Passione Domini nostri Jhesu Christi[94]
Prayer in verse
Prayer in verse
Ricardus Herimita super versiculo, Oleum effusum nomen tuum, in Cantic. etc.

93 Lyarde is a comic poem within a group of romances.

94 A tract by William Nassyngton, former advocate of the York council, concerning the Trinity and its unity, with a declaration about the works of God, and concerning the Passion of our Lord, Jesus Christ.

Narracio. A tale that Richerde Hermet (made)[95]
A prayere that the same Richerd Hermet made
Ympnus quem composuit Sanctus Ambrosyus (a hymn composed by St Ambrose)
Two tales from Hampole *de inperfecta contricione* (concerning imperfect contrition)
Moralia Richardi Heremite de natura apis (a moral tale by Richard the Hermit concerning the nature of the bee)
A tale from Hampole, *De vita cujusdam puelle incluse proptter amorem Christi* (A story of a certain young girl enclosed for the love of Christ)
Two short Latin extracts from *Richardus Herymyta*
A notabille tretys off the ten comandementys, drawene by Richerde the hermyte *off* Hampulle
Item idem de septem donis Spiritus Sancti (Likewise the same concerning the seven gifts of the Holy Spirit)
Item idem de dilectacione in Deo (Likewise the same on the [spiritual] joys of God)
Speculum Sancti Edmundi, Cantuar Archi(e)piscopi, in Anglicis (Mirror of St Edmund, Archbishop of Canterbury among the English)
Tractatus de Dominica oracione secundum, at the end of which is written: "Explicit. Amen. Thorntone. Amen." (Tract on the Lord's Prayer)
Metrical orison
Orison to Christ
Meditacione of the fyve woundes of oure Lorde Jhesu Criste, in Latin verse
Medytacione of the Crosse of Criste, with a prayere in Latin verse
A moral poem
Sermone that dane Johan Gaytryge made
Hymn to Christ
Prose tract on the love of God
A moral poem
Treatise on active and contemplative life
Treatise on sin
Of Sayne Johan the Evaungelist
Prose treatise on prayer
De gracia Dei. (concerning the grace of God)
Quedam revelacio (a certain revelation)
Two Latin hymns
Sayne Jerome Spaltyre, in Latin
Religio Sancti Spiritus. Religio munda (religion of the Holy Spirit, Religion undefiled)

95 Richard Rolle of Hampole, here referred to as "Richard the Hermit" and "Hampole"; Your name is like oil poured out, *Song of Songs*, 1: 2.

Part of a religious poem

De vij gaudia Beate Marie Virginis per sanctum Thomam et martirem, Cantuariensem archiepiscopum, edita (The Seven joys of the Blessed Virgin Mary edited by Thomas, Archbishop of Canterbury, saint and martyr)

Salutacioune tille oure lady of hir fyve joyes, in Latin verse

Ane antyme to the Fadir of Hevene, with a colett, in Latin

Another ant[h]yme of the Passyoune of Criste Jhesu, in Latin

A colecte of grete pardone unto Crist Jhesu, in Latin

A hymn to our Saviour, at the beginning of which is written: "*Thorntone. Misereatur mei Dei.*" (Thornton. Lord have mercy on me)

Preyere to the wounde in Crystis syde, in Latin

Memento, homo, quod sinis es, et in cenerem reverteris (Remember, man, that you are dust, and to dust you will return)

Liber de diversis medicinis (A book of various medicines)

(Lincoln Cathedral MS. A.i.17). c. 1440.

Philippa de Coucy (d. 1411) and Sibilla de Felton (d.1419)

Given the uncertain fate of so many medieval manuscripts, prey – as Richard de Bury notes – to destruction and neglect, it is surprising to be able to trace the transmission of a particular manuscript, but Susan Cavanaugh's careful research has allowed just that. Philippa de Coucy (d. 1411), wife to Robert de Vere, Earl of Oxford who was a close companion of Richard II in the early years of his reign, owned a maunscript which passed into the possession of Sibilla de Felton, Abbess of Barking Abbey, Essex, from 1393 to 1419, the year of her death. We know that both women owned the books described below because they inscribed their names in them, coincidentally leaving a record that allows us to imagine the kinds of exchanges that linked the two women through their books.

Among the books listed in Sibilla de Felton's will is a manuscript now titled Paris, BN MS. fr. 1038, a miscellany of religious texts, largely in French (translations by the editors):

La Vie des sainz Peres (Lives of the Holy Fathers)

Les Voiages que Saint Antoine fist en la terre d'Outremer (St Anthony's voyages in the Holyland)

L'estoire de Balaam et de Josaphat (Balaam and Josaphat)

L'Avenement Antecrist (The Coming of the Anti-Christ)

Si comme Nostre Sires vendra Jugier le Monde (How Our Lord Will Come to Judge the World)

L'Asumptiom Nostre Dame (The Assumption of Our Lady)

Recipe "for to makin aqua vite"

On f. l67b. of this manuscript one can read something of its history: "Cest livre est a Philipe de Coucy duchesse d'Ireland comtesse d'Oyenfordh,"

and on f. 4: "cest liviere achata dame Sibile de Felton, abbesse de Berchyng de les executeurs de dame Philipp Coucy duchesse d'Irland."
(*This book belongs to Philipa de Coucy, Duchess of Ireland, Countess of Oxford; Sibille de Felton, Abbess of Berkyng bought this book from the executors of Dame Philipp Coucy, Duchess of Ireland.*)

Other volumes belonging to Sibilla de Felton:

1. *Ordinale* in Latin and French (Oxford, University Coll. MS. 169): "Memorandum quod anno Domini millesimo quadringentesimo quarto domina Sibilla, permissione divina abbatissa de Berkyng, hunc librum ad usum abbatissarum in dicta domo in futurum existencium concessit et in librario ejusdem loci post mortem cujuscumque in perpetuum commoraturum ordinavit, donec electio inter moniales fiat. . . ."
(Be it noted that in the year 1404 Lady Sibilla, by divine permission abbess of Berkyng, granted this book to the use of the abbesses in the said house in the future and ordained that it be kept after her death perpetually in the library of that house, as long as the sisters choose.)

2. *The Clensyng of Mannes Sowle* (Oxford. Bodl. Lib. MS. Bodley 923). Inscriptions: "Anno domini 1401," and "Iste liber constat Sibille de Felton abbatisse de Berkyng." *(This book belongs to Sibille de Felton, Abbess of Berkyng.)*

3. *Mirror of the Life of Christ*, an English translation ascribed to Nicholas Love. On f. 4b.: "Iste liber constat domine Sibille de Felton' Abbatisse de Berkyng."

(Cavanaugh, pp. 337–8)

Sir John Fastolf (1377–1459)

John Fastolf was born in Norfolk in 1377. He maintained his close connection to Norfolk, and is a notable figure in the Paston Letters, being a supporter of John Paston.[96] *Fastolf fought in France in the Hundred Years' War and distinguished himself in battle, subsequently becoming wealthy through his connections with the nobility. He was appointed seneschal of the Duke of Bedford's household, and became governor of Anjou and Maine. He died in 1459.*

It may have been his connection to the Duke of Bedford that enabled him to gather a substantial library during his life, one that reflects a taste for humanist subjects and texts. A list of books in the inventory of Fastolf's goods at Caister Castle, his chief residence, is preserved in Magdalen College, Oxford (published in Hist. MSS Comm 8th Rtpt, part 1 p. 268 a). It is organized by categories and reflects a strong classical influence:

96 For the Pastons, see 3.7.

In the Stewe hous; of Frenche books:
the Bible.
the Cronycles of France.
the Cronicles of Titus Levius. (Livy's history of Rome)
a booke of Jullius Caesar.
lez Propretez des Choses. (perhaps a version of Trevisa's translation of *De Proprietatibus Rerum,* see 4.1)
Petrus de Crescentiis, Liber almagesti.
Liber geomancie cum iiij aliis Astronomie. (a book of geomancy and four others of astronomy)
liber de Roy Artour. (book of King Arthur)
Romaunce la Rose.
Cronicles d'Angleterre.
Veges de larte Chevalerie. (Vegetius on the art of war)
Instituts of Justien Emperer.
Brute in ryme.
Liber Etiques. (Aristotle's Ethics)
Liber de Sentence Joseph. [sic ?]
Problemate Aristotilis. (Problems of Aristotle)
Vice & Vertues
liber de Cronykes de Grant Bretagne in ryme (book of rhymed chronicles of Great Britain)
Meditacouns Saynt Bernard. (Meditations of St Bernard)

The inventory also includes books for Fastolf's chapel, and a manuscript of one of Christine de Pizan's major works, the Epistle of Othea: *Christinae Pisanae opus quod dicitur Epistola Otheae Deae ad Hectorem Trojanum, cum praefatione ad Johannem ducem de Berry metrica*[97], *in French (Oxford, Bodl. Lib. MS. Laud Misc. 570). l450. On f. 93 is Fastolf's motto: "Me fault fayre," and the date.*

(based on Cavanaugh, pp. 330–32)

Reading for Pleasure and Profit

5.8 A warning against reading for pleasure: from Robert de Gretham, *The Middle English "Mirror": An Edition Based on Bodleian Library, MS Holkham misc. 40,* ed. Kathleen Marie Blumreich (Turnhout: Brepols, 2002), pp. 1–2.

While such records as those above show that people owned books whose topics ranged across a wide spectrum of literature, recurrent claims for texts whose contents are

97 Epistle of Othea: a work of Christine de Pisan which is called the Epistle of the Goddess Othea to Hector of Troy with a preface to John, Duke of Berry, in rhyme.

wholesome and profitable to virtuous living reflect an abiding suspicion of the value of fictional literature in a culture where most actions were regarded as a part of a grand metaphysical exchange system in which deeds earned salvation or damnation. Reading books was no exception. In the passage below, taken from the prologue to the Middle English version of Robert de Gretham's Anglo-Norman Miroir*, a collection of edifying sermons compiled c. 1250–60 for a woman "who apparently had an unhealthy appetite for secular literature," (p. xiii) (possibly Aline [Elena] de Quency), we read a commonly expressed refutation of the value of fiction. Like Chaucer's Parson, who asked why he should sow chaff when he could sow wheat (ParsT 35–6),*[98] *Gretham's project is to affirm the superior value of meaning over expression, ultimately setting the Bible as the standard by which to judge the moral worth of all other writing:*

> . . . many men hyt ben that han inwylle[99] to heren rede romaunces & gestes. That is more then ydelschyp[100], & that I wol wel that alle men hit wyte.[101] Ffor they ben controued[102] thorw mannes wytte that setten her hertes to folyes & trofles.[103] As the lyer doth, he maketh his speche queyntlyche[104] that hit may ben delysious to mannes heryng for that hit scholde be the better listened. Ffor Salamon seyth he had enquered & sowght all thingus undur sunne, & then he fond in al nothyng but uanyte but that thyng that falles to Goddes worschyp[105] and to note of mannes sowle [Eccles. 1:13–14]. & therfore yche haue sette my herte for to drawe owt a lytel tretyce of dyuynyte,[106] that men that han wille for to here suche truyfles, that they mow turne here hertes therfro and yeue hem to thyngus that is profitabul both to lyf and to soule. God hit me graunt yyf hit be hys swete wylle.[107] And for men seyn that al thyngus that ben ywryten hit ben for to leuen,[108] & they gabben;[109] for they that maken thes songes and these gestes,[110] they maken hem aftur wenyng.[111] And men sey on olde Inglysche that wenyng is no wysdom. Loke now to Tristrem, other of Gy of Warrewyk, or of ony other, & thu ne schalt fynde non that ther nys many lesynges & gret.[112] Ffor they ben

98 *The Riverside Chaucer*, ed. Larry D. Benson, 3rd ed. (Boston: Houghton Mifflin, 1987).
99 Great desire.
100 Mere idleness.
101 And I wish that all men would understand this.
102 Composed.
103 Through the wit of men who have set their hearts on follies and trifles.
104 Cleverly.
105 Glory and honor.
106 Little treatise of divinity.
107 God grant me the achievement of this task if it be His will.
108 Worthy to be believed.
109 Lie.
110 Romance; poem or song about heroic deeds.
111 According to their supposition, idle fancy.
112 If you read the romance of Tristram or Guy of Warwick, or any other, you will find none that is not full of many and great lies.

nought drawen owt of holy wryt,[113] but iche man that maketh hem enformeth hem aftur the wylle of his herte, & thenketh that hit is al soth[114] & no for than is al uanyte for to here alle suche thyngus and undurstand hem that the soule ne may no gode leren. Ffor alle that thyng that doth no god to the sowle byfore God is nought worth. & mychel he lest[115] of his time that so settes his herte from God & trespaseth gretlyche.

Textual Apologies: The Value of Reading

From The Prologues and Epilogues of William Caxton, *ed. W. J. B. Crotch, EETS, o.s. 176 (London, 1928), pp. 11–13.*

5.9 William Caxton, Prologue, *The Game and Playe of the Chesse,* 2nd ed. 1483.

In this prologue Caxton argues the moral utility of the work he translates, and invokes a common medieval aphorism best known today from Chaucer's Canterbury Tales: *"all that is written is written for our doctrine."*

The holy appostle and doctour of the peple saynt Poule sayth in his epystle. Alle that is wryten is wryten vnto our doctryne and for our lernyng. Wherfore many noble clerkes haue endeuoyred them to wryte and compyle many notable werkys and historyes to the ende that it myght come to the knowlege and vnderstondyng of suche as ben ygnoraunt. Of which the nombre is infenyte[116]/ And accordyng to the same saith Salamon. that the nombre of foles[117] is infenyte/ And emong alle other good werkys. It is a werke of ryght special recomendacion to enforme and to late vnderstonde wysedom and vertue vnto them that be not lernyd ne can not dyscerne wysedom fro folye. Thenne emonge whom there was an excellent doctour of dyuynyte in the royame of fraunce of the ordre of thospytal of Saynt Johns of Jherusalem[118] whiche entended the same and hath made a book of the chesse moralysed, which at suche tyme as I was resident in brudgys in the counte of Flaundres[119] cam in to my handes/ which whan I had redde and ouerseen/ [me] semed ful necessarye for to be had in englisshe/ And in eschewyng[120] of

113 Not based on Holy Scripture.

114 But each man who composes them shapes them according to the will of his own heart, and thinks that it is all truth.

115 Lost, wasted.

116 Infinite.

117 Fools.

118 Jean de Vignay.

119 In Bruges in the country, territory of Flanders; literally the area ruled by an earl.

120 Avoiding.

ydlenes And to thende that somme which haue not seen it/ ne vnderstonde frensshe ne latyn. I delybered[121] in my self to translate it in to our maternal tonge/ And whan I so had achueued the sayd translacion/ I dyde doo sette in enprynte[122] a certeyn nombre of theym/ Whiche anone were depesshed[123] and solde. wherfore by cause thys sayd book is ful of holsom wysedom and requysyte[124] vnto euery astate and degree/ I haue purposed to enprynte it/ shewyng therin the figures of suche persons as longen to the playe. In whom al astates and degrees ben comprysed/ besechyng al them that this litel werke shal see/ here or rede to haue me for excused for the rude and symple makyng and reducyn[125] in to our englisshe/ And where as is defaute to correcte and amende/ and in so doyng they shal deserue meryte and thanke/ and I shal pray for them/ that god of his grete mercy shal rewarde them in his euerlastyng blisse in heuen/ to the whiche he brynge vs that wyth his precious blood redemed vs. Amen

5.10 In Praise of Chaucer's Art: from William Caxton, Proheme to *The Canterbury Tales*, second edition, 1484; From *The Prologues and Epilogues of William Caxton*, pp. 90–1.

In this prologue Caxton ventures away from the moral justification for his translations and offerings, moving beyond the merely edifying in his praise of Chaucer's artful writing. The passage is notable because it is an expression of fifteenth-century praise of Chaucer as the quintessential English writer, and because it includes an anecdote about Caxton's awareness of and anxiety about the unstable nature of the Chaucer canon. He expresses both a sense that a "standard" text may well exist, and an awareness of the great deal of variability which had crept into the body of works attributed to Chaucer over the course of the fifteenth century, in a literary culture which depended on scribes whose work was the combining and recombining of literary texts.

Grete thankes laude[126] and honour/ ought to be gyuen vnto the clerkes/ poetes and historiographs[127] that haue wreton many noble bokes of wysedom of the lyues/ passions and myracles of holy sayntes of hystoryes/ of noble and famous Actes/ and faittes[128]/ And of the cronycles sith the begynnyng of the creacion of the world/ vnto thys present tyme/ by whyche we ben dayly

121 Thought carefully; deliberated.
122 I caused to be printed.
123 Fr. Depecier, dispose of; here, dispatch.
124 Requisite, necessary.
125 Translation.
126 Praise.
127 Historians.
128 Deeds.

enformed/ and have knowleche of many thynges/ of whom we shold not haue knowen/ yf they had not left to vs theyr monumentis wreton/ Emong whom and inespecial to fore alle other we ought to gyue a synguler laude vnto that noble and grete philosopher Gefferey chaucer the whiche for his ornate wrytyng in our tongue may wel haue the name of a laureate poete/ For to fore that he by hys labour enbelysshyd/ ornated/ and made faire our englisshe/ in thys Royame was had rude speche and Incongrue[129]/ as yet it appiereth by olde bookes/ whyche at thys day ought not to haue place ne be compared emong ne to hys beauteuous volumes/ and aournate[130] writynges/ of whom he made many bokes and treatyces of many a noble historye as wel in metre as in ryme and prose/ and them so craftyly made/ that he comprehended hys maters in short/ quyck and hye sentences/ eschewing prolyxyte/ castynge away the chaf of superfluyte/ and shewyng the pyked greyn of sentence/ vtteryd by crafty and sugred eloquence[131]/ of whom emonge all other of hys bokes/ I purpose temprynte by the grace of god the book of the tales of cauntyrburye/ in which I fynde many a noble hystorye/ of euery astate and degre/ Fyrst rehercyng the condicions/ and tharraye of eche of them as properly as possyble is to be sayd/ And after theyr tales whyche ben of noblesse/ wysedom/ gentylesse/ Myrthe/ and also of veray holynesse and vertue/ wherin he fynysshyth thys sayd booke/ whyche book I haue dylygently ouersen[132] and duly examyned to thende that it be made acordyng vnto his own makyng/ For I fynde many of the sayd bookes/ whyche wryters haue abrydgyd it and many thynges left out/ And in somme place haue sette certayn versys/ that he neuer made ne sette in hys booke/ of whyche bookes so incorrecte was one brought to me vj yere passyd/ whyche I supposed had ben veray true and correcte/ And accoryng to the same I dyde do enprynte a certayn nombre of them/ whyche anon were sold to many and dyuerse gentyl men/ of whome one gentylman cam to me/ and said that this book was not accoryng in many places vnto the book that Gefferey chaucer had made/ To whom I answred that I had made it accordyng to my copye/ and by me was nothyng added ne mynusshyd[133]/ Thenne he sayd he knew a book whyche hys fader had and moche louyd/ that was very trewe/ and accordyng vnto hys own first book by hym made/ and sayd more yf I wold enprynte it agayn he wold gete me the same book for a copye/ how be it he wyst wel/ that hys fader wold not gladly departe fro it[134]/ To whom I said/ in caas that he coude gete

129 Incorrect.

130 Ornate.

131 That he expressed his matter in short, quick, and elevated sentences, avoiding wordiness, casting away the chaff of superfluity, and showing the select grain of substance, expressed by artful and sugared eloquence.

132 Overseen.

133 Nor removed (diminished).

134 Be separated from it.

me suche a book trewe and correcte/ yet I wold ones endeuoyre me to enprynte it agayn/ for to satysfye thauctour/ where as to fore by ygnouraunce I erryd in hurtyng and dyffamyng his book in dyuerce places in settyng in somme thynges that he neuer sayd ne made/ and leuyng out many thynges that he made whyche ben requysite to be sette in it/ And thus we fyll at accord/ And he ful gentylly gate of hys fader the said book/ and delyuerd it to me/ by whiche I haue corrected my book/ as here after alle alonge by thayde of almyghty god shal folowe/ whom I humbly beseche to gyue me grace and ayde to achyeue/ and accomplysshe/ to hys laude honour and glorye/ and that alle yet that shal in thys book rede or heere/ wyll of your charyte[135] emong your dedes of mercy/ remembre the sowle of the sayd Gefferey chaucer first auctour/ and maker of thys book/ And also alle we that shal see and rede therin/ may so take and vnderstonde the good and vertuous tales/ that it may so prouffyte/ vnto the helthe of our sowles/ that after thys short and transitorye lyf we may come to euerlastyng lyf in heuen/ Amen

5.11 Literature and Action: from William Caxton, Epilogue to *Godefroy of Bologne*, 1481, p. 48.

One of the three modern worthies among the nine worthies of medieval culture,[136] *Godefroy of Bologne was a popular figure because of his heroic deeds in the Holy Land. This prologue suggests the political as well as spiritual uses of history and of reading history. The vicarious experience of reading about Godefroy might well inspire readers to take up the Cross as soldier-pilgrims who pledge to recover the Holy Land from the Saracens to the glory of God and the honor of Christ, a theme that recurs in English literature well into the early modern period.*

Thus endeth this book Intitled the laste siege and conquest of Jherusalem with many other historyes therin comprysed/ Fyrst of Eracles,[137] and of the meseases[138] of the cristen men in the holy londe/ And of their releef and conquest of Jherusalem/ and how Godeffroy of boloyne was first kyng of the latyns[139] in that royamme and of his deth, translated and reduced out of ffrensshe in to englysshe by me symple persone Wylliam Caxton to thende that euery cristen man may be the better encoraged tenterprise warre for the defense of Cristendom, and to recouer the sayd Cyte of Jherusalem in whiche

135 Charity.

136 The nine worthies comprised three groups: the three pagans, Hector, Alexander the Great, and Julius Caesar; three Biblical heroes, Joshua, David, and Judas Maccabeus; three "modern" heroes, Arthur, Charlemagne, and Godfrey.

137 Hercules.

138 Sufferings.

139 Europeans.

oure blessyd sauyour Jhesu Criste suffred deth for al mankynde. and roose fro deth to lyf/ And fro the same holy londe ascended in to heuen. And also that Cristen peple once vnyed in a veray peas[140]/ myght empryse[141] to goo theder in pylgremage with strong honde for to expelle the sarasyns and turkes out of the same that our lord myght be ther seruyd and worshipped of his chosen cristen peple in that holy and blessyd londe in which he was Incarnate and blissyd it with the presence of his blessyd body whyles he was here in erthe emonge us/ by whiche conquest we myght deserue after this present short and transitorye lyf the celestial lyf to dwelle in heuen eternally in ioye without ende Amen/ Which book I presente vnto the mooste Cristen kynge, kynge Edward the fourth. humbly besechyng his hyenes to take no displesyr at me so presumyng. whiche book I began in marche the xij daye and fynyshed the vij day of Juyn/ the yere of our Lord M. CCCC. lxxxj and the xxj yere of the regne of our sayd sauerayne lord kyng Edward the fourth. and in this maner sette in forme and enprynted the xx day of nouembre the yere a forsayd in thabbay of Westmester by the sayd wylliam Caxton.

Further Reading

Aston, Margaret, *Lollards and Reformers: Images and Literacy in Late Medieval Religion* (London: Hambledon Press, 1984).

Connolly, Margaret, *John Shirley: Book Production and the Noble Household in Fifteenth Century England* (Aldershot: Ashgate, 1998).

Driver, Martha W,. *The Image in Print: Book Illustration in Late Medieval England and its Sources* (London: British Library, 2004).

Driver, Martha W. and Michael T. Orr, *An Index of Images in English Manuscripts from the Time of Chaucer to Henry VIII, c.1380–c.1509* (New York City, Columbia University–Union Theological, London: Harvey Miller Publishers, 2007).

Green, D. H., *Women Readers in the Middle Ages* (Cambridge: Cambridge University Press, 2007).

Hudson, Anne, *Lollards and Their Books* (Ronceverte, W. Va.: Hambledon Press, 1985).

Hudson, Anne, *The Premature Reformation: Wycliffite Texts and Lollard History* (Oxford: Clarendon Press, 1988).

Justice, Steven, *Writing and Rebellion: England in 1381* (Berkeley: University of California Press, 1994).

Justice, Steven and Kathryn Kerby-Fulton, eds, *Written Work: Langland, Labor, and Authorship* (Philadelphia, Pa.: University of Pennsylvania Press, 1997).

Kerby-Fulton, Kathryn and Maidie Hilmo, eds, *The Medieval Reader: Reception and Cultural History in the Late Medieval Manuscript* (New York: AMS Press, 2001).

Kerby-Fulton, Kathryn, *Books Under Suspicion: Censorship and Tolerance of Revelatory Writing in Late Medieval England* (Notre Dame, IN: University of Notre Dame Press, 2006).

140 Once united in a true peace.

141 Undertake, plan.

Kuskin, William, *Caxton's Trace: Studies in the History of English Printing* (West Bend, IN: University of Notre Dame Press, 2006).

McCash, June Hall, ed., *The Cultural Patronage of Medieval Women* (Athens, GA: University of Georgia Press, 1996).

Meale, Carol M., ed., *Women and Literature in Britain, 1150–1500* (Cambridge: Cambridge University Press, 1993).

Mooney, Linne R., "Some New Light on Thomas Hoccleve," *Studies in the Age of Chaucer*, 29 (2007), pp. 293–340.

Mooney, Linne R., *The Design and Distribution of Late Medieval Manuscripts in England* (York: York Medieval Press, 2008).

Olson, Linda and Kathryn Kerby-Fulton, eds, *Voices in Dialogue: Reading Women in the Middle Ages* (Notre Dame, IN: University of Notre Dame Press, 2005).

Pearsall, Derek, *New Directions in Later Medieval Manuscript Studies* (York: York Medieval Press, 2000).

Riddy, Felicity, ed., *Regionalism in Late Medieval Manuscripts and Texts: Essays Celebrating the Publication of A Linguistic Atlas of late Mediaeval English* (Cambridge: D. S. Brewer, 1991).

Scott, Kathleen L., *The Caxton Master and his Patrons with a Preface by J. A. W. Bennett* (Cambridge: Cambridge Bibliographical Society, 1976).

Scott, Kathleen L., *Later Gothic Manuscripts, 1390–1490* (London: H. Miller, 1996).

Scott, Kathleen L. *Dated & Datable English Manuscript Borders, c. 1395–1499* (London: Bibliographical Society/British Library, 2002).

Scott, Kathleen L., *Tradition and Innovation in Later Medieval English Manuscripts* (London: British Library, 2007).

Smith, Lesley, and Jane H. M. Taylor, *Women and the Book: Assessing the Visual Evidence* (London: British Library, 1997).

Watt, Diane, *Medieval Women's Writing: Works by and for Women in England* (Cambridge, UK: Polity Press, 2007).

6

Producing and Exchanging: Work in Manors and Towns

The documents in this chapter might, on first encounter, encourage a view of the period 1350 to 1500 as a particularly conflictual era in medieval English society and culture, an era of struggles often explained by the demographic catastrophe associated in the early fourteenth century with particularly harsh climatic change, hunger and even starvation; or by the plague, first felt in 1349 but continually re-experienced over the following century, which sharply reduced the English population, devastated families and communities across the land, and led to new battles over the land as well as terms of service and work among both aristocracy and peasants; or by the long and complicated struggles between English and French warriors that we now label the Hundred Years' War, sometimes a source of wealth and resources for the aristocracy, but often a drain upon the monarchy and the realm; or by the rivalry between Lancastrians and Yorkists, eventually resolved in the precarious but ultimately successful claim by Henry Tudor to the crown; or by some combination of all of the preceding.

It may, however, be a mistake to concentrate too heavily upon the demographic crisis, the external struggle generated by the English crown's claim to the French kingdom, or the internal struggles originating in rivalries among English aristocrats. Instead, what is worth noting at the outset is the extraordinary achievement of English rulers and subjects in the centuries preceding these various conflicts and crises, an achievement that rested on a system of manorial production which in turn sustained major overseas trade, especially in wool; an achievement that included an elaborate and sophisticated royal administration, capable of collecting taxes for warfare and administering justice throughout the country, howbeit more effective "justice" the closer to London the administration; and an achievement which also included a network of parishes and dioceses, alongside major and minor monastic houses and their estates, giving Christianity a strong, creative, if also potentially oppressive, presence in most communities of the realm. Whatever the evidence for conflict and crisis during the period after 1350, we should not overlook the strength and resilience of the institutions constructed by that date, institutions strong enough to shape the struggles over resources and power, even as those struggles illustrated the tensions and contradictions within the same institutions.

At heart, the re-shaping of communities during the late Middle Ages may be best understood as a re-negotiation of the terms of work, within manors where peasants usually acknowledged but sometimes contested their subordination to lords both lay and ecclesiastical, and in towns and cities, where artisans and craftsmen depended upon but also challenged merchants who ordinarily dominated civic government. Late medieval England remained a society and polity organized hierarchically, but status was always vulnerable, or open, to revision. Villein or servile tenure, after all, was taken for granted, by both lords and tenants at the beginning of our period; it had become the exception for peasants in England by the end. Such a change surely owes something to the creativity and imagination of those who struggled over what work should be done, to whose benefit, and by whom, during these years.

6.1 Work and the Rule of Custom, from R. Sharpe France, "Two Custumals of the Manor of Cockerham, 1326 and 1483," *Transactions of the Lancashire and Cheshire Antiquarian Society Publications* 64 (1955), pp. 42–52.

Here, two customaries from the lordship of Cockerham, Lancashire, are included because they offer detailed description of the rules governing land and work to be enforced by lord and community alike, as well as extensive information regarding what peasants owed the lord of the manor; because they enable us to grasp the complex relationship of governance and agrarian production characterizing rural life in the late Middle Ages; and because the subtle but important contrasts between the earlier of the two – in Latin, recorded in 1326 – and the later – recorded in English in 1483 – afford some guidance to continuities and changes in agrarian society and the dynamic, even violent, relationship between lords and peasants in the late Middle Ages. Given the insight the customary of 1326 offers into agrarian life and into the lives of a majority of English people of the era, it is reproduced at length; only a few clauses of the later customary, largely relating to relations between lords and their tenants, are reproduced, but they should be enough to encourage reflection on changes in what lords expected of their tenants and servants by the end of this period. Does the language of duties and obligations in this English-language customary point to increased power and authority by lords over their lands and laborers? Or does it indicate a struggle to hold onto seigneurial rights, and reflect the attempt by lords to renew effective control over land and labor, control weakened or at least modified by the initiative of peasant tenants and laborers ready to take advantage of demographic or political crises for their own advantage? Clearly, lordship remains a given of agrarian production and life more generally at the end of the fifteenth century – but it may not be precisely the same kind of lordship exercised in the early fourteenth century. The translation below of the Customs of 1326 is that of R. S. France; so also, his glosses and emendation, in brackets, within the 1483 customary have been retained, with the exception of "no" for "na" and "if" for "and"; after the first appearance of each in the document; it seemed sensible simply to substitute "no" and "if" thereafter.

The Customs of 1326 [Latin]

The customs of the manor of Cockerham in the county of Lancaster diocese of York and archdeaconry of Richmond observed of old in the said manor of Cockerham and ordained from time to time in the court of the same manor of the aforesaid lord and in a court which was held by Brother William Geryn, cellarer of the monastery of the Blessed Mary of Leicester in the year of our Lord one thousand three hundred and twenty-six [1327] and in the first year of the reign of King Edward the third after the conquest of England.

It was ordered that the tenants and [blank] shall not dig more turves. than they can conveniently and sufficiently use for burning, and the fuel from the holdings shall not be provided for strangers under pain of half a mark.

And the tenants of each Crymbyill [Great Crimbles and Little Crimbles] shall maintain the dikes of the mill pond so that the pond does not burst for the lack of them.

And no tenant shall go to other mills.

And the tenants of the marsh shall maintain the sea dikes each of them at his own place under payment of half a mark.

Item no tenant shall call any of his neighbours a thief or a robber . . . under pain of 40d.

And no tenant shall call any of his neighbours whore . . . if he does so he shall give the lord 12d.

Item no tenant shall prevent the cattle or animals of his neighbours from being taken into the lord's pound when an offence has been committed under pain of 40d.

Item no tenant shall dare to put cattle or animals in the lord's pound or in any way drag them out by night or furtively lead them away under pain of 6s. 8d.

Item no tenant shall implead his neighbour or his fellow for any injury he has suffered in another court outside the aforesaid lordship under pain of the seizing of his holding.

Item no tenant shall allow his holding or his houses to fall into ruin under pain of making full reparation and of the seizing of his holding.

No tenant shall bring fuel for his salt cote from outside his holding or take the fuel which has been assigned to one holding to another without the licence of the lord under pain of 40d.

No tenant shall sell his turves [peat] to anyone without the grant of a licence from.the lord under pain of 20d.

No tenant shall keep on a marsh, that is to say a common pasture, horses of less value than half a mark which are called in English Nasaldes[1] or Tyttes[2] under pain of 6s. 8d.

---

1 Asses.

2 A small kind of horse.

No tenant shall keep a scabby horse or horses under pain of 6s. 8d.

Item no tenant of his own authority shall alter the boundaries of any sands or turf which has been assigned from ancient times under pain of half a mark.

Item no tenant shall in any way deprive his neighbour of the turf which has been assigned to him under pain of half a mark. Item no tenant shall destroy in any manner the ancient and appointed way on our moss which in English is called Morethweyte or dig turves thereon under pain of 40d.

Item none of our tenants whether in our court or outside shall, either as a whole or singly, falsify any inquest under pain of paying half a mark to the lord, and similarly to each man who is upon the inquest.

None of our tenants shall in any way remove his neighbour's fences under pain of 12d. Item none of our tenants in the place called the Bankhouse shall keep the ditches closed which reach from the moss to the sea causing thereby a stifling of his neighbour's corn, nor shall he prevent those who are concerned from opening them under pain of half a mark.

Item no brewer who brews for sale shall refuse to sell beer up to four gallons under pain of 6d. Item anyone holding his tenement for any time after the Feast of the Nativity of St John the Baptist [24 June] and not rendering a penny in the manor of the lord shall be held wholly and fully in account for the whole of the following year until the same Feast although in the meantime he has left his tenement.

Item no tenant shall by himself or his cattle break the dike of the water mill in any way or make a path through the middle of it under pain of 40d. for each time.

Item no tenant shall receive servants whether men or women against the will and command of the lord under pain of 6s. 8d.

The tenants of the Great and Little Crymbles shall maintain and preserve the dike of the aforesaid water mill from harm and breach under pain of 40d. each place being responsible for the part of the dike anciently assigned to it under pain of the sum aforesaid.

Item each tenant having four acres of arable land shall plough with the lord with one ox twice a year or he shall give the lord 6d., and if he has eight acres he shall give 12d. and so in a mounting scale in proportion to the quantity of his land, 12d. for a plough.

And each tenant shall give gifts to the lord in autumn as they are contained in the rental or 12d. for each gift and 12d. for each hen.

And each tenant shall give a 1/2d. a year for the making of the fold and likewise the elders [superiores] of the town give 'outlane halpenyes for the cauce [causeway]'. And on his death each tenant shall give the lord his best beast.

Item the lord shall be paid one penny for any stray animal belonging to the tenants caught in the corn, the meadow, or the pasture of the lord.

And no tenant within the manor of Cockerham shall keep a pig in his house unless it be in chains under pain of 40d. but he shall keep his pigs on the common pasture of Wiyrsdall and then he owes [blank] to the warden of the manor for them. And no tenant shall allow the aforesaid pig to enter onto the lord's demesne under pain of 40d. for each time and no tenant shall keep the aforesaid swine within the lord's demesne under pain of 40d. for each, always excepting Adam Slaven, senr. and Randolph Hoggesson; and the reason for this is that these tenants aforesaid may keep them in the pasture unharmed and free from the interference of their neighbours the one in the wood of Forton and the other in his own field.

And no tenant of the manor of Cockerham shall live anywhere other than on his holding in the manor of Cockerham with his family, and if he does so his holding will be seised and taken into the lord's hand.

And no tenant shall set to farm or in any other way sublet his land, pasture, or moss without licence under pain of the seizing of his holding. And no one shall keep she-goats within the boundary of the manor of Cockerham, and if they do shall be heavily amerced.

Item whoever has a holding of four acres of land shall bring one ox to plough with the lord's team twice a year or he shall give the lord 12d. for the ox if he does not have it, and should he have eight acres of land he shall bring two oxen or give the lord 2s. and if he has more he shall give more, and if less he shall give less according to the number of acres which he holds unless he has a full plough team and then he shall plough with the lord twice a year.

And no one shall fell any trees or cut branches in the lord's woods or receive any who have done so and if he does he shall be heavily amerced. And when damage of this kind has been done an inquest of the inhabitants of the wood shall be held in the lord's court of those who have done the damage and if they cannot be apprehended by this inquest then the inhabitants will be amerced to the amount of the damage done; a special penalty is imposed however for oak and ash namely 40d. . . .

No tenant shall hire servants whether men or women for the period of hay making until the lord has chosen whom he will at or near the Feast of St Peter in Chains [1 August]. Tenants summoned to mow with the lord shall come on the day appointed or on the next day immediately following under pain of 2s. Item no tenant shall receive any men or women who although resident in the lordship refuse to reap in August if they then take themselves off to other service, and he shall not take any such reapers or binders into his service until the warden of the manor has expressed a wish to have them or not; if he does so he shall be heavily amerced. Item when all the tenants have been summoned to plough or reap with the lord on a certain day they shall not fail to come on the day on which they were summoned, except when they are reasonably prevented and then they shall come on the morrow of the aforesaid day; if they default then distraint shall be made of all their animals until they submit to the will of the warden.

Item no tenant shall pasture his animals along the dikes of the lord or on his holding, if he does so he shall be heavily amerced.

Item no tenant shall implead or complain against his neighbour in another court or take part with a stranger or relative against his neighbour for any injuries, but he shall abide by the decision of the lord's court; if he disobeys his land shall be taken into the lord's hand until he has made sufficient amends. Item no one shall appear in the court of Gobyr Weyt[3] under pain of a heavy amercement.

No tenant in his digging for turves shall encroach upon the ancient boundaries assigned to the salt marsh as far as a place called the Grene under pain of 40d.

No tenant shall trap any of the animals on the warren by any device or contrivance without the licence of the lord under pain of 20d.

No one shall agist[4] in his own or on the common pasture any animals called in English forinnote[5] that is to say acquiring for him profit in money except for the purpose of work of tilling the soil under pain of 40d.

No tenant selling meat in the market under the price at which others buy outside shall deny it to his lord.

No ale-wife of the aforesaid lord shall sell a gallon of ale at a dearer price than a silver halfpenny so long as the price of a quarter of oats does not exceed 2s. 6d. without the licence of the lord under pain of 40d.

No tenant of the Bankhouse shall trade his fuel with the strangers who come looking for mussels under pain of 40d.

It is ordered that no tenant of the Bankhouse shall keep any animals in the pasture for two years excepting only one cow; if he has a horse or a mare there he shall pay 48d. a year to the lord for each of them. And accordingly he shall pay the lord agistment for the other animals which he has and may bring with him but he shall not have geese or pigs or any of that kind.

The customs of 1483

Thies ben the customs of Cokyrhame mad[e] by the lord and his offycers ever to be observyd and kepyd in tyme to cum. In the fyrst, that and [if] a tenond[6] be agayns hys lord in any maner of wyse whilk [which] ys the lord's matter he schall forfett hys place. Or if a tenond conseyll[7] ony of hys rente or ony of hys servys he schall forfett his place. Or if ony tenond seyke hym master-shippe or frenschippe without Cokyrham agayns the lord or agayns ony tenond, he sall forfett hys place. Or if any tenond brynge in to Cokyrham onv owt men, or resett [receive] ony of thaym agains the lord or onv man that is

3 The court of the manor of Nether Wyresdale was held at Gubberthwaite in Cabus.

4 Turn out to grass.

5 Possibly foreign neat, i.e., cattle from outside the manor.

6 Tenant.

7 Conceal.

within the lordschape,[8] for if he do he sall forfett hys place. Or if oni tenond lett hys howse ga [go] downe bot yf [unless] that thay be made sufficient onse in the yer when thay ar[e] seyne, he forfett hys place.

Ther sall na [no] tenond hald [hold] no place unless he dwell oppon yt with hys meyneyth [household] he sall forfett yt to the lord. Also ther sall no tenond halde [hold] no place unless he saw [sow] ii partys of hytt in the yer, or ells he sall forfett hytt to the lord. Also ther sall no tenond sett [let] hys place ne [nor] taveryn [subdivide] his land nor hys mosse withowt leve of the lord, bot he sall forfett hys place. Also ther sall no tenond sett [let] his cowte [saltcote], nor taveryn [subdivide] hitt nor his mosse[9] withowt the lycense of his lord, bot lay down the thryd [third] parte well and take halfe for that fredom [privilege], pay in the yer a quarter of salte to the lord, or ells he sall forfett hvs cowte [saltcote]. Also ther sall no tenond ynprow [improve] nane [no] intake of the comwen [common] pastur[e] unless it be acent [assent] of the lord and ber [bear] hym rente yeyrly, for if he do he sall forfett hys place. Also ther sall no tenond resett [receive] no man nor woman that vs forbedyn the iordschepe, of payn of vi^{s} viij^{d}. Also ther sall no tenond cutt nor pull up by the rotes nedar [neither] ashys nor akys [oaks] nor welos [willows], nor na [any] grawand [growing] wood, of payn of dowbyll [double] mercymendys [amercements = fines]. Who suever fellys awdor [either] asche or ake [oak] without leve, for ilke [each] pece to the lord iii^{s} iiij^{d}. Ther salt no mon pele [take the bark off] no trese of payn of grevus mercymendys.

Thyes ar the payns of Cokyrham sett by the lord and his offycers for to be haldyn [holden]: Whosuver brekys any arest mad by the lord or any of his offycers vi^{s} viij ^{d}. A rescows [rescue] of strys [strays] vj^{s} viij$^{d.}$ A fold brech vj^{s} viij$^{d.}$ Who as gas [goes] to any owt mylne vj^{s} viij$^{d.}$ vj*s* . Who as haldys [holds] one scabyd [scabbed] capulls[10] odar [either] hors or mare, a piece, vj$^{s.}$ viij$^{d.}$ Who as haldys [holds] any aysold[11] vj^{s} viij$^{d.}$ vjs. Who suver sellys twrfe vj^{s} viij$^{d.}$. Who suver ledys ony twrfe fra [from] his howse-mosse to hys salte cote, or fra hys salte cote mosse to hys hawse vj^{s} viij$^{d.}$. Who suver skyftys [shifts] ony mer [boundary mark] betwys [between] tenond and tenond vjs viijd. Who suver falsys[12] any sworn man[13] vj^{s} viij$^{d.}$. Who suver stoppys any waters that is pwt to go by sworn men vj^{s} viij$^{d.}$. Ther sall no tenond hyre no servand before the lord be servyd, of payn vj^{s} viij$^{d.}$. Who suver falsys any sworn whest [inquest] they sall pay to the lord vj^{s} viij$^{d.}$ and to ylke [each] mon that is on the whest xij^{d} Ilke [each] tenond that wonys [lives] in the marshe sall uphald the se[a] dykys anente [against] hys haldyng under payn vj^{s} viij$^{d.}$. Who suver

8 Lordship.

9 A separate allotment of moss was made to provide peat for household and saltcote.

10 An uncertain type of horse.

11 An ass.

12 Commits perjury against.

13 Officers and jurymen of the manor.

hawkys or hwntys vj^{s} viij^{d}. If they sle [slay] ony best of warand [warren], for ilke [each] pece xx^{d}, a dowfe [dove] xij^{d}, a partrike [partridge] vj^{d}, a larke vj^{d}, a whayle [quail] iijd. Who suver falcys ony mon that is sworne in.the lordes cowrte for to do ony offyce: to lwke howsys,[14] yardes, dykes, bowndys, merkys [marks], merys [meres:: boundary marks] betwys tenond and tenond, thei sall forfett to the lord as ofte tymes as thei ar fawty vj^{s} viij^{d}.

* * *

All theis forsaid usages and laudabull customs we John, Abbott of the hows .of Owr Ladye of Leicester, and Co[n]vent of the same, wyll and comaund that thai be dwlye observyd and kepyd in our dayes in lyke wyse as thei have byne afore tymes, be [by] the oversight and discrecon of owr farmar onely under payne and payns afore rehersed; and also we will and stretly chardge and comawnd all owr tenondes within the saide lordschepe that thei meddull not no[r] oder [other] wyse contrarie to our customs afore writtun, but be [by] the avyse and assent and wyll of our farmar, to whome only we gyfe full power in our absence be [by] theis presentes of all thinges to the said lordschepe belonging for hys farme and covenandes betwene hus rehersed in speciall endenture.

Given in our monastery the second day of the month of September in the first year of the reign of king Richard the third after the conquest of England [1483].

Each and all these ordinances we have had copied in these presents under the seal of our Exchequer at the instance or request of our aforesaid subject John Calverte gentleman. In witness whereof we have caused these our letters to be made patent. Witness Roger Manwood, knight, at Westminster the twelfth day of February in the twenty first year of our reign.

6.2 Peasant Suits in a Lord's Court: Manorial Court Proceedings at Barnston (Essex),[15] 7 October 1449, TNA DL 30/58/721, in *Select Cases in Manorial Courts: Property and Family Law. 1250–1500*, ed. L. R. Poos and Lloyd Bonfield, Selden Society Publications 114 (London, 1982), pp. 91–92 [Latin].

Evidence of the way in which such manorial courts allowed negotiation among peasants may be found in the following documents, which show how tensions among the peasants themselves were addressed, tensions which suggested that rivalries within families and within peasant communities may have been no less important than friction between

14 The house-looker was responsible for seeing that no one built a house where he liked, and also saw that any dangers of fire were removed.

15 This manor was not ancient demesne.

lords and their peasants and laborers. We can, that is, read the following records of manorial courts either as signs that peasants acted to defend their "private" property interests against each other, or as indications that the lord's court could be appropriated by his tenants and dependants to balance individual and private interests against the common welfare of the community.

Worth emphasizing is the complexity and sophistication of the litigation undertaken by peasants within these local courts, and the strong implication in such manorial records that peasants could negotiate a complex legal process with considerable skill when important interests were at stake, even if those interests might seem trivial compared with litigation over aristocratic estates pursued in the common law courts at Westminster. Although peasants might in most cases be limited in the use that they might make of the royal bureaucracy, and especially of the common law system of courts and legal processes developed since the twelth century for the benefit of landed aristocrats, the gap between aristocratic legal maneuvers, and the resort to legal process within manors by peasants, should not be exaggerated. Peasants may have had similar interests in the rule of law as their social betters, even if they more often referred to custom than to law when pursuing their interests. Law, and custom that both contrasted with and mirrored law, provided to both lords and their tenants a common linguistic and conceptual framework for cooperation, and for conflict.

Litigation among rival claimants to land in the manor of Barnston, Essex, of which we have reproduced here a part only of a lengthy court record preserved by the lord and his officers there, overlapped what may have been an effort by that lord of the manor to retain control over land and, more importantly, the labor of those who lived on it. Significant for us is the formula by which the land in question was held, i.e., "at the lord's will according to the custom of this manor." If at the lord's will, had the tenant then no protection? But if by the custom of the manor, was the lord therefore limited in his exercise of will? Within this formula, peasants and their manorial lords managed to negotiate an accommodation that preserved lordship of land, even as peasants found ways to limit exploitation by lords of their time and energy. Despite the seeming contradiction, this formula became by far the most common description of peasant holdings within manors (and eventually by others, including some from the seigneurial elite itself in time).

Land forfeited

Whereas at the last court preceding a complaint was had and moved between William Tanner the son and heir of William Tanner, plaintiff, and John atte Wode, defendant, in a plea of land, namely of and upon the right, title and possession of a messuage[16] and half a yardland[17] of customary land called

16 A plot of land containing a dwelling house and outbuildings.

17 Equivalent to a virgate, or quarter of a hide, i.e., a standardized villein holding of c. 30 acres.

Pyes in Barnston, whereof a plea is pending in the same court between the aforesaid parties, a day was then given to the same parties to be here at this day to hear judgment of and upon certain articles and enrolments touching the manner and custom of this manor used and approved of old, as appears more fully of record in the rolls of the same court etc. Nevertheless as in various preceding courts a day was likewise given to the said John atte Wode for repairing the ruinous and badly wasted houses of his said tenement called Pyes, and this under penalty of grave forfeiture etc., most recently at the court held here on the Tuesday [15 July 1449] next before the feast of St Margaret the Virgin in the twenty-seventh year of the said lord king it was ordered by the lord's steward that the same John correct and repair the ruinous houses of his said tenement,[18] and this under penalty of forfeiture of the same tenement and land by himself and his heirs for ever. And because afterwards at the said last court it was found and presented by the entire homage,[19] being there, that the aforesaid John atte Wade has not as yet repaired his said wasted tenement in any way, nor does he have the means to repair the said tenement, nor has he offered any security to the lord of this manor at this court for repairing the said tenement as the same John was ordered and warned at the said court then last preceding etc., therefore it was ordered by the then steward of the lord that the bailiff of this manor seize into the lord's hands the said lands and tenement with all their appurtenances as forfeit, and answer therein concerning the profit until etc. Whereupon now at this court it was adjudged by the said steward that process should cease between the aforesaid parties upon the demand of the aforesaid tenement, and that the said John should go without day etc.

And the lord, being thus seised[20] and in full possession, afterwards in this same present court, by the advice and consent of Robert Dooyle and Richard Warner, chaplains and fellows of the College of Pleshey and of Thomas Darell and others of the council of the same college, being at this court, both for the lord's profit and for various causes moving the court, granted by his steward from his hands the aforesaid tenements and lands called Pyes with all their appurtenances to the abovesaid William Tanner, the son and heir of William Tanner, to whom seisin therein was delivered, to hold to himself, his heirs and assigns[21] for ever by the rod at the lord's will according to the custom of the manor by all the old rent, suits, services and customs owed to the lord therein and accustomed etc., always saving the right of each etc. And he gives the lord a fine to have entry, as appears etc.

The condition however of this demise and grant is such that if the aforesaid William Tanner on the Wednesday on the morrow of this court, namely

18 Land held of another – in this case, a peasant's holding from the lord of the manor.

19 Jury, consisting of manorial tenants who had rendered "homage" to its lord.

20 Possessed; "seisin" denotes possession, not ownership.

21 Assignees, or persons Individuals to whom property is or may be transferred by conveyance, will, descent, etc.

on the eighth day instant of the month of October, should appear personally at Pleshey before John Stangryff, clerk, master of the College of Pleshey aforesaid, lord of this manor, and provide the same master sufficient security, both for the repair of the said tenement called Pyes, to be done and repaired well and sufficiently by a certain reasonable day to be limited to him then by the said lord, and for paying a fine for the said tenement and lands to the said lord then and there, and also toward the same master and his successors and all his other officials and ministers for all and singular actions, suits, complaints, disputes and demands, both real and personal, and whatever impleadings, vexations or grievances in whatever manner pertaining or accruing to the aforesaid master and his successors or his aforesaid officials and ministers at the suit, incitement, procurement or abetting of John atte Wode of Barnston, his heirs or assigns or of any others in his name claiming, challenging or pretending right, claim or title of and in the aforesaid tenement and lands or in any parcel therein, by reason or cause of the abovesaid grant, thenceforth such grant and demise of the said tenement and lands made above to the aforesaid William and the livery of seisin therein should stand in all its force and effect etc. Otherwise, for lack of the aforesaid security to be provided by the same William to the lord in the foregoing manner and form above noted, as he freely offered to the lord to do in open court, it would be freely permitted to the said lord and his successors to seize again into his hands, re-take and retain the same tenement and lands with their appurtenances and to dispose and provide therein at his pleasure, the aforesaid grant, demise or seisin delivered therein to the said William notwithstanding in any way etc.

New grant/ fine 100s./ condition

6.3 Legislating the Value of Work: The Statute of Labourers, 1351, TNA C 65/15, m. 1 (*RP* II. 233–235; *SR* I 311–13, 25 Edward III, St. 2, cc. 1–7), from Mark Ormrod, ed., "Edward III: Parliament of February 1351, Text and Translation," in *The Parliament Rolls of Medieval England*, ed. C. Given-Wilson et al., item 47, Internet version at http://www.sd-editions.com/AnaServer?PROME+0+start.anv+id=EDWARDIII, accessed on 11 September 2009. Scholarly Digital Editions, Leicester, 2005 [Anglo-French].

Manorial records make clear efforts by English lords to maintain direct control over not only land but also the persons of those who worked directly on the land. In the long run, English lords of land and men proved unable, or unwilling, to preserve either serfdom or direct management of the time and energy exacted from agrarian laborers. Challenges to lords' rights over villeins and their control of labor essential to manorial production were especially evident in the fourteenth century, in the aftermath of climatic changes that radically reduced production, and in the wake of plague, from 1349, which radically reduced population. That peasants took advantage of changed demographic circumstances to improve their working conditions is hardly surprising, nor for that matter is the effort by lords to deny them these improvements. What is striking, however, is the forum in which much of the conflict occurred, or was monitored: parliament. Parliamentary history of the late Middle Ages readily tracks the negotiations, and sometimes bitter conflicts, between king and aristocracy over taxes, and over who should pay for the king's bureaucracy, and especially for his wars; less attention has been devoted to parliament as the venue within which members of the landed aristocracy worked out new structures for ensuring that they, and not peasants or laborers, were the primary beneficiaries of agrarian production.

The period after 1349 saw vigorous experiments in collaboration between the central government and local landlords in maintaining the subordination of laborers, especially agrarian laborers, to landlords. The language of the first major effort by England's propertied governors to preserve subordination of laborers, The Statute of Laborers in 1351, argues strongly that those at the top England's social and political hierarchy took for granted a "natural" order in which labor was owed them, and owed them on traditional, customary terms; they shared, that is, the conviction that custom coincided with right, even as they were taking steps "to make" a law preserving their superior position against enterprising peasants and workers entirely willing to take advantage of demographic shifts that made laborers increasingly precious. It also provides a handy survey of the kinds of work that mattered enough to England's rulers, local and national, to regulate.

> Recently, against the malice of servants who were idle and unwilling to serve after the pestilence without taking the most outrageous payments, our lord the king, with the assent of the prelates, nobles and others of his council, ordained that such manner of servants, both men and women, should be obliged to serve, receiving the salaries and wages customary in the places where they would have served in the twentieth year of the reign of our said lord the king, or five or six years before, and if the same servants refused to serve in like manner, they would be punished by imprisonment of their bodies, as is more fully contained in the same ordinance; wherefore commissions were made out to various people in each county to seek out and punish all those who offended against the ordinance. And now, because it has been suggested to our said lord the king in this present parliament by the petition of the commons that the said servants, having no regard for the said ordinance but only for their ease and their own greed, withdraw themselves from serving great men or others, unless they have liveries and payments double or treble that which they were accustomed to take in the said twentieth year and before, to the great damage of the great men and to the impoverishment of all the said commonalty; for which remedy was prayed by the same commons. Wherefore in the same parliament, by assent of the prelates, earls, barons and other great men and

of the said commons assembled there, in order to restrain the malice of the said servants, the points written below were ordained and established. That is to say, that each carter, ploughman, driver of ploughs, shepherd, swineherd, dairymaid and all other servants shall take the liveries and payments accustomed in the said twentieth year, and four or three years before; so that in areas where wheat is usually given, they shall take 10d. for each bushel of wheat at the will of the giver, until it shall be ordained otherwise. And that they shall be hired to serve for one whole year, or for other usual term, and not by the day. And that in times of weeding or hay-making no one shall take more than 1d. for each day; and mowers of meadows 5d. for each acre or 5d. for each day; and reapers of corn 2d. in the first week of August and 3d. in the second and so on until the end of August, and less in areas where less is usually given, without food or other favours being demanded, given or taken. And that such workers publicly carry their tools in their hands to market vills, and be hired there in a common and not in a private place. Also, that no one shall take more than 2½d. for threshing one quarter of wheat or rye; and 1½d. for a quarter of barley, beans, peas and oats if so much used to be given. And in areas where it is the custom to pay reapers by the sheaf and threshers by the bushel, no more shall be taken in any other manner than as was accustomed in the said twentieth year and before. And that the same servants shall be sworn twice a year before the lords, stewards, bailiffs and constables of each vill to uphold and observe these things. And that none of them shall leave the vill where they dwell in the winter to serve in the summer, if they may have service in the same vill, taking wages as is aforesaid; saving that the people of the counties of Stafford, Lancaster and Derby and the people of Craven and of the marches of Wales and Scotland and other places may come and work in other counties in August, and return safely as they were accustomed to do before this time. And those who refuse to take such oath or to perform that which they have previously sworn or undertaken shall be put in stocks for three days or more by the said lords, stewards, bailiffs and constables of the vills, or taken to the nearest gaol, there to remain until they are willing to submit to justice. And that stocks shall be made in each vill for this purpose between now and Whitsun. Also, that carpenters, masons, tilers and other roofers of houses shall not take more per day for their work than is customary, that is to say a master carpenter 3d. and others 2d., a master mason of freestone 4d. and other masons 3d. and their servants 1½d., a tiler 3d. and his assistant 1½d. and other roofers of reed and straw 3d. and his assistant 1½d. Also, plasterers and workers of clay walls and their assistants, shall be paid in the same manner, without food or drink, that is to say from Easter until Michaelmas, and from this time less according to the requirements and discretion of the justices who shall be assigned for this. And that those who make carriage by land or by water shall not take more for making such carriage than they were accustomed in the said twentieth year or four years before. Also, that cordwainers and shoemakers shall not sell boots, shoes or any other thing touching their craft, in any manner other than as they were accustomed in the said twentieth year. And that goldsmiths, saddlers, farriers of horses, spurriers, tanners, curriers, pelterers, tailors and all other workers, craftsmen and labourers and all other servants not specified here shall be sworn before the said justices to perform and practise their crafts and offices in the manner in which they did in the said twentieth year and in earlier times, without refusing because of this ordinance. And if any of the said servants, labourers, workers or craftsmen, after making such oath, shall contravene this ordinance, he shall be punished by fine, ransom and imprisonment at the discretion of the said justices. Also, that the said stewards, bailiffs and constables of the said vills shall be sworn before the same justices to inquire diligently in every appropriate way they can, concerning all those who contravene this ordinance and to certify the same justices of their names; and that each time the justices come into the area to hold their sessions, they shall have certification from the same stewards, bailiffs and constables of the names of rebels, and shall have them attached by their bodies to be before the same justices to answer for such contempts, so that they shall make fine and ransom to the king in the event that they shall be attainted, and shall furthermore be commanded to prison, there to remain until they have found security to serve and take wages, and to do their work, and to sell goods, in the aforesaid manner. And in the event that any of them shall contravene his oath, and be attainted of this, he shall be imprisoned for forty days. And if he is convicted again, he shall be imprisoned for a quarter of a year, so that each time that they commit trespass and are convicted the penalty shall be doubled. And each time they come there the same justices shall inquire whether the said stewards, bailiffs and constables have made good and loyal certification or concealed anything by bribe, procurement or affinity, and punish them by fine and ransom if they shall be found guilty. And that the same justices shall have power to inquire into and impose due punishment upon any of the said officials, workers, labourers and other servants whatsoever; and also upon hostellers, innkeepers and those who sell victuals in retail and other items not specified here, whether at the suit of the party or by presentment, and to hear and determine and put the matter in execution by exigent after the first capias if it shall be necessary; and to appoint as many deputies as they consider shall be best for the keeping of this same ordinance. And those who would sue against such servants, workers and labourers for taking excess from them, if they are attainted at their suit, may reclaim this excess. And in the event that no one will sue in order to reclaim this excess, it shall then be levied from the said servants, workers, labourers and craftsmen and delivered to the collectors of the fifteenth, in alleviation of the vills where such excess was taken. Also, that sheriffs, constables, bailiffs and gaolers, clerks of justices or of sheriffs and other officials whatsoever should take nothing by reason of their office from the same servants for fees, suit of prison or in any other manner. And if they take anything in such manner, they shall cause it to be delivered to the collectors of the tenth and fifteenth in aid of the commonalty for the time that the said tenth and fifteenth are in force, both for all past times and for times to come. And that the said justices shall inquire in their sessions whether the said officials have received anything from the same servants, and that which they find through such inquests to have been received by the said officials, the same justices shall cause to be levied from each of the said officials and delivered to the said collectors, together with the excess and fines and ransoms made, and also the amercements of all those who shall be amerced before the said justices, in alleviation of the vills, as is aforesaid. And in the event that the excess found in one vill surpasses the total of the fifteenth of the same vill, the remnant of such excess shall be levied and paid by the said collectors to the poorest of the neighbouring vills in aid of their fifteenth, by the advice of the said justices; and that the fines, ransoms, excesses and amercements of the said servants and labourers for the time to come, while the said fifteenth is in force, shall be delivered to the said collectors in the aforesaid form, by indenture to be made between them and the said justices; so that the same collectors may be liable on their account by the same indentures in the event that the said fines, ransoms, amercements and excess are not paid in aid of the aforesaid fifteenth. And when the same fifteenth ceases, the money shall be levied to the king's use, and answered for to him by the sheriff of the county. Also, that the said justices shall hold their sessions in every county of England at least four times a year, that is to say at the feasts of the Annunciation of Our Lady, Saint Margaret, Michaelmas and Saint Nicholas, and also whenever it shall be necessary at the discretion of the justices. And that those who speak in the presence of the said justices, or do anything else in their absence or presence, in encouragement or maintenance of the said servants and labourers to the contrary of this ordinance, shall be grievously punished at the discretion of the said justices. And if any of the said labourers, craftsmen or servants flee from one county into another because of this ordinance, the sheriffs of the counties where such fugitives shall be found shall cause them to be taken at the command of the justices of the counties from which they have fled and shall put them in the chief gaol of this same county, there to remain until the next session of the same justices. And that the said sheriffs shall return such demands before the same justices at their next sessions. And that this ordinance shall be upheld and observed in the city of London as well as in other cities and boroughs and elsewhere throughout the land, inside as well as outside franchises.

6.4 A Commons' Petition against Rebellious Villeins, 1377, TNA C 65/32, m. 11 (RP III. 23; SR II. 1–5, St 1 Ric. 2 c. 6) from Geoffrey Martin, ed. and trans., "Richard II: Parliament of October 1377, Text and Translation," in *The Parliament Rolls of Medieval England*, ed. C. Given-Wilson et al., item 88, Internet version, at http://www.sd-editions.com/AnaServer?PROME+0+start.anv+id=RICHARDII, accessed on 11 September 2009, Scholarly Digital Editions, Leicester, 2005 [Anglo-French].

Evidence that landed Englishmen were more concerned to enforce service than to insist on their independence of royal authority is found in several petitions from the parliamentary Commons to the king, including one below from 1377, when we might expect friction over Richard II's autocratic behavior to have hindered such cooperation. This evidence of aristocratic appeals to royal power and authority should caution us against assuming that peasants and laborers shared their lords' conviction that either serfdom or obligatory labor on behalf of lords was "natural," whatever the surprise expressed in 1351 by landed Englishmen that laborers and even tenants were not willing to stay put, or by similar parliamentary members in 1377 perplexed and distressed by "rebellious" behavior by villeins who refused to acknowledge their servile status, whatever the occasional advantage to some of them caught up in the imperfect but oppressive machinery of the Statute of Laborers.

To our lord the king and to the council of parliament the commons of the realm show: that in many parts of the kingdom of England the villeins and those holding lands in villeinage, who owe services and customary dues to lords for whatever reason within various lordships, as well of holy church as of lay lordships, have by counsel, procurement, maintenance and manipulation of certain persons, for money received from the aforesaid villeins and tenants, purchased in the king's court exemplifications from Domesday Book, concerning the manors and lands in which the said villeins and tenants reside; by colour of which copies, through the evil intention of the same, and through wicked interpretations provided by the said counselors, procurers, maintainers, and abettors, they have withdrawn and do withdraw the customs and services they owe from their lords, claiming that they are entirely released from all manner of service as well of their bodies as for their aforesaid holdings: and have prevented the ministers of the said lords from distraining them to perform the aforesaid customs and services, and have formed leagues and confederacies forcibly to oppose their said lords and ministers: and each is supported by the others when they are distrained for that reason; and they threaten to kill the ministers of their said lords if they distrain them for the aforesaid customs and services, so that the lords and their ministers do not distrain them for their customs and services, through fear of death which might arise from their rebellion and resistance. And therefore the said lords lose and have lost large profits from their lordships, bringing about their disinheritance and injury to their

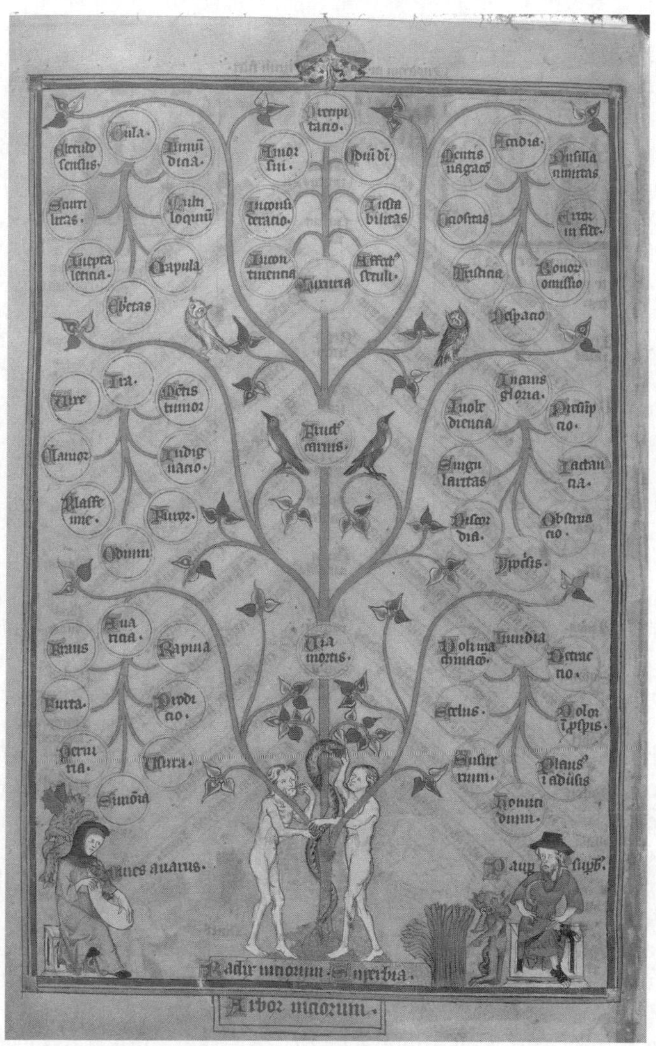

Figure 2 The Tree of Vices (Arbor viciorum), De Lisle Psalter (© British Library Board. MS Arundel 83 II, fo. 128v, c. 1339). Lucy Freeman Sandler, in *The Psalter of Robert De Lisle* (New York: Oxford University Press, 1983), p. 48, draws attention to the bottom of the page, where the vices are exemplified pictorially, first by the fall of man, the prototype example of pride, and second by a topical scene of the sort used by the friars in sermons to war against the besetting sins of secular society, pride and avarice. Especially relevant to documents shown here in 6.4 and 6.5 is the roughly clothed peasant on the right, who despite his appearance is presented in the posture of kingly authority, with a leg crossed over the other. Sandler notes that a contemporary English poem, "Handlyng Synne," similarly condemns overweening pride of the sort imputed to a peasant here.

estate, and the crops of many in the realm remain unreaped, and have perished forever for that reason, to the great injury of all the community; so it is feared, if remedy be not swiftly provided, that war might arise within the same kingdom because of their aforesaid rebellion, or that they might ally themselves to the enemies from overseas to seek vengeance on their lords, if the said enemies make some inroad. And for the support of such misdeeds they have collected amongst themselves large sums of money, to meet costs and expenses. And many of them have now come to court to gain support for their aforesaid purpose.

Wherefore may it please our said lord the king and the council to ordain a swift and fitting remedy for this, against the said counsellors, procurers, maintainers, and abettors, as well as against the said villeins and tenants, and especially against those who have appeared here now, as has been said, in order that those staying in the household might have knowledge of their punishment and to avert the kind of peril which has previously arisen in the kingdom of France through such rebellions and alliances of villeins against their lords.

Answer

As for the copies granted and made in the chancery, it was declared in parliament that these could not nor should not have value or force in respect of the franchise of their persons, nor change the condition of their tenure and customs due of old, nor work to the prejudice of the lords enjoying their services and customs as they used to long ago: and let the lords have letters patent made under the great seal on this declaration, if they wish to have them. And as for the rest of the article, let the lords who feel aggrieved have special commissions under the great seal to the justices in the counties, or to other worthy persons, to enquire about all such rebels, and their counsellors, procurers, maintainers, and abettors: and those who shall be indicted before them, both in time past as well as time to come, let them be imprisoned and not released without the assent of their lords by mainprise, bail, or any other means, until they be attainted or acquitted. And if they be attainted thereof, the said rebellious tenants shall not be freed in any way until they have paid the king a fine, and have the assent of their said lords: saving always with regard to the said fines the franchises and liberties of the lords who have the fines and amercements of their tenants. And as for the counsellors, procurers, maintainers, and abettors let there again be such a process, similarly carried out, and they shall never be freed until they have paid the king a fine and compensated the lords thus aggrieved in accordance with their estates, and the degree of their wrongdoing, if the same lords wish to proceed against them by writ or by vill. Saving the franchises and liberties of the lords, as said above.

6.5 Trial and Execution of John Shirle, July, 1381, TNA Just 1/103 (Justices in Eyre, of Assize, of Oyer and Terminer, and of the Peace, etc: Rolls and Files), m.5d, from R. B. Dobson, "Introduction to the second edition," *The Peasants' Revolt of 1381*, ed. R. B. Dobson, 2nd edn (London and Basingstoke: Macmillan, 1983), pp. xxviii–xxix.

The worries expressed by English lords of land and men in 1377 (and on other occasions between 1349 and 1381) were far from groundless. Whatever the disruption to institutions and conventional assumptions about social and political order produced by plague in 1349 and subsequently, the challenge launched by peasants and laborers in 1381, against both royal and seigneurial exactions and authority, would resonate for centuries among England's governors, and those whom they claimed to govern. The major chroniclers of the period provide descriptions of a world that seemed to most of them "turned upside down" by a rebellion in which England's warrior class appeared largely helpless to defend either themselves or the king against "mobs" of ill-armed but remarkably well-organized peasants. Thomas Walsingham's conviction that immorality ultimately must account for such a social cataclysm may well have been common, even if his decision to lay primary blame on friars is probably eccentric.[22] *Instead of reproducing here his explanation, we offer another perspective, perhaps not uncommon among peasants in the aftermath of the rebellion's suppression, a view that the king's judges, in suppressing, preserved for us. The record of John Shirle's execution after an arrest for vagrancy and dangerous language – language starkly different from Walsingham's or other chroniclers' at the time – demonstrates the crown's determination to restore the status quo ante; it also indicates why such a goal would not be easily achieved.*[23]

John Shirle of the county of Nottingham was taken because it was found that he had been a vagabond (vagabundus) in various counties during the whole time of the late disturbance, insurrection and tumult, carrying lies as well as silly and worthless talk from district to district, whereby the peace of the lord the king could rapidly be broken and the people be disquieted and disturbed. Among other damaging words, namely after the proclamation of the peace of the lord the king made on the aforesaid day and year, when the justices assigned by the lord the king were holding sessions in the town, he said in a tavern in Briggestrete [Bridge Street] in Cambridge, where many were assembled to listen to his news and worthless talk, that the stewards of the lord the king as well as the justices and many other officers and ministers of the king were more deserving to be drawn and hanged and to suffer other lawful pains and torments than

22 Walsingham's explanation for the revolt, along with other contempory interpretations of events in 1381 offered by the Chancellor, Sir Michael de la Pole, in 1383, and Jean Froissart, may be read in R. B. Dobson, ed., *The Peasants' Revolt of 1381*, 2nd ed. (London: Macmillan Press, 1983), pp. 362–72.

23 Ralph Hanna III, in *Pursuing History. Middle English Manuscripts and Their Texts* (Stanford: Stanford University Press, 1996), pp. 267–79, reconsiders the Miller's intrusion into the Canterbury tale-telling in light of Shirle's case.

John Ball, chaplain, a traitor and felon lawfully convicted. For John Shirle said that he [Ball] had been condemned to death falsely, unjustly and for envy by the said ministers with the king's assent; because he was a true and worthy man, prophesying things useful to the commons of the kingdom and telling of wrongs and oppressions done to the people by the king and the aforesaid ministers; and Ball's death would not go unpunished but within a short space of time he would well reward both the king and his said ministers and officers. These sayings and threats redound to the prejudice of the crown of the lord the king and to the contempt and manifest disturbance of the people. And thereupon the said John Shirle was immediately brought by the sheriff before the said justices sitting in Cambridge castle; and he was charged about these matters and was diligently examined as regards his conversation, his presence [in Cambridge] and his estate; and when these things had been acknowledged by him before the said justices, his evil behaviour and condition was made plainly manifest and clear. And thereupon trustworthy witnesses in his presence at the time when the abovementioned lies, evil words, threats and worthless talk had been spoken by him, were requested; and they, being sworn to speak the truth about these matters, testified that all the aforesaid words imputed to him had indeed been spoken by him. And he, examined once again, did not deny the charges laid against him. Therefore by the discretion of the said justices he was hanged; and an order was made to the escheator to enquire diligently about his lands and tenements and his goods and chattels, and to make due execution thereof for the lord the king.

6.6 The Continuing Burden of Villeinage: Netheway v. Gorge, 1534, TNA REQ 2/5/21, from *Select Cases in the Court of Requests, 1497–1569*, ed. by I. S. Leadam, Selden Society Publications, Vol. 12 (London, 1898), pp. 42–6.

Another record from a royal court, Netheway v. Gorge, leaves little doubt that some lords intended, even at the end of our period, to take every advantage of traditional lordship, including the enforcement of burdens associated with servile status. An appeal to the king's justice launched by someone claimed as a serf, at the end of the period covered by this volume, leaves no doubt that serfdom remained part of the law of the land in the sixteenth century, and it presents the unattractive picture of at least one lord who had no scruples about taking advantage of his rights over an alleged serf to acquire an ox for free. What is most interesting about the case, however, is the alleged serf's description of Sir Edward Gorge's conduct, when the latter may have refused to pay for the ox, and invoked as justification William Netheway's status as his bondman; such conduct, the alleged bondman insisted, was simply not appropriate for a knight. Villeinage remained legal; but had it become socially unacceptable, not only for the bondman, but for the knight who depended on bondage for his position? Certainly, by the early sixteenth century, despite the survival of personal bondage, most peasants held their land, not in villeinage, but "at the will of the lord according to the custom of the manor," to which we have earlier referred.

To the Kynge our souereygne lord

In moost petuose manor complaynyth vnto your moost noble hyghnes your trewe and feythfull subject and legeman William Netheway of Walton in the countie of Somerset husbandman that wher of late oon Edward Gorge[24] Knyght of the sayd countie sent his seruaunt callyd John Ballard vnto your humbly besecher to by of hym an oxe ffor his sayd master his howsholde youre sayd supplyant was ther with contentyd to sell hym an oxe pryse xxvj *s*. Whiche oxe your sayd suppliant delyuered to the sayd John Ballard to the vse of his sayd master, whiche oxe the sayd Ballard receyvyd att the same pryse and when your sayd besecher demaundyd of the sayd Edward his money for the sayd oxe the sayd Edward fferr byyond good ordere of knyghthod and good gravyte to that degre & ordre apperteynynge in moost ragyouse maner[25] sayd vnto your poore Oratour theis wordes in effect folowynge that is to saye Thow schalt have noo money of me ffor that oxe butt swerynge grete and detestable othis that he wolde have your sayd humble subgett his goodes ffor that he toke hym as his bondman and that he would sease his londes that he hyld of other men and kepe them dewerynge[26] his lyfe and that he wolde ffeche hym att an horse tayle and make hym to tvrne a broch in his kechyn and ferder with lyke ffurye sayenge to youre supplyant iij or iiij tymes he wolde thrust a dagger thoroght his chekes by occasyon of whiche crewell & extreme demenour youre seyd humble supplyant nott yett recompensyd ffor the sale of the sayd oxe and beynge soo thretenyd in fforme aforsayd darnot nor knowyth nott what to doo or howe to goo or labor abowte his besyne ffor the lyvynge of hymselfe his powre wyffe & syxe powre chyldern lest that the seyd sir Edward wolde take or imprison hym ffor a bondman, your sayd supplyant & his auncetors beynge ffreemen and of free condition and neuer bond to the sayd Sir Edward nor none of his auncetours ffor the which pleasith hit your hyghnes in consyderacion that your sayd humble subgett is a very powre man and nott able to trye for his sayd libertie and dutie in the premysses declared with the said sir Edward by the ordre of the comen lawe the sayd Sir Edward beynge a man of grett allyans myght and pover in the sayd countie pleasyth hit youre grace in the waye of cherytie to graunt vnto your humble supplyant Youre gracious letters of prevy seale to be directid to the sayd Edward, commandynge hym be the same to appere before youre

24 Sir Edward Gorge, or Gorges, of Wraxall, Somerset, eldest son of Sir Edmund Gorges, K.B., by Anne, daughter of John Howard, Duke of Norfolk, was knighted in 1513 for his conduct at Flodden. He was High Sheriff of Somerset and Dorset in 1514. In December of the same year he was granted the office of bailiff of the Manor of Portbury, Somerset, a grant renewed to him in 1525 and 1538. In 1529 he served as High Sheriff of Devon.

25 Outrageous manner.

26 During.

moost honerable counsell att a certeyne daye and vnder a certeyne payne there to answer to the premysses and youre sayd humble supplyaunt schall dayly pray to gode ffor Your moost noble & Ryall astate longe to indewer.[27]

6.7 Advice to the President of Magdalen College, Oxford, on Manorial Administration: Thomas Ely to Richard Mayhew, late fifteenth century, from W. Denton, *England in the Fifteenth Century* (London: George Bell and Sons, 1888), pp. 318–20.

The Peasants' Revolt did not revolutionize manorial administration and estate management, but it may well have prompted lords both spiritual and temporal to lighten the direct exactions of lordship, or perhaps more often, to explore alternative sources of income and wealth that would in time lead to an agrarian capitalism which depended on the farming of their estates by intermediaries who had strong motives to achieve greater production through more efficient organization of both land and laborers on it. Lords whose well-being depended, even in part, on the labor of serfs became the exception over the period from 1350 to 1530, and much more frequent are signs that English landlords chose instead to monitor more closely, and to exploit more vigorously, their tenants, whether free or unfree.

Analyzing the conflict between the material self-interest of a landlord and his political and social obligations to his own and the king's subjects, Thomas Ely, a priest and schoolmaster writing near the end of the fifteenth century,[28] cautioned the president of Magdalen College against a style of estate management that would put the income of the college ahead of the well-being of a peasant community likely to suffer, and perhaps to disappear, were the president indeed to let the entire estate in question to a single tenant instead of continuing to deal directly with the present tenants. The triumvirate of landlord, tenant, and landless laborers which would characterize the agrarian capitalism of early modern England can be seen, at least in dim outline, behind the management decision against which Ely cautioned the president of Magdalen College; we need not move the origins of modern capitalism forward to the fifteenth century, to find in Ely's caution a dilemma for English landholders, poised as they were between maintaining the more or less willing subservience of an agrarian labor force, and the equally pressing need to make the most possible from their landed estates.

Rygth wryschypful ser, I recommaunde me unto yowe, desyryng and prayng yowe in god tenderly to remebur the welfare of owre cherch of quynton and the supportacion of owre poer towne[29] qwych[30] fallys fast in decay and nere to the poynt of destruccion except ye stand goud lord and turne more favourable to yowre tenantes: for yowre howsynge gose downe, xx marke[31] wyll nott sett up

---

27 Endure.

28 Ely obtained the benefice of Quinton in summer, 1486; he died there no later than August, 1493.

29 Village.

30 Which.

31 Just over £13.

ageyn that ys fallyn within thys iiij yere,[32] and as long as ye kepe thys way to lett yowre lordschyp to one mane[33] to preferre hym and he to kepe under[34] yowre tenantes and have all the vayle[35] and thay the burdyn wyll there none tenantes come to the towne; and more over thes ij ploys[36] that ye have, there be no moo bott[37] the fre alder,[38] they wyll not falow[39] if M. Rose ocupy styll as they say, I remembur ser that ye sayd my lord byschope[40] in hys last days, and allso yower maysterschyp syn[41] my lord desessyd,[42] dyd stand in maner of a wavereyng mynd wethere it were more expedient to the welfare of yowr place to have one mane to yowre tenant or the tenantes of the towne. Ser, savyng yowr reverence and yowr descrecion, aftur my sympull reson me think it is more meritory to support and succur a comynte[43] then one mane, yowr tenantes rathere then a stronge man, the pore and the innocent for[44] a gentylman or a gentylmans man, nott wytth standdyng, peraventur ye thynke yff thys way be more meritory, the othere way wald[45] be more vayle to yowre place, in so much as they wyll gyff more then yowr tenantes, for mane[46] men wyll ley owt more to kepe under the pore then for to help thaym; ser, it may be thowgth so for a sesyn,[47] bott in long space I thynke for dyvers consyderacions it were better to lett the tenantes have it. One is thys, ther as ye be wyrschypfull men of saddnes in yowre place and dyuynes[48] yff ye suld[49] support a synglere[50] man to dryve yowr tenantes owt and lett downe yowre tenandres,[51] as they doo, and destroy the cherch and the towne for a lytyll valye to yowre place, it walld be grettly spokyn of that ye suld be in fecth[52] with covetyse amang men of wyrschype and other commenty,[53] and allso a ensampylle[54] to lay pepulle to cast down towns,

32 Four years.
33 Man.
34 Oppress.
35 Value, i.e., profit.
36 Two ploughs.
37 No more except.
38 The freeholder.
39 Follow.
40 William Wainfleet, bishop of Winchester.
41 Since.
42 Deceased.
43 Community.
44 Before.
45 Would.
46 Many.
47 Season.
48 The president and fellows of the college.
49 Should.
50 Single.
51 Tenements or holdings?
52 Infected.
53 Communities.
54 Example.

another consyderacion is thys, yff the towne were replenyscht[55] with tenantes the cherch sulde the better be support, the parsonage better in tythys[56] oblacions[57] and many thyngs, the pore pepull better relevyd and allso a veyle to yowr place wat in aryotts,[58] fynes[59] and sutth of cowrte[60] were now yowr farmor[61] takes in and lettes at hys wylle with owt fyne or aryott to yowe. Sere I understand that yowre maysterschypp walld nowe [th]at the tenantes suld have it, bott I meruell[62] grettly that ye stryke so sore to make thaym to gyffe more then othere men hase gyffyn afore consyderyng that a man that kepys non howsalld[63] a pon itt bott brynges all to the peny[64] and no tenant fare better for hym[65] may better pay than he that kepys a hows, wer fore,[66] I be seche yowe to schewe yowre tenantes favore and lett thaym hafe it for xxx li and I sall gyff yow to yowr plesure Lyerd[67] my horse. And ther as ye desyryd me to take a part there of, I wyll for yowre plesur and the wellfare of my neghburs to sett thaym in a rowlle[68] putt me selfe in dawnger[69] and tyll[70] more trobyll and yff it plese yowe to take my way there as is bott iij ploys in the towne nowe by thys day ij yere there sall be viij with the grace of god, and the lordschyp to be devydyd equale amange thos viij. and wether ye wyll that thes viij be takers togeder, or ye wyll that I and iij of thaym, or ij, or i sall answer yowe, it sall be aftur yowre plesure etc. now benedicite. . . .

Colin Richmond, in a brief but illuminating note on the selection from Ely's letter above, contrasted it with another in Magdalen College archives, written between 1517 and 1537 by John Basse to John Claymond, while the latter was president of Corpus Christi College. Basse, according to Richmond, articulates attitudes much more typical than Ely's. Claymond was rector of Bishop's Cleeve, Gloucester, and Basse was his curate.[71]

---

55 Replenished.
56 Tithes.
57 Offerings or donatons to God or his church.
58 Heriots, animals owed to lords of the manor upon deaths of tenants.
59 Entry fines, owed upon inheritance or succession to a tenement held at the will of the lord according to the custom of the manor, i.e., by copyhold.
60 Suit of Court.
61 Farmer, the person who in return for a fixed payment manages, and enjoys the profits of, a manor or estate – or the losses from the same.
62 Marvel.
63 Household.
64 Is penny-pinching.
65 No tenant getting anything from him.
66 Wherefore.
67 My grey horse.
68 Rule.
69 Debt.
70 Cultivate.
71 Colin C. Richmond, "The Transition from Feudalism to Capitalism in the Archives of Magdalen College, Oxford: a Note," in *History Workshop Journal* 37 (Spring 1994), pp. 165–9; The first part of

Ryght Worsshypffull Master, my dewty doyng I recommend me unto your Masterschype, glade for to hyre of your bodely helthe, wyche long to contenowe to the plesyar of gode, the whyche dayly I schall praye, sertefyyng you that I wyth all youre parysshionys were yn goode helthe at the makynge here of, thankyde be gode. there hathe ben berryde of the comun syknesse viij personse forthe of iij howsys yn a towne callyd Sowtham [Goucestershire]. of theyre sowlys[72] Jhesu have marcy. for I have greet besynes with the Cure and small profyttes. I have no bedrolle nor masepens[73] as yet, but I truste your Masterschype wyll say that I shall have the maspens, for hyt ys costyn[74] yn alle places save only here. or else, yeff yt plese your Masterschyppe, that I may cum to oxforde at owre lady day nexte cumyng, for I am wery of the servys be cawse I have no preste with me; for youre parysshnares[75] wyll hyre no preste whyle youre farmer dwellythe apon the parsonage; and as for hym, he spekyth feyre wordys but hys dedys be contrary to hys seyyng, as ye schall hyre of youre parysshnares, and I sertefy you, that there schall never be love and charyte wyth them as longe as he contynowe farmer, as for the artycullеs that be a yenste[76] hym I schall you showe at youre cumynge to Cleve with the grace of gode, to whome I commyte you; and me to youre prayers. the xth daye of Desembre.

Be youre parysshe preste and bedman[77] John basse

6.8 Enclosure and Depopulation, Late Fifteenth Century, from *Domesday of Inclosures, 1517–18*, II, ed. I. S. Leadam (1897), pp. 431–2, in *Documents of English Economic History*, Vol. 1*: England from 1000 to 1760*, ed. H. E. S. Fisher and A. R. J. Juřica (London: G. Bell & Sons, 1977), p. 117 [Latin].

The President of Magdalen's moral dilemma, at least as Thomas Ely (in his letter above, 6.7) *described the choices confronting him, may hint of radical re-organization of agrarian production that would force the majority of England's producers onto the labor market, but the enclosures that would consolidate aristocratic landed estates into property leased to a farmer employing wage labor and driven by market forces to more efficient production still lay far in the future at the end of the fifteenth century.*

Ely's letter, included here, appears on pp. 167–8; Basse's letter is included in fn. 12, p. 169. For another valuable perspective on Quinton and the "transition from feudalism to capitalism," see Christopher Dyer, *An Age of Transition? Economy and Society in England in the Later Middle Ages* (Oxford: Clarendon Press, 2005), pp. 78–85.

72 Souls.

73 No income either from saying obits or from singing masses for the dead.

74 Custom.

75 Parishioners.

76 Against.

77 Beadsman; petitioner, suppliant.

Conversion of arable land into pasture, however, provided an extraordinarily attractive choice for many landlords eager to minimize negotiations with both peasant tenants and laborers on arable holdings; sheep required grass, not lots of agricultural workers, and wool production promised large returns, so long as the market for wool or woolen textile remained strong.

Below, a brief excerpt from records of a broad inquiry into enclosures in 1517 illustrates responses by the central government to a broad anxiety that the advantages offered by a pastoral economy to landlords might be disadvantageous to political and social stability. Although the government's actions probably did little to inhibit conversions from arable, it does indicate one other fault line within the ruling elite, as monarchs, in the interest of stability, attempted to protect peasant producers against the self-interested enterprise of landlords who arguably needed protection against themselves. King and the parliamentary Commons of the fourteenth century had tried to put a limit on employers' readiness to undercut their neighbors by paying higher wages to agricultural workers. The majority of those ruling England at the beginning of the sixteenth century were hardly more compassionate towards workers, either on the land or in the manufacture of cloth, than their fourteenth-century predecessors; but literate and articulate English people may have understood more fully that protecting the governing elite required protections for both peasants and wage laborers imperiled by market developments, in land and labor as well as in goods [Latin].

Stretton super Street, Warwickshire.

And the aforesaid jurors say that Henry Smith was recently seised in his demesne as of fee[78] of 12 messuages[79] and 4 cottages, 640 acres of arable land to the annual value of £50 with appurtenances in Stretton super Street in the aforesaid county; and with each of the aforesaid messuages 40 acres of arable land, suitable for and ordinarily in cultivation, were accustomed to be let, farmed and occupied from time immemorial. Thus was the same Henry Smith seised on the 6th December 9 Henry VII.[80] He enclosed the messuages, cottages and lands with ditches and: banks and he wilfully caused the same messuages and cottages to be demolished and laid waste and he converted them from the use of cultivation and arable husbandry into pasture for brute animals. Thus he holds them to this day, on account of which 12 ploughs that were employed in the cultivation of those lands are withdrawn and 80 persons, who similarly were occupied in the same cultivation, and who dwelled in the said messuages and cottages, were compelled to depart tearfully

78 To be seised in demesne as of fee was to hold land from another, enjoying not only direct and independent control but also an estate of inheritance, so long as services owed the lord were performed, often trivial by this date.

79 A landed holding with a dwelling house.

80 1493.

against their will. Since then they have remained idle and thus they lead a miserable existence, and indeed they die wretched. What is more to be lamented is [that] the church of Stretton on that occasion fell into ruin and decay, so that the Christian congregation, which used to gather there to hear the divine offices, is no longer held there and the worship of God is almost at an end. In the church animals are sheltered from the storms of the air and brute animals feed among the tombs of Christian bodies in the churchyard. In all things the church and burial-place are profaned to the evil example of others inclined to act in such a manner.

6.9 "On England's Commercial Policy," temp. Edward IV, from *Political Poems and Songs Relating to English History*, II, ed. Thomas Wright, Rolls Series (Longman, Green, Longman, and Roberts, 1861), pp. 282–7.

Supplying food for townsmen might bring lords and their tenants into market transactions in towns, but wool and textile production linked the rural world even more tightly into local, national, and even international markets. The importance to the kingdom of the wool market and textile production received powerful expression in the wool sacks on which the king's highest judges sat when parliaments convened, from the time of Edward I. By the late fifteenth century, however, sheep may have displaced wandering peasants as the focus for worries that aristocratic self-interest and greed threatened the order, stability, and well-being of the entire kingdom. The selections below, from Edward IV's reign, attest a growing awareness that work, wealth, and the welfare of the realm were interdependent, and that poverty and social distress might require something more than Christian charity and the generosity of the rich. Striking about this poem is the author's distress over workers either threatened by unemployment or denied an equitable return on their labor, a concern that seeks a solution not through moral imperatives directed towards the greedy rich, but in legislative action that would regulate the market in favor of wage laborers. His analysis and conclusion engages directly a market in which labor itself is perceived as a commodity, and it is hard to imagine, even today, a clearer statement of the powerful bonds between the material conditions of workers' lives and the welfare of the kingdom as a whole than the poet's declaration that "every man must have met, drynk, and clothe."

The author of "The Book of English Policy" was scarcely typical in his appeal for more equitable wages for laborers in the clothing industry, but he was not the only thoughtful, articulate Englishman of the late Middle Ages to grasp the connection between economic changes, English productivity, and the wealth and welfare of the kingdom as a whole. Few found imagery as graphic as Thomas More in his Utopia, *when he attributed to his character Raphael Hythlodaeus the observation that English sheep "which are usually so tame and so cheaply fed, begin now, according to report, to be so greedy and wild that they devour human beings themselves and devastate and depopulate fields, houses, and towns."*[81] *More's – or more precisely, Hythlodaeus's – criticism of "noblemen, gentlemen, and even some abbots" who enclosed land for pasture, in order to support an "idle and sumptuous life," may remind us that fourteenth-century writers also centered their explanations for the peasants' revolt of 1381 on greed, but both the analysis in "The Book of English Policy" and the more famous description of ravenous sheep in* Utopia *imply greater willingness, after almost a century and a half of agrarian struggle and parliamentary practice of legislating, to propose political solutions shaped by analyses of markets and production, not simply to advance moral injunctions as remedies.*

Anglia, proper tuas naves et lanas, omnia regna te salutare deberent[82]

* * *

Ffor ther ys no reme[83] in no maner degree,
Butt they have nede to our Englysshe commodyte;
And the cawse theroff I wylle to yow expresse,
The wiche ys soth as the gospelle of the masse.

Ther ys noothir pope, emperowre, nor kyng,
Bysschop, cardinal, or any man levyng,
Of what condicion or what maner degree,
During theyre levyng thei must have thynges iij.

Mete, drynk, and cloth, to every mannes sustynaunce
They leng[84] alle iij, without varyaunce.
For whoso lacketh any of thyse iij things,
Be the popys or emperowrs, or soo royall kynges,

Yt may not stonde with theym in any prosperity;
For who so lackyth any of thyse, he suffryd adversyty;
Whiles this ys sooth by your wyttes dyscerne,
Of alle the remes in the worlde this beareth the lanterne.

Ffor of everyche of thyse iij. by Goddes ordynaunce,
Wee have suffycyenly unto oure sustynaunce,
And with the supplusage of oone of thyse iij. thyngs
We myght rewle and governe alle crystyn kynges.

---

81 Thomas More, *Utopia*, ed. Edward Surtz (New Haven: Yale University Press, 1964), p. 24.
82 O England, on account of your ships and wool, all realms. Ought to salute you.
83 Realm.
84 Belong.

And paynymys[85] also mygthe mak theym ful tame,
Ffor the cause we take no hed we be mykylle[86] to blame;
For of alle the pepylle that be lyvyng on grounde
To praye and to please God we be most bownde.

Ffor thow thei have met, drynke, in every kyngges londe,
Yet they lacke clothe, as y undyrstonde;
And for to determyn that the trouthe ys soe,
Lestyn wel to me, and ye moste accord therto.

* * *

Therfor let not owre woole be sold for nowghte,
Neyther oure clothe, for they must be sowth;
And in especyalle restrayne strayttly the wool,
That the comyns of thys land may wyrke at the fulle.

And yf any wooll be sowlde of thys londe,
Lete yt be of the worst bothe to ffre and bonde,
And noone othr in [no] maner wyse,
Ffor many dyverse cawsys, as y can devyse

Yf the woole be coarse, the cloth ys myckle the worse,
Yet into lytylle thei putt owte of purse,
As myche for gardyng,[87] spynnyng, and wevyng,
Ffullyng, rowing,[88] dying, and scheryng.

And yet when suche clothe ys alle ywrought,
To the maker it waylyth[89] lytylle or nowghtte,
The pryce ys sympylle, the cost ys never the lesse,
They that wyrkkyd[90] soche wool in wytte be lyke an asse.

The costes into lytyll trewly at the fulle
Ys as myche as yt were made of fyne wool,
Yet a yerde of that oon ys worth v. of that other;
Better can I not seye, thow yt were to my brother.

85 Pagans.
86 Much.
87 Carding.
88 Roving.
89 Availeth.
90 Worked.

Take hed to my lessoun that y have shewyd here,
Ffor yt ys necessary to every clothyer,
And the most prevalye to them that may be fownde,
Yf they wylle take hede therto and yt undyrstonde.

A ordynaunce wolde be maad for the poore people,
That in thyse days have but lyttle avayle,
That ys to say for spynners, carders, wevers also,
Ffor toukers[91], dyers and schermyn[92] thereto.

For in thyse days ther ys a hewsaunce,[93]
That puttyth the pore pepylle to grett hynderaunce,
By a strange mene that ys late in [the] londe
Bygun and usyd as y undyrstonde

By merchaundes and cloth-makers, for Godys sake take kepe,
The wyche makythe the poreylle to morne and wepe;
Lytyll thei take for theyre labor, yet halff ys merchaundyse;
Alas! For rewthe,[94] yt ys gret pyte.

That they take for vjd, yt ys dear ynow[95] of iij,
And thus thei be defrawdyd in every contre,[96]
The pore have the labur, the ryche the wynnyng;
This accordythe nowghtte, it is a hevy partyng.

Butt to voyde fraude, and sett egallyté,
That syche wyrfolk[97] be payd in good mone,
Ffrom this tyme forthe by suffycyent ordynaunce
That the poreylle no more be putte to suche grevaunce.

For and ye knew the sorow and hevynees
Of the pore pepyll levyng[98] in dystress,
How thei be oppressyd in alle manner of thyng,
In yevyng[99] theym to myche[100] weythe[101] into the spynnyng.

91 Tuckers.
92 Shearmen.
93 Usage, practice.
94 Truth.
95 Enough.
96 Country.
97 Workfolk.
98 Living.
99 Giving.
100 Too much.
101 Weight.

For ix^li I wene they schalle take xij,
This ys very trewthe, as y know my selff;
Theyre wages be batyd, their weyte ys encresyd,
Thus the spynners and carders avaylys be alle seased.[102]

[The poet continues with an argument for developing more silver mines, coupled with the establishment of mints, in order to expand employment and the wealth of the kingdom in general. He returns, however, to his earlier emphasis on the importance of cloth-making to England's welfare:]

And so to contynow owtt of hevyness,
Fro penowry[103] and need, and to be put owt of distress
And for to cawse owre enmyss[104] be this ordynaunss
To seke love and pese withowtt varyaunss.

And ffulle fayne that they may be subyet[105] to this lond
Yf we kepe the woolys straytly owt of theyre hond;
For by the endraperyng[106] theroff they have theyre sustynaunce
And thus owre enmys be supportyd to owre gret hynderaunce.

And therfor, for the love of God in trinyté,
Conceyve welle these matorss,[107] and scherysshe[108] the comynalté,[109]
That theyre pover levyng synfulle and adversyté
May be altratyd[110] unto welth, rychess, and prosperyté.

Here endythe the boke of Ynglysshe polysye,
That may cause alle the worlde yt to obeye;
There may no man denye but that it ys soothe,
For every man must have met, drynk, and clothe.

102 Ceased.
103 Penury.
104 Enemies.
105 Subject.
106 Converting wool to clothing.
107 Matters.
108 Cherish.
109 Commonalty, community.
110 Altered.

6.10 Regulating Weavers in Shrewsbury, 1448, from Shrewsbury Borough Archives, Assembly Book 1, f.342, in *English Historical Documents,* Vol. 4: *1327–1485,* ed. A. R. Myers (London: Eyre & Spottiswoode, 1969), pp. 1094–5 [English].

The document below alerts us to the close bonds between what might be the fate of agrarian workers displaced by landlords more interested in raising their revenues than preserving rural communities, and the work of cloth manufacturers and merchants in towns and cities, on whom rural producers, whether of food or wool, depended. As peasant tenants in the kingdom's manors attempted within their lord's courts to preserve social harmony through regulation of their common economic interests, so also townsmen, and in particular guildsmen, energetically crafted what they hoped would be rules that balanced self-interest against common goals and social harmony. Significantly, members of Shrewsbury's guild of weavers took for granted that economic activity could not be regulated without regulation of their members' moral conduct. Difficult as it may be to think that bigamy was common among the weavers of Shrewsbury, the guild sharply warned its members against consorting with any man accused of having two wives. Less surprising is a provision against widows of weavers who might take over their late husbands' businesses, unless it were for only one quarter of the year during which she could finish projects begun before his death – and perhaps most importantly, so long as she accepted the rule and governance of the craft's wardens and stewards during that time.

To all those who shall chance to see or hear this writing Richard Hadnall, John Ynce, William James, and John Hager, wardens of the craft of weavers, Thomas Ferton and Morris Reede, stewards of the said craft of the town of Shrewsbury, send greeting in God everlasting. Know ye that we for the good rule governance peace and tranquillity of all the said craft in the honour and worship of God, as well by the advice and consent of all the masters of the said craft as by the licence and agreement of our masters William Boorley and Richard Stury, bailiffs of the town and liberty of Shrewsbury, have ordained and established certain articles for our said craft for ever to endure in the following manner and form. In the first place, that no manner of foreign men of any foreign shire of England, that is to say, no man dwelling in any shire of England except those who dwell in Shropshire, Herefordshire, or the March of Wales, shall sell any kind of linen cloth except canvas cloth within the town or franchise of Shrewsbury but only at the time of the fairs of Shrewsbury and that time while the said fairs last, upon pain of forfeiture of the said cloth, one half to the bailiffs of the said town and their successors for the time being and the other half to the said commons of the said town. And that the wardens and stewards of the said craft of weavers and their successors or two of them to be assigned thereto by the said craft, with one of the serjeants of the said town, to be assigned thereto by the bailiffs or their successors, shall have power to attach or take such cloth at all times except only the fair times within the town and franchise aforesaid as often as it shall happen to be so forfeited to the use of the said bailiffs and commons and their successors as it is stated above. Also that no man of the said craft of weavers shall take any servant to serve him as apprentice for less than the term of seven years and that no man shall keep more than one apprentice weaving with shuttle and lathe until the time that the term of six years of one apprentice be fully completed and passed, if he live so long, on pain of 20*s* of lawful money of England, to be forfeited and paid in the following manner, that is to say, 6*s* 8*d* to the bailiffs of the said town and their successors for the time being to the use of the said bailiffs and their successors, 6*s* 8*d* to the common avail of the said town to the use of the said commons, 6*s* 8*d* to the wardens and stewards of the said craft of weavers to the maintenance and increase of the light of the said craft of weavers and their successors at the feast of Corpus Christi day to the use of the said craft. Also that no woman shall occupy the craft of weaving after the death of her husband except for one quarter of the year, within which time it shall be lawful to her to work out her stuff that remains with her unwrought, so that she be ruled and governed by the wardens and stewards of the said craft during the said terms as for the good rule of the said craft. And we the said William Boorley and Richard Stury, bailiffs of the town and liberty of Shrewsbury aforesaid, considering that the premises are conceived and proposed for the good rule and governance of the said craft, at the special request and supplication of the said wardens and stewards by advice of all the masters of the said craft of weavers, have affixed the seal of office in witness of the foregoing. Given in the Guildhall of the town of Shrewsbury the Monday next after the feast of Saint Thomas Martyr Archbishop the 27th year of the reign of our sovereign lord King Harry the Sixth after the conquest [30 December 1448]. Also if any man of the said craft happen to be defamed that he should have two wives and so live in adultery, and that it may be so proved as the wardens and stewards of die said craft by their wisdoms can in short time be advised for the welfare of the said craft, that then none of the said craft, whether he be master or journeyman, have anything to do with him, nor help him until such defiance be duly amended, on pain of 10*s* to be forfeited in the following manner, that is to say, 3*s* 4*d* to the bailiffs of the said town and their successors for the time being, 3*s* 4d to the commons of the said town, 3*s* 4*d* to the wardens and stewards of the said craft, to the use of the said craft. [In Latin] This agreement specified above was thus enrolled, and exemplified and enlarged in the time of Roger Eyton and John Hoord, Bailiffs of the town of Salop, 28 Henry VI.

Also this agreement thus specified was enrolled and exemplified in the time of John Colle and Philip Grace, Bailiffs of the town of Salop, 32 Henry VI.

6.11 Contesting Authority over Urban Workers: The Mayor of Exeter et al. v. Stoden and Others, 1477, TNA STAC 2/26/393, in *Select Cases before the King's Council in the Star Chamber*, Vol. 1: A.D. 1477–1509, ed. I. S. Leadam, Selden Society Publications 16 (London, 1903), pp. 1–6.

The weavers of Shrewsbury who attempted to regulate and protect the craftwork of their members were scarcely exceptional, in such an effort to balance cooperation on behalf of common interests against the interests of individual members and families. Craft guilds, however, were seldom able to manage their internal affairs and external relations free from interference by urban or municipal authorities, authorities that usually had more concern for the well being of merchants than solicitude for the makers of what moved, locally and nationally, in commerce. Parties on all sides of conflicts in urban communities, of course, claimed that their conduct was intended to bring peace, harmony, and good order to the king's subjects; and a recurring theme in the documents below is the invocation of royal authority to resolve these local conflicts – or an implicit acknowledgement that royal authority may have contributed, directly or indirectly, to the conflict itself.

Rivalries between civic authorities and the masters and wardens of guilds gave the central government frequent occasion to intervene; indeed, such rivalries made almost inevitable the king's involvement in the affairs of towns and cities, whatever the inclination of any particular monarch to manage the local affairs of London, or York, or Exeter, from which we have the record below from Star Chamber proceedings. The mayor of Exeter's petition to the king and his councilors in 1477 lays out a fairly simple case against several people identified as tailors, for riot, assault, and disturbance of the king's peace; the tailors accused of such riot, however, responded that they were simply exercising their responsibility, under a royal grant incorporating the Guild of Tailors, for maintaining a high standard of production among those engaged in their craft within the town. The case takes an intriguing turn in the mayor's response to the tailors' claim, when he invokes the "liberties" of the bishop, and also of the Dean and Chapter, of the cathedral, themselves usually an irritant to civic authorities resentful of their exclusion from such liberties within the city, to insist that the defendants in the case usurped rights belonging to others when they conducted their searches for defective tailoring. Both sides agreed that cooperation and communal responsibility should trump self-interest and self-advancement; but in each case, the question of who should determine terms of cooperation and assess communal responsibilities received radically different answers from the opposing parties.

To the kyng oure Soueraigne lord

Shewyth vnto your highnesse your trew liegemen and Subgettes the Mayre Bailifs and comynaltie of your Cite of Excestre in the Counte of Deuons greuously compleynynge, that where oone John Stoddon Richard Tournour[111]

111 This name and that of William Seyngyll afford the clue to the date of this case, which, as well be seen from the reference, has been sorted among the papers of Henry 8. The case was heard at

Thomas Penhall Water Kent Symon Davy Robert Crisshaue William Seyngyll John Martyn Thomas Blakechawe and John Tylham of the seid Cite Tayllours confedered and accompaigned with dyuers other mysdoers and riotous persones being of the mystere of Tayllours withyn the seid Cite and brekers of your peas, in maner of werre arrayed with force, that ys to say jakkes,[112] doublettes of defence, Swerdes, Bokelers, Gleyves,[113] and Staves and other weapons defensible, the Saturday nexte after the fest of Seynt Marke last passed[114] at Excestre aforesaid in riotous wyse made assaute vppon oone Thomas Davy of the seid Cite and hym bete wounded and evill entretid, that he was in dispayre and jupardie of his lyfe and so manassed and put hym in suche fere that he dar not dwell withyn the seid Cite And also the seid mysdoers and riotours contynuyng their vnlaufull confederacy and mysdoyng, assembled theym the Fryday next after[115] the seid fest of Seynt Marke in the seid Cite with grete force and in riotous wyse came to the house of oone Richard Longe and there made assaute vppon hym being in his house manassyng[116] to sle hym without he wold be of their confederacy or els departe oute of the seid Cite and dwell not withyn it, and this the seid mysdoers by coloure of youre letters patentes[117] for theym and other of the seid mystere[118] opteigned contrarie to the old libertees customes and laufull vsages of the seid Cite had and vsed, accompaigneth theym with many evyll disposed and nasty persones and maykyth dayly dyuers conuenticles confederacions and vnlaufull assembles contrarie to your lawes, disobeying the seid Maire and other officers of the seid Cite and woll not be corrected by theym tto the grete disturbance of your liege people and of youre peas withyn the seid Cite and in subuersion of the old libertees customes and rules vsed and had for the welle peas and good gouernell[119] of the same Cite, not oonly to evill and perilous example, but also finally to the distruccion of the seid Cite, without youre good grace beshewyd in this behalfe, it Please therefore your highnesse of

Westminster before the King (Edward 4) in Council, and the judgement delivered on February 22, 1477, 16 Ed. 4, at the prayer of Richard Tournour and William Sengill, proctors and attorneys of the Master and Wardens of the Taylors.

112 Jack, a kind of sleeveless tunic or jacket formerly worn by foot soldiers and others, usually of quilted leather, and in later times often plated with iron.

113 Galive, gleyve, &c. A name given at different periods to three distinct kinds of weapons, viz. lance, bill, and sword. Ibid. s.v. In this context it would probably be a bill or halberd, a common meaning of the word in the fifteenth century.

114 St Mark's Day is April 25. This was Saturday, 29 April 1475.

115 The context seems to indicate that the Friday next after the Saturday following St Mark's Day is intended, i.e., 5 May.

116 Menacing.

117 A written grant by the king, conferring property, privileges, or other benefits on the recipient or recipients, whose title to the same would subsequently depend on this "open" letter.

118 Guild.

119 More commonly "goernail": government.

youre most habundant grace to considere the premysses and theruppon forasmoche as the seid John Stoddon Richerd Turnour and John Tylham be here[120] withyn youre Cite of London to commaunde theym by a seriant of Armes to appere afore youre highnesse and the lordes of youre most honourable Councell to Aunswere to the premysses. And ouer this it please youre good grace to graunte seuerall letters of privie seall directe to the other the seid mysdoers commaundyng theym by the same to appeare afore your highnesse and the lordes of youre seid Councell at a certeyn day to Aunswere to the premysses. And ouer that such correccion to be had in thus behalf as it may be an example to other so mysdoynge, And thus for the loue of God.

Indorsed. The maire and bailiffs of the Citee of Excestre versus John Stoddon Richard Turnour and other of the same.

This is the Aunswere of John Stoden and Richard Tournour to the bill of complaint of the Maire Bailiffes and Cominaltie of the Cite of Exceter.

The seid John Stoden and Richard Tournour seyen that as for eny thing surmitted to be done by them or eny of theym with force and armes riotously or ageynest the kynges peace they be therof not gyltye And that they be redy to prove by all suche meanes and weyes as your wysedomes and good lordeshippes shall assigne And as for eny thing surmitted to be done by them to the seid Thomas Davy and Richard Longe they seye that the kyng oure soueraign lorde of his grace especiall and for othere diuerse consideracions hym moving by his letters patentes[121] redi to be shewed among othere thynges graunted to his liege men of the mistere of taillours within the Cite of Exceter A Gylde or a Fraternite in the worship of Seint John the Baptist[122] And that Gylde or Fraternite soo vnyed[123] founded create erecte and stablisshed have hold and the same enjoye to theym and theire successours for euer to endure And that they the same Gylde or Fraternite may encresse and augment as often shall please or shaalbe nedefull to theym for the gouernaunce kepyng and regiment of the seid Gylde or Fraternite imperpetuyte as it shall best please theym And ouer that oure seid soueraign lord of his habundaunt grace by his seid letters patentes hath graunted to the seid maister and wardens and here[124] successours that they the foresid Gylde Fraternite or Craft within the seid Cite and in the suburbies of the same may ordeign and rule and the defaictes of the same of here seruauntes by the

120 It would seem from this that the plaintiffs had promise of an immediate hearing. The historian of Exeter, John Vowell (alias Hoker), Chamberlain of the city during Elizabeth's reign, states that two years elapsed between the riots and the judgment. Large expenses were incurred by the Corporation in getting evidence and making journeys to London, "pro material cissorum."

121 These are dated November 17, 1466. The tenor of the patent is correctly set forth by the defendants.

122 A patron saint of tailors, e.g. of the Merchant Taylors' Company of London.

123 United.

124 Their.

menyng of the worthiest and most sufficient men of that Craft to correcte and amend And also that the seid maister and wardens and theire successours for euer haue and make full serche in and of the seid Craft And all othere persones wheche bene or shalbe priuilegied with the seid Craft within the seid Cite of Excetour and the Suburbies of the same and of suche Craftes as they or eny of theym vsen or vseth or before tymes haue vsed And all defautes amonge theym founden after theire discression by the surveieu of the mayre of the seid Cite for the tyme being thei may correcte and reforme, After whech grauntes so made and notwithstondyng the same the maire and the Bailiffes of the same Citee nowe being will not suffer the seid maister and wardens to plede or implede eny persone within the Courte of the same Citee nor in anny Accion to Appere by the name of there corporacion contrarie to the lawe and all maner justice And for asmuche as the seid Thomas Dauy and Richard Longe occupieden and exercised the mistere and craft of Tayllours within the said Cite And that it was enformed the seid John Stoden than being maister of the said mistere And Richard Tournour than being oone of the wardens of the seid mistere that the said Thomas and Richard Long occupied the said mistere and were not of connyng nor able to vse the seid mistere and also mysse vsed the same to the gret hurte of the kynges Liege peple Thei for the welt of the same peple according to the seid letters patentes come to the dwelling houses of the seid Thomas Dauy and Richard Longe within the seid Citee in pesible wyse to serche and see howe and in what maner of wyse they occupied and excersised the seid mistere And than and there willed And on the kynge oure soueraign Lorde is behalve chargied theym that thei shuld occupie and excersise trulie the seid mistere soo that the kynges Liege people were not by them desceyved And theruppon the maire of the seid Citee and Bailiffes of the same by the sturryng of the seid Thomas Davy and Richard Longe with gret multitude of people assembled with gret force and in riotouse wyse assauted the seid John and Richard Tournour soo that the seid John and Richard Tournour dare not abide and dwell in the seid Citee for fere of their lyves.[125] All wheche matiers the seid John Stoden and Richard Tournour be redy to proue as your gret wisdames and Lordeshippes will a ward And prayeth that they maye be dismissed fro this Courte as all good faith and trought require And that your Lordshippes wold cause the seid maire and Bailiffes to content vnto the seid John and Richard Tournour theire costes and exspences that they have wrongfully susteynned in this behalve And also to comaund the seid maire Bailiffes and Cominaltie and eueryche of theym to kepe the kyngis peace ayenst the seid John and Richard Tournor vppon suche a peyne as shalbe thought by your gret wysdomes most requisite and behofull in that be halve And this for the love of Jhesu and in the wey of Charitee.

125 Retaliatory violence was inflicted by the guild on those members who were induced by the corporation to renounce the guild, according to the editor of this case.

This ys the Replicacion of the Maire Baillifes and Cominalte of the Cite of Excestre to the Aunswere of John Stoddon & Richard Turnour.

The seid Maire Baillifes and Cominalte sayen that the seid Aunswere is insufficient to put theym to Aunswere vnto, Wherfor they pray that for the nonsufficiente therof, that the said John and Richard may be punysshed according to their deserte &c. And ouer this the said Maire Baillifes and Cominalte sayen that the seid John Stoddon and Richarrd Turnour bene gylte of the riottes brekyng and disturbaunce of the Kynges peas in maner and forme as ys alleged in their said bille, and that the said Cite is an old Cite and of tyme that no mynde ys hath bene corporat of Maire Baillifes of the same Cite for the tyme being by all the said tyme haue vsed and had all serches correccion and punysshement of all maner offences and defaltes by any persone aswell artificers as other done withyn the liberte of the said Cite, and in like wyse the Reuerend Fader in God the Bysshoppe of Excestre and his predecessours withyn their fee called Seynt Stevynes fee withyn the same Cite, and also the Dene and Chapiter of Excestre and their predecessours withyn their fee called Seynt Sydwellis fee in the Suburbes of the said Cite by their officers by all the said tyme haue vsed and held serches correccion and punysshement of all defautes and offences done by any persons artificers or other withyn the same fees, so forasmoche as the said John Stoddon and Richard Turnour claymeth in their seid Aunswere such serches correccion and punycion withyn the seid Cite and fees by color of the Kyunges letters patentes,[126] it apperith that it is contrarie to the Customes libertees and vsages of the seid Cite and fees and grete derogacion of the seid Bysshoppe Dene and Chapiter and of the seid Maire Baillifes and Cominaltie and likely moche more hereafter to be if due remedy theryn be not had. Wherefor forasmoche as the said John and Richard confessith and withsaith not the mater comprised in the seid bille of compleynt nor aunswerith to the riot manassyng and evyll entretyng of the said Thomas Davy and Richard Longe namyd in the said bille, the said Maire Baillifes and Cominalte prayen that they may be punysshed according as right requyrith. And ouer this the said Maire Baillifes and Cominalte sayen in all things as they haue alleged in their said bille. Without that they made any assaute or manassed the said John Stoddon and Richard Turnour in maner and forme as is supposed in the seid Aunswere. All whiche maters the said Maire Baillifes and Cominaltge bene redy to proue as shall to youre good Lordshippes and gret Wysedomys bethought reasonable.

126 "And they shall have full scrutiny of the mistery within the city and suburbs," Letters Patent of November 17, 1466.

6.12 Civic Regulation of Work and Morals in Coventry, 1475, 1477, and 1492, in the *Coventry Leet Book*, Part II, ed. by Mary Dormer Harris, EETS, o.s. 135 (London,1908), pp. 416–19, 422, and 544–55.

Further illustration of the urban struggles between craft and artisan organizations or collectives on the one hand, and the governors of the cities or towns in which such producers' organizations pursued their work, comes from Coventry, only a couple of years before the mayor of Exeter brought his grievances against overly independent associations of craftsmen and artisans to the king's attention. The city's rulers decreed that at least once a year, all craftsmen should be reminded that, should they wish to make ordinances, they must first obtain approval of the mayor and common council. In both Exeter and Coventry, all sides agreed that cooperation and communal responsibility should trump self-interest and self-advancement; but in each case, who should determine terms of cooperation and assess communal responsibilities received very different answers from the opposing parties. Especially interesting about the ordinance below regarding independent "unions" of workers in Coventry is its appearance in the record of a governing assembly that ordered every city craft to show up for "processions and Ridyng" as customary. In light of the vigorous scholarship devoted to civic celebrations of Corpus Christi in recent years by both historians and literary scholars of medieval drama, it is tempting to see a similar investment of imagination and energy in the prohibition against independent confederacies of craft laborers, an investment both by the craftsmen themselves, in their obvious campaign to achieve collective power, and by civic governors who insisted on their own vision of "community" for Coventry.

Regulation of work and workers was a routine responsibility of Coventry's governors, and royal intervention in struggles over urban workers, while scarcely routine, was far from uncommon. Coventry's records, however, contain an unusual example of a king's involvement in civic supervision of work. Edward IV's letter of 1477, below, ordering Coventry's rulers to afford John French the secure conditions that he would need to practice alchemical transformations, may add further weight to the evidence above (4.8, 4.9) that alchemy was taken seriously; but it also hints that, without explicit royal instructions, French might have faced harassment and prosecution from Coventry's residents and governors.

Some years later, whatever people in Coventry may have thought about alchemy, its benefits and its dangers, the city's rulers took several decisions that illustrate how firmly they took for granted their responsibility, and their right, not simply to regulate work within the city, but to take whatever steps seemed appropriate to the welfare of citizens' souls. Coventry's governing council in 1492 appears curiously even-handed, establishing on the one hand an ordinance designed to discourage adultery by its (male) officers, while on the other banning single women from a potential source of independent income and requiring them to enter service until marriage "released" them from the obligation of servitude. The city's rulers sought to protect apprentices and servants from spending money on any "woman of evell name," although the wording of the prohibition leaves some ambiguity, whether an apprentice's master could license such behavior. Perhaps most significantly, civic authorities required all crafts in the city to hire priests to sing daily prayers, thereby expanding divine service in the city. What better justification, for monitoring and regulating craftsmen and artisans, than the preservation of their souls and the establishment of a "holy" city? But if political and economic benefits might accrue to Coventry's rulers from their duties to enforce moral rectitude and spiritual growth, their vision of themselves and their city included a moral dimension to work itself. Whatever else these ordinances of the late fifteenth century may illustrate, they remind us that, in a late medieval world in which all work was subject to supervision and often to regulation, however imperfect and vulnerable to challenge and evasion such supervision may have been, women were surely the most consistently and closely monitored of all who produced England's wealth in these centuries.

View of Frankpledge, Monday after the close of Easter, 15 Edward IV [April 8 1475]

[Ordained] that euery Craft within this Cite com with their pageantes accordyng as hit haith byn of olde tyme, and to Com with their processions & Ridyng[127] also, when the byn required by the Meire for the worship of this Cite [upon] pene of x li at euery defalt.

* * *

ffor-as-much as both be the tyme that no mannes mynde is Contrari,[128] & by full laudabull ordenaunce by autorite of letes holden within this Cite, hit bath byn vsed & attorissed that Crafty men of no Craft nor occupacion within this Cite shulden amonges them within ther Craft make any Conventicle, confederacie, caue[129] nor ordenaunce ayens good rule of this Cite or to hurt of the Comen Weyle of the same; & the mastres of euery Craft within this Cite shuld yerely at the Commaundement of the Meire, deliuer hym all the ordenaunces of their Craftes to be seen by hym & the Councell of the Cite, the good & laufull ordenaunces in that partie made to [be] by them affermed, and the vnlawfull to be be them adnulled, & this to be don & duly & performed vp certen peynes in dyuers ordenaunces by auctorites of diuerse letes made [and] conteyned, as in the same ordenounce apperetb. Contrary to which good ordenaunce, diuerse Crafty men of this Cite nowe late haue made diuerse conuenticles & ordenaunces vnlawfully ayenst the Comen publique of this Cite. And a-monges other, the Craftesmen of diuerse[130] Craft haue made a vnlafull ordenaunce, that is to say, that non of them shuld Colour ne dye but

127 On St John Baptist's and St Peter's Eves, when the armed watch rode through the city.

128 I.e., remembrance.

129 Rule or Injunction.

130 Sic: it should be "dyers".

vndur a certen forme amonges them selfe ordeigned, vp certene peynes by wrytyng ordeyned by surte of wrytyng & othes unlaufull in that behall[f]. Hit is therfor ordeyned by this lete, and by the auctorite of the same, as well the seid vnlauftill & hurtfull ordenaunces made by the said dyers, and all other vnlafull & hurtfull ordenaunce made in euery other Craft within this Cite be the Craftesmen of the same Crafts, that the vnlaufull othes and. wrytynges made for the same be vtterly vuyde,[131] cassed,[132] adnulled & of non effect; & that from hensforth eny persone, beyng of any Craft of this Cite, by eny suche ordenaunce vnlafull be not bounden nor Compelled by the Meister of any Craft to performs such ordenaunce; and that no Master of any Craft of this Cite from hensfurth sewe nor trobull in eny lawe eny persone for non-performyng of eny such ordenaunce, upon the peyne to forfet at euery defalt x li., the Meir to haue xiij s. iiij d. & the sheryffes to haue vj s. viij d., & the remennant to the Chaumber of this Cite to be applied. The same forfet to be demed and determed by due examinacion of the Meire of this Cite [and] vj of his Brethern taken with hym and the lerned Councell of this Cite.

This ordenaunce to be pro-Clamed euery yere, ones at the lest, that all Craftesmen may haue knolege theroff.

* * *

[6 Jan., 1477]
Mem.[133] that the vjth day of Januare the yere aforeseid, the forsaid Maire[134] resceyued a priuie signet be the handes of a servaunte of the kynges, the tenor wherof hereafter ensueth.

By the kyng.
Trusty and wele-beloued, we grete you wele. And late you wite that it hath ben shewed vnto vs that oure wele-beloued, Joh. ffrench, oure seruaunt, commonly conuersyng[135] and abydyng in oure Cite there, entendeth be his labour to practise a true and a profitable conclusion in the Cunnying of transmutation of metails to oure profyte and pleasure, and, for to make a clere shewing of the same Joh. French before certen oure seruauntes and Counsellours by vs therfore appointed, is required a certain tyme to prepare his materials; we, not willing therfore oure seid servant to be trobled in that he shall so werk or prepaire for oure pleasure and profits, woll & charge yews that ye ne suffre hym in any wyse by any persone or persones to be letted, troubled, or vexed, of his said labour and practise, to thentent that he, at his

131 Void.
132 Quashed.
133 Memorandum, Be it remembered.
134 John Seman.
135 Living or dwelling (in a place).

goode liberte, may shewe vnto vs and such as be by vs therfore appointed, the clere effect of his said conclusion. Yeuen vnder oure signet at our palays of Westm[ynstre] the xxix[ti] day of December.

To ours trusty and wele-belotted, the Maire and his Brethern of oure Cite of Couentre, and to the Recordour of the same, and to euery of thaim.

* * *

View of Frankpledge, Michaelmas 8 Henry VII, 1492

Hit is ordeyned at this present lete that all maner men that haue swynsties[136] within the walles of this Cite that they avoide theym betwixt that [and] Christemas then next folowyng, vppon the peyn to lese at euery defalt vj *s* viij *d*.

It is also ordeyned that yf hereafter eny man of worship within thie Citie that hath be Maire or eny person that be sclandred[137] in the synnes of avowtre,[138] ffornicacion or vsure[139] which haue be warned to amend them of such vices & woll not, but contynue in the same, and therof detected, that then such person, yf he haue be Maire to be deprived of his cloke, & of the Counceill of this Cite, never to precede farther to other office of worship as Meister of the Gilds or other; & to be eloyned[140] from all worship & goode companye till he fynde sufficient and suer caution or suertie of amendement: and in like wyse yf such offendour haue be shirrif or other officer or comiener[141] they never to precede nor to be called to farther worship, nor auaunced but utterly to be estraunged from all goods company, as is aforeseid.

Also that all Craftes and mysteries within this Cite that fynde pristes to syng & pray for them, that they gyfe straitly in charge to their said pristes to kepe the quer dayly aswell vppon the werk daies as vppon the holy daies, in encreasyng of dyuyn seruice dayly to be songon in the parish Chirches of this Cite.

Also that no person within thie Cite ffrohensfurth kepe, hold, resceyue nor fauour eny Tapster, or Woman of evell name, fame or condition to whom eny resorte is of synfall disposicion, hauntyng the synne of lechery, vppon the peyn of euery householder to lese at euery defalt xx *s*. And that euery person that hath such tenaunt kepyng such suspect persones in his house after

136 Pig sties.

137 Brought into ill repute, or suspected of evil; the subject of public outcry, notoriety, or public scandal.

138 Adultery.

139 Usury.

140 Removed to a distance.

141 Freeman, citizen or burgess.

knowlech be made to hym of such guydyng be an officer, but yf he voids such tenaunt, he to lese xl *s*.

Also that no Tapster nor other persons frohensfforth resceyue nor fauour any mannes prentes or seruaunt of this Cite in his house ther to spend eny money or to company with eny woman of evell name, or other person of vnsadde disposicion, or other person diffamed, ayenst the will of his maister, vppon the peyn to lese at euery defalt vj *s* viij *d*.

Also that no senglewoman, beyng in good hele & myghty in body to labour within the age of L yeres, take nor kepe frohensforth houses nor chambres be them-self; nor that [they] take eny Chambre within eny other persone, but that they go to seruice till they be maried, vppon the peyn who doth the contrarie to lese at the first defalt vj *s*. viij *d*. & at the ij[de] defalt to be comyt to prison, there to abide tyll they fynde suerte to go to seruice. And that euery such persons [that] resceyue eny such persones, or set them eny house or Chambre, to lese at the first defalt xx *s*., at the ij[de] defalt xl *s*. & at the iij[de] defalt to be comyt to prison, there to remayn till he fynde suerte to conforms hym-selfe to this ordeneunce.

Further Reading

Bennett, Judith M., *Women in the Medieval Countryside: Gender and Household in Brigstock before the Plague* (Oxford: Oxford University Press, 1987).

Bennett, Judith M., *Ale, Beer and Brewsters in England: Women's Work in a Changing World* (Oxford: Oxford University Press, 1996).

Bridbury, A. R., *Medieval English Clothmaking: An Economic Survey* (London: Heinemann Educational, 1982).

Britnell, R. H., *The Commercialization of English Society, 1000–1500*, 2nd edn (Manchester: Manchester University Press, 1996).

DeWindt, Anne, and Edwin Brezette DeWindt, *Ramsey: The Lives of an English Fenland Town, 1200–1600* (Washington, DC: Catholic University of America Press, 2006).

Dyer, C. C., *Lords and Peasants in a Changing Society: The Estates of the Bishopric of Worcester, 680–1540*. Cambridge: Past and Present Publications (Cambridge: Cambridge University Press, 1980).

Fryde, E. B. *Peasants and Landlord in Later Medieval England* (New York: St Martin's Press, 1996).

Goldberg, P. J. P., *Women, Work, and Life-cycle in a Medieval Economy: Women in York and Yorkshire c.1300–1520* (Oxford: Clarendon Press, 1992).

Hatcher, John and Mark Bailey, *Modelling the Middle Ages. The History and Theory of England's Economic Development* (Oxford: Oxford University Press, 2001).

Holt, R. and G. Rosser, eds, *The Medieval Town: A Reader in English Urban History, 1200–1540* (London: Longman, 1990).

Kermode, Jennifer I., *Medieval Merchants: York, Beverley and Hull in the Later Middle Ages* (Cambridge: Cambridge University Press, 1998).

Masciandaro, Nicola, *The Voice of the Hammer. The Meaning of Work in Middle English Literature* (Notre Dame, IN: University of Notre Dame Press, 2007).

Miller, Edward, ed., *The Agrarian History of England and Wales,* Vol. 3, 1348–1500 (Cambridge: Cambridge University Press, 1991).

Palliser, D. M., *The Cambridge Urban History of Britain,* Vol. 1 (Cambridge: Cambridge University Press, 2000).

Palliser, D. M., *Towns and Local Communities in Medieval and Early Modern England* (Aldershot: Ashgate Variorum, 2006).

Poos, Lawrence Raymond, *A Rural Society after the Black Death: Essex, 1350–1525* (Cambridge studies in population, economy and society in past time, 18) (Cambridge: Cambridge University Press, 1991).

Raftis, James Ambrose, *Peasant Economic Development within the English Manorial System* (Stroud: Sutton, 1997).

Razi, Z. and R M. Smith, eds, *Medieval Society and the Manor Court* (Oxford: Clarendon Press,1996).

Robertson, Kellie and Michael Uebel, eds, *The Middle Ages at Work. Practicing Labor in Late Medieval England. The New Middle Ages* (Basingstoke: Palgrave Macmillan, 2004).

Schofield, Phillipp R., *Peasant and Community in Medieval England 1200–1500* (Basingstoke: Palgrave Macmillan, 2003).

Swanson, Heather, *Medieval British Towns* (Basingstoke and New York: Macmillan and St Martin's Press, 1999).

Swanson, Heather, *Medieval Artisans: An Urban Class in Medieval England* (Oxford: Basil Blackwell, 1989).

Whittle, J., *The Development of Agrarian Capitalism: Land and Labour in Norfolk 1440–1580* (Oxford: Clarendon Press, 2000).

7

Polity and Governance, Unity and Disunity

Although debates continue about the chronology and dynamics of state formation in England, and about the relative contributions of Anglo-Saxon monarchy and Norman feudal lordship to the process, England by the fourteenth century had achieved a remarkable degree of centralization and administrative unity, with a monarch that could, at least on occasion, raise taxes from subjects throughout the territory that acknowledged his kingship, summon troops for the king's wars, and administer justice in courts whose judges he appointed. Appearances were, to be sure, not always consistent with practice, as the evidence makes clear; but whether or not the people on the island who acknowledged him to be their king thought of themselves as part of a English "nation" or not, that acknowledgment was more than nominal, and royal institutions of police, taxation, and justice gave some substance to the claim that he ultimately ruled "England" and "Englishmen." England approximated a unitary state, even if it was not yet a nation-state; but such unity as it possessed, under the king and the aristocracy on whom he depended, and with whom he fought often, required constant attention, frequent justification, and repeated negotiations, often accompanied by violence, between rulers and ruled.

The documents here include not only works immediately recognizable to modern readers as "political theory" or "social criticism," but also works of advice, conduct and "etiquette" books that may initially strike our readers today as more relevant to domestic and private life than affairs of state. But a major theme of this chapter is the misleading nature of sharp distinctions, at least for this period, between "public" and "private" realms of experience and thought, and how unsatisfactory modern notions of individual autonomy prove when applied to late medieval literature, despite repeated emphasis on the moral accountability of individuals.

These sources, while too limited to provide a comprehensive survey of political institutions during this period, should illustrate the range of arenas in which English people found ways to manage competing needs and interests. Not only documents used in this chapter but many of those throughout this collection drawn from government archives testify to the role that judicial institutions played in people's lives and imaginations – and to the innovation and imagination that people brought to using and manipulating those institutions. People complained vigorously about inadequacies of royal justice and abuses of the king's courts, but we know their complaints because so many were using the courts, and because the courts produced lots of records.

7.1 Challenging Bondage and Using Parliament: Petition of Thomas Paunfeld of Cambridgeshire, 1414. TNA, SC 8/23/1143A, in *An Anthology of Chancery English*, ed. John H. Fisher, Malcolm Richardson, and Jane L. Fisher (Knoxville: University of Tennessee Press, 1984). pp. 198–204. (The Petition is also accessible online at "Anonymous. An Anthology of Chancery English," Electronic Text Center, University of Virginia Library, at http://etext.lib.virginia.edu/etcbin/toccer-new2?id=AnoChan.sgm&images=images/modeng&data=/lv1/Archive/mideng-parsed&tag=public&part=163&division=div1.)

One place to begin an investigation of English polity, and the institutions that both expressed that polity and constructed it, might be an early 15th-century petition that makes clear the fundamental importance of "justice" in the ideological and material formation of an "England' centered around and focused on a king whose principal job was to see justice done. The following petition illustrates how the processes of justice within the king's courts were far from impersonal, and how readily they could be used and abused in ways that look, from a modern perspective, deeply corrupt. But it also illustrates that the courts indeed provided a place where conflicts over interests and rights could be, and were, conducted, and how strong was the conviction that the courts were an appropriate and useful place to negotiate, sometimes with violence to be sure, differences over interests and rights.

Evident in the account of Thomas Paunfeld's troubles[1] *are the several institutions*

1 Evidence of trouble in Chesterton between tenants, who claimed privileges of ancient demesne, and the Prior and Canons of the Augustinian Priory of Barnwell, appears in a memorandum on the royal Close Rolls for August, 1405, recording an undertaking by the prior and canons to "procure no hurt or harm to the tenants of the town of Chesterton . . . and to keep all things contained in an act made before the king and council touching disputes and debates whatsoever between him and the said tenants: ("Close rolls, Henry IV: August 1405", *Calendar of Close Rolls*, Henry IV: volume 2: 1402–1405 (1929), pp. 513–514. URL: http://www.british-history.ac.uk/report.aspx?compid=102121 Date accessed: 26 September 2009.) Customary tenants had protested excessive labor services, arbitrary entry fines, exclusion of tenants from common rights, and the prior's demands for oaths of fealty to him as chief lord instead of to the king, threatening their status as ancient demesne tenants and reducing them to the status of ordinary bondmen or villeins; the prior retaliated with indictments under the Act of 1377 banning villeins' appeals to Doomsday Book, see 6.4 above. The award by king and council referred to in 1405 points to efforts by the central government to mediate the dispute, but legal proceedings largely favored the prior and canons; only Thomas Paunfeld, it appears, remained active in resistance to the Priory's lordship a decade after the award of 1405.

constructed over the previous several centuries that would give coherence and integrity to "England": courts of justice acting in the name of the king, a parliament that represented the various interests of the realm, and of course, the king himself. But more interesting than what the case has to say about the strength of royal judicial institutions, or about the way in which such institutions incorporated readily the play of lordship and patronage, is what it reveals about the deep connections among concepts of "freedom," " justice," and the institutions of the king's justice among English people whose birth and status did not *entitle them to bear arms.* (In *An Anthology*, parentheses are used within the document to indicate rubbed areas of the manuscript.)

To the worshipful and wyse syres and wyse Communes that to this present parlement ben assembled

Besecheth mekely youre pore Bedeman[2] Thomas Paunfeld oon of the fre tenentes of oure liege lord the kyng of his maner and tounshipe[3] of Chestreton in the Shyre[4] of Cambrigg: that ye wole considere how that I pursuede diuerse billes by fore oure liege lord kyng henry the four the fader to oure liege lord the kyng that now is and hise worchepeful lordes and comunes in his parlement holden at Westminstre that x day of ffeuer[5] the xiiij yer of his regne:

To the whiche billes myne aduersaries replieden by mouthe[6] and enformeden the kyng and the worshepeful lordes spirituelx and termporelx in that parlement: how that I was outelawed[7] by heye record of trespace[8] wherethurgh[9] that I ne oughte not to ben herd nor answered of no maner compleynt in my billes writen but yif (it) so were that I hadde brought my Chartre[10] in myn hand wherby that I myghte haue answered in lawe to alle

"Chesteron: Economic History", *A History of the county of Cambridge and the Isle of Ely: Volume 9: Chesteron, Northstowe, and Papworth Hundreds* (1989), pp. 18–26. URL: http://www.british-history.ac.uk/report.aspx?compid+15309 Date accessed: 15 September 2009.

2 Beadsman, i.e., suppliant or petitioner.

3 Manor and township.

4 Shire or county.

5 February.

6 Answered orally.

7 Outlawry was a step in compelling appearance of defendants in legal actions, technically putting an individual who had failed to appear beyond the protection's of the king's law; in practice, it was an inconvenience, lifted in a number of ways, including the purchase of a pardon (John Baker, *An Introduction to English Legal History*, 4th ed. (London: Butterworths, 2002), p. 65). In this case, however, outlawry appears to have served Paunfeld's opponents as a device to deflect his charges against them – for, inter alia, manipulating the legal system itself.

8 Trespass, an action at common law alleging force used to achieve an unlawful end.

9 Wherefore, as a consequence of which.

10 Pardon. Paunfeld is arguing that his opponents had delayed his prosecution of his complaints by insisting that his outlawry required a pardon before the substance of his petitions for justice could be considered.

maner of persones that ony replicacions[11] wolden haue maked ayeyns any article of my billes:

And worchepeful and discrete sires that myghte I not done that tyme: for (I wi)ste[12] not how I was endited and outelawed of what maner trespace: but as Iohan Cokayn the Justice recordede byfore the kyng and made mencion at that tyme. whiche I trustede to god to haue proued by lawe by fore the kyng and the worchepeful lordes and comunes in that parlement that the processe of myn outelawerye was vnlawefully made and al that longeth[13] ther to: yif Johan Cokayn the Justice wolde haue brought in that record by fore the kyng in the parlement and there to haue ben determyned byfore hym and hise lordes and Comunes afore seyde (yo)r[14] they hadde departed thennes

ffor byfore hene[15] of the persones that weren and ben Commissioners vp on myn enditement wherby that I was outelawed: I myghte not haue ben remedied ne myne neyghebores nother so sone at that tyme lyk as we oughten to haue ben of right and as me thoughte we shulde ben here:[16] and that was for cause of meyntenance[17] that was ayeyns vs and yit is. and that made me cause to come to that heye Court of rightwisnesse: (T)heder to pleyne[18] for to han declared thilke[19] record ayeyns my neighboures and me vnlawefully mad and there sounere[20] to han ben remedied of the wronges that we haue had by the Priour and Chanons of Bernewelle and her meyntenors these x. yer (and) more vnduely and vngoodly:

And now thanked be god and the rightwisnesse of the discrete and trewe Juges Sire william hankford and hise felawes: han[21] after the laws of the lond made me able for to yeve[22] myne answeres in lawe as my symple wittes wole semen me to alle maner persones that any replicacions wolde maken ayeyns ony of the articles of my billes after the forme that sueth yif it like to the kyng: with swich conseil as he hath a(ss)igned, to me and shal by the grace of god: for to declaren the entente of my billes for the kynges auantage and for fortherynge of his trewe lieges better than I can in this heye Court of rightwisnesse:

---

11 In legal process, a plaintiff's response to a defendant's answer to the original complaint; but here, it probably means simple a reply or response to Paunfeld's earlier bills of complaint.

12 Know.

13 Belonged.

14 Ere, before.

15 Any.

16 Heard.

17 Wrongful interference in a lawsuit on behalf of one or the other parties to litigation, or to defendants in criminal inquiries and proceedings.

18 Complain.

19 That.

20 Sooner.

21 Have.

22 Give.

And by cause that I am of no power to pursue these materes in any other Court saue in this heye Court of rightwisnesse where as most truste and hope to haue rightwisnesse and lawe rather than I shulde in any other Court byfore ony of tho persones that weren and aren Commissioneres vp on myn enditement: for the heye meyntenance that I knowe wel shuld be made ayeyns me:

Also worchepeful sires: we beseche yow at the reuerence of god: that ye wole praye to oure liege lord the kyng: that he wole fouche[23] saf of his special grace and his Ryal prerogatyf[24] in this heye Court: to graunte me durynge my pursuyte by the auctorite[25] of his parlement to walken at large to pursue these materes that ben folwynge in my bille. . . .

And sithe the tyme that I was resseyued to meynprise[26] by cause that I was endited of trespace as an accessorie and not endited as a principal and delyuered out of prison at large by the kynges commaundement in strengthyng and enhaunsyng of his Rial prerogatif that he grauntede to me by the auctorite of his parlement:

Yit myne aduersaries han pursued me nowe and holden me in prison sithen seynt katerynes day twelve monthes last passed in to this tyme. ayeyns (the kynges graunt &) ordinaunce no consideracion ne tendernesse hauynge in my pore persone that am goddes cristene[27] creature of my longe contynnance in prison (for these materes that ben) folwynge vij. yer and more to destroye me to the uttereste that I shulde no more haue come to the kynges presence to pursue my right but for to kepe (me stille in prison til I hadde) deyed for defaute of socour and helpe. and as it semeth to my symple wittes there is litel charite of priestes whiche shulden cherice[28] goddes christene crature[29] as the kynges trewe liege man:

And therfore I beseche yow that ye wole prayen to oure liege lord the kyng of his special grace that swich remedie may be mad at this present parlement by the auys[30] of hise wise lordes spirituelx and temporelx in sauynge and encresynge of the kynges prerogatif in tyme comynge and in fertherynge of hise trewe lieges after that he hath graunted hise graciouse grauntes to ony of hise lieges: that fro hennes forward no persone of his Rewme deferre ony of hise lieges fro hise graciouse grauntes that he hath graunted in esement and in fortheryng of hise trewe lieges: and that vp on a suff(is)ant peyne payinge to the kyng and a nother peyne payinge to the partie so defferred fro the kynges graunt:

* * *

23 Vouch.
24 Royal prerogative.
25 Authority.
26 Surety, a guarantee of appearance when required by legal process.
27 Christian.
28 Cherish.
29 Creature.
30 Advice.

And also to praye oure liege lord of his special grace that the peticions afore rehersed and alle othere petitions that ben folwynge after hise graciouse (grauntes) mowe ben enacted in the parlement rolle: and also to yeue in charge to the Clerk of the parlement: that I may haue (a copye) of the same for the loue of god and of seynt Charite:

Also to yow worechepeful and wyse Comunes greuouseliche compleynen alle the kynges tenentes of the Ryal lordshipe and tounshipe of Chestreton in the Shyre of Cambrigge[31]: the whiche holden of the tenure of anxien demeyn of the Rial Coroune longynge to oure souereyn lord the kyng as it sheweth by oure euydence of old record in the book called Domesday thus begynnynge. Dominica villa regis E &c in the kynges eschekker[32] at Westminstre:

Also we greuouseliche compleyne vs vp on the Priour and Chanons of Bernewell[33] in the Shyre of Cambrigg byfore seyd and vp her predecessour that was the kynges fermour how that they han cleymed and yit cleymen[34] the regalite and the frehold of the kynges lordshype and tounshipe of Chestreton in the Shyre byfore seyd as for her owne with oute ony exception wher it is wel knowen by alle manere of euydences that the[35] konne shewen for hem self or ony man for hem that they were but fermours to the kyng: and now they are not as it sheweth by her chartres of king henry the thridde:

And vnder colour of the regalite and of the frehold whiche they presumen wilfully to haue: they haue cleymed and yit cleymen the kynges trewe lieges that ben hise fre tenentes annexed to his coroune: as for her bonde bore men and her bonde lond holderes: wher it is wel knowen by alle manere of euydences that they konne shewe for hem self or any man for hem that they ben fre tenentes and fre holderes to the kyng in chief and the chiefte resert and principalite of the same lordshipe and tounshipe shal retourne to the kyng and to his forseide Coroune as for oure chief and perpetuel lord of the fee:

* * *

31 The argument here is that Chesterton was ancient demesne, part of the royal estates at the time of Edward the Confessor, identified as such by its listing as a royal manor in the Domesday Book compiled on order of William the Conqueror, at the end of the twelth century. Tenants of such manors, although technically villeins or serfs, enjoyed exceptional privileges, including rights of inheritance, fixty of their rents and services, and access to royal courts in defense of their titles. On ancient demesne, see Marjorie Keniston McIntosh, "The Privileged Villeins of the English Ancient Demesne", *Viator* 7 (1976), pp. 296–328, and McIntosh's outstanding study of an ancient demesne manor, its local governance and its relationship to royal authority and jurisdiction, during the late Middle Ages, *Autonomy and Community: The Royal Manor of Havering atte Bower 1200–1500* (Cambridge: Cambridge University Press, 1986).

32 Exchequer, the office or agency of royal government that monitored and collected the king's revenues, including income from his estates and his feudal rights over his tenants, taxes, and the "profits" of his courts.

33 Prior and canons of Barnwell, who claimed lordship and the profits of Chesterton.

34 Have claimed and yet claim.

35 They, i.e., the tenants protesting the prior's conduct.

And for cause that we haue pursued to oure liege lord the kyng as for oure chief lord of the fee for to haue remedie and socour of the grete wronges mischiefs and diseses the whiche we haue suffred these .x. yer and more vnduely and vngoodly: The forseide Priour and Chanons han pursued ayeyns vs a Commission of oyer and termyner[36] after the forme of a statut mad vp on bond bore men and bond land holderes: which statut was made the ferste yer of kyng Richard the seconde in his tendre age with oute mencion exception or declaracion made of the same fre tenentes of the fre tenure of the ryal coroune byfore seid:

And by strengthe and colour of the forseide statut so generaly mad vp on bonde bore[37] men and bonde londe holderes:[38] the forseide Priour and Chanons han vs endited by men of her owne clothyng[39] and also by enquestes enbraced[40] as for her bonde bore men: to the which statut we fre tenentz of the coroune owe[41] not obeye: for we be not in the cas of the statut and ne oughte not to answere lyk as bonde men of byrthe shulde: for the whiche the forseide statut was made:

ffor we be fre tenentz and fre lond holderes annexed to the worthy coroune of oure most souereyn lord.the kyng and that we wele proue and declare by oure euydence wreten in the kynges eschekker at Westminstre: wherfore we wole answere as fre men oughte to done and proue that the suyte of the commission byfore seide which is mad vp on bonde bore men and bonde land holderes: was wrongfully taken ageyns vs and al the proces that longeth ther to with oute auctorite and power and that shal we proue by the grace of god:

* * *

And thus worchepeful sires yif this be suff(red): the freest knyght or Squyre of the Rewme yif they be dwellynge tenentes vnder ony of the religious that haue swiche lordshipes of the kynges to ferme[42] may be put in prison by swych cohercion and compulsse[43] as (the) mischeuouse statut byfore seid sheweth and declareth: for to ben the moste bonde tenentes of al the Rewme: also in the contre[44] they shullen ben endited by enquestes enbraced by these

36 Literally, a commission to "hear and determine," i.e., a special panel authorized by the king to conduct criminal inquiries and proceedings in a particular locality, or addressing a particular incident.

37 "Born bond," i.e., a bondman by birth.

38 Tenants who might be free by birth but hold land in villeinage

39 I.e., by men who have received livery of the prior and canons.

40 Embraced, i.e., by juries corrupted or bribed by the prior and canons.

41 Ought.

42 "To farm" in this context means to manage and take the revenues of a manor or estate at the lease or grant of another, in this case, of the king.

43 Compulsion.

44 Country.

dede religiouse fermours: and that for cause of the grete profites and the grete extorcions that the Sherreues[45] of the Shyres resceyuen and done: they mowe haue no remedie of the lawe but onely enprisonned manaced and oppressed: and yif ony consaill of the lawe hem wolde helpe after the cours and fourme of lawe: they shulle ben put in prison as her conseilloures fa(c)tours and abettouers[46] and as they were bonde men to these religious byfore seide in so moche that they shulle non other mercy haue ne non other remedie but only for to yolden hem[47] to ben her bond cherles[48] for euere more and her heyres[49] (alle the dayes) of her lyues to these dede religious fermours:

Wherfore we beseche yow mekely discrete and wyse Comunes of this present parlement: that ye praye for (vs to ouer liege lord) the kyng and to hise worchepeful lordes of (this present) parlement. . . .

That is to seyn that he wole at youre instance and prayer in sauynge of his owne right and in fortherynge of (his) trewe lieges: ordeyne at this tyme or[50] ye departen hennes fro this present parlement with auys of hise wise lordes and also by the assent of (yow wyse) and worchepeful comons: such remedie that fro hennes forward none swiche commissions be take nor pursued ayeyns the kynges fre tenents annexed to his worthy coroune by no religious fermours that (han such manors) and tounshipes of the kynges to ferme: til that it be pleynly determyned byfore hise Iustices of that on benche or of that other by comon lawe: whether the forseid tenentes ben fre or bonde and whether they ben worthy to ben punysshed by that forseide statut or non and that vp on a suffisant peyne payinge to the kyng and a nother peyne payinge to the partie pursued and greued for such sute:

* * *

Besechinge also (to) oure liege lord that he wole haue compassion and pyte vp on vs that euere haue ben trewe lieges and trewe fre tenentes to his worthy coroune of his worthi maner[51] and tounshipe of Chestreton byfore seide that these greuouse meschiefs that ben done to vs mowen ben amended now at this tyme or ye departen hennes and this commission mowe be repeled and the obligacions to ben adnulled and to ben delyuered to ech man his owne obligation for (the loue), of god and of seynt[52] charite:

45 Sheriffs.

46 Lawyers, that is, would be charged with maintaining, or abetting, freemen, if those freemen could be claimed as bondmen or villens by religious houses such as Barnwell.

47 Yield themselves.

48 Churls.

49 Heirs.

50 Before.

51 Manor.

52 Holy.

7.2 Ruling Well and Doing Justice: "The III Considerations Right Necesserye to the Good Governance of a Prince," University College, Oxford. MS 85, translated in the fifteenth century from the French original, in *Tracts of the Later Middle Ages*, ed. Jean-Philippe Genet, Royal Historical Society Publications, Camden Fourth Ser. 18 (London: Royal Historical Society, 1977), pp. 196–200 and 202–6.

Thomas Paunfeld's petition, preceding, makes emphatically clear that kingship in late medieval England should be understood in terms of personal lordship, not as sovereign authority exercised through an impersonal bureaucracy. Paunfeld makes a powerful claim to free status, for himself and other tenants of the ancient demense manor of Chesterton; but such a claim rests ultimately on the king's personal lordship of the manor from the past, not on an inherent right of all men to free status. In short, by claiming privilege by virtue of their status as tenants to the king, he and his fellows of Chesterton concede that freedom originates in ancient submission to the king's lordship, not as a right available to all subjects of the king.

Not surprisingly, systematic discussions of how the king should govern often focus sharply on the king's personal behavior and morality, emphasizing the importance of the king's personal adherence to high moral standards; a good king necessarily was a good man – not a bad basis for effective kingship, to be sure, when kingship depended on the personal ties that bound at least the king's greatest subjects to his person. Excepts here from III Considerations *illustrate the strong emphasis on the king's moral instruction that was assumed to make for strong and effective kingship. The selections from this tract included below are designed to show the fundamental responsibility of a king – to see justice done – but also to illustrate a perennial problem for a medieval monarch whose personal responsibility for governance required heavy reliance on subordinates, some of whom might well think themselves his equal, not only in wisdom, but in material resources. The discussion of offices remains firmly within the framework of personal moral choices and ethical commitments; but in advising how most effectively to select officers and ministers of the government, observers and critics of royal governance could find an opening for a more systemic and structural analysis of politics and political administration, an analysis that by the late fifteenth century, in the writings of Sir John Fortescue (below), would produce a new perception of the state and the necessity for something other than personal moral standards for the achievement of strong and effective governance.*

(XIII) Of the vertue of justise and how it apperteyneth sovereignly unto a Prince

Here siwyngly[53] it is in partie to treete of the vertue of justise with out which no reaume ne lordshippe may well be governyd ne long endure. And aftir the

53 Perhaps Anglo-Norman form, meaning following or ensuing.

Lawe Civile, the diffinicion of justise is suche: justise is perpetuell, ferme and constaunt will to yive unto every persoone his owne right and that he ought of dutie for to have.[54] And the right of justise yiveth unto every man III commaundementz: the first is to lyve honestly and mesurably, the secunde is to noon to doo wronge ne iniurie, the thridde is to yive and surende to every man his right and dutie. The wise man seith that justise is as the mothir of all vertues, for alle vertues have and comprehende in theyme the nature of justise. And verily, whan a Prince loveth justise and executeth it, he hath a greete resemblaunce and similitude unto God, as the Philosophre seith in this boke of Politiques, for God dooth no thinge but that he dooth by justise, loving the good and punisshing the yvell; as it is well shewed at the begynnyng of the worlde, for as soone as Lucifer, the first aungell, with his assenteers synnyd by pryde ayenst God, anoon by wey of justise God commaunded hem to a perpetuell deth in helle, and theyme chaced and devoicid[55] from the joyes of heven, nevyr to have mercy.[56] And the aungellys that hym obeyed, he stablissht and confermed in glorye and joye evyrlastingly perdurable. And also, as soone as God had made the worlde and had fourmed Adam and Eve and sett theyme in the blisse of paradyse, for so moche as they disobeide his commaundement and presumed to eyte[57] of the frute whiche he had theym streytly defendid,[58] he put theyme from paradise terrestre and theyme condempnyd by justise to spirituell deeth and bodily, as it is well expressed in the bible.[59] And thus God by his justise governyd as well in heven and in erthe. And this was for to yive ensaumple[60] to kynges, Princes and greet lordys of this worlde that they governe in like wyse whan they cometh to their lordshippe and that they doo justise. . . . And for this cause a kynge or a Prince that will nat doo justise by reson shall soone be with oute lordshippe. And yf he desire that his lordshippe shall longe abide and that he and his heires shall it longe tyme reioyse, he most doo right greete diligence to execute justise and it susteyne. And for this cause, a kinge or a Prince shuld chiefly and principally doo twey[61] thinges. The first is he shuld doo justise be duly kept through his lande and alle his obeisaunce. The secunde is that he love especially and principally the comyn[62] profite of the peeple and of subgites,[63] and that he yive noon attendaunce to his especial, private or

54 'Iustitia est constans et perpetua voluntas ius suum cuique tribuens' (the opening words of Justianian's Institutes).

55 Separated.

56 Isaiah 14: 12.

57 Eat.

58 Prohibited.

59 Genesis 3: 23, 24.

60 Example.

61 Two.

62 Common.

63 Subjects.

particuler profyte so moche and so ferforthly that he leve[64] to doo the comyn profite above seide. . . . And soo shall they kepe truly justise, the whiche yf they will have well kept of theire subgites, it is full covenable[65] that they principally kepe it in theym self and in theire owne persoones, for the wyse man seith that every vertu begynneth at hym self. That is to sey, who soo will doo any good vertu, he most begynne at hym self first chiefly And also he that desireth to have othir folke juste, he oweth to doo justise first in his owne persoone and in his lignage,[66] in his peeple, his servauntz and all his maynee,[67] for it is reson that the Prince doo good right and justise in his owne persoone, on his lignage and freendys, on his peeple and maynee, as well as upon his othir subgites. And it is greet laude and preisinge to a kinge or Prince whan he kepith truly the lawe whiche he commaundeth to be kept in his lande. And so dyd oure lorde Crist Jhesu, Goddys sone: he kept in hym self the lawes and the justises that were ordeyned to be kept in othir[68] as the lawe of deeth, of circumcision and othir, as hooly scripture witnessith in divers manyers. . . . And a Prince shuld nat yive credence in any wyse to any of his counsellours that yiveth him counseill unto the contrarie as unto such counsellours as beth flaterers and untrue, and lyeth in awaite to seeche[69] meenys[70] to their ownee preferrement, avauncement and promocion, by conduyt of yvell counseill. And the good proverbe[71] seith that he ne is lorde of his owne cuntree that is hated of his subgites. And therfore a kinge or Prince owith[72] with all his cure[73] and bisinesse take heede to keepe and execute justise. And whan he shall it so putte in execucion, also to doo it with softnesse and with attemperaunce.[74] And for so moche as mercy and pitee is it that oweth to attempre the rigoure and streitnesse of justise, it is to ben towched now aftirwarde of mercy, how she is necessarie unto the governaunce of a Prince whan she is medled[75] with justise.

64 Neglects.
65 Appropriate or suitable.
66 Lineage, family.
67 Perhaps Anglo-Norman "maneez", i.e., household?
68 By others, i.e., by Jews.
69 Seek.
70 Means.
71 'N'est pas seigneur de son pays/Qui de son pays est hay' (*Livre des proverbs francais*, ii, p. 99).
72 Ought.
73 Care, duty, responsibility.
74 Moderation, restraint.
75 Mixed together, blended, mingled.

(XV.) How and in what maner and with whiche circumstaunces a Prince shulde cheese his officers and servauntes

Aftir that it is before shewid[76] and meevid somwhat of the good governaunces perteynyng unto king, Princes and othir greet lordys, it seemyth convenient and resonable now siwyngly to entreete[77] of the cheesing[78] and eleccion of theire officers and servauntes. And for soo moche as it is greetly nedfull that they have officers with outen the whiche the lordes may never well governe, as seneshallz,[79] ballifz,[80] vicowntes,[81] provotz,[82] capteynes[83] of placez and many othir, they shulde knowe that for to have the good governementz of these above seide, the kinge or the Prince or the greet lorde shuld doo alle the good diligence that he might to have good and sage and true persoones in theire offices. And whan they have putte into suche offices the moost covenable persoones that they can finde, they shulden ley upon theyme greete charges and peynes, and doo theyme well to wyte and knowe how they shall well and truly bere theym and demeene theyme[84] in the seid offices, ffor right as it is according that every lorde yilde[85] unto God reson[86] and streyght accounte of his lordshippe and admynistracioun that he hath hade in this worlde, as holy scripture seith, right so also shall he answere for the defaute of his eville servauntz, that they by favoure or affeccion or necligence putteth into offices yf they ne puniysh theyme ne correct theyme duly for theire trespaces. And therfore especially they shuld doo greete peyne and diligence to take good, wyse and true officers, nat by meenys of prayer, affeccion or favoure. . . .

7.3 A Prince Rules Personally: Prince Arthur's Reception in Coventry, 1498, from *Coventry Leet Book: or Mayor's Register*, ed. by Mary Dormer Harris, Part III, EETS, o.s. 138 (London: 1909), pp. 589–92.

It was a source of royal strength and power that the king personally might claim the ultimate authority to dispense justice, and his responsibility for justice often provided rhetorical justification for his (self-interested) actions. But it was also a duty to be

76 Now that is has been shown.
77 Take up, consider.
78 Choosing, or choice.
79 Stewards.
80 Bailiffs.
81 Vicounts; Sheriffs.
82 Provosts.
83 Captains.
84 Demean or carry themselves.
85 Yield or give.
86 Here, perhaps "explanation," from the Anglo-Norman "reson".

invoked by subjects, and his personal responsibility could be a constraint on kingship, as well as a source of strength. The king's personal burden for seeing justice done (as well as some indication of how strongly the story of Arthur played in the consciousness of England's various local governors, including those in Coventry) is well illustrated by a royal visit to Coventry in 1496, in this case by Prince Arthur, Henry VII's son and presumptive heir at the time. Arthur himself was surely too young to play a major part personally in solving local controversies; but his presence offered a strong possibility of reconciling persistent local differences over rights and interests there. Equally intriguing about the entry in local records describing the prince's reception is testimony to the pageantry and dramatic imagination provoked by his visit. Spirituality found expression in communal theater, especially in the Corpus Christi plays, in Coventry and elsewhere;[87] *clearly, the civic record here confirms that governance – or politics – contributed also to dramatic practice in the late Middle Ages.*

Mem. that this yere the Wensday the xvij day of Octobre anno xiiij^{o} *Regis* H. vij, prince Arthur, the ffirst begoton son of kyng Henre the vijth, then beyng of the age of xij yeres & more, cam first to Couentre & there lay in the priory fro Wensday unto the Munday next suying,[88] at which tyme hie removed toward London. Ayenst whos comyng was the Spon-strete-gate garnysshed with the ix worthy[s], and kyng Arthur then hauyng thus spech, as foloweth: –

[KING ÁRTHUR.] Hayle, prynce roiall, most amyable in sight!
Whom the court eternally thurgh prudent gouernaunce,
Hath chosen to be egall ons to me in myght,
To sprede our name, Arthur, & actes to auaunce,
And of meanys victorious to have such habundaunce,
That no fals treitour, ne cruell tirrant,
Shall in eny wyse make profer to your lande.

And rebelles all falce quarels schall eschewe,
Thurgh the fere of Pallas, that favoreth your lynage[89]
And all outward Enmyes[90] laboreth to subdue,
To make them to do to yewe as to me dyd homage.

87 See above, 2.14; and among essays that reveal a debate among historians over the origins, purpose, and politics of communal drama, see Margaret Aston, "Corpus Christi and Corpus Regni: Heresy and the Peasants' Revolt," *Past & Present* 143 (May, 1994), pp. 3–47; Gail McMurray Gibson, "Bury St Edmunds, Lydgate, and the N-Town Cycle," *Speculum* 56:1 (Jan., 1981), pp. 56–90; Mervyn James, "Ritual, Drama and Social Body in the Late Medieval English Town," *Past & Present* 98 (Feb., 1983), pp. 3–29; Retha M. Warnicke, "More's Richard III and the Mystery Plays," *The Historical Journal* 35:4 (Dec. 1992), pp. 761–78.

88 Following.

89 Lineage.

90 Enemies.

Welcome therfore, the solace & comfort of my olde age,
Prince pereless, Arthur, Icome of noble progeny,
To me & to youre Chambre with all this hole companye!

And at the turnyng into the Croschepyng before *Maister* Thrumpton's durre,[91] stode the barkers paiant[92] well appareld,[93] in which was the Quene of Fortune with dyuers other virgyns, whech quene has this spech folowyng: –

[QUEEN OF FORTUNE.] I am dame Fortune, quene called, full expedient
To Emprours & princes, prelates, with other moo[94]
As Cesar, Hectour, & Fabius, most excellent,
Scipio, exalted Nausica, & Emilianus also,
Valerius, also Marchus, with sapient Cicero.
E and noble men, breuely the truth to conclude, all
My favour verily had, as storys maketh rehersall;

With-oute whom, sithen non playnly can prospere,
That in this muitable[95] lyfe as nowe procedyng,
I am come thurgh love. Trust me intiere[96]
To be with yewe & yours Evirmore enduryng,
Prynce, most unto my pleasure of all that ar nowe reynyng;
Wherfore, my nowne hert[97] & best beloved treasure,
Welcome to this yours Chaumbre of whom ye be inheriture.[98]

And the Crosse in the Croschepyng was garnyssbed, & wyne there rennyng, and angels sensyng & syngyng, with Orgayns and others Melody etc. And at the Cundyt,[99] ther was seynt George kyllyng the dragon, and seynt George had this speche folowyng: –

[Saint George.] O most soueraign lorde, be dy[vy]ne[100] provision to be
The ruler of cruell Mars & kyng Insuperable!
Ye reioyce my corage, trustyng hit to se,
That named am George, your patron fauorable;
To whom ye ar & euer shal be so acceptable,

91 Door.
92 Pageant.
93 Appointed, decorated, apparalled.
94 More.
95 Mutable, changeable, transitory.
96 Entirely, completely.
97 The heart in my chest? "Nowne" may here mean "chest," and "hert" is probably "heart."
98 Inheritor.
99 Conduit.
100 By divine.

That in felde,[101] or Cite, where-so-ever ye rayne
Shall I neuer fayle yewe, thus is my purpose playn.

To protect your magnyficence myself I shall endevour,
In all thynges that your highnes shall concerne,
More tenderly then I yit did ever;
Kyng, duke, yerle, lords, or also berne,[102]
As *ye* be myn assistence in processe shall lerne,
Which thurgh your vertue, most amorous knygh[t],
I owe to your presence be due & very right.

Like-wyse as this lady be grace I defended,
That thurgh myschaunce chosen was to dye,
ffro this foule serpent whom I sore wonded;
So ye in distresse preserve ever woll I
ffro all parell and wyked veleny,[103]
That shuld your noble persona in eny wyse distrayn,
Which welcome is to this your Chambre & to me right fayn.

And this balet[104] was song at the Crosse:

Vivat le pryncc Arthur.

Ryall prince Arthur,
Welcome nowe, tresur,
With oure hole Cur,[105] to this your cite!
Sithen in vertue dere,
Lorde, ye haue no pere,[106]
Of your age tendre, as all we may see

Cunyng requyred,
All hath contrived,
And so receyued – your intelligence

That Yngland, all playn,
May nowe be right fayn
Yewe long to remayn, to their extollence[107]

101 Field or countryside.
102 Baron.
103 Churlishness, rudeness.
104 Ballad.
105 Heart.
106 Peer, equal.
107 Extolling, celebration.

Syng we ther foll all;
Also let us call .
To God Immortal that he yewe defend!

In this breve beyng
Youre astate supporting,
And vertue ay spredyng, to your lyfes yend!

[The Prince and Local Disputes, Oct. 18, 1498]

And vppon Thursday in the mornyng the Maire with his Brethern cam vnto rhe princes Chambre and there presented hym with a gilt Cup to the value of x marc, & C marc of gold therin, which was gadered in the x wardes accordyng as the xv^{te}[108] is.

And on the Morowe the Maire presented a bill to the said prince desiryng be the same that he wold please to desire the priour of Couentre to pay at his desire the Murage[109] money which he had with-drawen the space of xx yeres: and also shewed his grace be the same bill howe the Citezenis of Couentre were trobled be there merchandisez in Bristoll, Gloucestre, & Worcestre & compelled to pay tholl[110] & other customez[111] contrarie to their liberteez. Vppon which bill lettres went out to Bristoll, Glouceetre & Worcestre desiryng be the same that the seid Citezenis of Couentre myght passe fre without eny custome paying after their liberte, or els they to apper at London crastino S. Martini[112] then next folowyng *etc.* And vppon this the priour & his Couent were bounde to my seid lord prince in v^{c} li.[113] to abide the awarde of my lordes of Lincoln & Couentre & other of the Counceill of the said prince etc. and in like wyse the Maire & Cominalte[114] bounde to the seid prince in like some;[115] the transcript of which obligacion here ensueth. .And the obligations both remaynen in the kepyng of the seid prince.

108 The Fifteenth, or tax levied by king and parliament.
109 A tax for the building and maintenance of a town's walls.
110 Tolls.
111 In this case, duties or taxes levied on commercial transactions.
112 The morrow of St Martin.
113 £500.00
114 Commonalty.
115 Sum.

7.4 Strong Kingship and a Strong Kingdom: The Governance of England by Sir John Fortescue, 1471–5, in *The Politics of Fifteenth-Century England. John Vale's Book*, by Margaret Lucille Kekewich, Colin Richmond, Anne F. Sutton, Livia Visser-Fuchs, and John L. Watts (Alan Sutton Publishing for Richard III & Yorkist History Trust, 1995), pp. 226–50.[116]

Fortescue's "Governance," in contrast to works such as "III Consideration," not only explicitly acknowledges that kings commanded only if they also gave, and gave generously, to those who in turn could command, by their own generosity, the loyalty of others below them; it also provides some guidance to kings and their servants who needed to remain above factional conflicts within the aristocracy, or at least to manage those conflicts to the king's advantage. Although Fortescue's analysis begins with and frequently cites old authorities, and draws heavily on examples from the scriptures, his grasp of the opportunities and risks of royal patronage are sophisticated and practical. His "Governance" lets us see clearly how justice itself could be regarded as essential to the reciprocities, usually very material reciprocities, that bound rulers to those ruled at all levels of the political and social hierarchy. That English royal government was already markedly bureaucratic in its operations is clear, not only from the voluminous records of royal courts upon which we can draw, but also from Fortescue's advice that the king hoard royal offices for his own patronage, not that of great landlords who sought places in the royal administration for their own dependants and subjects. England had a working royal bureaucracy, but it was far from impersonal.

[Chapter 1] The difference bitwene ij kingdomes that oon called dominium regale[117] and thetother dominium politicum et regale[118]

There beene twoo kyndes of kyngdomes of the whiche that oon ys callid in latyn DOMINIUM REGALE and that other is called DOMINIUM POLITICUM

116 The copy of Fortescue's "Governance" excerpted here occurs in what its editors describe as "an unrivalled collection of letters, amnifestos and other material from the early fifteenth century to the 1480s." John Vale, the scribe responsible for the original collection, was servant to the family of Thomas Cook, junior, alderman and mayor of London. Although the editors admit uncertainty about the purpose of the collection, and wonder whether a single motive can explain a collection made over 40 years, they conclude that Vale was "not writing a book, he was recording and reflecting some of the practical and theoretical concerns of Londoners and those in government during several turbulent decades of the fifteenth century" (p. xi). Kekewich refers readers to Charles Plummer, *The Governance of England: Otherwise Called The Difference between an Absolute and a Limited Monarchy, by Sir John Fortescue* (Oxford. Oxford University Press, 1885, photographic reproduction, 1926), for detailed notes and comments on the text, pointing out that Plummer also lists variant words and phrases from the early versions (pp. 159–68). For a recent edition of Fortescue's major works on politics, in modern English and with useful notes, see *Sir John Fortescue, On the Laws and Governance of England*, ed. Shelley Lockwood, Cambridge Texts in the History of Political Thought (Cambridge: Cambridge University Press, 1997).

117 Royal Dominion.

118 Political and Royal Dominion.

ET REGALE. The firste king may rewle his peopull by suche lawes as he maketh hym selfe and therfore he may sette upon theim tailes and imposicions suche as he woll him selfe withoute their assente. The secunde king may not rewle his peopull by other lawes thanne suche as they will assenten unto, and therfore he may sette upon theim noon imposicions withoute their owne assente. This diversite is weele taughte by Seint THOMAS in his booke whiche he wrote, AD REGEM CIPRI DE REGIMINE PRINCIPUM.[119] But yit yt ys more playnly treated in a boke called COMPENDIUM MORALIS PHILOSOPHIAE[120] and sumwhat by Giles in his boke DE REGIMINE PRINCIPUM.[121] To the children of Israell as seithe Seint Thomas[122] after that God had chosen theym, IN POPULUM PECULIAREM ET REGNUM SACERDOTALE,[123] they were rewled by hym under judges REGALITER ET POLITICE unto the tyme that they desired tahave a kyng, as thoo had the gentyles whiche we calle paynemes[124] that hadde no king but aman that reigned upon theim REGALITER TANTUM. With whiche desire God was gretly offended and ther with displeased as wele for theire folye as for their unkindenesse, that sythen they hadde a king whiche was God reigning upon theime politikly and roially and yit wolde chaunge hym for a kynge, a verrey man, that wolde reigne uppon theyme oonly royally. And therfore God manasing theime and made theyme to bene aferde by thundres and other gastefull thinges from the hevene above. And whanne they wolde nat leve therby theyre foly desire, he charged the prophete SAMUEL to declare unto theim the lawe of suche a kyng as they desired tahave, whiche amonge other thinges saide that he wolde take from theyme theire londe and gyve it to his servants and sette theire children in his cartes and doo to theyme suche other many harmefull thinges as in the viij^the^ chapitre of the firste boke of kynges it may apere.[125] Where as before that tyme they were rewled by God oonly roially and politikly under juges, in whiche tyme hit was not lefull tany[126] man for to take from theyme any of their goodes or to greve theire children that had not offended. Wherby it may apere that in thoo daies REGIMEN POLITICUM ET REGALE was distincte a REGIMINE TANTUM REGALE and that it was bettir to the people to be reuled politikly and roially thanne to be reuled oonly royally, for Seint Thomas in his boke praiseth DOMINIUM POLITICUM ET REGALE by cause the prince that regneth by suche lordship may nat frely falle into tyrannye as may the prince that regneth REGALITER TANTUM.[127] And yit they bothe biene egall

119 Aquinas, *On Princely Government.*

120 Roger of Waltham, c. 1300, *Compendium of Moral Philosophy.*

121 Giles of Rome, c. 1243–1316, *On Princely Government.*

122 Pseudo-Aquinas, *De Regimine Principum.*

123 Deuteronomy 14: 2 and Exodus 19: 6.

124 Pagans.

125 1 Samuel 8:10–18.

126 To any.

127 Only royally (Aquinas, *On Princely Government* I.vi).

in estate and power as it may lightly be shewed and proved by infallible reason.

* * *

[Chapter 3] ***The frutes of ius regale and of ius politicum et regale***

And how so be it that the Frenshe king regneth upon his peopull DOMINIO REGALI, yet Seint Lowes,[128] sumtyme king ther, nor any of his progenitours sett never tailes nor other imposicions upon the peopull of that londe withoute thassente of the iij estates. Whiche whanne they biene assembled biene like to the courte of the parliamente in Englonde. And this order kepte many of his successours into late daies that Englisshe menne made suche werre in Fraunce that the iij estates durste nat come to geder. And for that cause and for the grete necessite of that londe he toke upon hym to sette tailes and other imposicions upon the commones withoute thassente of the iij estates. But yit he wolde nat sette any suche charges or hathe sette uppon the nobles for fere of rebellion and by cause the commones therthrough hadde grugge and were hardy to rebelle, the Frensshe king hathe yerly sithen sett such charges upon theym and so augmented the same charges, that the same commones bene so enpoverisshed, kepte under and as who seithe destroyed, that they mowne unnethe lyve. They drinken water and eten apples with righte browne brede made of rye. . . . But verily they lyven in the mooste extreme necessite, povertie and misere that any cristen men lyvith, and yit they dwellen in oon of the mooste fertile reaume of the worlde. Wherthroughe the Frenshe king hathe nat menne of his owne reaume able to defende it, excepte his nobles whiche beren noon suche imposicions, and therfore they bene righte likly and personable of theire bodyes, by whiche cause the seide king is compelled to make his armyes and his retynues for the defence of his lande of straungeres as Scottys, Spaynardes, Arragoneres, men of Almayne and of other nacions or ellis alle his enemyes mighte ovur renne hym, for he hathe no defence of his owne peopull suche as bene called his commones, but oonly resortithe and kepithe his castellis and fortressis. Loo this ys the frute that comyth of this IUS REGALE.[129] Yif the reaume of Englonde which is but an ile, and therfore it may natt lightly gete socours ne helpe of peopull of other landes, were reuled under suche alawe and suche aprince hit wolde be thanne a praye tall[130] other landes and nacions that wolde conquerre, robbe or devoure it. . . . But blessed be God this londe is reuled under a bettir lawe and therfore the peopul therof biene not in suche penurie, disease nor misere nor therby hurte in theire personnes but they bene welthy and have all thinges necessarie to the sustenaunce of nature. Wherfore they bene mighti and able to

128 St Louis, or Louis IX, 1226–1270.

129 Royal Law.

130 Prey to all.

resiste their adversaries and enemyes and to bete other reaumes that wolde do hem wronge. Loo this is the frute of IUS POLITICUM ET REGALE under whiche we lyve. Sumwhat now have I shewed you the frewte of bothe thise ij lawes UT EX FRUCTIBUS EORUM COGNOSCETIS EOS.[131] etc.

* * *

[Chapter 9] ***The periles that mowe falle to a kyng by ovur mighti subgiettes*** Now sithen the seide extraordinarie chargis biene so uncertayne that they bene not estymable, it is not possible to putt in certainte what lyveloode[132] wil yerly suffice to bere hem. Wherfore we nede in this caas to use coniecture and imaginacion as to thinke that ther is no lordes liveloode in Englonde sufficiente to bere thextraordinarie charges. Than nedith it that the kynges lyveloode, above suche revenues as shulne[133] be assigned for his ordinari charges, biene gretter thanne the lyvelood of the grettest lorde in Englonde. And peraventur whanne lyvelood sufficiente for the kinges ordinarie charges is lymyted and assigned therto, it shal appere that divers lordis of Englande have also moche lyveloode of in theire owne as than shal remaigne in the kinges handis for his extraordinarie charges, whiche were inconvenience and wolde be to the king right dredfull. For thanne suche alorde may dispende more than the king, considering that he is charged with noon suche chargis extraordinarie nor ordinarie as is the king excepte an howsholde, whiche is but litil in comparison off the kinges hous. Wherfore yif it be thus, it shalbe necessarye that therbe purveyed for the king moche gretter livelode than he hathe now. For mannys corage is so noble that naturelly he aspirith to highe thinges and to be exalted and therfore he enforsith hym selfe to be alwey gretter for which the philosophur seithe: OMNIA A MAIUS SED PRINCIPARI MAIUS.[134] Wherof it hathe comen that often tymes, whanne a subgiet hathe had also grete lyveloode as his prince, he hathe anoon aspired to thastate of his prince, whiche by suche a man may sone begote. For the remenante[135] of the subgiettes of such a prince seying that yif so mighti a subgiet mighte obteigne thestate of their prince, thei shulde thanne biene under aprince double so mighti as was their olde prince, whiche encrease every subgiet desyrethe for his owne discharge of that he bereth to the sustenance of his prince, and therfor they wilbe righte glad to helpe such a subgiet in his rebellion. . . . We have also late in our reaume knowen somme of the kinges subgiettes given hym bataill, by occasion that their lyvelode and offices weren the gretteste of the londe, and elles they wolde nat han done soo. Thise erles of Leycestre and Glowcestre which weren the grettest lordes of the londe,

---

131 And by their fruits shall you know them.

132 The means to procure the necessities of life; property, land, rent, or income.

133 Should.

134 "a maius" is a scribal error for "amamus": We love all, but we love the prince the most.

135 Remainder, rest of.

roose ageyne their king HENRY THE III^{de} and toke hym and his soone prisoneres in the felde. Whiche maner of demeaning the king of Scottes that laste deyed, dreding the same to be practised in his londe, put oute of the same londe therle Douglas whos lyvelode and mighte was nerehande[136] equivalente to the kinges owne, the whiche king was moved therto by noon other cause saufe oonly dreede of his rebellion. . . . And also it may nat be eschewed but that the grete lordis of the lande by reason of newe discentes falling unto hem and by reason also of mariages, purchases and other titles shulne oftyn tymes growe to be gretter thanne thei be now, and peradventure some of hem to be of lyvelode and power like a kyng. Whiche shalbe righte good for the londe while they aspire to noon higher degree or estate, for suche was the duc of Lancaster that werred upon the kyng of Spayne, oon of the moste mightiest kynges cristen, in his owne reaume. But this is wretyn oonly tothentente that it bee wele understande how necessarie that it is that the kyng have grete possessions and particuler lyveloode for his owne suretie, namely whan any of his lordis shuln happen to be so excessyfly grete as ther myghte ther by growe perile to his estate. For certaynly ther may no gretter perile growe to a prince thanne tahave a subgiet equipolente[137] to hym selfe.

[Chapter 10] ***How that the crowne may beste be endowed***

Now that the lyklynesse of the kinges charges ordinarie and extraordinare biene shewed, and ovur that how necessarie it is that he have grete livelode above the same charges in whiche it nedeth that he excede gretely ovur evere man of his londe, whiche lyvelode undoubted he hathe nat at this day, hit is therfore behovefull that we now serche how the king may have suche lyvelode, but firste of what commodites it may beste arise and be take. . . . Wherfore me thinketh that yif he mighte have his livelode for the sustenaunce of his estate in grete lordshippes, maneres,[138] feefermes and soche other demaynes,[139] his peopul not charged, he shulde kepe to hym hooliche theire hertes and excede in lordshippes and riches alle the lordes of his reaume, And than shulde noon of hem growe to be like unto hym, whiche is thing moste to be fered of alle the worlde. . . .

* * *

[Chapter 14] ***Here is shewed whi it nedeth that ther be a resumpcion and grant of good made to the king***

This serche whiche we now have made for to undirstonde how harmefull it wolde be to the kyng and to his reaume yif his comones were pouer, it hathe

---

136 Nearly.

137 Equivalent.

138 Manors.

139 Demesnes = landed estates; more specifically, manorial estates.

biene a digression from the matier in whiche we labour, that is to saye for to undirstonde how the kyng may beste have sufficiente and perdurable liveloode for the sustenacioun of his estate. . . .

* * *

[Chapter 17] ***Here folowen thadvertisementes for geving of the kynges offices*** Yiff it wolde like the king to geve noon office unto the tyme that his intente therinne be communed with his counseill and their oppynioun by his highenesse undirstonde in the same, he shall more rewarde so his servantes with offices, as there shall litil nede to geve hem moche of his lyvelode, and his offices shall thanne be gevun to soche as shal oonly serve hym selfe. Wherthroughe he shall thanne have agrete mighte and agarde of his officeres whan he liste to call theim, thanne he hathe now of his other feode[140] men undre thestate of lordis. For the mighte of the londe, after the gret mighte of the lordis therof, stondith moste in the kinges officeres, for they mow[141] beste reule the contreyes where as their offices biene, whiche is in every parte of the londe. Apore bayle[142] may do more in his baylewic thanne any man of his degree dwellyng withinne his office. Somme forster[143] of the kinges that hathe noone other lyveloode thanne his forstership may bringe moo men into the felde wele arayed, and namely for shotyng, thane may somme knighte, squier or gentilman of righte grete lyvelode dwelling by hym and having noon office. What thanne may gretter officeres doo as stiwardes of grete lordshippes, receyvours, constables of casteles, maister forsteres and suche other officeres, besides the highe officeres as justices of forester, justices and chambreleynes of contreies, the warden of the portes and suche other? For sothe it is nat lightly estymable what mighte the king may have of his officeres yif everyche of hem had but oon office and served noon other man but the kyng. Nor it is nat esey to be estemed how many men mow be rewarded with office, and how greately it prevaileth soo yif thei be discretely gevun[144]. . . . Forsothe the gretteste lordes lyvelode in Englande may nat suffice to rewarde so many men, thoughe he wolde departe it everydell[145] amonge his servantes, nor ij the gretteste lordes of Englonde may make so grete a mighte as the king may have oonly of his officeres, yif they were hooliche[146] and oonly his servantes and everiche[147] of theyme had but oon

140 Feed men, men receiving fees in return for service.

141 May.

142 Bailiff.

143 Forester.

144 Given with discretion.

145 Divide all of it.

146 Wholly.

147 Each.

office. To this suche lordes sayne and other men suche as asken of ye king offices for their servantes that they and all theire servantes shulne alwey serve the king, and his officeres shuldo hym the better service, by reasoun that they bene in theire service for they wil helpe hym to do soo and suffre noon in theyre company but suche as wil do soo. Wherto maybe seid that ys trewe they shuln do the king service while they be in their companye, but so shulde they have doone thoughe the king had nevur made hem his officeres, wherfore the king shal nat be the better served that he hathe geven his offices to their servantes but rather worse, for our lord seith NEMO POTEST DUOBUS DOMINIS SERVIRE.[148] And so the king shall lese the offices as for any singuler service and thanke that he shat have for hem. Or that the same officeres shul thinke hym selfe beholde unto the kinges highenesse for their offices, whiche his highenesse hathe gevun hem at the contemplacioun of theire maistres and for no rewarde of any service that they have doone or shul doo unto hym selfe. By consideracioun wherof theyre olde maistres shuln he better served by hem thanne they weren beforne and be more mighty in the contreyes to do what hym liste, and the king in lasse mighte and have the fewer officeres to represse hem whanne they do amysse. . . . Whiche matieres throughly considered it semeth verely good that no man have any office of the kinges gifte, but yif he be firste sworne that he is servant to noon other man or wil serve any other man or take his clothing or fee while he serveth the king of any other man. And that no man have moo offices than oon, excepte that the kinges bretheren mow have ij offices and that suche men as serven the king aboute his persone or in his counsaill mow have in their contres aparkership for their disporte whan they come home, or suche another office as they mow wele kepe bi their deputes.

* * *

[Chapter 19] ***Here shewithe what good wil growe of the ferme endowing of the crowne***

And whan the king bi the meanes forsaide or otherwise hathe geten agein his livelode, yif thanne it wolde like his moste noble good grace testablisshe, as whoo saithe amortise, the same liveload to his crowne, so as it may never be aliened therfro withoute thassente of his parliamente. Whiche than wolde be as anewe foundacion of his crowne, he shalbe therby the grettest foundur of the worlde. For ther as other kinges have founded bisshopriches, abbeyes and other houses of religeoun, the king shal thanne have founded an hole reaume and endowed it with gretter possessions and better than evur was any reaume in cristendome. This maner of foundacion may nat be ageinste the kinges prerogatif or his liberte no more than is the foundacion of an abbey, fro

148 No man may serve two masters, Matthew 6: 24.

whiche he may take no parte of their possessions whiche he hathe oones given hem, withoute thassente of their covente. But this maner of endowing of his crowne shalbe to the king a gretter prerogatif, in that he hathe thanne enriched his crowne with such riches and possessions as never king shal mow take from it, withoute thassente of his hole reaume. . . .

7.5 Royal Offices, Noble Patronage, and Importunate Gentry: Godfrey Greene to Sir William Plumpton, 8 November [?1477], in *The Plumpton Letters and Papers*, ed. Joan Kirby, Royal Historical Society Publications, Camden Fifth Series 8 (Cambridge: Cambridge University Press, 1996), pp. 51–53 (no. 28).

The following letter to Sir William Plumpton, a northern gentlemen of substantial estates, from one of his counselors, not only suggests that Fortescue was fully justified in the attention that he gave the distribution of royal offices, and the emphasis with which he encouraged the king to maintain a monopoly over their distribution, but also illustrates the obstacles that either Edward IV or his successors might face in acting on Fortescue's advice. Evident in Greene's language is recognition that the sheriff's office lay in the king's gift; but no less evident in his report on the Earl of Northumberland's treatment of this royal office is the nobleman's critical role in dispensing justice, and his conviction that it was his duty, no less than the king's, to mediate and resolve controversies among local rivals in the region. Without doubt, however, royal offices – as deputies to sheriffs, bailiffs of royal estates, justices of the peace – clearly constituted the resource described by Fortescue: a resource for building loyalties, but a resource that also placed heavy strains on loyalties, between king and noblemen, between noblemen and the gentlemen who on occasion found themselves played by, and able to play, the competition for their service by king and nobles.

Right worshipfull Sir, I recommend me vnto your good maistershipp. . . . Also, Sir, now of late I have receaued from you diuerse letters of the which the tenure and effect is this: one, that I shold labour to Sir John Pilkinton[149] to labor to my lord of Glocester or to the king, they to moue my lord of Northumberland that ye might occupie still in Knaresborough. Sir, as to that, it is thought here by such as loues you at that labour should rather hurt in that behalue then[150] availe, for it is as long as my lord of Northumberlands patent thereof stands good, as long will he haue no deputie but such as shall please him and kan him thank for the gift thereof, and no man els, and also doe him servise next the king. So the labour shalbe fair answered and turne to none effect but hurt.

149 Sir John Pilkington of Chevet Hall, near Wakefield, knight at Tewkesbury, 1471; chamberlain of receipt of the Exchequer, April 1477; dead by 8 March 1479.

150 Than.

And as to another point comprised in your writing, that is to enforme the lords and their counsell of the miscouernances of Gascoin[151] and his affinitie. Sir, ye understand that in euery law the saying of a mans enemies is chalengeable, and rather taken a sayin[g] of malice then of treuthe, whereby the correction of the [same] default, the complainer hath no availe.[152] And so, certainly by your counsell, is thought here that it wold be soe taken, and in no other wise, how be it that it be trew, and also a disworship[153] to my lo:[154] of Northumberland that hath the cheif rule there vnder the king. And as for the matter to enforme my lord of Northu[mberland's] counsell how ye were entreated[155] at Knaresboro: Sir, we enformed my lords counsell, according to your commaundement, and they enformed my lord, and my lord said he wold speak with us himselfe, and so did, and this was the answerr: that the cause why he wrote that no court of sheriff turne[156] shold be holden was [for] to shew[157] debate betwixt you & Gascoins affinitie vnto time he might come into the cuntry and se a deraction[158] betwixt you; & that he wold that the 3 week court were holden for discontinuance of mens actions;[159] & that he entended not to dischardge you of your office,[160] ne will not as long as ye be towards him; and that as soune as he comes into the cuntry he shall see such a direction betwext his brother Gascoin and you as shalbe to your harts ease & worship. And that I vnderstand by his counsell that it shalbe assigned vnto you by my lord & his counsell what as longes[161] to your office, & Gascoin nott meddle therewithall; & in likewise to Gascoyne.

And as for the labour for the bailiships & farmes: Sir, your worship vnderstands what labour is to sue therefore: first, to haue a bill endorsed to the king, then to certein lords of the counsell (for ther is an Act made that nothing shall

151 Sir William Gascoigne, of Gawthorpe (d.1487), brother-in-law of the 4th earl, appointed deputy at Kanaresborough after the earl's appointment as steward etc. in 1470. In October 1471 he gave a bond to keep the peace towards Sir William Kirby.

152 The writer is cautioning Plumpton that should he pursue complaints against Gascogine's misbehavior, they will likely be dismissed as self-serving and little more than confirmation of Plumpton's enmity.

153 Insult.

154 Lord.

155 Treated.

156 The sheriff's court or tourn was the most basic local jurisdiction exercised on behalf of the king and the king's responsibility for punishing crime and maintaining order; much of its earlier responsibility for criminal justice had by this date passed to the Justices of the Peace.

157 Eschew, or defer.

158 Direction, agreement, or compromise.

159 The Earl explained that he had not intended to discontinue actions of parties to lawsuits in the sheriff's court, but did not wish the court held until he could resolve the rivalry between Plumpton and Gascoigne.

160 The bailiwick of Knaresborough, granted to Sir William by the duke of Gloucester, 29 September 1472, for 12 years.

161 Belongs.

passe from the king vnto time they haue sene it) and soe to the privie seale & chauncellor. So the labour is so importune that I cannot attend it without I shold do nothing ells, and scarcely in a month speed one matter. Your mastership may remember how long it was or we might speed your bill of iustice of the peace, & had not my lord of Northumberland been, had not been sped, for all the fair promisses of my lord chamberlaine.[162] And as for the message to my lord chamberlain, what time I labored to him that ye might be iustice of the peace,[163] he answerred thus: that it seemed by your labor & mine that we wold make a jelosie[164] betwixt my lord of Northumberland & him, in that he shold labor for any of his men, he being present. Sir, I took that for a watch word for medling betwixt lords. As for any matter ye haue to do in the Law, how be it that it be to me losse of time and costly to labor or medle, as yett I am & always shalbe readie to doe you service & pleasure therein. With the grace of God, who haue you euerrnore in his lessed protection. Written att London, the eight day of Nouember.`

Your servant Godfrey Greene

Endorsed To his right worshipfull maistre Sir William Plompton kt

7.6 Temporal and – or? – Spiritual Authorities: Earl of Arundel v. Bishop of Chichester, TNA KB 27/419, m.29 (1365), in *Select Cases in the Court of King's Bench under Edward III*, ed. G. O. Sayles, Selden Society 82 (London, 1965), pp. 143–5 [Latin].

The distinction between "public" and "private" may not be very useful in understanding the politics and political ideas current in late medieval England, but another distinction – that between "spiritual" and "temporal" authority – played a critical role in shaping governance and politics. As royal courts and royal jurisdiction expanded, they did so alongside, and sometimes in rivalry with, ecclesiastical courts and the spiritual jurisdiction of Christian clergy. In some measure, the rivalry was between an English monarch and a "foreign" pope; but from another perspective, it was a conflict within the ruling elite of England, complicated by the ties of kinship and patronage that closely linked the institutions of monarchy and those of the church. Even as the laity, and particularly the lay aristocracy, found it convenient on occasion to play one kind of authority off against the other, the relationship readily became a complicating aspect of other, more fundamental arguments about Christian faith and belief. That Wycliffe, eventually condemned, howbeit only formally after his death, should have found strong

162 Sir William Hastings, appointed king's chamberlain for life, 31 July 1461, raised to the peerage.

163 Having made his peace with the Yorkists, Sir William reappeared on the commission in February 1472, but was dropped in November 1475 when the number of JPs was reduced. His reappointment in December 1476 was due to Northumberland's good offices.

164 Jealousy or rivalry.

support in the royal court and among some English magnates and lesser aristocrats, owes a lot to the persistent tension between secular and ecclesiastical authorities, a tension that Wycliffe resolved in favor of the former – opening the way, by implication, for the laity to benefit from a major transfer not only of jurisdiction, but also of landed property.[165]

Not many Englishmen were willing in the late Middle Ages to embrace fully Wycliffe's claims for royal authority and their corollary, the insulation of clergy from secular authority and the power of property. The risk posed by Lollards to the existing order of power and authority meant that such a transfer did not occur until the sixteenth century and the Reformation; and even then, it did not mean an end to "spiritual" jurisdiction distinct from the secular jurisdiction of the king's court, although the former was firmly subordinated to the latter. But suppressing Lollardy did not mean that the English laity, and especially the king, would meekly yield to either the pope or local clergy when either insisted on the autonomy, much less the supremacy, of spiritual authorities. A case of 1365 in King's Bench below illustrates endemic tensions between royal and ecclesiastical jurisdiction, as it also points to the importance of parliament's support for the king's judicial monopoly, at least with respect to issues of property.

Whatever the tensions between temporal and spiritual authorities throughout the period of this volume, and whatever the resentment lay and ecclesiastical officers directed towards each other over jurisdictional boundaries, collaboration, especially collaboration in the interests of both as landlords dependent on peasant tenants, characterized the relationship more often than overt conflict. Without underestimating the significance of rivalry between ecclesiastical and secular hierarchies of authority and governance during this period, common interests kept such rivalries within manageable limits, at least until the early sixteenth century.

London

The king sent his writ close to the sheriffs of London in these words:

Edward, by the grace of God king of England, lord of Ireland and of Aquitaine, to the sheriffs of London, greeting. Whereas it has been provided and ordained by common counsel of our realm in our last parliament held at Westminster[166] that all those who have sued out or prosecuted, or shall henceforth presume to sue out or prosecute, personal citations against any of our realm on any

165 See above, 2.22. For a middle English version of Wycliffe's arguments against any forms of authority or power in temporal affairs by clergy – and by implication, his case for depriving clergy of ttheir landed property – see "Tractatus de Regibus," in *Tracts of the Later Middle Ages*, ed. Jean-Philippe Genet, Camden, 4th ser., Vol. 18 (London: Royal Historical Society, 1977), pp. 1–19. It was issued by Wycliffe or one of his followers.

166 38 Edward III, statute 2, c. 1 (SR, i, 305 f).

fictitious or false suggestions or propositions, made in the Roman curia in deception of our most Holy Father to compel them to appear there to answer on and upon causes whereof the cognisance[167] and final determination is known to pertain to us and our royal crown, shall have a period of two months by warning given to such impetrants in their own places of residence if they have any places of residence or in our courts or county courts or before our justices in their sessions or in any other adequate way to answer thereon to us and to the party aggrieved in this matter and to await and stand trial in the said case before us and our council, and they are to be punished thereon in accordance with the manner and form contained in the statute made in such case in the twenty-seventh year of our reign;[168] and it has been shown to us by the plaint of our beloved and faithful Richard, earl of Arundel, that William, bishop of Chichester, residing at the Roman curia, procured the citation of the said earl in person, by false and fictitious suggestions made there by the bishop, to answer there with respect to those matters whereof the cognisance and final determination is known to pertain particularly to us and our royal crown within our realm, and he is there prosecuting a plea thereon against him, to our contempt and prejudice and the destruction and manifest disherison of our royal crown and dignity and the very serious loss of the said earl and in contravention of the aforesaid provision and ordinance; we, wishing the aforesaid provision and ordinance to be observed and those contravening them to be punished and chastised according to the force and effect of the same, command you that, if the earl gives you security that he will prosecute his suit, then you are to have the bishop summoned by upright and law-worthy men of your bailiwick to be before us at a Fortnight after St John the Baptist's Day wherever we may then be in England to answer not only to us for the aforesaid contempt and prejudice but also to the earl for the trespass committed against him in this respect. And you are to have there the names of pledges, and the names of those by whom you made the said summons, and this writ. Witness myself at Westminster the first day of May in the thirty-ninth year of our reign.[169]

* * *

And, after consultation with Robert of Thorp, John Mowbray and John Knyvet, the king's justices of the common bench, as well as with William Skipwith and Thomas of Ludlow, the king's barons of the exchequer, it is awarded that the bishop is to be put outside the protection of the king, and that all the temporalities and other lands and tenements of the said bishop are to be seized into

167 Jurisdiction, the responsibility to hear pleas.
168 27 Edward III, c. 1 (SR, i. 329).
169 1 May 1365.

the king's hands, and that all his goods and chattels are to be forfeited to the said king in accordance with the terms of the statute and ordinance in such case provided. And as regards judgement for the arrest of the person of the aforesaid bishop, let this be postponed until the court is advised thereon.

7.7 Civic Disunity and the Riot called "Gladman's Insurrection," in *The Records of the City of Norwich*, Vol. 1, ed. William Hudson (Norwich: Jarrold & Sons, 1906), pp. 340–1 and 343–6.

The case preceding testifies to rivalry over jurisdiction between king and clergy, between "state" and "church," even as the suppression of Lollard critics of the church makes evident the crown's continued reliance on and cooperation with ecclesiastical authorities. A similar rivalry over jurisdiction and political authority expressed itself in local communities, and not least in the towns and cities where civic authorities fought vigorously to maintain control over crafts, and over craft workers and artisans. Records from mid-fifteenth-century conflicts in Norwich, the second largest city of the realm, offer some perspective on the deeply embedded ties between secular and ecclesiastical authorities in governing urban communities in England; they also illuminate the strong competition between those authorities, as well as divisions within each.

The preoccupation of Norwich's governors – or more precisely, citizens aspiring to govern the city – produced in 1449 an exceptionally detailed picture of how civic authorities there imagined conditions of work necessary for civic peace, in an ordinance tightly constraining the conduct of workers who might be tempted to act collectively on their own behalf.[170] *Instead of reproducing here the authorities' blueprint for peace and stability through regulation of artisans and craftsmen, however, we offer evidence of the bitter divisions with the city's government, and sustained and vigorous rivalry between it and the cathedral priory there, that characterized the decade preceding 1449. So severe were the divisions, so contentious the struggle, that the king and his councilors saw no remedy but to seize Norwich's liberties and to impose his own appointee as governor of the city for four years, between 1443 and 1447.*

Equally noteworthy in the records of "Gladman's Insurrection," however, are the strong hints that citizens engaged in festive practices might be easily mistaken for traitors challenging, or at least mocking, the king and his authority. Or were they indeed appropriating, inappropriately, the "dramatic" practices with which their noble and royal superiors legitimized authority? When does local drama and pageantry become rebellion or insurrection, these Norwich events which some labeled an insurrection may lead us to ask. And how often might festive or carnival conduct treated as evidence of

170 *The Records of the City of Norwich*, Vol. II, ed. John Cottingham Tingey (London: Jarrold & Sons, 1910), pp. 278–96; and see above, 6, for other civic struggles over work and its organization and regulation.

folkways by later observers mask – or testify to, however obliquely – challenges to social and political superiors?[171]

Here follows a recital of the disturbances as reported at an Inquisition held at Thetford [Latin].

In 21 H. VI. on Thursday after the feast of St Mathias Apostle[172] before Fortescue and Westbury Judges assigned to enquire into treasons etc. 12 sworn men of Norfolk presented that the Mayor, William Hempstead merchant, and the Commonalty of the city on Tuesday[173] next before the feast of the Conversion of St Paul in the said 21st year in the said city having in purpose to make common insurrection and commotion of all the Lord King's lieges in the city and country adjacent were so violent that they made Thomas Bishop of Norwich, John Abbot of St Benet of Hulm and John Prior of the Church of Holy Trinity of Norwich by threats of burning release divers actions of theirs which they had against the said Mayor and. Commonalty and very many more of the said city; and caused that the Lord King did not dare nor had the power to punish John Gladman of the aforesaid city merchant for riding there as a King with a crown and sceptre and sword carried before him by 3 men unknown, and Robert Suger of Norwich souter,[174] Robert Hemmyng of the same osteler, Richard Dallyng coteler and others to the number of 24 persons for riding there in like manner before John. Gladman with a crown upon their arms and with bows and arrows as valets of the crown of the Lord King; and they ordered 100 other persons now unknown with swords bows and arrows as well on foot as on horseback then and there to follow John Gladman; and on the day of the Conversion of St Paul[175] in the aforesaid year . . . they struck and caused to be struck divers bells in turn and the said Mayor and Commonalty with many other unknown persons of the city to the number of 3,000 gathered to them by the striking of the bells by force and arms caused them to cross over to the Priory of the

171 For an illuminating examination of "Gladman's Insurrection," see Philippa C. Maddern, *Violence and Social Order: East Anglia 1422–1442* (Oxford: Clarendon Press, 1992), pp. 175–205, and especially pp. 202–3, where she explains how "Gladman's Insurrection" fit within the context of other civic processions, including an elaborate celebration on St George's Day. She also points out, pp. 198–9, that Gladman, although not an office-holder and largely unknown outside the records generated by the riot, was a member of good standing in the city's elite fraternity, the Guild of St George, and almost certainly a respectable citizen and burgess. Also useful in interpreting Gladman's "disporte" is Ben R. McRee, "Peacemaking and its Limits in Late Medieval Norwich," *English Historical Review* 109:433 (September 1994), pp. 853–66; both McRee and Maddern emphasize divisions within the governing elite at the heart of Norwich's troubled politics in the 1430s and 1440s, not conflict between governors on the one hand, laborers and servants in the city on the other.

172 28 February 1443.

173 January 22, 1443.

174 shoemaker.

175 25 January 1443.

Cathedral Church shouting and saying, We will burn the Priory and kill the Prior and Monks thereof; and then they dug under the gates of the Priory to enter in, and they carried logs [ligna] there to burn the gate and they placed engines, viz. guns against the Priory. And from the day of the Conversion of St Paul to the 4th hour after noon on Tuesday then next following with force and arms they continued such insurrection whereby by threats they made Richard Walsham and John Wichyngham fellow monks of the Prior there to deliver to them a certain evidence sealed with the common seal of the city by which the Mayor etc. were bound to William Worstead Prior to pay a rent of 4 shillings and also to hold no plea nor any Sheriff's tourn in Conesford Meadows or in Brakendale, Eton, Lakenham and Erlham; and they carried off the evidence and from the Monday next after the Conversion of St Paul to the Monday then next following[176] they kept the city with gates closed and with armament as a city warring against the Lord King, and they kept outside the city John Duke of Norfolk from Tuesday after the feast of the Conversion of S' Paul for week thereon following[177] John Veer Earl of Oxford and other ministers of the Lord King from Monday after the feast of St Matthias Apostle in the aforesaid year to Wednesday next following, whom the Lord King by his letters patent of commission assigned to take the insurgents and rioters, and would not permit the said Duke and Earl to enter the city for those times.

Presentments[178] connected with the foregoing disturbances prepared against Tudenham, Heydon and others, c. 1448. [From Manuscripts in Norwich Muniment Room]

These be the extorcions oppressions meynteinances perjuryes imbraceryes and wrongs don to the Meir Aldermen and Commonalte of the Citie of Norwich and to other singular persones of the same Citie by Sr Thomas Tudenham, Knyght, John Heydon and others.

First the said Meir and Comonalte compleyn of that, that where ye said City of Norwich was an auncyent Cite and of old tyme had bailiffs and a comonalte corporat in hem self of tyme that no mynde is of, and wher King Herry the fourth [separated it and all its suburbs etc. from the County of Norfolk], which precincte and circuite extendith hymself by all the touns hameletts etc., " ut rei veritas est,[179]" nevertheless the said John Heydon, maliciously disposid, causid certeyn presentments to be made agayn the meir and comonalte of the seid Cite of that, that the said late meir and comonalte shuld haf incroched to theym the hameletts and touns aforesaid etc.; And the

176 28 January to 4 February.

177 29 January to 5 February.

178 Findings by jurors; charges or accusations.

179 As indeed is the truth of the matter.

said John Heydon, that tyme being recorder and of the special counsail and trust of the same Cite, confederid with the priour of the church of the trinite of Norwich, and with out ony knowing of the said meir and comonalte aperid to the said presentments and of his untrouth himself put into the kyng's courte pleggs[180] for the seid meir and comonalte and made fyne for them in such some with the Kynge agayn reson and trouthe wher they wold and myghte by the law a traversed the said presentment; to that ende and intent that the same meir and comonalte shuld, by that untrue fyne makyng, be barrid and stoppid at ony tyme to plede the said hameletts and circuites to be parcels of their forsaid Cite or in any wyse contrary to the mater conteyned in ye presentment. And of the said fyne the said Heydon was one of the pleggs with out warant of the said meir and comonalte; as in a copy of the said presentments and of the said fyne made, it is pleynly conteyned. And to that intent that this untrouth thus done shuld be longe hidde and unknow to the seid meir and comonalte the said John Heydon of his ymaginacion causid the said fynes of xxviii^{li} affexed[181] upon the said meir and comonalte and upon other persones for the said acrochment[182] supposid with disseyte[183] for to be paid in secrete maner, the said mair and comonalte not knowyne.

Item. Wher it was so that Alice Dutchess, that tyme Countess, of Suffolk late in hire persone cam to the said Cite disguised lyke an huswife[184] of the countre and the said Sir Thomas Tudenham and two other persons with her also disguysed etc. [Hudson here summarizes a story explaining why Tudenham and the Countess set themselves afterwards against the City and its jurisdiction, a consequence of a decision by one of the keepers of the City Ditches, not recognizing or knowing who they were, to prevent their entry into Norwich.]

And it is so over more that when John Heydon[185] late was recorder[186] of the said Cite, takyng of the said Meir and citeseyns a resonable fee, as to the recorder theer is accustomed, he so beyng recorder interlacid hymself with the pryour of Norwich that tyme being in travers[187] with the said meir and comonalte and discovered the prevyte of the evidence of the said Cite to the

180 Pledges or sureties, to guarantee observance of legal process.

181 Assessed?

182 Encroachment.

183 Deceit.

184 Housewife.

185 The Paston family (above, 3.7) may have shared resentment of John Heydon's role in local controversies; Margaret Paston referred to him as a "false shrew." See Norman Davis, ed., *The Paston Letters: A Selection in Modern Spelling* (London: Oxford University Press, 1963), pp. 15, 18, 91, 92.

186 A Recorder was often one of the most important civic officials, chosen by the mayor and magistrates (unless the king or a local potentate intervened) to provide legal counsel, generally direct the administration of justice within the city, and speak for it in dealings with the central government and royal agents.

187 Controversy, dispute, conflict.

said Priour, because whereof the meir and comons of the said Cite dischargid the said Heydon of the said condicion of recorder; because of which the said Heydon took also a displesir agayn the said Cite. By malice of which displesires of the said Duchesse Sr Thomas Tudenham and John Heydon, ye Duke of Suffolk then Erle in his persone, upon many suggestions be the said Tudenham and Heydon to hym made that the meir aldermen and comonalte forsaid shuld have misgoverned the said Cite, laboured and made to be take out of the chauncery a commission of oyer determyner. And therupon at a session holden at Thetford the Thursday after the fest of Seynt Mathy thappostle the seer etc.,[188] the said Sir Thomas and John Heydon fyndyng in their conceyt no maner mater of trouthe wherof they myght cause the said meir and comonalte ther to be indited, ymagyned thus as insueth: first they sperde[189] an Inqueste[190] ther take in a chaumbre at on Spilmer's house in which chaumbre the said T. logged[191] and so kept thayme sperd.

And wher that it was so that on John Gladman of Norwich which was ever and at this oure is a man of sad[192] disposicion and true and fethful to God and to the King, of disporte[193] as is and ever hath ben accustomed in ony Cite or Burgh thrugh al this reame on fastyngong tuesday[194] made a disporte with his neighburghs having his hors trapped with tyneseyle[195] and otherwyse dysgysyn[196] things crowned as King of Kristmesse in token that all merthe shuld end with the twelve monthes of the yer, afore hym eche moneth disgysd after the seson therof, and Lenten cladde in white with redde herrings skinnes and his hors trapped with oyster shelles after him in token that sadnesse and abstinence of merth shulde followe and an holy tyme; and so rode in diuerse stretes of ye Cite with other peple with hym disgysed making merthe and disporte and pleyes; the said Thomas and John Heydon amongs many other ful straunge and untrue presentments made by perjury at the seid Inquest caused the seid meir and comonalte and the said John Gladman to ben indited of that, that thei shuld an ymagined to a made a comon rysyng and a corouned the said John Gladman as kyng coron ceptre[197] and diademe wher thei never ment it ne never suych thyng ymagined as in the said

188 28 February 1443.

189 Locked up.

190 A jury.

191 Lodged.

192 Serious.

193 Amusement, leisure or pleasurable activity, entertainment

194 Shrove Tuesday; Hudson, in his introduction to Gladman's insurrection, pp. lxxxviii–xcii, points out the perplexing reference to Shrove Tuesday, which that year would have been 5 March; Gladman's procession, then, on 24 or 25 January, occurred some weeks before the appropriate holiday, which raises questions about the claim that he was simply engaged in seasonal festivities.

195 Cloth interwoven with gold or silver thread.

196 Decked out, elaborately attired.

197 Scepter.

presentment it shewith more pleyn; and by that presentment, with many other horrible articles theryn comprised so made by perjury thei caused the fraunchise of the said Cite to be seasid into the Kyng's handes to the harmes and costs of the seid meir and comonalte of X$^{m\ li}$.

7.8 Reporting on the Workings of Parliament: An Account by Thomas Christmas and John Vertue, Burgesses of Colchester, 1485, in Nicholas Pronoy and John Taylor, *Parliamentary Texts of the Later Middle Ages* (Oxford: Oxford University Press, 1980), pp. 185–9.

Although the king's courts no doubt played a more frequent role in the lives and interests of propertied English people during the late Middle Ages, parliament was to occupy an increasingly larger part not only in the affairs of the aristocracy, but also in the lives and choices of the vast majority of the population, peasants and laborers as well as aristocrats, over this period. Although the dominant voices in parliament were aristocrats, the nobility in the House of Lords, and lesser but nonetheless collectively significant landholders representing the shires in the Commons, one of the most detailed accounts of a parliament originates in a report from burgesses representing the interests of Colchester in one of Henry VII's parliaments. Municipal governors, to whom we probably owe this precious item of evidence on the proceedings at Westminster in the late fifteenth century, were better able to insist on written reports from their chosen delegates, than the freeholders who, under the presidency of sheriffs, elected the representatives of counties.[198]

Maister Baillies, and all my masters. Accordyng unto our deute we went to Westmynestr the vijth day of Novembr,[199] the yere aboveseid, by ix of the clocke, and there we gave a tendawnse[200] upon the Kyngs grace withyn that same oure it pleased the Kyngs high grace, and all his lords speritualx and temporalx that was there present; soo cam downe oucte of the parlement chambir in to the cherche of Westmynestre, and there was seid the masse of the Holy Gost.[201] In that while that masse wasse a seyyng cam my Lord Stuard[202] in to the parlement chambir, and there comaunded a proclamacion for the Kyng, that every knyght that wear chosyn for the sheris,[203] and ever(y) citzener for ceties, and every burgessez for borrowes[204] that they

198 Ellipses in this entry indicate lacunae in the original. Words in parentheses, now illegible in the original, are from later transcripts.

199 In 1485 November 7 was a Monday.

200 Attendance.

201 The Mass of the Holy Ghost was the usual Mass for parliament: Powell and Wallis, *House of Lords in the Middle Ages*, pp. 530 n. 27, 555.

202 The Lord Steward was Thomas Stanley, Earl of Derby and Henry VII's stepfather through marriage with Margaret Beaufort.

203 Shires.

204 Boroughs.

shuld answer be ther names[205]; and so they ware callid and resseyved in to the parlement chambir; and son after that doon it pleasid the Kyngs grace and all his lords spirituall and temporall cam in to the parlement chambir . . . ryall estat, and all his lords spirituall and temporall (and all his jugges) . . . Kyngs grace for to comaunde my Lord Chaunseler[206] for to show the . . . a worshipful sermon, in that he shewe many worshipful! points (for) . . . this lond. That don, the Kyng comaunded my Lord Chaunseler (that he) . . . all Knyghts, settnarirs[207] and burgeyssys, that they shuld semble to the parlement. . . . The vijth day of Novembr, be ix of the clokke, so for to procede un to a (leccion[208] for) . . . chose a Speker. So the leccion gave hir voyse unto Thomas Lovel, a (gentilman) . . . Lyncolnes Inne. That doon, it pleased the Knyghts that there there present (for to ryse from) ther sets and so for to goo to that plase where as the Speker stode and . . . set hym in his sete. That don, there he thanked all the maisters of the plase. (Than) . . . the Recorder of London for to shew the custume of the place.[209] This was his seyeng; . . . Speker, and all my maisters, there hath ben an ordir to this place in tymes (passed that) ye shuld commaunde a certeyn of Knyghts and other gentilmen, such as it pleaseth (you) . . . to the nombre of xxiiij, and they to goo togedir un to my Lord Chaunceler, (and there) to show unto his lordship that they have doon the Kyngs commaundement in (the chosyn) of our Speker, desyrng his lordship if that he wold shew it un to the Kyngs (grace. And) . . . whan it plesith the Kyng to commaunde us when we shall present hym a fore his (high grace) Yt pleased the Kyng that we shuld present hym upon the ix day of Novembre. (That) same day, at x of the cloke, sembled Maister Speker and all the Knyghts, sitteners and burgeyses in the parlament howse, and so departed in to the parliament chambir[210] (be fore) the Kyngs grace and all his lords spirituall and temporall and all his Juggs, (and so) presented our Speker before the Kyngs grace and all his lords spirituall and temporall.

The xth day of Novembre there was red a byll for the Subsedy[211] be twen the (kyng and) the merchaunts, whiche byll was examyned amonges us and oder divers person (maters) and non conclusyon.

205 Roll calls were an essential feature of the parliaments of the sixteenth century.

206 The Lord Chancellor was John Alcock, Bishop of Worcester. He declared the cause of the summoning of parliament, RP VI. 267.

207 Citizens.

208 Election.

209 It is worth noting that a later Recorder of London, William Fleetwood, had in his possession a copy of the Modus, Harvard Law Library MS. 21. Fleetwood was, however, also a legal antiquarian.

210 Note that the account identifies the "parliament chambir" as the place where the Lords sat. The Commons usually met in the chapter house of Westminster Abbey. There can be no doubt that the chamber was the Painted Chamber in the palace of Westminster.

211 For the financial grants made to the King see RP VI. 268–70. In the second session of parliament he enriched the Crown by an enormous act of resumption, not referred to in this account, RP VI. 336–84.

The xjth day of Novembre the same byll was red afore us and there passed (as) an aucte. And that doon, Maister Speker commaunded iiij gentyll men for to ber (it) to my Lord Chaunseler, desyryng his lordship that he wold certifie the Kyngs (good) grace withall.

The xijth day of Novembre there cam a byll from the Qwene Elizabeth[212] that was, (and so) red, for such certeyn desyrs for castells and for oder possessions that she was (possessed) of in King Edward's day, and so red.

The xiijth day of Novembre it was Sonday.

The xiiijth day there were arguments for such to non conclusyon.

The xv day of Novembre there passed a byll with Master Hawte[213] for to have (restore) hym un to his londs, the whiche he was a teynte[214] be awcte of parliament in Kyng Richards day.

The xvj day of Novembre there ware qwescionns moved for the comenwell of thise false persons whiche hath reyned many dayes amongs us, and (non) conclusyon.

The xvij day of Novembre there cam in the Counteys of Warwik, and there she shewd a pytelous compleynt, and therupon she delyvered so a (byll).[215]

(The xviij day of Novembre) it pleased the Kyngs good grace to send us downe a byll that he . . . ettyed[216] with his lords be advyse of an othe that no man shuld supporte . . . (un) lawfull mayntenaunce by the mene[217] of the lyveres gevyng,[218] neyther be non other menes.[219]

(The xix day) Sir John Wynkefeld brought in a byll of suche wronges and hurts . . . (he felt) hym agreved of, and so delyvered a byll.

The xx day it was Sonday.

(The xxj) day of Novembre ther passyd a byll as an awct[220] for to restore blyssed Kyng Harry and Qwene (Marget) and Prince Edward, upon such atteynt[221] as was shewed by awct of parliament be (Kyng) Edward the iiijth. Also ther passed a byll[222] for my lady the Kyngs moder for to restore hyr (of suche) possessyons as she was a teynt of by the parliament of Kyng Richard, Kyng in ded and (not) of ryght. Also ther passed a byll the same day as an awcte[223] for Sir Jamez Loterell, to restore (hym of) his londs suche as he was

212 Bill concerning Queen Elizabeth, RP VI. 288.

213 Richard Hawt of Ightam (Kent) was one of the Maidstone group of rebels in Buckingham's rebellion of 1483, RP VI. 245.

214 Attainted.

215 The bill was not in fact passed in 1485. It came again before the 1487 parliament and was passed then, RP VI. 391–2.

216 An illegible fraction of a word omitted before ettyded.

217 Means.

218 Giving of liveries.

219 This account is a simple man's version of the oath against maintenance as administered in this parliament, RP VI. 287–8. The oathtakers included minors whose names do not appear on the chancery list.

220 Act reversing attainder on Henry VI, RP VI. 288.

221 Attainder.

222 Act restoring estates to Margaret Beaufort as Countess of Richmond, RP VI. 284–5.

223 Act restoring Hugh Luttrell to the estates of his father, *Ibid.*, pp. 297–8.

a teynt of, and all hys heirez, be awcte of parliament by (Kyng) Edward, the fyrst yer of his reigne.

(The) xxij day of Novembre ther cam in a byll by Duke of Bedford of compleynte upon a teynt, (the whiche) passed by an aucte[224] of parliament in Kyng Edwards dayes, the whiche that (is restored) of as that aute[225] had never be made.

(The) xxiij day of Novembre ther cam in a byll of compleynt by the Bysshop of Ely and the Bysshop of Salusbury, and be the Bysshop of Excetyr. They desyred to be restored of that (they) were a teynt of, be awcte of parliament, in Kyng Richards dayes; and so passed as an aucte, and so restored.[226]

The xxiiij day of Novembre, Knights and Sqwrs and other gentyllmen and yemen of the Crowne, and with odir yomen, to the numbre of vj score, they were rest(ored) aftir the forme as is above rehersed.

The xxv day of Novembre ther were red certeyn bylls, and therupon were arguments, and nothing passed that day.

The xxvj day of Novembre we gave a tendaunce in the Cheker[227] for to dyscharge our ffe fferme[228] with Appylton and with Tynt and Hynkley; and the Chambleyn was there present.[229]

The xxvij day it was Sonday.

The xxviij day of Novembre there was a comonyng[230] for the comen well of all the lond for to se a remedy for this fals money which that reyneth in the lond,[231] disseyvyng[232] of the Kyngs leige people; and so continued the xxix.

The xxx day of Novembre cam downe the Clerke of the Crowne, by the commaundement of the Kyng and his lords spirituall and temporall, with xij bylls; so resseyved and red that day.[233]

The first day of Decembre ther passed a byll with Th. Thorp ageyn John Colte for such certey(n) londs that he hath holde of his to his wronge; and so he was restored.[234]

224 Act restoring estates to the Duke of Bedford, *Ibid.*, 278–9. An act of 1478 deprived George Neville of the dukedom of Bedford because of insufficient means to support his dignity, RP VI. 73. Jasper Tudor was created Duke of Bedford in 1485 on the accession of his nephew, Henry VII.

225 As if that Act.

226 No separate petition appears on the roll. Those listed in this group of petitioners include all those attainted by Richard III including the three bishops. The list is headed by Bedford and the bishops, RP VI. 273–5.

227 Exchequer.

228 Fee farm, the annual rent by which the city enjoyed its corporate statue.

229 It was part of the duties of the Colchester burgesses to pay in the fee farm of the town at the Exchequer, Colchester's due were fixed at £35, RP VI. 300.

230 Meeting, discussion, conference.

231 Land.

232 Deceiving.

233 It is not possible to establish what these bills might have been.

234 Thomas Thorp was a Baron of the Exchequer in the time of Henry VI and Speaker in 1453. For the act annulling Colt's recovery of the lands, RP VI. 294–5. This brief and matter of fact reference hides one of the most remarkable recorded examples of the personal feuds that could develop as a

The second day of Decembre there passed a byll with Sir Ts Wrylond, as an aucte, for certeyn londs and ten'tz[235] of that he was a teynt of be aucte of parliament, in Kyng Edwards dayes; and there upon he was restored. The same day there passed a byll with Sir John Weynescotte, as an aucte, for to restore hym a geyn unto his londs.

The iijde day of Decembre the(r) came downe ix bylls by the Kyngs . . . his lords spiritual) and temporall, delyvered unto us by (the clerke of). . . . So they ware red for that day, with odir maters that ware (resoned).[236]

The iiijth day it was Sonday.

The vth day of Decembre ther passed a byll with Sir John Gylford (as anaucte) . . .[237] hym of his londs that he was a teynt of be aucte of parliament.[238]

The vj day of Decembre ther passed a byll, as an aucte[239], with therle (of Oxynf[240]), and his brodir[241] George Fear,[242] and his broth Th. Fear, to restore (them of . . .) ther londs whiche as they ware a teynt of be aucte of parliament, (in) Kyng Edwards day. The same day passed a byll, as an aucte,[243] (with Lord Wells) to restore hym to all his lands that he was a teint of be aucte (of parliament). The same day passed a byll, as an aucte,[244] with my Lord Hungerford, to (restore) hym agayn to his londs that he was a teint of be aucte of parliament, in Kyng Edwards dayes.

---

result of officials acting in their official capacity against a powerful magnate, particularly if that magnate was none other than Richard, Duke of York. Thomas Thorp, the father of Roger Thorp who was the petitioner, in his capacity as baron of the Exchequer took possession of the warlike accoutrements of York (harness and other apparatus of war) after he had fallen into the King's hands. York pursued Thorp with undying vengeance for the return of these articles. His agent in this was Thomas Colt, M.P. for Warwick in 1453–4. A Middlesex jury found for the duke in 1454, and Thorp was committed to the Fleet for a time.

235 Tenements.

236 It is probable that these are the statutes listed after the end of the first session, RP VI. 335.

237 The missing words may include "to restore."

238 No separate petition appears on the roll. Sir John Guildford was included in the general reversal of Richard III's attainder.

239 Repeal of the act of attainder against the De Veres, RP VI. 281–2. John de Vere commanded the archers at Bosworth.

240 Oxyenford=Oxford.

241 Brother.

242 Vere.

243 The attainder of John Welles, and those of his brother and nephew were reversed in 1485, RP VI. 286–7. The Welles lands were restored to him. Among other appointments he was made Constable of Bolingbroke.

244 19 Act reversing attainder on Lord Hungerford, RP VI. 305–6. Lord Hungerford and Moleyns (attainted 1461) was taken prisoner and beheaded in 1464. His son, Sir Thomas, was convicted of treason in 1469 and beheaded. The property was divided between the heir general and the heir male.

The vij day of Decembre ther passed a byll with Foster as an aucte[245] (for to restore) hym of all his londs that he was a teint be aucte of parliament. (The same) day there passed a byll[246] with Maister Wilby[247] as it is above said. The same (day) there passed a byll[248] with Maister Tressom[249] after the same manner of forme.

The viij day it was oure lady day.[250].

The ix day came in the byll of a teynt and sore was questioned with. (The same) day cam in a byll, with the erle of Stafford and with his moder, my (lady of) Bedford, savyng hym the tytyll of his lords and his moders joynter[251] (and) so was red the same day.

The x day ther passed the same byll of a teynt.[252] The same day passed a byll, as aucte,[253] with therle of Stafford and with my lady his moder, to (restitucion) of there londs. The same day there passed another byll that there (should) no man take non accion a genst non of tho[254] that had eny patent, (nor) no byll assyned, nor non that was proved that had occupied (in his) owne wronge in tyme the parliament be ended. Also the same day (there) passed a byll for the Court of Request that it is annulled, and it (shall) be occupied no more.[255] The same day it pleased the Kyng and (all) his lords for to sende for Maister Speker and all the howse in(to the) parliament chambir. And we cam theder and wayted upon his (grace). So it pleased his grace for to commaunde my Lord Chaunseler to (proloye[256] his) high Court of parliament in to the xxiij day of Januarie.[257]

---

245 Act restoring estates to John Forster, RP VI. 332.

246 Act restoring estates to Robert Willoughby, *Ibid.*, pp. 287, 325–6. 532.

247 Willoughby.

248 Act restoring John Tresham to estates of his father, RP VI. 317–18. Sir Thomas Tresham was a noted Lancastrians and Speaker in the parliament of 1459.

249 Tresham.

250 Conception of the Virgin Mary, 8 December.

251 Jointure.

252 Richard III and his principal supporters were attainted. Those who had opposed Henry at Bosworth were declared to be rebels, RP VI. 275–8.

253 Act restoring lands to Catherine, Duchess of Bedford, RP VI. 284–5. The bill was "read" on the ninth day and "passed" on the following day.

254 Those.

255 There is no evidence of any act concerning the Court of Requests.

256 Adjourn.

257 As regards the payment of the Colchester burgesses for their parliamentary duties, "an annuity of £1. 6s. 8d. being the rent from two mills 'at the New Hythe' was set aside for Thomas Christemasse."

7.9 Paying for War and Promoting "English" Unity: Edward IV's instructions to Thomas Cook, alderman of London, 13 March 1462, in *The Politics of Fifteenth Century England: John Vale's Book*, by Margaret Lucille Kekewich, Colin Richmond, Anne F. Sutton, Livia Visser Fuchs, and John L. Watts (Alan Sutton Publishing for Richard III and Yorkist History Trust, 1995), pp. 135–7.

Colchester's burgesses, who produced the account above, would scarcely have reported on proceedings at Westminster had the citizens whom they represented been indifferent to what happened when members of the landed aristocracy, the most important clergy of the realm, and burgesses from towns and cities responded to parliamentary summons. Parliament provided dominant figures in English communities – landlords and civic authorities – an occasion and a means to bend royal authority to their needs, but from the king's perspective, parliament mattered because it afforded him a highly convenient means to supplement the income of his estates, a chronic necessity despite the wishes of his subjects that he should "live of his own."

Fortescue saw the wealth and power of the monarchy in offices within the king's gift, as well as in the king's own estates; but immediate needs of English kings during the late Middle Ages drove them to tap directly their subjects' wealth, and especially wealth potentially available from urban populations. Whatever else the towns and cities of England contributed to construction of cultural values and social institutions, they supplied the central government with a resource no monarch could afford to forgo, especially when his aristocracy fought among itself.

Evident in the following letter by Edward IV is the importance of London to the financial well-being of the king; equally obvious are divisions within the landed elite at the time, whose cooperation was fundamental to the political stability of any late medieval regime. Edward IV, after all, had deposed his predecessor, as had Henry IV deposed his predecessor, and as Edward III's mother had organized the removal of his father, Edward II. No one in the fifteenth century likely imagined an end to royal government; indeed, the several depositions may signify how attractive some nobles found royal authority, and the resources of centralized authority within the realm. But the vigor and resilience of the late medieval English state did not mean that English monarchs of the era could relax their guard or take for granted the support of their subjects, high or low. Edward IV, in appealing for the generous financial support of Londoners, points here an accusing finger at France and Scotland, and plays upon fear of a "malicious wymman"; but at heart, his precarious seat on the throne reflected the chronic necessity to negotiate rival and conflicting interests on behalf of a unity and harmony more often invoked than enjoyed. Edward invoked English blood and the English language to justify the financial burden that would fall upon his subjects in his defense; but he also promised good value on the money he asked that they invest in his survival.

A lettre of prive seale /direct to Thomas Cook aldirman of London speciali studied and devised in maner folowing.

Edward bi the grace of God king of Englande, of Fraunce and lorde of Irelande. To oure trusty and welbeloved Thomas Cook aldreman of oure citie of London, greting. Forasmuche as we by divers meaner beene credibly enfourmed and understanden for certayne that oure greate adversarie Henry[258] namyng hym selfe king of England, bi the malicious counsaill and excitacion of Margarete his wife namyng her selfe quene of England, have conspired, accorded, concluded and determyned with oure outewarde ennemyes aswele of Fraunce and of Scotland as of othre divers countrees, that oure saide outewarde ennemyes in grete numbre shall in all haste to thayme possible entre into this oure reaume of Englande to make in the same suche cruell, horrible and mortall werre, depopulacion, robberye and manslaughter ashere before hathe not biene used among cristen people. And with all wayes and meanes to thayme possible to distroye uttirly the people, the name, the tongue and all the blood Englisshe of this oure saide reaume, inso moche that in the seide conspiricie amonges other thinges it is agreed and accorded by oure saide adversary Henry, moved therto bi the malicious and subtill suggestion and entycing of the seide malicious wymman Margarete his wife, that incas[259] thei shall nowe perfourme this thaire malicious and cruell purpoose, whiche God defende,[260] that thanne her oncle called Charles of Angieu[261] with othre Frenshemen shal have the domynacion, ruel and gouvernaunce of this oure reaume aboveseid. And ovir this among other wicked and detestable thinges attempted in this partie bi the seide Henry and Margarete his wife to thentent that oure seide outeward ennemyes of Fraunce and Scotlande shulde rather condescende and applye theyme to thaire malicious entente and to the distruccion of this lande, the same Henry oure adversary bathe graunte and sente unto oure adversarie Loues de Valois namyng hym selfe king of Fraunce a renunciacion and relees of the righte and title that the corowne of Englande hathe unto the reaume and corowne of Fraunce, and also to the duchies and coutrees of Guyenne and Normandie, of Angieu and Mayne, Caleis and Guysnes, with thaire marches and appertenaunces. And ovir that hathe graunted to the same entente to the Scottys not oonly the towne and castell of Berwik now by his delyveraunce hadde and occupied by the same Scottys, but also agrete partie of this oure reaume of England. Which thinges above reherced weele and diligently considered, it openly apperith that the seyde Henry and Margarete his wife biene not oonly to us but also to all this oure reaume and alle oure trewe liege people of the same, mortall and moste cruell ennemyes. We entending with all oure mighte and power to resiste the grete cruel[te]e and malicious purpos of oure saide adversarie and enemyes, and therin inno wise

258 Henry VI.
259 In case.
260 Prevent.
261 Anjou.

to spare oure personne, body or goodes, neither to refuse any aventure, jepardie or peril for the tuicion and defence of this our reaume and our trew subgettes of the same, desire and pray you in the moost special wise that ye immediately uppon the receipte of thes our lettres make to be called and assembled before you alle the househoIderes and inhabitauntes withinne your warde aswele citezeins as forainers, and declare unto theym thabove malicious, furious and cruell entent of our said adversarie and enemyes. And ovur that on owre behalve, exhort, induce and hertly pray theyme with such gentill langage and wordis of benyvolence as shalbe thoughte to you hehovefull that they for the defence and seuretee of thayme selfe and of all this lande and in theschewing of the grete and orribie mischeves and inconveniences aboverehersed, wol at this tyme in this grete and moost urgent necessite shewe effeetuelly and in deede thaire good willis, zele and affeccion that they bere unto us, to the comune weele of this lande and prosperite of thayme selfe. And that into the relevyng and supportacion of the grete charges, expenses and costes that us must of necessite daile bere in this partie, thaye and everyche of thayme woll graunte unto us of thair goodnes and frewill somme certayne somme of money suche as they shall mow bere withoute thaire hurte and grevaunce, lating theyme wete[262] for certayne that we have wele in oure fresshe and tendre remembraunce the grete and manyfolde charges that they herebefore have borne, and that yif we mighte bany[263] meane othirwise doo, we wolde nat at this tyme any thing desire to thaire charge, trusting nevurthelesse somoche in thaire good disposicions and discrecions that that wol nat suffre wilfully alle this reaume and thayme selfe to perisshe and uttirly be distroied. Considering namely that wee desire no thing of thayme by waye of imposicion, compulcion or of precedent or example therupon hereaftir to be taken, but all only of thaire humanite and good willis, trusting in the infinite goodnes, grace and rightwisnes of all mighti God, whiche herebefore in just batell by victorie and confusion of our enemyes hathe juged and declared openly and in dede for our righte and title, that yif oure trewe and feithefull subgettes woll at this tyme doo thaire parte and applye thayme benyvolently to oure desir in this behalfe, we shal for oure parte semblably[264] so behave us, and so from all suche perilles and myscheves preserve and defende theyme and all this lande, that withinne fewe daies thay shall have cause to thynke that thay never herebefore better bestowed, besette[265] or spended any money. . . . Geven undir our prive Beall at our towne of Stampford the xiij day of Marche the second yere of oure reigne.

262 Letting them know.

263 By any.

264 Similarly, accordingly.

265 Bestow, allot.

7.10 Lords Doing Justice to Lords: Henry Percy[266] to William Plumpton, 18 September [before 19 May 1527], in *The Plumpton Letters and Papers*, ed. Joan Kirby, Royal Historical Society Publications, Camden Fifth Series 8 (Cambridge: Cambridge University Press, 1996), p. 201.

Political rivalries, armed and verbal conflicts, even civil war, can easily dominate modern views of political life and institutions in the late Middle Ages. And we could argue – as some of the historians of bastard feudalism have argued – that propertied Englishmen took advantage of weak kingship to manipulate and distort the processes of royal justice to personal advantage during the late Middle Ages, leading to a virtual breakdown in the judicial system. Certainly, the evidence for continuing concern over liveries, retaining, bribery and maintenance, embracery, and other abuses of the system are not hard to find, in either parliamentary or judicial records, and in the correspondence of landed families.

But we could also argue that, given weak kingship, landed aristocrats were only trying to see justice done, at least to their families, kin, and dependants, and that they were in effect performing their "natural" responsibility for administering justice, whether to their own tenants or to those whom they recruited to their service. In either case, it seems clear that whatever the commentators on kingship might argue about the king's responsibility for justice, the preservation of the polity of England was seen by those aristocrats as their responsibility no less than that of the king, and that they acted on the responsibility, no doubt because it benefited them, but also because it was their duty.

Right trusty and welbeloued, I great you hardy well, and whear there is done & trau(ersed) betwixt you and the tennants of Folefeit Poole, of my lord and father lordship of Spofforth, for our courte in this time within his said township of Folefout, and, as I vnderstand, ye ar contented to bide the order of me and others of the said lord and my fathers cowncell of and vpon the premises, so that an end wear maid[267] before months day next. And so it is now at this time that I haue had, and yet hath, such buisenes as I can not attent it this time; wherfore I pray you be contented to giue sparing to[268] the next head cort[269] at Spoforth, at which time ye shall haue an end, with my lord and fathers fauor and mine. And if you doe break and make iij or iiij gaps in Folefout feild, as ye clame to doo, of coustam[270] yearly, thearwith I am content at this time, so that ye doe make noe more buisenes therin to the

266 Henry Percy succeeded his father the 5th earl of Northumberland on the latter's death, 19 May 1527. The two had recently been on bad terms.

267 Were made.

268 Await, be patient until.

269 Court.

270 Custom.

time when the said matter be ordered or determined. And herof at this time, I pray you faile not, as my trust is in you. Written at the castle of Wresill the xviij day of September.

H: Pearcy

Endorsed: To my right trusty and welbeloued William Plompton esquire

7.11 Advice to Aristocratic Wives on Mediation and Goverance, c.1404, from Christine de Pizan, *A Medieval Woman's Mirror of Honor. The Treasury of the City of Ladies*, trans. Charity Cannon Willard, ed. Madeleine Pelner Cosman (Persea Books, 1989), pp. 85–87, 168–70 [French].

We see in aristocratic correspondence an acceptance of mediation and conciliation as fundamental to effective governance and social well-being. We also see it, interestingly enough, in Christine de Pisan's manual for the conduct of women in the late middle ages, a manual that gave substantial space to how the wives of the aristocracy should serve the interests of their husbands but also of society at large – precisely by managing well the family estates, managing that was both an exercise of patronage, and an administration of justice in many cases. Women, even when their job was obviously "domestic," governed, when the domestic "realm" so often overlapped "public" government.

Book I, chapter 9

Wherein it is explained how the good and wise princess will attempt to make peace between the prince and his barons if there is any difficulty between them.[271]

If any neighboring or foreign prince wars for any grievance against her lord, or if her lord wages war against another, the good lady will weigh the odds carefully. She will balance the great ills, infinite cruelties, losses, deaths, and destruction to property and people against the war's outcome, which is usually unpredictable. She will seriously consider whether she can preserve the honor of her lord and yet prevent the war. Working wisely and calling on God's aid, she will strive to maintain peace. So also, if any prince of the realm or the country, or any baron, knight, or powerful subject should hold a grudge against her lord, or if he is involved in any such quarrel and she foresees that for her lord to take a prisoner or make a battle

271 See Carolyn Collette, "Anne of Bohemia and the Intercessory Modes of Ricardian England," in *Performing Polity. Women and Agency in the Anglo-French Tradition, 1385–1620* (Turnhout, Belgium: Brepols, 2006), pp. 98–121, for a vivid example of the practice encouraged by Christine de Pisan.

would lead to trouble in the land, she will strive toward peace. In France the discontent of an insignificant baron (named Bouchart[272]) against the King of France, the great prince, has recently resulted in great trouble and damage to the kingdom. The *Chronicles of France* recount the tale of many such misadventures. Again, not long ago, in the case of Lord Robert of Artois,[273] a disagreement with the king harmed the French realm and gave comfort to the English.

Mindful of such terrible possibilities, the good lady will strive to avoid destruction of her people, making peace and urging her lord (the prince) and his council to consider the potential harm inherent in any martial adventure. Furthermore, she must remind him that every good prince should avoid shedding blood, especially that of his subjects. Since making a new war is a grave matter, only long thought and mature deliberation will devise the better way toward the desired result. Thus, always saving both her own honor and her lord's, the good lady will not rest until she has spoken, or has had someone else speak to those who have committed the misdeed in question, alternately soothing and reproving them. While their error is great and the prince's displeasure reasonable, and though he ought to punish them, she would always prefer peace. Therefore, if they would be willing to correct their ways or make suitable amends, she gladly would try to restore them to her lord's good graces.

With such words as these, the good princess will be peacemaker. In such manner, Good Queen Blanche,[274] mother of Saint Louis, always strove to reconcile the king with his barons, and, among others, the Count of Champagne. The proper role of a good, wise queen or princess is to maintain peace and concord and to avoid wars and their resulting disasters. Women particularly should concern themselves with peace because men by nature are more foolhardy and headstrong, and their overwhelming desire to avenge themselves prevents them from foreseeing the resulting dangers and terrors of war. But woman by nature is more gentle and circumspect. Therefore, if she has sufficient will and wisdom she can provide the best possible means to pacify man. Solomon speaks of peace in the twenty-fifth chapter of the *Book of Proverbs*. Gentleness and humility assuage the prince. The gentle tongue (which means the soft word) bends and breaks harshness. So water extinguishes fire's heat by its moisture and chill.

Queens and princesses have greatly benefitted this world by bringing about peace between enemies, between princes and their barons, or between

---

272 The count of Corbeil.

273 The nephew of Mahuat, countess of Artois in the reign of Philip VI (1328–1350), he challenged her claim to the title, inventing false documents to that end. The French king had designs on Artois, a questionable claim contributing to the Hundred Years' War.

274 Regent for Louis IX, who was twelve at the death of his father, managing her and her son's passage through a revolt of barons and some princes of the royal blood.

rebellious subjects and their lords. The Scriptures are full of examples. The world has no greater benevolence than a good and wise princess. Fortunate is that land which has one. I have listed as examples many of these wondrous women in *The Book of the City of Ladies.*

What results from the presence of such a princess? All her subjects who recognize her wisdom and kindness come to her for refuge, not only as their mistress but almost as the goddess on earth in whom they have infinite hope and confidence. Keeping the land in peace and tranquility, she and her works radiate charity.

Book II, chapter 9

Which speaks of the lady baronesses and the sort of knowledge which may be useful to them.

Now it is time to speak to the ladies and demoiselles who live in castles or other sorts of manors on their own lands, in walled cities, or in smaller market towns. For them this advice should helpful. Because their estates and powers vary, we must differentiate among them in our discussions of certain things: their status and their style of living. As for their morals and good deeds on God's behalf, certainly they can profit from our advice in the earlier chapters to princesses and women living at court. All women can learn to cultivate virtue and avoid vice. However, the women I address now are powerful women: baronesses and great land owners who nevertheless are not called princesses. Technically, the name "princess" should not be applied to any but empresses, queens, and duchesses. Yet in Italy and elsewhere, wives of men who because of their land holdings are called princes, after the names of their territories, may be called princesses. Although countesses are not universally called princesses, because they follow duchesses in rank according to the importance of their lands, nonetheless we have included them among the princesses. First we address these baronesses of whom there are many in France, in Brittany, and elsewhere.

These baronesses surpass in honor and power many countesses, even though their titles are not as distinguished. Certain barons have enormous power because of their land, domains, and the nobility that goes with them. Thereby, their wives have considerable status. These women must be highly knowledgeable about government, and wise – in fact, far wiser than most other such women in power. The knowledge of a baroness must be so comprehensive that she can understand everything. Of her a philosopher might have said: "No one is wise who does not know some part of everything." Moreover, she must have the courage of a man. This means that she should not be brought up overmuch among women nor should she be indulged in extensive and feminine pampering. Why do I say that? If barons wish to be honored as they deserve, they spend very little time in their manors and on their own lands. Going to war, attending their prince's court, and traveling are the three primary duties of such a lord. So the lady, his companion, must represent him at home during his absences. Although her husband is served by bailiffs, provosts, rent collectors, and land governors, she must govern them all. To do this according to her right she must conduct herself with such

Figure 3 An embracing man and woman, probably peasants, from Bodleian Library MS. Rawl. D. 939, section 3 recto, an astrological and ecclesiastical calendar in six pieces of the late fourteenth century. According to the caption provided by the Bodleian Library, the embracing couple accompany a Thunder chart; they signal "Peace and Concord among the people, with abundant crops of fruit and corn," which contemporary adherents of astrological wisdom could anticipate if they experienced thunder in December. In light of sources 7.11, 7.12 and 7.13, we might well regard the comfort and support each figure offers the other indeed fundamental to social peace and political order, and economic productivity. Their isolation, on the other hand, is not easy to reconcile with abundant evidence, in these pages, that describe a dense network of relations in which men and women, peasants or lords or merchants, lived their lives and, for that matter, joined together as couples. And surely, the artist's choice of a simply-clad couple to convey harmony, peace, and fertility lets us speculate that contemporaries, however mindful of hierarchy and the rights of governance attributed to the aristocracy, also acknowledged that the welfare of England's "natural" governors depended on peaceful and productive peasants and laborers. The latter mattered, and mattered critically, even if they ordinarily enter the historical record as objects of aristocratic initiative.

wisdom that she will be both feared and loved. As we have said before, the best possible fear comes from love.

When wronged, her men must be able to turn to her for refuge. She must be so skilled and flexible that in each case she can respond suitably. Therefore, she must be knowledgeable in the mores of her locality and instructed in its usages, rights, and customs. She must be a good speaker, proud when pride is needed; circumspect with the scornful, surly, or rebellious; and charitably gentle and humble toward her good, obedient subjects. With the counsellors of her lord and with the advice of elder wise men, she ought to work directly with her people. No one should ever be able to say of her that she acts merely to have her own way. Again, she should have a man's heart. She must know the laws of arms and all things pertaining to warfare, ever prepared to command her men if there is need of it. She has to know both assault and defense tactics to ensure that her fortresses are well defended, if she has any expectation of attack or believes she must initiate military action. Testing her men, she will discover their qualities of courage and determination before overly trusting them. She must know the number and strength of her men to gauge accurately her resources, so that she never will have to trust vain or feeble promises. Calculating what force she is capable of providing before her lord arrives with reinforcements, she also must know the financial resources she could call upon to sustain military action.

She should avoid oppressing her men, since this is the surest way to incur their hatred. She can best cultivate their loyalty by speaking boldly and consistently to them, according to her council, not giving one reason today and another tomorrow. Speaking words of good courage to her men-at-arms as well as to her other retainers, she will urge them to loyalty and their best efforts.

Such courses of action are suitable for the wise baroness whose absent husband has given her the responsibility and commission to take his place. This advice would be useful if an aggressor or some baron or powerful man should defy her. So, also, the baroness will find particularly expedient the advice in the chapter on widowed princesses. For if during a baron's lifetime his wife knows everything about the management of his affairs, then if left a widow, she will not be ignorant of her rights if anyone dares to try to take advantage of her and make away with her inheritance.

7.12 Seeking Patrons and Arranging Marriages among England's Governors: Two Letters, 1535/6 and 1496/7, from *The Plumpton Letters and Papers*, ed. Joan Kirby, Royal Historical Society Publications, Camden Fifth Series 8 (Cambridge: Cambridge University Press, 1996), pp. 205–6 and 118–19.

The search for lordship was the inverse of patronage, and the pressure on superiors from their dependants and potential dependants could be strong and persistent, as the Paston correspondence illustrates well, and as the letter below from Robert Plumpton shows us. Robert Plumpton's letter to his mother, gently begging for further money, more importantly urges her and his father to more effective intervention with potential patrons whom he hopes to serve. His practical necessities are obvious; but anxieties about his own future co-exist easily with concern for his mother's spiritual well-being, as he recommends a copy of the New Testament to her – and thereby reminds us of the controversies over reformation of the church intensifying rapidly at the end of our period.

Patronage was by no means limited to offices and service; it can be seen again and again in the arrangement of marriages, and almost certainly we should view women as critical to the preservation of social order, not only when they contributed directly to such order by means described above by Christine de Pisan, but as objects in the creation or reinforcement of social and political connections. Surely, affection and simple attraction played a role in negotiations over marriage; but given the importance of families within the maintenance of good governance generally, wives and potential wives were never simply wives, but political, social, and economic assets. Obedience of wives to husbands, and servants to masters, was no less important than obedience to royal authority in maintaining the English polity of the late Middle Ages. Obedience, however, seldom implied passivity.

Robert Plumpton[275] to Mrs Isabel Plumpton, 12 January [c.1535/6]

Right worshipful mother, I humbly recommend mee unto you, desiring you of your dayly blessing, praing Jesu long to continew your helth to his pleasur. Mother, I thank you for the [blank] at you send mee, for yf you were not, I were not able to liue, for this same Christmasse hath cost mee as much as you send mee. Wherfor I am afraid I shal not haue money to serue mee to Easter. Also I wold desire you to send mee word of the letter that I wrote to my father and you, for to mooue my Lady Gascoin[276] to write to my lord her brother[277] not to bee only his seruant, but of his houshold and attending unto him, for els he wold do as other lords do, knowes not half their seruants. Wherfor I desire you that you wil mooue my Lady Gascoin to writ so to my lord that I may bee his houshold seruant.

Also, mother, I wold desire you to mark wel my letter that I sent you by Mr Oughtred.[278] And here I send you a godly New Testament by this bearer, and yf the prologues bee so small that ye cannot wel reade them, ther is my

275 William and Isabel's eldest son, who died 1546.

276 Margaret daughter of Richard, Lord Latimer (d.1530) was the 2nd wife of Sir William Gascoigne (d. 1551).

277 John Neville, Lord Latimer (d. 1542) joined the Pilgrimage of Grace but claimed that it was against his will. His third wife, Katherine, daughter of Sir Thomas Parr, later married Henry VIII.

278 Robert Ughtred of Kexby, son of Sir Henry (d. 1510).

fathers book, and they are bothe one, and my fathers book hath the prologue printed in bigger letters. Yf it wil please you to read the Introducement ye shal see maruelous things hyd in it. And as for the understanding of it, dout not, for God wil giue knowledge to whom he will giue knowledg of the Scriptures, as soon to a shepperd as to a priest, yf he ask knowledg of God faithfully. Wherfore pray to God, and desire Jesus Christ to pray for you and with you. No more to you at this tyme, but God fill you with al spiritual knowledge, to the glory of God, helth of your soule, and the profit of your poor nieghbor. Written at the Temple, the 12 day of January.

By your sonn Robart Plompton

Endorsed: To his mother at Plompton be this letter deliuered

Edward Plumpton to Sir Robert Plumpton, 2 March [1496/7]

In my right humble & most hartyest wyse I recomend me vnto your good mastership & to my singuler goode lady. Sir, yt is so that certaine lovers & frinds of myne in London hath brought me vnto the sight of a gentlewoman, a wedow of xl yeres & more, & of good substance. First, she is goodly & beautyfull, womanly and wyse, as euer I knew any, none other dispraysed, of a good stocke & worshipfull; hir name is Agnes. She hath in charge but one gentlewoman to her daughter, of xij yer age. She hath xx mark of good land within iij myle of London, & a ryall[279] maner buyld [. . .] thervpon, to giue or sell at hir pleasure. She hath in coyne in old nobles cl, in ryalls – cl,[280] in debts xl*li*,[281] in plate cx*li*, with other goods of great valour; she is called worth iij*li* beside her land.

Sir, I am bold vpon yor good mastership, as I haue euer bene, & if yt please God & you that this matter take effect, I shalbe able to deserue althings done & past. She & I are agreed in onn mynd & all one, but her frinds that she is ruled by desireth of me xx marke iointor[282] more than my lands come to, & thus I answeered them, saying that your mastership is so good master to me that ye gaue to my other wyfe xij marke for hir ioyntor, in Studley Roger,[283] & now, that it wyll please your sayd mastership to indue this woman in some lordship of yours of xx marke duryng her life, such as they shalbe pleased with; & for this, my sayd frinds offer to be bonden in M*li*.[284] Sir, vpon this they intend to know your pleasure and mynd preuely, I not knowing. Wherfore I

279 Sufficient.

280 The ryall, first minted in 1463, was valued at 10s. It replaced the noble, valued at 6s 8d.

281 £10.00

282 Jointure, a provision for a wife in the event of her husband's death.

283 On 10 December 1483 Edward Plumpton entered into a bond to release a rent out of Nether Studley granted to him and his first wife, Agnes.

284 £1,000.00.

humbly besech your [good mastership], as my especiall trust is & euer hath bene aboue all earthly creators, now, for my great promotion & harts desire, to answere to your pleasure & my well & [. . .] poore honesty; & I trust, or yt come to pass, to put you suertie to be discharged without any charg. For now your good and discret answere may be my making, for & she & I fortune, by God & your meanes, togyther our too goods & substance wyll make me able to doe you good service, the which good seruice & I, now & at all tymes, is & shalbe yours, to ioperde[285] my life & them both. Sir, I besech your good mastership to wryte to me an answere in all hast possible, and after that ye shall here more, with Gods grace, who preserue you & yours in prosperous felicyte long tyme to endure. Wrytten in Furnywall Inne in Oldborn, the ij day of March 1496.

Your humble seruant Ed: Plompton

Endorsed: To my master Sir Robt Plompton kt

7.13 Custom, Order, and Adultery, 1486, from Hil., 1 Henry VII, pl. 3, fos. 6–7v, in *Year Books*, Vulgate edition (1679–80, a reprint of black-letter editions of the 16th century) [Translation from law French by HGG].

How deeply personal was the basis of political order, and how deeply dependent on what we would regard as personal relationships was the maintenance of good order and social stability, we can see in the following case, which nicely illustrates both the commitment to social harmony, and the anxiety about threats that were inherent in the very relationships on which social unity and harmony were constructed. In this report of lawyers' arguing about legal process within a royal court, we find many of the themes touched upon in other documents: the relationship of custom to law; the fit between morality and legality on the one hand, between secular and spiritual authority on the other; and the centrality of women to anxieties about political order and social stability, a centrality that testifies to their perceived value, even as it illustrates the constraints within which they might assert agency. And most importantly, this debate over a London constable's response to allegations of adultery reminds the modern scholar and student that the political imagination of medieval Englishmen renders irrelevant distinctions between public matters and private affairs and resists interpretations that contrast public authority with private interest.

On the second day of the term, Vavisour rehearsed how a person had brought a writ of trespass for assault, battery, and imprisonment lasting for two days, which the defendant had committed against him in the Ward of B., London. The defendant pleaded in bar to the action as follows: that they had a custom in London, that if an information should be made to a Constable of London,

285 Hazard, put in jeopardy.

that someone within their jurisdiction were with any woman in adultery, then he should call the Bedel and others within the same parish, who would go to the house with him. And if they should find a man in adultery, that they should take him to the Counter prison, and there they should leave him. And they say in fact, at another time and parish [than those alleged in the charge], which they specify precisely, an information was given to this defendant, then and previously the Constable of the same parish, that the plaintiff was engaged in adultery with a certain woman in the same parish. By virtue of this information, he called to him the other defendants, who according to the said custom went to the house, etc., and there they found the plaintiff in adultery, wherefore they took him and led him to the Counter, and delivered him to the warden of the prison. . . .

And the plaintiff demurred in law on this; and now he prayed his judgement, because the plea was not valid. For one reason, that such a thing cannot lie in our law, because it is merely spiritual. . . .

Colow disagreed, and Townsend argued that the plea was good. Firstly, he said that the matter lay well in prescription, because it was good for conserving good rule and peace. For in each adultery, there is a wrong in our law to a third party, that is, to the husband. For it is not lawful to anyone to take any woman; and if he should do so, this is a wrong to the husband, and this is shown by the husband's right to have an action of trespass, for trespass done to his wife, and also for taking and leading away his wife, which illustrates well the wrong to a third party; the which wrong moreover is not only done to the husband but is also a disturbance of the peace and a grievance to all the neighbors. And since it is a wrong to someone and a common disturbance to all the neighbors, a prescriptive right to correct such behavior may be invoked. And as to the argument that it is a spiritual offence, etc., and should have spiritual correction, this is not particularly to the purpose; for by the law of Holy Church, if the husband should find one in adultery with his wife, he can kill the man and his wife for the wrong done to him, without penalty. And this law proves that it is a wrong done to the husband. It is a great sin and peril according to the law of God and man, and such an occurrence can destroy a whole city or borough, for the neighbors will call the husband a cuckold, and on this shall develop a grudge, and from this battery and manslaughter, and so a great disturbance of the peace and of good governance, the which is prohibited, according to Bracton, by the law of the Romans, the French, and the English. And the king of England prohibits all of these things upon grievous temporal pains. And also, it was prohibited by the Civil Law, for Phineas killed one of the sons of Israel who slept with a wife of a gentile and Placuit multum deo, as it appears, percussit Phineas & cessauit scelus. Moreover, a wife taken in adultery shall be dead according to law. And these things show clearly that this custom could have a lawful origin, wherefore, etc. . . .

* * *

Townsend: I think that the plea is good, and that the matter lies well in custom. For adultery is a temporal matter, as well as spiritual, and against the peace of the land. For the peace of the land is that each man shall be in peace within his home with his wife, children, goods, and chattels; and he who wrongly troubles any of them does break the peace and public weal of the same borough and city. And if any person enter his home to rob him, it is a felony or burglary. And it be to take his goods, it is a felony, or at least a trespass; thus to take and misuse the wife is a greater trespass, a larger shame and villainy, and a major threat to the peace and public weal of the same city. And in each adultery, there is a wrong to the husband, who is a third party, and the breaking of his home, etc., wherefore, etc. And as to the argument that he has not said what shall be done with him when he is led to prison, it is not necessary, for the defendants are only officers, and it is sufficient for them to allege sufficient matter to excuse themselves. As if a constable should see a man stealing, he may arrest him, and commit him to ward, without saying further what would be done with him then, etc.

Gatesby: This is true, for the case of stealing is at common law, and we say that we know the procedures in such a case. But we do not know in the case of a private custom in London, etc.

Townsend: This is not a private custom, but for the advantage of the public weal, and a custom which is lawful in each city, borough, and town throughout the realm.

Gatesby: If it be so, then I agree, although he ought to show what the fine shall be, etc. . . .

(The report ends with an adjournment. N.B., the translation above omits argument on various technical faults alleged in the pleadings by the defendant.)

Further Reading

Archer, Rowena E., *Crown, Government and People in the Fifteenth Century*, The Fifteenth Century series, 2 (Stroud: Sutton, 1995).

Archer, Rowena E. and Simon Walker, d. 2004, eds, *Rulers and Ruled in Late Medieval England: Essays Presented to Gerald Harriss* (London & Rio Grande (OH): Hambledon, 1995).

Baker, J. H., *An Introduction to English Legal History*, 4th ed. (London: Butterworths, 2002).

Baker, J. H., *The Oxford History of the Laws of England, Vol. VI: 1483–1558* (Oxford: Oxford University Press, 2003).

Bennett, M. J., *Community, Class and Careerism: Cheshire and Lancashire in the Age of Sir Gawain and the Green Knight* (Cambridge: Cambridge University Press, 1983).

Britnell, R. H. and A. J. Pollard, eds, *The McFarlane Legacy* (Stroud: Sutton, 1995).

Carpenter, Christine, *The Wars of the Roses: Politics and the Constitution c.1437–1509* (Cambridge: Cambridge University Press, 1997).

Clough, C. H., ed., *Profession, Vocation and Culture in Later Medieval England* (Liverpool: Liverpool University Press, 1982).

Davies, R. G. and J. H. Denton, eds, *The English Parliament in the Middle Ages* (Manchester: University of Manchester Press, 1981).

Goheen, R. B., "Peasant politics? Village community and the crown in fifteenth century England", *American Historical Review*, 96 (1991), pp. 42–62.

Harding, Alan, *Medieval Law and the Foundations of the State* (Oxford: Oxford University Press, 2002).

Harvey, I. M. W., *Jack Cade's Rebellion of 1450* (Oxford: Clarendon Press, 1991).

Kaeuper, R., *War, Justice and Public Order: England and France in the Later Middle Ages* (Oxford: Clarendon Press, 1988).

McIntosh, M. K., *Controlling Misbehaviour in England, 1370–1600* (Cambridge: Cambridge University Press, 1998).

Maddicott, J. R. and David Michael Palliser, eds, *The Medieval State: Essays Presented to James Campbell* (London and Rio Grande (OH): Hambledon, 2000).

Musson, Andrew and W. M. Ormrod, *The Evolution of English Justice: Law, Politics and Society in the Fourteenth Century* (London: Palgrave Macmillan, 1999).

Palmer, R. C., *English Law in the Age of the Black Death* (Chapel Hill, NC: University of North Carolina Press, 1993).

Powell, E., *Kingship, Law, and Society: Criminal Justice in the Reign of Henry V* (Oxford: Clarendon Press, 1989).

Ormrod, W. M., *Political Life in Medieval England, 1300–1450* (Basingstoke: Macmillan; New York: St Martin's Press, 1995).

Scattergood, V. J. and J. W. Sherborne, eds, *English Court Culture in the Later Middle Ages* (London: Duckworths, 1983).

Watts, J., *Henry VI and the Politics of Kingship* (Cambridge: Cambridge University Press, 1996).

Further Reading

General introductions to medieval English literature

Christopher Cannon, *Middle English Literature : a Cultural History*. Malden, MA: Polity, 2008.

Douglas Gray, *Later Medieval English Literature*. Oxford University Press, 2008.

James Simpson, *1350–1547: Reform and Cultural Revolution*. Oxford University Press, 2007.

A Companion to Medieval English Literature and Culture, c.1350–c.1500, ed. Peter Brown. Blackwell, 2007.

The Cambridge Companion to Medieval English Literature, 1100–1500, ed. Larry Scanlon. Cambridge University Press, 2009.

Middle English, ed. Paul Strohm. Oxford University Press, 2007.

Language and Culture in Medieval Britain: the French of England c.1100–c.1500, ed. Jocelyn Wogan-Browne et al. York Medieval Press, 2009.

Introductions to and surveys of medieval English history

Richard Britnell, *The Closing of the Middle Ages? England 1471–1529*. Wiley-Blackwell Publishing, 1997.

Christopher Dyer, *An Age of Transition? Economy and Society in England in the Later Middle Ages*. Oxford: Clarendon Press, 2006.

John Gillingham and Ralph Griffiths, *Medieval Britain: A Very Short Introduction*, Oxford University Press, 2002.

P. J. P. Goldberg, *Medieval England. A Social History 1250–1550*. London: Hodder Arnold, 2004.

Gerald Harris, *Shaping the Nation. England 1360–1461*. The New Oxford History of England. Oxford University Press, 2005.

C. Warren Hollister and Judith Bennett, *Medieval Europe: A Short History*, 10th ed. McGraw Hill, 2006 (an 11th ed., authored solely by Judith Bennett, has been announced for 2011).

Rosemary Horrox and W. Mark Ormrod, *A Social History of England 1200–1500*. Cambridge: Cambridge University Press, 2006.

S. H. Rigby, (ed.), *A Companion to Britain in the Later Middle Ages* (Blackwell Companions to British History). Oxford: Wiley-Blackwell Publishers, 2003.

S. H. Rigby, *English Society in the Later Middle Ages: Class, Status and Gender*. Basingstoke: Macmillan, 1995.

Nigel Saul, *The Oxford Illustrated History of Medieval England*. Oxford University Press, 2001.

Anthony Tuck, *Crown and Nobility: England 1272–1461*, 2nd ed. Wiley-Blackwell Publishing, 1999.

Printed source collections relevant to the late middle ages (in addition to published sources and source collections cited in the body of this book)

Emily Amt, ed., *Medieval England, 1000–1500: A Reader,* Readings in Medieval Civilizations and Cultures Series. University of Toronto Press, 2000.

Laurel Amtower and Jacqueline Vanhoutte, eds., *A Companion to Chaucer and his Contemporaries. Texts and Contexts*. Broadview, 2009.

Chris Given-Wilson, ed. and trans., *Chronicles of the Revolution 1397–1400. The Reign of Richard II,* Manchester Medieval Sources Series, Manchester: Manchester University Press, 1993.

P. J. P. Goldberg, *Women in England c. 1275–1525: Documentary Sources*. Manchester University Press, 1995.

Matthew Boyd Goldie, *Middle English Literature. A Historical Sourcebook*. Oxford: Blackwell Publishing, 2003.

John Shinners, *Medieval Popular Religion 1000–1500. A Reader*. 2nd ed., Readings in Medieval Civilizations and Cultures Series, University of Toronto Press, 2006.

Faith Wallis, ed., *Medieval Medicine: A Reader,* Readings in Medieval Civilizations and Cultures Series, University of Toronto Press, 2010.

Websites containing information, bibliographical guidance, and sources useful to students of the late middle ages (in addition to those cited in the body of this book)

[URLs below were all accessed on or shortly before March 31, 2010. Descriptions below in quotation marks are from the sites themselves.]

Netserf: the Internet Connection for Medieval Resources
http://www.netserf.org/
Perhaps the most useful entry point to other websites with primary materials from the middle ages.

Orb: On-line Reference Book for Medieval Studies,
at the College of Staten Island, City University of New York.
http://www.the-orb.net/

> "The ORB is an academic site, written and maintained by medieval scholars for the benefit of their fellow instructors and serious students. All articles have been judged by at least two peer reviewers. Authors are held to high standards of accuracy, currency, and relevance to the field of medieval studies. NOTE: ORB'S OCLC number is 35987956. Quick connect to other major medieval studies sites."

The Labyrinth:Resources for Medieval Studies
Sponsored by Georgetown University
http://labyrinth.georgetown.edu/

Internet Medieval Sourcebook, located at the
Fordham University Center for Medieval Studies.
http://www.fordham.edu/halsall/sbook.html

The National Archives (UK),
http://www.nationalarchives.gov.uk,
Although basically a guide and catalogue of governmental archives, this site provides access to various collections of online documents, including Ancient Petitions, Henry III–James I (TNA SC 8), described as "Free of charge (funded by the Arts and Humanities Research Council). Petitions pursuing grievances which could not be resolved at common law, or requests for a grant of favour." http://www.nationalarchives.gov.uk/documentsonline/browse-refine.asp?CatID=25&searchType=browserefine&pagenumber=1&query=*&queryType=1

British History Online
http://www.british-history.ac.uk/,

> "British History Online is the digital library containing some of the core printed primary and secondary sources for the medieval and modern history of the British Isles. Created by the Institute of Historical Research and the History of Parliament Trust, We aim to support academic and personal users around the world in their learning, teaching and research."

Legal History: The Year Books
An Index and Paraphrase of Printed Year Book Reports, 1268–1535, located at Boston University
http://www.bu.edu/law/seipp/
compiled by David J. Seipp (Seipp's Abridgement)

Medieval English Towns
http://users.trytel.com/~tristan/towns/towns.html

> "The aim of the Medieval English Towns site is to provide historical information about cities and towns in England during the Middle Ages, with particular but not exclusive emphasis on medieval boroughs of East Anglia and on social, political and constitutional history. A growing selection of primary documents (translated into English) relevant to English urban history is included."

EEBO: Early English Books Online
http://eebo.chadwyck.com/home

> "From the first book printed in English by William Caxton, through the age of Spenser and Shakespeare and the tumult of the English Civil War, Early English Books Online (EEBO) will contain over 125,000 titles listed in Pollard and Redgrave's Short-Title Catalogue (1475–1640), Wing's Short-Title Catalogue (1641–1700), the Thomason Tracts (1640–1661), and the Early English Tract Supplement – all in full digital facsimile from the Early English Books microfilm collection."

Corpus of Middle English Prose and Verse, located at the University of Michigan
http://quod.lib.umich.edu/c/cme/

> "This collection of Middle English texts was assembled from works contributed by University of Michigan faculty and from texts provided by the Oxford Text Archive, as

well as works created specifically for the Corpus by the HTI. The HTI is grateful for the permission of all contributors. For more information on the source of individual titles, please consult the bibliography. All texts in the archive are valid SGML documents, tagged in conformance with the TEI Guidelines, and converted to the TEI Lite DTD for wider use.

"The Humanities Text Initiative intends to develop the *Corpus of Middle English Prose and Verse* into an extensive and reliable collection of Middle English electronic texts, either by converting the texts ourselves or by negotiating access to other collections produced to specified high standards of accuracy. At present, fifty-four texts are available; several others will be added soon. HTI wants to include in the corpus all editions of Middle English texts used in the MED, and the more recent scholarly editions which in some cases may have superseded them. Large scale expansion of the Corpus will not take place until the MED and the HyperBibliography are further advanced, but text conversion continues at a modest rate as time and money permit. The Corpus is provided with a full array of search mechanisms, and texts may be searched individually, in user designated groups. or collectively."

Middle English Dictionary, also located at the University of Michigan
http://quod.lib.umich.edu/m/med/

Medieval Writing: History, Heritage, and Data Source.
http://medievalwriting.50megs.com/writing.htm
This site is created and maintained by Dr Dianne Tillotson, freelance researcher and compulsive multimedia and web author.

Medieval Calendar Calculator
http://www.wallandbinkley.com/mcc/mcc_main.html

Reviews in History, at the the Institute of Historical Research, Senate House, Malet Street, London WC1E 7HU
http://www.history.ac.uk/reviews/

"Launched in 1996, this e-journal publishes reviews and reappraisals of significant work in all fields of historical interest. To date, we have published over 800 reviews, reaching thousands of readers via the Internet and the free email alert."

The Medieval Review, sponsored by the Medieval Studies Institute and the College of Arts and Sciences at Indiana University, Bloomington
https://scholarworks.iu.edu/dspace/handle/2022/3631

"Since 1993, The Medieval Review (*TMR*; formerly the Bryn Mawr Medieval Review) has been publishing reviews of current work in all areas of Medieval Studies, a field it interprets as broadly as possible. The electronic medium allows for very rapid publication of reviews, and provides a computer searchable archive of past reviews, both of which are of great utility to scholars and students around the world."

Index